W9-DBC-761

CHURCHILL

AND

THE JEWS

BOOKS BY MARTIN GILBERT

The Churchill Biography

Volume III: The Challenge of War, 1914–1916
Document Volume III (in two parts)
Volume IV: World in Torment, 1917–1922
Document Volume IV (in two parts)
Volume V: The Coming of War, 1922–1939
Document Volume V: The Exchequer Years, 1922–1929
Document Volume V: The Wilderness Years, 1929–1935
Document Volume V: The Coming of War, 1936–1939
Volume VI: Finest Hour, 1939–1941
Churchill War Papers I: At the Admiralty, September 1939–May 1940
Churchill War Papers II: Never Surrender, May–December 1940
Churchill War Papers III: The Ever-Widening War, 1941
Volume VII: Road to Victory, 1941–1945
Volume VIII: Never Despair, 1945–1965
Churchill: A Photographic Portrait
Churchill: A Life

Other Books

The Appeaser (with Richard Gott)
The European Powers, 1900–1945
The Roots of Appeasement
Children's Illustrated Bible Atlas
Atlas of British Charities
Atlas of American History
Atlas of the Arab-Israeli Conflict
Atlas of British History
Atlas of the First World War
Atlas of the Holocaust
Atlas of Jewish History

Atlas of Russian History
The Jews of Russia: Their History in Maps
Jerusalem Illustrated History Atlas
Sir Horace Rumbold: Portrait of a Diplomat
Jerusalem: Rebirth of a City
Jerusalem in the Twentieth Century
Exile and Return: The Struggle for Jewish Statehood
Israel: A History
Auschwitz and the Allies
The Jews of Hope: The Plight of Soviet Jewry Today
Shcharansky: Hero of Our Time
The Holocaust: The Jewish Tragedy
The Boys: Triumph over Adversity
The First World War
The Somme: The Heroism and Horror of War
The Second World War
D-Day
The Day the War Ended
In Search of Churchill
Churchill and America
Empires in Conflict: A History of the Twentieth Century, 1900–1933
Descent into Barbarism: A History of the Twentieth Century, 1934–1951
Challenge to Civilization: A History of the Twentieth Century, 1952–1999
Never Again: A History of the Holocaust
The Jews in the Twentieth Century: An Illustrated History
Letters to Auntie Fori: The 5,000-Year History of the Jewish People and Their Faith
The Righteous: The Unsung Heroes of the Holocaust
Kristallnacht: Prelude to Destruction

Editions of Documents

Britain and Germany Between the Wars
Plough My Own Furrow: The Life of Lord Allen of Hurtwood
Servant of India: Diaries of the Viceroy's Private Secretary, 1905–1910

CHURCHILL AND THE JEWS

A LIFELONG FRIENDSHIP

MARTIN GILBERT

Henry Holt and Company
NEW YORK

Henry Holt and Company, LLC
Publishers since 1866
175 Fifth Avenue
New York, New York 10010
www.henryholt.com

Henry Holt® and ® are registered trademarks of Henry Holt and Company, LLC.

Published in Great Britain in 2007 by Simon & Schuster UK
Published in Canada in 2007 by McClelland & Stewart Ltd.

Library of Congress Cataloging-in-Publication Data

Gilbert, Martin, 1936-
Churchill and the Jews : a lifelong friendship / Martin Gilbert.—1st ed.
p. cm.
Includes bibliographical references and index.
ISBN-13: 978-0-8050-7880-0
ISBN-10: 0-8050-7880-0
1. Churchill, Winston, Sir, 1874–1965—Views on Zionism. 2. Zionism—Great Britain—History—20th century. 3. Palestine—History—1917–1948. 4. Great Britain—Foreign relations—Palestine. 5. Palestine—Foreign relations—Great Britain. 6. Israel—History. I. Title.
DA566.9.C5G4454 2007
320.54095694092—dc22

2007014812

Henry Holt books are available for special promotions and premiums.
For details contact: Director, Special Markets.

First U.S. Edition 2007

Printed in the United States of America

3 5 7 9 10 8 6 4 2

To Esther

CONTENTS

List of Maps · *xi*

List of Photographs · *xiii*

Preface · *xv*

Acknowledgements · *xvii*

Chapter One
EARLY YEARS: 'THIS MONSTROUS CONSPIRACY' · 1

Chapter Two
SUPPORTING THE JEWS · 7

Chapter Three
THE FIRST WORLD WAR AND ITS AFTERMATH · 23

Chapter Four
'A STRUGGLE FOR THE SOUL OF THE JEWISH PEOPLE' · 37

Chapter Five
RESPONSIBILITY FOR THE JEWISH NATIONAL HOME · 45

Chapter Six
PLEDGES IN JERUSALEM · 52

Chapter Seven
BUILDING ON THE BALFOUR DECLARATION · 67

Chapter Eight
AN ANTI-SEMITIC LIBEL, PALESTINE, AND MOSES · 86

Chapter Nine
THE RISE OF HITLER · 97

Chapter Ten
DEFENDER OF ZIONISM · 108

Chapter Eleven
THE PARTITION DEBATE: 'A COUNSEL OF DESPAIR' · 121

Chapter Twelve
NAZISM RAMPANT: 'ABOMINABLE PERSECUTION' · 135

Chapter Thirteen
PALESTINE: THE LEGITIMATE JEWISH HAVEN · 149

Chapter Fourteen
THE BLACK PAPER: 'THIS MORTAL BLOW' · 157

Chapter Fifteen
THE FIRST NINE MONTHS OF WAR · 163

Chapter Sixteen
PRIME MINISTER: THE PALESTINE DIMENSION · 172

Chapter Seventeen
'THESE VILE CRIMES' · 186

Chapter Eighteen
PALESTINE: A VIGILANT EYE · 202

Chapter Nineteen
SEEKING TO SAVE JEWS · 211

Chapter Twenty
'IF OUR DREAMS OF ZIONISM ARE TO END . . .' · 221

Chapter Twenty-One
THE SAUDI ARABIAN DIMENSION · 231

Chapter Twenty-Two
FROM WAR TO PEACE: 'I SHALL CONTINUE TO DO MY BEST' · 239

Chapter Twenty-Three
THE KING DAVID HOTEL BOMB: 'WE ARE TO BE AT WAR WITH THE JEWS OF PALESTINE' · 253

Chapter Twenty-Four
'A SENSELESS, SQUALID WAR WITH THE JEWS' · 261

Chapter Twenty-Five
THE STATE OF ISRAEL ESTABLISHED: 'AN EVENT IN WORLD HISTORY' · 268

Chapter Twenty-Six
'AN OLD ZIONIST LIKE ME' · 280

Chapter Twenty-Seven
'A GREAT NATION' · 293

Epilogue · 307

Maps · 311

Bibliography · 325

Index · 331

LIST OF MAPS

1. Great Britain 312
2. Cities in Europe in which Emery Reves placed Churchill's Articles, 1937–9 313
3. Western Europe 314
4. Central and Eastern Europe 315
5. Britain's Promise to the Arabs, 1915 316
6. Zionist Desiderata for Palestine, 1919 317
7. The British Mandate for Palestine, 1920–1948 318
8. Churchill's Journey to Jerusalem, 1921 319
9. Churchill in Palestine, 1921 319
10. Churchill's Middle East Journey, 1934 320
11. The Peel Commission Proposals for Palestine, 1937 321
12. The United Nations Partition Plan, and the State of Israel, 1948–1967 322
13. Jerusalem 323

LIST OF PHOTOGRAPHS

1. Lord Rothschild and Lord Randolph Churchill
2. Churchill and his Manchester Jewish constituents
3. Churchill and Dr Joseph Dulberg
4. Churchill and his Jewish Constituents
5. Churchill and Sir Ernest Cassel
6. Winston and Clementine Churchill
7. 'Zionism versus Bolshevism' article
8. Churchill and Balfour
9. Outside Government House, Jerusalem
10. Churchill on Mount Scopus, Jerusalem
11. Churchill and Mayor Dizengoff in Tel Aviv
12. Chaim Weizmann
13. Pinhas Rutenberg
14. Vladimir Jabotinsky
15. Churchill and Albert Einstein at Chartwell
16. Churchill and Leon Blum
17. Churchill and Emery Reves
18. Eugen Spier
19. James de Rothschild
20. Churchill and Stefan Lorant at Chartwell
21. Randolph Churchill in Partisan-Held Yugoslavia
22. Victor Rothschild
23. King Ibn Saud and Roosevelt
24. Churchill and Ibn Saud
25. Churchill, his daughter Sarah and Emery Reves
26. Churchill and Bernard Baruch
27. Oscar Nemon and his bust of Churchill
28. Churchill, Eliahu Elath, and Sir Isaac Wolfson
29. Churchill and David Ben-Gurion
30. Ben-Gurion and Edmund de Rothschild

PREFACE

Individually, Churchill, Jews, and Zionism have long been subjects of interest. Combined, they form a study of the interaction of a remarkable man and a remarkable people, both surrounded by challenges and controversy. Almost forty years have passed since I began to collect material for this book. It was on 12 September 1969 that I spent the day with General Sir Edward Louis Spears, who had been Churchill's friend for many years: a fellow soldier, historian and parliamentarian. In the reposeful setting of his home in the English countryside, Spears urged me, as Churchill's biographer, to paint a true portrait, warts and all, of the Great Man whose official biography was then in its early stages. Once he was convinced that I was indeed determined to paint a true portrait, he went on to confide: 'Even Winston had a fault. He was too fond of Jews.'

The general's comment gave me the idea that one day I would look into this 'fault' in greater depth than was possible in the biography. How did it manifest itself? What effect did it have on the course of history? Did this 'fondness' affect the fate of the Jews during the Second World War? Did it influence the emergence of the State of Israel in 1948? Why was it seen as a fault? Was it mere 'fondness' or something deeper?

For more than half a century Churchill's life intertwined with Jewish issues. As a young Member of Parliament from 1904 to 1908 with many Jews among his constituents; as a Cabinet minister in 1921 and 1922 responsible for determining the future status of the Jewish National Home in Palestine; as a war leader from 1940 to 1945 confronted by the military power and tyranny of Nazi Germany; and as peacetime Prime Minister from 1951 to 1956, in the early days of the State of Israel, he was aware of Jewish concerns, and sympathetic to them. Although such a sympathetic stance was unpopular with many colleagues, parliamentarians and contemporaries, Churchill rejected what he called 'the anti-Semitic lines of prejudice', and strove to support Jewish aspirations, both as citizens of Britain participating fully in national life, and as advocates and participants in the creation of Israel.

For his support of Zionist enterprise in Palestine, Churchill was warned publicly by one Member of Parliament that as a result of his efforts he would find himself 'up against the hereditary antipathy which exists all over the world to the Jewish race.' Churchill was not deterred. While never an uncritical supporter of Zionism, he was one of its most persistent friends and advocates. In a world where Jews were often the objects of scorn, dislike, distrust and hostility, Churchill held them in high esteem, and wanted them to have their rightful place in the world. At a time when he was criticising Jewish terrorist acts against the British in Palestine, he told a Jewish friend who was uneasy about his criticisms: 'The Jewish people know well enough that I am their friend.' This was true: he was both a friend in their hours of need, and a friend in deed.

London
5 February 2007

ACKNOWLEDGEMENTS

I am grateful first and foremost to those Jews with whom Churchill was in contact, and who, over many years, shared their recollections with me. Andre Maurois – then Captain Emile Herzog – recalled his meetings with Churchill on the Western Front in 1916. Hannah Ruppin, Churchill's hostess in Jerusalem in 1921, took me to the scene of his banquet with the Jewish community there, and shared with me her memories of the occasion. Dorothy de Rothschild, another of those who was with Churchill in Jerusalem in 1921, talked to me about the friendship between herself, her husband James de Rothschild and Churchill. Emery Reves gave me the benefit of his recollections of placing Churchill's newspaper and magazine articles, and later his books, in a large range of foreign countries. Eugen Spier, a refugee from Hitler, told me of the formation and working of Churchill's Anti-Nazi League that same year. Stefan Lorant, one of the first Jews to be sent to Dachau concentration camp, gave me details of the campaign he helped co-ordinate, when picture editor of *Picture Post*, to 'bring back Churchill' in 1939. In his studio at St James's Palace, Oscar Nemon told me of his conversations with Churchill while sculpting him in the 1950s. Eliahu Elath recounted his meetings with Churchill, as Israeli Ambassador, when we found ourselves on a station platform in Hampshire with an hour until the next train. Sir Maurice Shock recalled his work as one of Churchill's literary assistants in 1956–7. President Yitzhak Navon gave me an account of Churchill's last meeting with David Ben-Gurion, in 1960, at which Navon was the note-taker. David Ben-Gurion himself, in 1972 in his desert 'hut' in the Negev, told me about the influence Churchill's war leadership had on him when he had to confront the prospect of defeat in 1948.

Among non-Jews, Harford Montgomery Hyde gave me the transcript of the two legal actions involving Lord Alfred Douglas and his allegations that Churchill had been in the pay of the Jews during and before the First World War. Randolph Churchill – for whom I was then working – recalled a visit by Chaim Weizmann to Chartwell at the height of the 1930 White Paper discussions. Churchill's grandson Winston recounted a conversation with a survivor of the Warsaw Ghetto revolt of April 1943. Eve Gibson gave me an account of a meeting with Churchill in July 1943. Sir Laurence Grafftey Smith told me of his attempt in 1945 to prevent Churchill raising with King Ibn Saud of Saudi Arabia the desirability of a Jewish State in Palestine. Sir William Deakin described Churchill's shocked reaction to the news of the fate of the family of his Jewish literary agent. Anthony Montague Browne told me of Churchill's reaction to an accusation of 'black ingratitude' on the part of the Jews.

The Ben-Gurion Archive in Beersheva, the Central Zionist Archive in Jerusalem, and the Weizmann Archive in Rehovot, have put at my disposal a wealth of documentation. In the early years of my researches, the Mayor of the Jewish village of Rishon-le-Zion, then in Mandate Palestine, gave me access to the records of Churchill's visit there in 1921. Ben Gale recalled the moment in Tel Aviv in 1940 when news came that Churchill had become Prime Minister. Dr Igo Feldblum recalled a wartime slogan in Mandate Palestine.

I am grateful to those who, over the past thirty-five years, have asked me to lecture about Churchill and the Jews, among them the Weizmann Institute, Rehovot, Israel; Tel Aviv University; the Hebrew University, Jerusalem; the Jewish Public Library, Montreal; the Tauber Institute, Brandeis University; Princeton University; and the University of California, San Diego.

In the course of my research, many people and institutes have sent me archival material, and given me access to their holdings, among them, at the Churchill Archives Centre, Churchill College, Cambridge, Allen Packwood, Director, and Caroline Herbert, Katherine Thompson and Claire Knight; Hana Pinshow, Ben-Gurion

Archives; the National Archives (formerly Public Record Office) London; and Simon Blundell, Librarian, the Reform Club, London. I am also grateful to Anna D. Charin, Librarian, *Jewish Chronicle*; Sian King, Assistant Librarian, Library of the House of Lords; Ruth Mackinlay; Andrew Roberts; and Lord Rothschild. Particular thanks are due to Niv Hachlili, Peter Joy, Merav Segal, Yad Chaim Weizmann, Rehovot; Victoria Stubbs, Acting House Manager, Chartwell; Margaret Shannon, Tim Hughes (Tim Hughes & Associates) and Mich'ael Yagupsky for help in the tracking down of archival material. On bibliographical matters, I am indebted, as are all historians who write about Churchill, to Ronald I. Cohen, Churchill's bibliographer, who also read my text in its penultimate stage and made many helpful suggestions.

For help in acquiring the photographs, I am grateful to Reuven Koffler and Nechama Kaner, Central Zionist Archives, Jewish Agency for Israel; Jodi Lack, Assistant Art Editor, *Jewish Chronicle*; Jerry Moeran, Studio Edmark, Oxford; Kenneth Rose; Major Edmund de Rothschild; Taffy Sassoon; Merav Segal, Director, Weizmann Archives, Rehovot; Lady Soames; Katherine Thomson, Archivist, Churchill College, Cambridge; Dr C. M. Woolgar, Head of Special Collections, University of Southampton Library; and Masha Zolotarevsky, Archivist, Jabotinsky Institute in Israel.

For help in organising the mass of material involved in this study, I am grateful to Elżbieta Czernecka, and to Kay Thomson, who also helped manage a formidable amount of correspondence and reference material, and gave the text the benefit of her close scrutiny.

My publishers, John Sterling, Jennifer Barth and David Patterson at Holt (New York), Andrew Gordon and Rory Scarfe at Simon & Schuster (London), and Chris Bucci at McClelland & Stewart (Toronto), have been supportive throughout, as has my agent Caradoc King and his support team at A. P. Watt. Robyn Karney, copy-editor, gave the text the benefit of her expertise. Tim Aspden once more prepared maps of the highest quality.

CHAPTER ONE

EARLY YEARS: 'THIS MONSTROUS CONSPIRACY'

Churchill had no Jewish ancestry; his claim to an exotic origin came from a possible American Indian ancestor. But from his early years the Jews held a fascination for him. As a schoolboy at Harrow, the stories of the Old Testament were an integral part of his education and imagination. One of his earliest surviving essays was 'Palestine in the time of John the Baptist'. Writing about the Pharisees, Churchill asked his reader – in this case his teacher – not to be too censorious about that 'rigid' Jewish sect. 'Their faults were many,' he wrote, and went on to ask: 'Whose faults are few?' At the age of thirteen he could himself be forgiven for describing the 'minarets' of the Temple of Zion.[1]

In Churchill's family circle, his father Lord Randolph Churchill was noted for his friendship with individual Jews. The butt of a popular clubland jibe that he only had Jewish friends, he was even rebuked by members of his family for inviting Jews to dine with him at home. On one occasion, when a guest at an English country house, Lord Randolph was greeted by one of the guests, a leading aristocrat, with the words: 'What, Lord Randolph, you've not brought your Jewish friends?' to which Lord Randolph replied: 'No, I did not think they would be very amused by the company.'[2]

Churchill, a devoted son eager for his father's approval, took his

1 Essay dated 26 May 1888: Churchill papers.
2 An exchange recounted on many occasions by Churchill's son Randolph during the author's time as one of his research assistants (1962–1967).

father's side in this pro- and anti-Jew debate. The Jews whom his father knew and invited to dine were men of distinction and achievement. One was 'Natty' Rothschild, 1st Baron Rothschild, the head of the British branch of the Rothschild banking family, who in 1885 became the first Jew to become a member of the House of Lords. Another was the banker Sir Ernest Cassel, born in Cologne, a close friend of the Prince of Wales, later King Edward VII.

When Churchill's father despaired of his son succeeding in the army examination in 1892, he wrote to Churchill's grandmother that if the boy failed again in the examination, 'I shall think of putting him in business.' He was confident that he could get the young Churchill 'something very good' through Rothschild or Cassel.[3] Shortly before Churchill's nineteenth birthday, his father took him to Lord Rothschild's country house, Tring Park. The visit went well. 'The people at Tring took a great deal of notice of him,' Lord Randolph wrote to Churchill's grandmother.[4]

It was just before his eighteenth birthday that Churchill had reported to his mother how 'young Rothschild' – Nathaniel, second son of the 1st Baron Rothschild – had been playing with him at Harrow School, 'and gorged eggs etc some awful sights!'[5] Fifty years later, the son of 'young Rothschild', Victor Rothschild, who succeeded as third baron shortly before the Second World War, was to be responsible for checking Churchill's wartime gifts of food and cigars to make sure they did not contain poison. For Victor Rothschild's bravery in dismantling an unexploded bomb hidden in a crate of onions – a bomb timed to explode in a British port – Churchill would recommend him for the prestigious George Cross.[6]

Another branch of the Rothschild family whom Churchill knew was the family of Leopold Rothschild, at whose house at Gunnersbury, just outside London, he dined while he was an army cadet in 1895, and whose son Lionel, later a Conservative MP, he befriended at that time.

---

3 Letter dated September 1892: Churchill papers.
4 Letter of 24 October 1893: Churchill papers.
5 Letter of 12 October 1892: Churchill papers.
6 Kenneth Rose, *Elusive Rothschild: The Life of Victor, Third Baron*, pages 68–70.

Lionel was at school with Churchill's younger brother Jack. 'He is a nice little chap,' Churchill wrote to Jack, 'and the Leo Rothschilds will be very grateful to you if you look after him.' Churchill added: 'Their gratitude may also take a practical form – as they have a charming place at Gunnersbury.'[7]

Also a Jewish friend of Churchill's parents was the German-born throat specialist, Sir Felix Semon. In 1896, shortly before Churchill left Britain for India as a soldier, he consulted Semon about his speech defect, the inability to pronounce the letter 's'. An operation was possible, but Semon advised against it; with 'patience and perseverance' he would be able to speak fluently.[8] 'I have just seen the most extraordinary young man I have ever met,' Semon later recalled telling his wife. After telling Semon of his army plans, Churchill confided: 'Of course it is not my intention to become a mere professional soldier. I only wish to gain some experience. Some day I shall be a statesman as my father was before me.'[9]

Churchill's parents were also friendly with the Austrian-born Baron Maurice de Hirsch, a leading Jewish philanthropist, at whose house in London they were frequent guests. The Baron's adopted son, Maurice, known as 'Tootie', later Baron de Forest, first met Churchill in the late 1880s at Hirsch's racing home near Newmarket. During one of his school holidays, he was a guest at Hirsch's house in Paris.

Paris at the time of Churchill's visit in 1898 was in turmoil following the trial and imprisonment of Captain Alfred Dreyfus, a Jewish officer in the French army, accused of being a German spy. Emile Zola had taken up the captain's cause, and in a powerful article headed 'J'Accuse', denounced the government and the anti-Semitism of the French army, and exposed the falsity of the charges. 'Bravo Zola!' Churchill wrote to his mother. 'I am delighted to witness the complete debacle of this monstrous conspiracy.'[10]

---

7 Letter of 30 September 1895: Churchill papers.
8 Randolph S. Churchill, *Winston S. Churchill*, Volume One, page 293.
9 Henry C. Semon and Thomas A. McIntyre (editors), *The Autobiography of Sir Felix Semon*, page 191. In his recollections, Semon misdated this meeting to 1900.
10 Letter dated 8 September 1898; Churchill papers.

After Lord Randolph Churchill's death in 1895, shortly after Churchill's twentieth birthday, his father's Jewish friends continued their friendship with the son. Lord Rothschild, Sir Ernest Cassel and Baron de Hirsch frequently invited him to their houses. In an aside in the first volume of the official biography, Churchill's son Randolph wrote, with a verbal twinkle: 'Churchill did not confine his quest for new and interesting personalities and friends to Jewish households. During this period he was sometimes invited into Gentile society.'[11]

While soldiering in India in 1897, Churchill was keen to find a newspaper willing to take him on as its war correspondent. 'Lord Rothschild would be the person to arrange this for me,' he wrote to his mother, 'as he knows everyone.'[12] On his return from India in the spring of 1899, eager to embark on a political career, Churchill again found Lord Rothschild a willing facilitator. He was pleased to find, while dining at Rothschild's London house, that another of the guests, the Chancellor of the Exchequer, A. J. Balfour, 'markedly civil to me – I thought – agreed with and paid great attention to everything I said.'[13]

It was his father's friend, Sir Ernest Cassel, who offered to look after Churchill's finances after his father's death. Churchill, having made his first earnings through his writing, told Cassel, 'Feed my sheep.'[14] This the banker did, investing Churchill's eventually considerable literary earnings both wisely and well. Cassel made no charge for his services.

In preparing to go to South Africa as a war correspondent in 1899, Churchill sought funds for his kit and provisions. Lord Rothschild gave him £150 and Cassel gave him £100: a total sum that was the annual income for many middle-class families. In 1902, Churchill's second year in Parliament, Cassel secured him a £10,000 stake in a loan offered that year by the Japanese government.[15] On

11 Randolph S. Churchill, *Winston S. Churchill*, Volume One, page 288.
12 Letter dated 21 April 1897: Churchill papers.
13 Letter dated 3 May 1899: Churchill papers.
14 Winston S. Churchill, *My Early Life*, page 369.
15 In the money values of today, £500,000 ($250,000).

that investment, Churchill wrote to his brother Jack, 'I hope to make a small profit.' In 1905, Cassel furnished a library for Churchill's bachelor flat in London's Mayfair. Cassel's help to Churchill was continuous. Bonds that he bought for Churchill in the Atchison, Topeka and Santa Fe Railway in 1907 provided him with the salary he paid to his typist – twice over. When Churchill married in 1908, Cassel gave him and Clementine a wedding present of £500: some £25,000 in the money values of today.

Churchill valued his friendship with Cassel. When Cassel died in 1921, Churchill wrote to Cassel's granddaughter Edwina Ashley that her grandfather was 'a good and just man who was trusted, respected and honoured by all who knew him. He was a valued friend of my father's and I have taken up that friendship and I have held it all my grown life. I had the knowledge that he was very fond of me and believed in me at all times – especially in bad times.'[16]

On 22 January 1901 Churchill was in Winnipeg, towards the end of a lecture tour about the war in South Africa – and his escape from a Boer prison camp – when he learned of the death of Queen Victoria. 'A great and solemn event,' he wrote to his mother, 'but I am curious to know about the King. Will it entirely revolutionise his way of life? Will he sell his horses and scatter his Jews or will Reuben Sassoon be enshrined among the crown jewels and other regalia? Will he become desperately serious? Will he continue to be friendly to you?'[17]

The King, Edward VII, did remain friendly to Churchill's mother, and did retain his friendship with the Baghdadi-born Jew Reuben Sassoon, whose nephew Philip Sassoon – a future Secretary of State for Air – was to become a friend of Churchill and, with his sister Sybil, a generous host at his home, Port Lympne, on the Channel coast. H. H. Asquith, soon to become Prime Minister and

16 Letter dated 25 September 1921: Mountbatten papers. (In 1922 Edwina Ashley married the future Admiral of the Fleet, Earl Mountbatten of Burma.)

17 Letter dated 22 January 1901: Churchill papers.

Churchill's patron, described the Jews in a letter to a female acquaintance – who, ironically, later converted to Judaism – as 'A scattered and unattractive tribe.'[18] Churchill made no such comments, publicly or privately. Indeed, in a letter to his mother in 1907, he warned her against publishing a story in her memoirs that was clearly anti-Semitic, about a leading politician, Lord Goschen. 'I do not think that the Goschen story would be suitable for publication,' he wrote. 'It would cause a great deal of offence not only to the Goschens, but to the Jews generally.' It might be a good story, but, he told his mother: 'Many good things are beyond the reach of respectable people and you must put it away from your finger tips.'[19]

Until 1904, Churchill's acquaintance with Jews was entirely social. But within four years of his entering Parliament, it was to become political, and decisive.

18 Venetia Montagu papers.
19 Undated letter, 1907: Churchill papers, 28/27.

CHAPTER TWO

SUPPORTING THE JEWS

Churchill's first political involvement in Jewish concerns came in 1904, when he was twenty-seven. That year, while still a Conservative Member of Parliament for Oldham, he had begun to support Liberal Party causes. His constituency Conservative Party at Oldham told him they would no longer support him. Needing a new parliamentary constituency, and a Liberal one, he accepted the invitation to stand for Manchester North-West, where a third of the electorate was Jewish.

The issue Churchill was called upon to take up at Manchester was a national one: the Conservative Government's Aliens Bill, aimed at curbing the influx of Jewish immigrants from Tsarist Russia, fleeing persecution and poverty. One of Churchill's principal supporters in the Manchester Liberal Party was Nathan Laski, a forty-one-year-old Manchester merchant, President of the Old Hebrew Congregation of Manchester, and Chairman of the Manchester Jewish Hospital, who enlisted Churchill's support, as a matter of urgency for the Jews, in seeking to prevent the passage of the Aliens Bill through parliament.

In May 1904, Nathan Laski sent Churchill a dossier of papers relating to the Aliens Bill, which included official government immigration statistics. Churchill prepared a detailed criticism of the Bill, which he sent both to Laski and as an open letter to the newspapers. 'What has surprised me most in studying the papers you have been good enough to forward me,' Churchill wrote in his letter, 'is how few aliens there are in Great Britain. To judge by the talk there has been, one would have imagined we were being overrun by the swarming invasion and "ousted" from our island through neglect of precautions which every foreign nation has adopted. But it now appears from the Board of Trade statistics that all the aliens in Great Britain do not amount to a one-hundred-and-fortieth part of the total population, that they are increasing only 7,000 a year on the average, and that, according to the report of the Alien Commission, Germany has twice as large and France four times as large a proportion of foreigners as we have. It does not appear, therefore, that there can be urgent or sufficient reasons, racial or social, for departing from the old tolerant and generous practice of free entry and asylum to which this country has so long adhered and from which it has so often greatly gained.'

Churchill's critique of the Aliens Bill also concerned the powers that the Bill would confer on those responsible for enforcing it. He feared 'an intolerant or anti-Semitic Home Secretary', noting that the custom in England 'has hitherto been to allow police and Customs officers to act and report on facts, not to be the judges of characters and credentials.'

Churchill had another objection, that an alien could be deported on the testimony 'of the common informer – perhaps his private enemy or a trade rival.' The whole Bill, Churchill concluded, looked like an attempt, on the part of the government, 'to gratify a small but noisy section of their own supporters and to purchase a little popularity in the constituencies by dealing harshly with a number of unfortunate aliens who have no votes . . . It is expected to appeal to insular prejudice against foreigners, to racial prejudice against Jews, and to labour prejudice against competition.' English working men, Churchill wrote, 'are not so selfish as to be unsympathetic towards the victims of circumstances or oppression. They do not respond in any marked degree to the anti-Semitism which has darkened recent Continental history, and I for one believe that they disavow an attempt to shut out the stranger from our land because he is poor or in trouble, and will resent a measure which, without any proved necessity, smirches those ancient traditions of freedom and hospitality for which Britain has been so long renowned.'[1]

'Pray accept my personal thanks for your splendid letter received this morning,' Nathan Laski wrote from Manchester. 'You have won the gratitude of the whole Jewish Community not alone of Manchester, but of the entire country.'[2] On 31 May 1904, the day Churchill's letter with its critique of anti-Semitism was published, he formally left the Conservative Party and joined the Liberal opposition. The Jews of Manchester had acquired a courageous champion.

On 8 June 1904 Churchill made his first speech from the Liberal Opposition benches: opposing the government's attempt to push the Aliens Bill through Parliament without a full debate. Despite his arguments, the Bill was sent – without scrutiny in the full House of Commons – to the far smaller Grand Committee, of which Churchill was one of four Liberal members; a daily and active participant in the committee's discussions.

Those Britons who opposed Jewish immigration appealed to popular anti-Semitic sentiment to make their case. The *Sun* newspaper alleged that Churchill's opposition to the Bill was on the direct orders of Lord Rothschild. This was the first but not the last time that Churchill was to be accused by his political opponents, and by anti-Semites, of being in the pocket, and even in the pay, of wealthy Jews. The accusation almost certainly arose from a short news item in the *Jewish Chronicle*, reporting a meeting in Manchester at which 'Mr Nathan Laski said he had interviewed Mr Winston Churchill, who had seen Lord Rothschild with reference to the Bill. The result of the interview was that Mr Churchill was practically leading the attack on the Bill in Grand Committee.'[3]

The Aliens Bill had eleven clauses, totalling 240 lines. Its opponents challenged each clause, however minor, with Churchill either

1 *The Times, Manchester Guardian*, and other newspapers, 31 May 1904.
2 Letter dated 31 May 1904: Churchill papers.
3 *Jewish Chronicle*, 1 July 1904.

proposing or seconding each of the many amendments. Major Williams Evans-Gordon, one of the Grand Committee members who opposed Jewish immigration, declared that Churchill 'was faithfully carrying out the instructions he had received from the party for which he was acting,' and hastened to add, defensively, that he 'did not say for anybody in particular.' This thinly veiled insinuation that he was acting on instructions from the Jews brought Churchill angrily to his feet. He then referred to the suggestion made in the *Sun* newspaper that he was acting under instruction from Lord Rothschild, telling the committee that he 'regretted that so foul a slander should be repeated here.'[4]

So determined were Churchill and his three fellow-Liberal opponents of the Bill on the committee to challenge its every word that, by the seventh day of the committee's deliberations, only three lines of a single clause had been discussed. A further ten clauses and 233 lines remained to be examined. Anxious to avoid the continuation of such thorough scrutiny, the government abandoned the Bill.

Churchill had supported the Jews, and prevailed. He had helped forestall legislation that would have posed a serious impediment to large numbers of Jews seeking to enter Britain; Jews who within a few decades were to make their contribution to Jewish life in Britain, and to the defence of Britain in both world wars, the second under Churchill's leadership.

The Russian Jews whose entry into Britain was being so strongly supported by Churchill in the House of Commons had good reason to want to leave the Tsarist Empire. For more than thirty years they had been subjected to spasmodic but often lethal outbreaks of violence: pogroms that continued into the twentieth century. In the Russian city of Kishinev, a three-day pogrom in April 1903 had led to forty-seven Jewish deaths – men, women and children – and more than seven hundred houses had been looted. A second pogrom took place in the same city in October 1905, when nineteen Jews were killed.

4 Reported in the *Jewish Chronicle*, 15 July 1904.

Jews worldwide were outraged at the continuing attacks. On 10 December 1905 a public protest meeting was called in Manchester. It was the day after Churchill had accepted his first government post, as Under-Secretary of State for the Colonies in the new Liberal administration, formed following the resignation of the Conservative Prime Minister, Arthur Balfour.

Churchill was the main speaker at Manchester. During the course of his speech, he told an audience of several thousand that they had met to protest 'against the appalling massacres and detestable atrocities recently committed in the Empire of Russia.'

Churchill went on to declare: 'The numbers of victims had been enormous. Many thousands of weak and defenceless people had suffered terribly, old people alike with little children and feeble women who were incapable of offering resistance, and could not rely at all on the forces of law and the regulations of order. That those outrages were not spontaneous but rather in the nature of a deliberate plan combined to create a picture so terrible that one could hardly distinguish it in its grim reality, even amid the darkness of Russia. They had met there to express, in no uncertain terms, how deeply moved the whole British nation were at such atrocious deeds.'[5]

Among those present on the platform when Churchill spoke was a Jewish chemist and active Zionist, Russian born Dr Chaim Weizmann, who had come from Geneva, where he was a lecturer in chemistry, to Manchester a year earlier. The two men, who were born three days apart, were to become closely associated in the evolution of Zionist needs and policies.

For the Jews of Britain in 1905 who were attracted to Zionism, the question was whether to press for a Jewish homeland in Palestine, then firmly under Turkish rule, or to seek some area of Jewish settlement, within the wide confines of the British Empire, where the persecuted Jews of Russia could find an immediate haven. The Zionist movement itself was divided. Some wanted all Jewish efforts to be focused on opening Turkish-ruled Palestine to Jewish immigration.

---

5 *Jewish Chronicle*, 15 December 1905.

Others, members of the Jewish Territorial Organisation – led by the Anglo-Jewish writer Israel Zangwill, and known as Territorialists – pressed the British Government to make some British colonial territory available. A favoured area was in the highlands of Kenya, part of British East Africa Protectorate – an area that today is part of Uganda. Another option, supported publicly by Lord Rothschild and already being financed by Baron de Hirsch, was for Jewish agricultural colonies in Canada and Argentina.

For Churchill, this question of Jewish national aspirations arose within a few days of his entry into government – and three weeks before the General Election called as a result of Balfour's resignation – when he was approached, on Boxing Day 1905, by a leading Jewish constituent, Dr Joseph Dulberg, who was Secretary of the Manchester Territorialists. On New Year's Day 1906 Churchill wrote to Dulberg, noting the 'numerous and serious difficulties which present themselves to a scheme of establishing a self-governing Jewish colony in British East Africa, of the differences of opinion among the Jews themselves, of the doubtful suitability of the territories in question, of the rapidly extending settlements by British colonists in and about the area, and of the large issues of general state policy which the scheme affects.'

Churchill was supportive, telling the Territorialists: 'I recognise the supreme attraction to a scattered and persecuted people of a safe and settled home under the flag of tolerance and freedom. Such a plan contains a soul, and enlists in its support energies, enthusiasms, and a driving power which no scheme of individual colonisation can ever command.' But what was needed was 'a definite detailed plan sustained by ample funds and personalities.'[6] Despite this positive suggestion, the Zionists who wanted Palestine or nothing won the day within the Zionist movement, and the focus of Jewish national aspirations turned back to the Turkish-ruled region between the Mediterranean Sea and the River Jordan, where, by 1905, fifty Jewish villages had been established, mostly by Jews from Russia.

*

6 Letter of 2 January 1906: Churchill papers.

At the beginning of 1906 Churchill published a two-volume biography of his father. In an extremely hostile review in the *Daily Telegraph,* the anonymous reviewer described Lord Randolph Churchill's treatment of his friends as 'often atrocious, sometimes not even honourable; he was very careless of the truth.' The reviewer went on to criticise Churchill, as author, for 'occasional lapses into execrable taste, which have not been wanting in his own career.' Churchill's cousin, the 9th Duke of Marlborough, was outraged that the manager of the paper was a Jew, Harry Levy-Lawson, and wrote to Churchill that he intended 'to administer a good and sound trouncing to that dirty little Hebrew.'[7]

In a letter to the *Daily Telegraph,* Marlborough described the review as using a method of attacking a dead man 'which appears to be essentially un-English.'[8] Sending a copy to Churchill, Marlborough commented: 'I trust the significance of the word "un-English" may not be lost to the understanding of those who may read my letters.' He would take the first opportunity, Marlborough added, of offering Levy-Lawson 'a public affront. I don't allow Jews to say members of my family are dishonorable without giving them back more than they expected.'[9]

The *Daily Telegraph* apologised. Marlborough continued to fulminate, writing to Churchill: 'Jews cannot be dealt with with that same good feeling that prompts the intercourse between Christians.' Churchill made no comment; already a member of the Liberal Government, he was busy electioneering, and on 12 January, at the General Election, was elected Liberal Member of Parliament for North-West Manchester. He spent his summer holiday that year travelling in Europe. His three hosts, Sir Ernest Cassel at the Villa Cassel in the Swiss Alps, Lionel Rothschild driving in Italy, and Baron de Forest at Castle Eichstatt in Moravia, were all Jews.

Back in Britain, Churchill married that October his 'darling

7 Letter of 2 January 1906: Churchill papers.
8 Letter of 3 January 1906, *Daily Telegraph,* 4 January 1906.
9 Letter of 3 January 1906: Churchill papers.

Clementine'. Then, in the first public meeting since his marriage, and accompanied by his wife, for her first ever public meeting, he was the main speaker at a meeting in Manchester in support of the Jewish Hospital Fund. His experience with Manchester Jewry had introduced him to the Jewish communal emphasis on social responsibility and self-help, with which he had been much impressed. He was a subscriber in his constituency to the Jewish Soup Kitchen, the Jewish Lad's Club, and the Jewish Tennis and Cricket Club.[10] *The Times* reported his visit to the Jewish Hospital, to the Talmud Torah religious school, and to the Jewish Working Men's Club, where he said that 'he could conceive of no better way of bringing members of the Jewish community together in friendly relationship than the extension of such clubs.' Churchill added that he had been 'much struck at the hospital and at the Talmud Torah School by the nature of the work that community had in hand.' He did not think that people could unite in communities 'unless they possessed some guiding principle. They in that part of Manchester had the spirit of their race and of their faith. He counselled them to guard and keep that spirit. It was a precious thing, a bond of union, an inspiration, and a source of great strength.'

In the afternoon Churchill attended a special service at the Great Synagogue in Cheetham Hill Road, a service held to raise funds for the Victoria Memorial Jewish Hospital. The Jewish Boys' Brigade formed a guard of honour. The Dean of Manchester, Bishop Welldon, Churchill's former headmaster at Harrow School, sent a message of support for the charitable object of their 'Jewish fellow-citizens'.

That night a mass meeting in support of the Jewish Hospital Fund was held in the Palace Theatre. After alluding to a 'pleasant and memorable day spent in North-West Manchester amidst the stir and hum of men and things,' Churchill said that 'we heard a great deal nowadays about corporate life, and he thought that if we were going to live decent lives in such great masses of people we would

10 'Manchester Subscriptions paid in 1906' and 'Subscriptions paid in 1907': Churchill papers, 1/55.

have to study the corporate organization of society in a way we had hitherto not attempted to do. We had got to band ourselves together for definite purposes.' The corporate life 'was worth nothing unless it had behind it personal effort. The mere mechanical arrangement of society, into larger combination, would be utterly sterile, unless those larger combinations were sustained by a great spirit of personal interest and of impersonal aspiration.' That was his sincere conviction. If they could get the people 'to make sacrifices to keep this special hospital going, depend upon it they would have created a new thing in the world; they would have brought from the realms of the infinite something new into the arena of mundane affairs. There they would have a lever which could remove vice, disease, sorrow and want, which could wipe away the grossnesses of our state in the world, and which would be of far greater value than any stereotyped or hidebound official organization because it carried the idea of the personal stamp and of the impersonal aspiration.'

He was 'quite sure of this', Churchill said, 'that if we were to have the higher corporate life we must have the higher corporate incentive, we must have the larger spirit, the larger driving power. The Jews were a lucky community because they had that corporate spirit, the spirit of their race and faith.' He would not stand there 'to ask them to use that spirit in any narrow or clannish sense, to shut themselves off from others'. He believed that to be 'far from their mood and intention, far from the counsels that were given them by those most entitled to advise. That personal and special driving power which they possessed would enable them to bring vitality into their institutions, which nothing else would ever give.' His advice was, 'if he might say it without disrespect': 'Be good Jews.' And he added, amid cheers: 'A Jew cannot be a good Englishman unless he is a good Jew.'[11]

Having fought so strenuously and successfully against the Conservative's Aliens Bill, Churchill was confronted by the Liberal Government's decision to introduce an Aliens Bill of its own. The

11 *The Times*, 22 October 1906.

new legislation, which was passed into law early in 1906, was a significant modification of the Conservative proposals, but it was restrictive nevertheless. On 8 February 1907 Churchill wrote in protest from the Colonial Office to the Home Secretary, Herbert Gladstone: 'I was concerned to find the other day how very bitter and disappointed the Jewish Community have become in consequence of the continuance of this very harsh and quite indefensible measure . . . I hope you will be able to do something to allay the feeling which is rife. I am sure the Liberal Party would support the repeal of such a foolish piece of legislation.'

Churchill then set out his criticisms. The Act did not prevent the entrance 'of all sorts of swindlers, rogues, vagabonds, thieves, of both sexes, so long as they can afford (with stolen money!) to come first or second class. But it does prevent poor but honest people from coming in.' Churchill went on to point out that those who were turned back 'from the land of promise to the regions of despair – from England to Russia – were so treated because they had not sufficient means, not because they were undesirable in the sense that the dishonest and the depraved are undesirable.' The officials responsible for working the Act used inconsistent and harsh criteria in their examinations and inspections. 'Children were parted from parents, and people have been sent back to their own country and thence returned here at the expense of charitable institutions, as first-class passengers. That shows the grotesque value of the Act. As long as a foreigner can beg, borrow, or steal the price of a first-class passage, he is welcome. Let him save his money and come third class, and he will be rejected, unless that money happens to be a certain sum, alterable at the whim of the Home Secretary.' The Act was both 'useless and vexatious.'[12]

On 14 March 1907 Churchill led a deputation of protesters against the high naturalisation fee in the Aliens Act to see the Prime Minister, Sir Henry Campbell-Bannerman. But despite this meeting, and a further initiative by Churchill a year later, the naturalisation

---

12 Letter of 8 February 1907: Herbert Gladstone papers.

fee remained too high for the poorer would-be immigrants. Churchill's efforts had not been successful. His concerns were genuine, and persistently expressed with facts and details to bolster his arguments, but on matters relating to Jewish immigration he was in a minority even within the Liberal Party.

Churchill's understanding of Jewish historical and national aspirations was put to the test at the beginning of 1908, a few months after his return from an official visit to East Africa. That January he was asked by a leading British Zionist, Rabbi Dr Moses Gaster, to send a message to the annual conference of the English Zionist Federation. The Federation was emphatic that Palestine, not East Africa, must be the Jewish national objective. In drafting the message he wanted Churchill to make, Gaster therefore stressed, in the second part of the draft, that Jerusalem must be 'the only ultimate goal' of the Jewish people, and that its achievement was 'one of the few certainties of the future.'

Churchill knew that this Jerusalem paragraph would be unwelcome to the Territorialists, strong in Manchester, who had not given up their hopes for a Jewish homeland under the British Crown in East Africa, and with whom he had been most closely associated since coming to Manchester two years earlier. He therefore did not include the Jerusalem paragraph in his message. Explaining this decision, Edward Marsh, Churchill's Private Secretary, wrote to Gaster that to Churchill's 'great disappointment and regret, he finds that he must postpone the expression of the opinions set out on the last part of the draft, touching as they do on delicate subjects, until he returns to a position of greater freedom and less responsibility.' Marsh added: 'He asks you to treat this as strictly personal to yourself.'[13]

Churchill's actual message, as sent on 30 January 1908 and based on Gaster's draft, stated: 'I am in full sympathy with the historical traditional aspirations of the Jews. The restoration to them of a centre of true racial and political integrity would be a tremendous

---

13 Gaster papers.

event in the history of the world. Whether the wide effort of the Jewish race should be concentrated upon Palestine to the exclusion of all other temporary solutions, or whether in the meanwhile some other outlet of relief and place of unification should be provided for the bitter need of those who suffer from day to day, are questions on which I could scarcely presume to express any opinion.'[14]

In April 1908 Churchill was appointed to his first full Cabinet position, as President of the Board of Trade. Under the parliamentary rules then current, he had to seek re-election. He did so, and was defeated. In order to take up his ministerial appointment he had to find a safe seat elsewhere, and did so at Dundee, in Scotland.

The friendships Churchill had made with the Manchester Jewish leaders were real and meaningful. One of them, Joseph Dulberg, wrote to commiserate on the election defeat. 'To me personally,' he wrote, 'like to very many others, the parting from you as our member seems almost like a bereavement and I cannot realise it. But I have the satisfaction that I have done my best for your success and that as far as the Jewish electors are concerned, you were not disappointed. Had the other sections of the electorate equally rallied round you, you would have won by a large majority. We reckon to have polled on our side 95% of the Jewish voters.'[15]

In the autumn of 1908, no longer its Member of Parliament, Churchill returned to Manchester to open a new wing of the Jewish Hospital in Cheetham. 'When he came among his Jewish friends in Cheetham,' Churchill said, 'there was always a good and hearty welcome awaiting him'. When he had been their Member of Parliament he took a special interest in the affairs of the Jewish community, 'and although he was no longer their member that interest still continued. He was very glad to have had the experience of watching the life and the work of the Jewish community in England; there was a high sense of the corporate responsibility in the community; there was a great sense of duty which was fostered on every possible occasion by their leaders.'

14 Letter of 30 January 1908: Gaster papers.
15 Letter of 25 April 1908: Churchill papers.

The Jewish Hospital, Churchill declared, was one of the instances 'of that corporate responsibility by which the Jews of Manchester were animated. There was so much sickness and so much destitution that one would have to possess a heart of stone to withhold sympathy and aid.' He knew that it was 'the glory of that hospital that it was open to all of whatever creed or race or whatever might be their condition of life.' He would always cherish the key to the hospital with which he had been presented, 'not only for his connection with the Hospital, but also as a memento and a token of the Jewish community in Manchester, from whom he had in the past received so many kindnesses and for whom he always cherished warm feelings of friendship and respect.'

In thanking Churchill for his 'handsome donation' to the hospital, the President of the Manchester Zionist Committee, and patron of the hospital, Dr Charles Dreyfus, stated that Churchill's name 'would go down to posterity as one who had endeared himself to the Jews in general, especially by those who had been oppressed and hit by the obnoxious Aliens Act against which he had fought so splendid a fight. They trusted that in his responsible position he might be able to do much to minimise the hardships of aliens and help them with his power and influence.'[16]

In 1910 Churchill became Home Secretary, responsible for the preservation of public order. A testing time came in the autumn of 1911, with a series of nationwide strikes in the docks, on the railways and in the mines. These were industrial disputes, centred on the call for better wages and better working conditions. For the Jews they had a tragic by-product: Britain's only pogrom. After the striking railway workers had agreed to settle their grievances by arbitration, there was a series of attacks on Jewish shops and homes throughout South Wales. The first outbreak came on 18 August, in the mining town of Tredegar, where thirty Jewish families lived among a population of 20,000. Seventeen of the breadwinners were shopkeepers,

16 *Jewish Chronicle*, 16 October 1908.

one was a mineral water manufacturer, another was a rabbi and three were pedlars. Only one derived his income from rents. But the word went around the town, and spread through the mining valleys, that Jewish landlords were evicting miners from their homes on a large scale, for non-payment of rents, and that when the tenants, in order to pay the inflated rents, took in lodgers, the Jewish landlords demanded even higher rents.

For three days the Jews of Tredegar were terrorised, their shops looted and their homes attacked. Churchill took immediate action. First, the police were ordered to block the entrances to the town to prevent attacks by rioters from neighbouring towns attracted by the prospect of loot. Then, on 20 August, the third day of the violence, after the police cordons had proved of no avail, Churchill arranged with the War Office to send a hundred soldiers to the town.[17]

The attacks continued, spreading from Tredegar to Ebbw Vale and then to other small towns in the valleys. No Jews were killed, but hundreds lost their livelihood. At Ebbw Vale, where the attacks on Jews and Jewish property started on 21 August, troops reached the town by midnight. 'While the looting was at its highest, a few minutes before midnight,' a report sent to Churchill from Ebbw Vale stated, 'the cry went round, "The soldiers are coming!" The effect was instantaneous. The looters fled to their houses like rabbits to their holes.'[18] When rioters armed with crowbars broke into a Jewish tobacconist's shop in Ebbw Vale and entered the living room, those hiding there, men, women and children, had, in the words of the *Jewish Chronicle*, 'to secrete themselves in an attic, and were rescued only by the arrival of the military. Upon being released from their hiding place, they found the shop totally wrecked and the goods stolen. Gas fittings had been wrenched off.'[19]

Similar reports about the destruction, and the beneficial effect of the arrival of troops reached Churchill on 22 August from

---

17 Home Office papers.
18 Home Office papers.
19 *Jewish Chronicle*, 25 August 1911.

other towns and villages in South Wales. His instructions to make use of troops to halt the anti-Jewish violence were everywhere carried out, and on 23 and 24 August no further outbreaks were recorded.

Churchill's despatch of troops brought criticism from both sides of the political spectrum. For trade unionists it was unpardonable to use the army against miners. For Conservatives it was a sign of unacceptable militarism to use troops at all. Yet Churchill had seen that his decision was effective, and despite the political attacks on him from both the Conservative and Labour ranks for his actions, he sent a further contingent of troops to the Sirhowy Valley, south of Tredegar, when violence against Jews broke out there.

Jewish leaders expressed their appreciation of Churchill's action. David Alexander, the President of the Board of Deputies of British Jews – the umbrella organisation protecting Jewish interests – said in an interview: 'I have it on the authority of the Home Office that there is no further cause for alarm amongst the Jewish community in South Wales. There are now ample troops in the district, and until all is absolutely quiet again these will not be withdrawn.' When Alexander reported to the Board Deputies on the outbreaks, he stated that he had come up to London on 21 August, at the height of the violence, and had gone to the Home Office, 'where he had been most cordially received and invited to come as often as he had anything to communicate. He had received adequate assurances as to the protection of the Jews from further outrages.'[20]

In the days after the attacks, Churchill ensured that as many as possible of the participants in the riots were arrested, brought before the courts, and sentenced to up to three months' hard labour. After the passing of the sentences, local populations called mass meetings and decided to collect signatures for a petition protesting against them. A deputation presented this petition to the Home Secretary,

20 Board of Deputies of British Jews Archive.

but Churchill replied, as the record of the meeting noted, that after having giving the evidence 'his careful and serious consideration, he cannot interfere with the decision of the local justices.'[21]

From his position of authority, Churchill had acted without hesitation to stamp on violence in Britain.

21 Home Office papers.

CHAPTER THREE

THE FIRST WORLD WAR AND ITS AFTERMATH

On 4 August 1914, following the German advance through Belgium, with which Britain had a treaty of alliance dating back more than seventy years, Britain declared war on Germany. Among those Jews then in Britain who immediately became enemy aliens was Theodor Herzl's son, Hans. 'Through Winston Churchill's influence,' recalled a leading British Zionist, Selig Brodetsky, 'Hans was naturalised when the war started.'[1]

Two other Jews, both Members of Parliament, were helped by Churchill after the outbreak of war. When his Austrian-born friend Baron de Forest, Liberal MP for West Ham North, was accused of belittling British naval effort and speaking in favour of a German victory, Churchill wrote to the Director of Public Prosecutions: 'I am satisfied of Baron de Forest's loyalty and sense of duty, tho' it is clear at times he has talked loosely and argumentatively.'[2] Churchill added that de Forest, who held the rank of Lieutenant Commander in the Royal Naval Volunteer Reserve, would be joining his unit in France 'next Saturday': which de Forest, urged to do so by Churchill, agreed to do, thereby avoiding possible prosecution. The previous year, Churchill had resigned from the Reform Club after de Forest had been blackballed for membership.[3]

---

1 Professor Selig Brodetsky, *Memoirs: from Ghetto to Israel*, page 70.
2 Letter of 29 September 1914: Churchill papers, 1/113.
3 Letter of 29 January 1913, Reform Club archive.

Also after the outbreak of war in 1914, German-born Major Frank Goldsmith, Conservative MP for Stowmarket, was accused of pro-German sympathies. His nephew Ernst von Marx had sent him a telegram from Germany: 'How can you consider fighting for anyone other than your Fatherland?' There were riots in Goldsmith's constituency. He even had to pay the hospital bills of those who defended him. Churchill, in the words of Goldsmith's son's biographer, was one of his few parliamentary colleagues who 'stood by him'.[4]

As the war at sea intensified, Churchill, as First Lord of the Admiralty, faced a growing shortage of acetone, the solvent used in making cordite: the essential naval explosive. Through the head of the powder department at the Admiralty, Sir Frederic Nathan, a Jewish chemical engineer, Churchill approached Chaim Weizmann, who had been working at Manchester University since his arrival in Britain a decade earlier. In his memoirs, Weizmann recalled their meeting: 'Mr Churchill, then a much younger man, was brisk, fascinating, charming and energetic. Almost his first words were: "Well, Dr Weizmann, we need thirty thousand tons of acetone. Can you make it?" I was so terrified by this lordly request that I almost turned tail.' But Weizmann did answer, telling Churchill: 'So far I have succeeded in making a few hundred cubic centimetres of acetone at a time by the fermentation process. I do my work in a laboratory. I am not a technician. I am only a research chemist. But, if I were somehow able to produce a ton of acetone, I would be able to multiply that by any factor you chose. Once the bacteriology of the process is established, it is only a question of brewing. I must get hold of a brewing engineer from one of the big distilleries, and we will set about the preliminary task. I shall naturally need the support of the Government to obtain the people, the equipment, the emplacements and the rest of it. I myself can't even determine what will be required.'

---

4 Ivon Fallon, *Billionaire*, pages 28–29. Goldsmith served in 1915 at Gallipoli with the Suffolk Yeomanry. In 1934, on a visit to Jerusalem, Churchill stayed at the King David Hotel, of which Goldsmith was one of the founders.

This explanation was satisfactory, and, as Weizmann recalled, 'I was given carte blanche by Mr Churchill and the department, and I took upon myself a task which was to tax all my energies for the next two years, and which was to have consequences which I did not foresee.'[5] Those consequences were the support shown by Churchill's successor at the Admiralty, Arthur Balfour, whom Weizmann won over to the prospect of British support for a Jewish National Home in Palestine once Turkey were defeated.

Within four months of the outbreak of war, fighting on the Western Front had become a bloody stalemate of trench warfare. As 1914 came to an end, Churchill proposed an attack on Turkey, based on a naval attack at the Dardanelles that would push past the Gallipoli Peninsula and threaten the Turkish capital, Constantinople. Churchill believed that the defeat of Turkey could help shorten the war, ending what he called the policy of 'sending our armies to chew barbed wire' on the Western Front.[6] In the fighting on the Gallipoli Peninsula between April and December 1915 an all-Jewish military force, the Zion Mule Corps, which had been recruited in Egypt mostly from Jews expelled from Palestine by the Turks, fought alongside the British, Australian and New Zealand troops.

The prospect of the defeat of Turkey stimulated British territorial ambitions. One of the two Jewish Cabinet Ministers, Sir Herbert Samuel – President of the Local Government Board – suggested that, once conquered, Palestine should be acquired by Britain as an eventual centre of Jewish self-government. Churchill felt it was time to make a 'clean sweep' of Turkey, suggesting, in a note to the Foreign Secretary, Sir Edward Grey, that 'Palestine might be given to Christian, Liberal and now noble Belgium.' Since the outbreak of war, Belgium had been suffering under harsh German occupation.

---

5 Chaim Weizmann, *Trial and Error: The Autobiography of Chaim Weizmann*, page 171. Weizmann misdated this meeting to March 1916, after Churchill had left the Admiralty and was serving as a soldier on the Western Front. As Home Secretary in 1910, Churchill had signed Weizmann's naturalisation papers.

6 Letter to H. H. Asquith (Prime Minister), 29 December 1914: Churchill papers, 26/1.

Ironically, it was Sir Herbert Samuel who had taken a lead in Britain in making Belgian refugees welcome.[7]

The failure of the naval attack on the Dardanelles led to Churchill's political eclipse. In December 1915 he resigned from the government and went to the Western Front, where he served as a battalion commander with the rank of lieutenant-colonel. The division he joined had a French interpreter, a thirty-year-old Jewish lieutenant, Emile Herzog, better known in later years as the writer André Maurois. When Churchill decided to provide his soldiers with hot baths, it was Maurois who went into the nearest town, Bailleul, to negotiate with the local brewery to provide their vats as baths. Later, at Churchill's request, Maurois helped obtain fresh mutton, vegetables and dairy products from farms behind the line for the men of Churchill's battalion. Maurois later wrote: 'I cannot hope he noticed that unknown Frenchman who looked at him with admiring eyes and said little.'[8] Churchill did indeed notice him, writing to Clementine of the 'very attentive and spruce' officer attached as an interpreter.[9]

In May 1916 Churchill returned to Britain and to his place in Parliament. That December, David Lloyd George became Prime Minister, charged with a more vigorous conduct of the war. In July 1917 he appointed Churchill as Minister of Munitions, with responsibility for the manufacture of the weapons, including tanks and aircraft, that were needed to defeat Germany. One of those with whom Churchill worked at his new Ministry was Sir Albert Stern, Director-General of Tank Production, a Jewish engineer who was a strong supporter of Zionism. Another of the senior civil servants on Churchill's Munitions Council was the Jewish explosives expert, Colonel Sir Frederic Nathan, then Director of Propellant Supplies, under whom Chaim Weizmann was working. Seven years earlier Churchill, as Home Secretary, had signed Weizmann's naturalisation papers.

7 Note of 15 March 1915: Sir Edward Grey (Viscount Grey of Falloden) papers.
8 André Maurois, letter to the author, 1969.
9 Baroness Clementine Spencer-Churchill papers.

In 1916 Weizmann had become the Director of the British Admiralty laboratories, where, by early 1917, he was using bacterial fermentation to produce substantial quantities of substances needed for the manufacture of explosives. Weizmann used the bacterium *clostridium acetobutylicum* – known as 'the Weizmann organism' – to produce the acetone for the cordite which was critical to the British and Allied war effort.

One main source of the bacterium was horse chestnuts. On 8 October 1917 several British newspapers reported that more than 25,000 tons of horse chestnuts, collected by schoolchildren, would reach the Ministry of Munitions by the end of the year. Churchill, who had not been told of the experiments, was puzzled by this activity. 'Pray explain to me why you are asking for chestnuts and what use you propose to make of them,' he wrote to Sir Frederic Nathan on 2 November 1917. Churchill underlined the words 'chestnuts'.[10] It was subsequently explained to him that the horse chestnuts were needed for Weizmann's experiments; and that acetone, of which there was a grave shortage, was needed for the production of cordite, the smokeless powder used as the propellant in rifle and artillery ammunition.

Churchill sent his letter enquiring into Weizmann's munitions activities on the same day that A. J. Balfour, Foreign Secretary in Lloyd George's government, sent a letter to the 2nd Baron Rothschild, a letter known ever since as the Balfour Declaration. The letter, on a single sheet of Foreign Office paper, read in full: 'His Majesty's Government view with favour the establishment in Palestine of a national home for the Jewish people, and will use their best endeavours to facilitate the achievement of this object, it being clearly understood that nothing shall be done which may prejudice the civil and religious rights of existing non-Jewish communities in Palestine, or the rights and political status enjoyed by Jews in any other country.'[11]

The War Cabinet hoped that, inspired by the promise of a

---

10 Ministry of Munitions papers.

11 Published in the *Jewish Chronicle*, 9 November 1917 (the British Government withheld publication for a week to enable the Jewish paper to carry it first).

national home in Palestine, Russian Jews would encourage Russia – then in the throes of revolution – to stay in the war, and that American Jewry would be stimulated to accelerate the military participation of the United States – already at war, but not yet active on the battlefield. To secure these results, Weizmann agreed to go first to the United States and then to Russia, to lead the campaign to rouse the pro-war elements among the Jewish masses in both countries. But on 8 November, before Weizmann could set off, the Bolsheviks seized power in Petrograd and declared that the war was over. The Bolshevik leader, Vladimir Ilych Lenin, had promised the Russian masses bread and peace: the first to be provided, within days of the revolution, was peace – followed by the unopposed German occupation of vast swathes of western and southern Russia.

The Balfour Declaration had been issued too late to affect the Bolshevik triumph. It did, however, encourage American Jews, especially those who had been born in Russia, to volunteer to fight in Palestine against the Turks as part of the British Army.[12] Churchill always recognised that the British Government's pledge to the Jews had been made as a result of the urgent needs of the war, and could not be set aside when, in later years, it became awkward to fulfil. The fact that the Zionist Jews had been prepared to try to prevent the Bolsheviks coming to power and pulling Russia out of the war, meant much to him. He saw the dangerous situation to Britain, France and the United States on the Western Front in March 1918, that resulted both from Russia's withdrawal from the war, and from the growing tyranny of Bolshevism inside Russia. Lenin's suppression of the democratically elected Constitutional Assembly, and the imposition of the harsh terror of the secret police, were anathema to Churchill.

In the United States, Churchill's transatlantic colleague in wartime munitions production and policy was the Jewish financier Bernard

12 Among those Russian-born American Jews who enlisted in the British Army in 1918 was Nehemia Rubitzov, who stayed on in Palestine, where, in 1922, his son, later known as Yitzhak Rabin, was born.

Baruch, who was Chairman of the War Industries Board in Woodrow Wilson's administration. Although Churchill and Baruch did not meet during the war, they exchanged many hundreds of detailed messages, as they worked in tandem to secure the raw materials essential for the continuing Allied war effort.

In France, Siegfried Sassoon, a member of the Sassoon family with whom Churchill had long been a social acquaintance, was writing powerful poems about the misery and futility of war. Churchill knew these poems by heart and often recited them. When Churchill was warned not to see Sassoon, he replied: 'I am not a bit afraid of Siegfried Sassoon. That man can think. I am only afraid of people who cannot think.'[13]

The First World War ended on 11 November 1918 with the German armistice. In Britain, the Prime Minister, David Lloyd George, called an election. The result was a predominantly Conservative House of Commons, which agreed to serve under Lloyd George in a broad-based coalition. On 26 December, while Lloyd George was forming his Cabinet, Churchill wrote to him, by hand, about its proposed composition: 'There is a point about Jews which occurs to me – you must not have too many of them.' Churchill went on to discuss the claims of the three Jewish contenders for Cabinet office in Lloyd George's Liberal Party. Two he wanted to see in the government, but as for the third, he wrote: 'Three Jews among only seven Liberal Cabinet Ministers might I fear give rise to comment.'[14] In the event, only one Jew was appointed. There were too many Conservatives who needed to be given high office if the coalition was to hold together.

In the Cabinet, Churchill was made Secretary of State for War, his first senior Cabinet post in five years. His first task was to carry out a smooth demobilisation scheme. Jewish soldiers had as much enthusiasm as their fellow comrades-in-arms for the scheme that

---

13 Recollection of Gilbert Hall (Churchill's pilot in 1918) in conversation with the author, 1971.

14 Letter of 26 December 1918: Lloyd George papers.

Churchill devised, whereby those who had served longest were sent home first.

Two years after the war, Churchill was asked to send a message for a book that listed all the Jews who fought, and those who were killed between 1914 and 1918, in the British and Empire forces. 'It is with great pleasure that I accede to your request to contribute a message . . .', he wrote. 'I feel, however, that any such message from me is unnecessary in view of the facts, which speak to themselves.' Churchill went on to point out that, although Jews formed only 'a small proportion of the population of the British Empire,' some 60,000 had fought in the war in Europe, Africa and Asia. Of these, 2,324 'gave their lives for the Cause' and a further 6,350 were wounded.

Churchill noted with appreciation that five Jewish soldiers won the Victoria Cross, 'the highest honour it is possible to obtain in our country,' while a further 1,533 won other awards for bravery. His message ended, 'I can truthfully say that this record is a great one, and British Jews can look back with pride on the honourable part they played in winning the Great War.'[15]

Churchill's main task at the War Office was to continue the government's policy, decided on before he had entered the government, of sending British war supplies to the Russian anti-Bolshevik armies, which were then seeking to drive the Bolsheviks from Petrograd and Moscow. On 2 June 1919 he read a statement by a leading anti-Bolshevik Russian that, once Petrograd had been taken from the Bolsheviks, 'great excesses' would be committed by the victorious troops. Churchill at once asked the Chief of the Imperial General Staff to prepare him a draft telegram to the general commanding the British troops in North Russia. Churchill pointed out to them that any force Britain supported even indirectly 'must proceed according to the recognised laws and customs of war and be guided by human considerations.'[16] The telegram as sent contained a sentence about the

15 Michael Adler (editor), *British Jewry Book of Honour*, page xix.
16 Letter of 2 June 1919: War Office papers, 32/5692.

widespread but far from universal Jewish support for the Bolsheviks, and its likely repercussions. 'In view of prominent part taken by Jews in Red terror and regime,' the telegram read, 'there is special danger of Jew pogroms and this danger must be combated strongly.'[17]

While fighting against the Bolshevik troops in southern Russia, the Volunteer Army commanded by General Denikin, an all-Russian force, turned savagely against the Jews in more than 160 towns and villages; many thousands of Jews were killed. Not only was there a deep anti-Semitic tradition in southern Russia and Ukraine that had seen pogroms and massacres in both the seventeenth and nineteenth centuries, but after the Bolshevik revolution in November 1917 many Jews, hoping for better times, had thrown in their lot with the Bolsheviks. A few Jews, whose deeds were much publicised and greatly feared, became political commissars, charged with the imposition of Bolshevik rule in southern Russia, and carrying out their tasks with cruelty and zeal.

Churchill knew this, but condemned the anti-Jewish terror; on 18 September 1919 he warned the senior British general in South Russia, General Holman: 'It is of the very highest consequence that General Denikin should not only do everything in his power to prevent massacres of the Jews in the liberated districts but should issue a proclamation against anti-Semitism.' Churchill added: 'The Jews are very powerful in England, and if it could be shown that Denikin was protecting them as his armies advanced it would make my task easier.'[18]

On October 14 Churchill announced that, although British troops had withdrawn from all fighting alongside the Russian anti-Bolshevik armies, British material support would continue. One result of continuing British aid, Churchill stated, will be 'of mitigating the anti-Semitism which the crimes of the Jewish Commissaries have so fearfully excited and which General Denikin has laboured faithfully to restrain.'[19]

---

17 Telegram of 6 June 1919 to General Gough: War Office papers.
18 Telegram of 18 September 1919: Churchill papers, 16/18.
19 Press statement, 14 October 1919: Churchill papers, 16/12.

The killing of Jews by Russian anti-Bolshevik forces continued. On 21 October Churchill drafted instructions to be sent to General Haking, the senior British officer attached to the anti-Bolshevik forces in the south. The instructions read: 'Everything will be done . . . to prevent indiscriminate or wholesale executions . . . Above all, anything in the nature of a Jewish pogrom would do immense harm to the Russian cause.'

Churchill's instructions continued with the threat of an arms embargo: 'All the influence of the British representative will be used in securing the safety of innocent Jews and a fair trial for all. To secure these objects General Haking is entitled to go all lengths in regard to refusal of further munitions or supplies. Using this great lever, he should be able to mitigate the ferocity of the situation which must undoubtedly arise.'[20]

After receiving a letter from Lloyd George about the continuing persecution and killing of Jews by the anti-Bolshevik Russian armies, Churchill wrote directly to Denikin: 'Your Excellency, I know, will realise the vital importance at this time, when such brilliant results are being secured, of preventing by every possible means the ill treatment of the innocent Jewish population. My task in winning support in Parliament for the Russian National Cause will be infinitely harder if well-authenticated complaints continue to be received from Jews in the zone of the Volunteer Armies. I know the efforts you have already made and the difficulty of restraining anti-Semitic feeling. But I beg you, as a sincere well-wisher, to redouble these efforts and place me in a strong position to vindicate the honour of the Volunteer Army.'[21]

A day after writing this letter, Churchill wrote to Lloyd George, 'I send you some papers about the treatment of the Jews by the Volunteer Army.' The first was that there was 'a very bitter feeling throughout Russia against the Jews, who are regarded as being the

20 Departmental note, 'Outline of Instructions for General Haking', 21 October 1919: Churchill papers, 16/18.
21 Letter of 9 October 1919: Churchill papers, 16/18.

main instigators of the ruin of the Empire, and who, certainly, have played a leading part in Bolshevik atrocities.' One result of this Russian view was 'fearful massacres' of Jews in Ukraine; they had been committed in large part by the soldiers of Simon Petlura, who had proclaimed himself head of the Ukrainian People's Republic, the anarchist warlord Nestor Makhno, and the soldiers of General Gregorieff, a former Tsarist general who had recently carried out a massacre of Jews in Odessa.

Churchill's second point was that anti-Semitism was shared by all the troops under Denikin, but that as his armies became increasingly disciplined and powerful, and as the administration behind them increased in authority, 'their feelings will be kept in strict restraint.' Churchill went on to point out that Denikin had, of his own initiative, 'constantly and repeatedly repressed by every means in his power all outrages on innocent Jews,' so much so that he had been attacked by the Petlurists and 'disgruntled' Ukrainians as the protector of the Jews and had been accused 'of being bought by them.'

Denikin's efforts to prevent the killing of Jews, Churchill told Lloyd George, 'are endorsed by General Holman, the Head of our Mission, who vouches implicitly for him and the Army Command. Indeed, the papers which you have sent me show that the Higher Command is exerting itself to its utmost.'[22]

As Secretary of State for War, Churchill also had responsibility for Palestine, which was then under British military administration. On 19 September Chaim Weizmann, as head of the Zionist Executive based in London, wrote to him, asking that he appoint as the new Chief Administrator of the British military administration someone sympathetic to Zionism. Weizmann suggested General Wyndham Deedes for the post. Although he did not say so, Deedes had been in charge of organising relief for the Jewish colonies in Palestine after the defeat of the Turks. Weizmann told Churchill he had already discussed the possibility of the appointment of Deedes with

22 Letter of 10 October 1919: Churchill papers, 16/12.

General Allenby at the Paris Peace Conference, and that Allenby had seemed 'in sympathy with such a proposal.'

Weizmann had other requests. The Zionist Organisation of which he was president 'is also very anxious,' he wrote, 'to have freedom to send to Palestine a variety of experts to make a general investigation of the country and to prepare plans, so that when the political adjustments in Paris have been made, the Jewish People can proceed, without loss of time, with the task of reconstituting Palestine as their National Home. In the course of my conversations with Lord Allenby in Paris, he urged this point rather strongly and indicated that the Zionists ought to utilise the present transitional period so as to be ready as soon as the political decision was taken.'

These were two 'concrete administrative measures', Weizmann explained, about which the Zionist Organisation was most concerned. 'I need not say that in general we desire and expect sympathetic treatment by the Military Administration of the whole Zionist Movement in Palestine. I do not wish to stress the past, but for a long time we had, under the Military Administration in Palestine, a most trying and unpleasant series of experiences. Happily, our most recent information is that the instructions sent out to the Administration of Palestine a few weeks ago have produced a very beneficial effect on the official atmosphere. The official conduct, instead of being cold and unsympathetic, is becoming appreciative of the Jewish destiny of the country. We shall be only too happy to learn that this tendency is maintained and strengthened.'[23]

Churchill sent this letter to Allenby, who replied on 15 October 1919: 'However much we may sympathise with Zionist aims, it must be borne in mind that Palestine is as yet merely occupied enemy territory, under a purely military administration. Therefore, the appointment of Chief Administrator is entirely the concern of the War Office; and not one in which the Executive of the Zionist Organisation should have any voice. This does not seem to be quite clear to Dr Weizmann.'[24] In the

23 Letter of 19 September 1919: War Office papers, 32/5732.
24 Letter of 15 October 1919: War Office papers, 32/5732.

event, Deedes was appointed six months later, and proved sympathetic to the Zionist position.

As Secretary of State for War, Churchill was concerned for the future of the Middle Eastern provinces of the defeated Ottoman Empire, fearing that the British Mandates proposed for both Palestine and Mesopotamia (Iraq) would lead to endless and costly conflict. Lloyd George had stressed to his colleagues that his aim in all foreign and overseas involvements was economy: economy of military effort and economy of expenditure. With this in mind, on 25 October 1919 Churchill wrote a memorandum for the Cabinet proposing that the Ottoman Empire should not be divided among the victorious powers, but preserved intact, and placed under the authority of the League of Nations. Such a plan would bring an end to the British Mandate in Palestine, and would lead to the abandonment of the Balfour Declaration pledge of a Jewish National Home.

In putting forward his case for an end to Britain's involvement, Churchill pointed out that the French were about 'to over-run Syria with hordes of Algerian troops' and would soon be involved 'in a protracted and bloody struggle with the Arabs who are defending their native land.' As this struggle proceeded, British sympathies would be increasingly on the side of the Arabs, causing 'serious injury' to Anglo-French relations. As to Palestine, Churchill wrote: 'Lastly, there are the Jews, whom we are pledged to introduce into Palestine and who take it for granted that the local population will be cleared out to suit their convenience.'

The above causes, Churchill warned, 'act and re-act' upon Britain's position as 'the greatest Mahommedan Power' – because of the twenty million Muslims in British India – and involve Britain 'in immense expense and anxiety.' He was therefore 'reluctantly drawn to the conclusion' that the policy of partitioning the Turkish Empire among the European Powers was a mistake.[25]

25 Cabinet memorandum, 14 October 1919: Churchill papers, 16/18.

Had Lloyd George responded positively to Churchill's suggestion, Britain's responsibility for the Jewish National Home would have come to an abrupt end. But Lloyd George was keen to retain British rule in Palestine, and committed to the Jewish National Home consequences of the Balfour Declaration. Within four months Churchill became a more articulate and determined advocate of this commitment.

CHAPTER FOUR

'A STRUGGLE FOR THE SOUL OF THE JEWISH PEOPLE'

In his determination to see Bolshevism crushed in Russia, Churchill studied the nature and organisation of the Bolshevik government in Moscow. He was familiar with the names and origins of all its leaders: Lenin was almost the only member of the Central Committee who was not of Jewish origin. Neither Churchill nor his colleagues, nor the Jews, knew that Lenin's paternal grandfather was a Jew.

In a speech in Sunderland on 2 January 1920, surveying the world scene, Churchill described Bolshevism as a 'Jewish movement'.[1] Churchill had nothing but contempt for what he described as 'the foul baboonery of Bolshevism.' A friend from his Admiralty years, Captain Cromie, had been killed on the steps of the British Embassy in Petrograd when the embassy had been attacked by a Bolshevik mob. Churchill had studied the Bolshevik terror against political opponents, democrats and constitutionalists, and he knew the significant part individual Jews had played in establishing and maintaining the Bolshevik regime.

For the several million Jews of Russia, caught up in the rapid and often ruthless spread of the Bolshevik revolution, three possibilities beckoned: to emigrate, either to Palestine or to the West; to seek to maintain Jewish social, religious and cultural institutions within Russia despite Bolshevik hostility; or to throw in their lot with the

1 *The Times*, 5 January 1920.

Bolsheviks. A minority chose the latter. It was with these facts in mind that, on 8 February 1920, a month after his Sunderland speech, Churchill wrote a long and closely argued article for a popular British Sunday newspaper, the *Illustrated Sunday Herald*, appealing to the Jews of Russia, and beyond, to choose between Zionism and Bolshevism. 'Some people like Jews and some do not,' Churchill wrote, 'but no thoughtful man can doubt the fact that they are beyond all question the most formidable and the most remarkable race which has ever appeared in the world.'

In a paragraph that the newspaper headed 'Good and Bad Jews', Churchill characterised the Jewish people in dramatic terms: 'The conflict between good and evil which proceeds unceasingly in the breast of man,' he told his readers, 'nowhere reaches such intensity as in the Jewish race. The dual nature of mankind is nowhere more strongly or more terribly exemplified.' Elaborating on this theme, he expressed his profound regard for an aspect of Judaism that had impressed itself upon him through his familiarity with the Old Testament. 'We owe to the Jews in the Christian revelation,' he wrote, 'a system of ethics which, even if it were entirely separated from the supernatural, would be incomparably the most precious possession of mankind, worth in fact the fruits of all other wisdom and learning put together. On that system and by that faith there has been built out of the wreck of the Roman Empire the whole of our existing civilisation.'

Jewish creativity was not, however, necessarily the final word. 'It may well be,' Churchill wrote, 'that this same astounding race may at the present time be in the actual process of producing another system of morals and philosophy, as malevolent as Christianity was benevolent, which, if not arrested, would shatter irretrievably all that Christianity has rendered possible.' This was Bolshevism. 'It would almost seem,' Churchill commented, 'as if the gospel of Christ and the gospel of Antichrist were destined to originate among the same people; and that this mystic and mysterious race had been chosen for the supreme manifestations, both of the divine and the diabolical.'

Churchill did not want to create a racial stereotype. There could be 'no greater mistake,' he wrote, 'than to attribute to each individual a recognisable share in the qualities which make up the national character. There are all sorts of men – good, bad and, for the most part, indifferent – in every country, and in every race. Nothing is more wrong than to deny to an individual, on account of race or origin, his right to be judged on his personal merits and conduct. In a people of peculiar genius like the Jews, contrasts are more vivid, the extremes are more widely separated, the resulting consequences are more decisive.'

At the present 'fateful period' of history, Churchill wrote, 'there are three main lines of political conception among the Jews, two of which are helpful and hopeful in a very high degree to humanity, and the third absolutely destructive.' First there were the Jews who, 'dwelling in every country throughout the world, identify themselves with that country, enter into its national life, and, while adhering faithfully to their own religion, regard themselves as citizens in the fullest sense of the State which has received them.' Churchill noted that such a Jew living in England would say, 'I am an Englishman practising the Jewish faith.' This, Churchill added, 'is a worthy conception, and useful in the highest degree. We in Great Britain well know that during the great struggle the influence of what may be called the "National Jews" in many lands was cast preponderatingly on the side of the Allies; and in our own Army Jewish soldiers have played a most distinguished part, some rising to the command of armies, others winning the Victoria Cross for valour.'

Churchill also pointed out that the 'National Russian Jews,' in spite of the disabilities under which they had suffered, 'have managed to play an honourable and useful part in the national life even of Russia. As bankers and industrialists they have strenuously promoted the development of Russia's economic resources, and they were foremost in the creation of those remarkable organisations, the Russian Co-operative Societies. In politics their support has been given, for the most part, to liberal and progressive movements, and they have been among the staunchest upholders of friendship with France and Great Britain.'

Turning to what he called 'International Jews', those Jews who supported Bolshevik rule inside Russia and Bolshevik revolution beyond its borders, Churchill told his readers: 'In violent opposition to all this sphere of Jewish effort rise the schemes of the International Jews. The adherents of this sinister confederacy are mostly men reared up among the unhappy populations of countries where Jews are persecuted on account of their race. Most, if not all, of them have forsaken the faith of their forefathers, and divorced from their minds all spiritual hopes of the next world.'

There was, Churchill continued – in the section of his article headed 'Terrorist Jews' – 'no need to exaggerate the part played in the creation of Bolshevism and in the actual bringing about of the Russian Revolution, by these international and for the most part atheistical Jews,' but he went on to write that the part they played 'is certainly a very great one; it probably outweighs all others. With the notable exception of Lenin, the majority of the leading figures are Jews. Moreover, the principal inspiration and driving power comes from the Jewish leaders.'

Churchill then listed some of the Jews who held real power, and the non-Jews whom they overshadowed. In the Soviet institutions, he wrote, 'the predominance of Jews is even more astonishing.' The 'prominent, if not indeed the principal, part in the system of terrorism applied by the Extraordinary Commissions for Combating Counter-Revolution' – the CHEKA – 'has been taken by Jews, and in some notable cases by Jewesses.' This was true, although the founder of the Cheka, Feliks Dzerzhinsky, a Pole, was not Jewish. Churchill might also have told his readers, as was well known, that in August 1918 the head of the Petrograd Cheka, a Jew, had been assassinated, by a fellow Jew, and that two weeks later a Jewess, Fanya Kaplan, had attempted to assassinate Lenin.

Outside Russia, Churchill told his readers, 'the same evil prominence was obtained by Jews in the brief period of terror during which Bela Kun ruled in Hungary. The same phenomenon has been presented in Germany (especially in Bavaria), so far as this madness has been allowed to prey upon the temporary prostration of the

German people.' Although in all these countries, Churchill reflected, 'there are many non-Jews every whit as bad as the worst of the Jewish revolutionaries, the part played by the latter in proportion to their numbers in the population is astonishing.'

Churchill then turned to the anti-Jewish pogroms in Ukraine, about which he had earlier protested to General Denikin. 'Needless to say,' he wrote, 'the most intense passions of revenge have been excited in the breasts of the Russian people.' The 'hordes of brigands' by whom Russia was 'becoming infested do not hesitate to gratify their lust for blood and for revenge at the expense of the innocent Jewish population whenever an opportunity occurs.' Anti-Bolshevik warlords 'signalised their every success by the most brutal massacres, everywhere found among the half-stupefied, half-infuriated population as an eager response to anti-Semitism in its worst and foulest forms.'

Churchill noted that 'the fact that in many cases Jewish interests and Jewish places of worship are excepted by the Bolsheviks from their universal hostility has tended more and more to associate the Jewish race in Russia with the villainies which are now being perpetrated.' This, he wrote, was an injustice on millions of helpless people: Jews who were themselves suffering under the Bolshevik regime. It was therefore 'specially important to foster and develop any strongly-marked Jewish movement which leads directly away from these fatal associations. And it is here that Zionism has such a deep significance for the whole world at the present time.'

Headed 'A Home for the Jews', the next section of Churchill's article was a public declaration in favour of Zionism. He was able to draw on both his recent correspondence with Weizmann and his experiences in Manchester twelve years earlier, when he represented a constituency in which Zionism had been much debated. 'Zionism offers the third sphere to the political conceptions of the Jewish race,' Churchill wrote. 'In violent contrast to international communism, it presents to the Jew a national idea of a commanding character.'

It had fallen to the British Government, Churchill explained, as the result of the conquest of Palestine, 'to have the opportunity and the responsibility of securing for the Jewish race all over the world a home and a centre of national life. The statesmanship and historic sense of Mr Balfour were prompt to seize this opportunity. Declarations have been made which have irrevocably decided the policy of Great Britain.' The 'fiery energies' of Dr Weizmann – 'the leader, for practical purposes, of the Zionist project, backed by many of the most prominent British Jews . . . are all directed to achieving the success of this inspiring movement.'

The small size of Palestine was another aspect of Zionism that Churchill had studied, but he saw the potential of the country for considerable growth. 'Of course,' he wrote, 'Palestine is far too small to accommodate more than a fraction of the Jewish race, nor do the majority of national Jews wish to go there. But if, as may well happen, there should be created in our own lifetime by the banks of the Jordan a Jewish State under the protection of the British Crown, which might comprise three or four millions of Jews, an event would have occurred in the history of the world which would, from every point of view, be beneficial, and would be especially in harmony with the truest interests of the British Empire.'

Churchill noted that Zionism had already become a factor in the 'political convulsions' of Russia, and was 'a powerful competing influence in Bolshevik circles with the international communistic system.' Nothing could be more significant, he pointed out, than 'the fury' with which the head of the Red Army, Leon Trotsky – who had been born Jewish but rejected Jewish national aspirations – 'has attacked the Zionists generally' and Weizmann in particular. The 'cruel penetration' of Trotsky's mind 'leaves him in no doubt that his schemes of a world-wide communistic State under Jewish domination are directly thwarted and hindered by this new ideal, which directs the energies and the hopes of Jews in every land towards a simpler, a truer, and a far more attainable goal.'

The lesson Churchill drew was emphatic: 'The struggle which is now beginning between the Zionist and Bolshevik Jews is little less than a struggle for the soul of the Jewish people.' It was therefore particularly important 'that the national Jews in every country who are loyal to the land of their adoption should come forward on every occasion, as many of them in England have already done, and take a prominent part in every measure for combating the Bolshevik conspiracy.' In this way they would be able 'to vindicate the honour of the Jewish name' and to make it clear to all the world that the Bolshevik movement was not a Jewish movement, 'but is repudiated vehemently by the great mass of the Jewish race.'

A 'negative resistance' to Bolshevism was not enough, Churchill stressed. 'Positive and practicable alternatives are needed in the moral as well as in the social sphere; and in building up with the utmost possible rapidity a Jewish national centre in Palestine which may become not only a refuge to the oppressed from the unhappy lands of Central Europe, but which will also be a symbol of Jewish unity and the temple of Jewish glory, a task is presented on which many blessings rest.'[2]

Although Churchill's article contained an outspoken endorsement of Zionism, its section on Bolshevik Jews infuriated the *Jewish Chronicle*, which blasted Churchill in a fierce editorial. 'The Secretary of War,' it wrote, 'charges Jews with originating the gospel of Antichrist with engineering a "world-wide conspiracy for the overthrow of civilisation."' He also charged the 'ex-Jew' Trotsky – 'who has jeeringly cast aside every connection with Judaism and refused even to listen to Jewish pleas for protection from massacre, with a scheme for "a world-wide communistic State under Jewish domination."' This, declared the editorial writer, was 'the gravest, as it is the most reckless and scandalous campaign in which even the most discredited politicians have ever engaged.' Nor was it 'rendered in any degree more tolerable by fantastic flattery of the Jews as "beyond all question the most formidable and the most remarkable race which has ever appeared in the world" – very much the reverse. We can dispense with Mr Churchill's double-edged appreciation in

2 Winston S. Churchill, 'Zionism versus Bolshevism: A Struggle for the Soul of the Jewish People', *Illustrated Sunday Herald*, 8 February 1920.

return for some approach to justice in the handling of matters which involve the lives and the honour of millions of men, women, and children. It is difficult to understand the object of this tirade, with its flashy generalisations and shallow theories.'[3]

The *Jewish Chronicle* did not know that a few weeks before writing the article, Churchill had been sent a copy of a new British edition of *The Protocols of the Learned Elders of Zion*: a Tsarist-era forgery portraying the Jews as seeking to dominate the world by conspiracy and guile. Aspects of this accusation were clearly echoed in the article. But Churchill's strong support in this same article for Zionism – an aspect of the article ignored by the *Jewish Chronicle* editorial – came at a time when the British wartime pledge to the Zionists was being much opposed in British political circles. This was particularly so in the Conservative Party, which formed an important element in Lloyd George's peacetime coalition. On 23 December 1920 a senior Conservative, the 17 Earl of Derby, wrote to Churchill: 'I look upon our Mandate for Palestine and the Zionist State as being dangerous in the extreme. In the first place it has made a lot of bad feeling between us and France, who for sentimental reasons think they should be a prominent power in Syria, and we are going to create a Zionist State composed of every Bolshevik Jew who will come there from the middle of Europe.'[4]

Churchill, with his high hopes for Zionism as a counterweight to Jewish Bolshevik sympathies, was keen for Britain to keep the Palestine Mandate, and also to ensure that the Jews who went there were free from the taint of Bolshevism. His chance to ensure this was about to come.

---

3 *Jewish Chronicle*, 13 February 1920.
4 Letter of 23 December 1920: Churchill papers, 2/111.

CHAPTER FIVE

RESPONSIBILITY FOR THE JEWISH NATIONAL HOME

In January 1921 Lloyd George appointed Churchill as Secretary of State for the Colonies, with special responsibility for Britain's two Mandates, Palestine and Mesopotamia (Iraq). In both places, his main purpose, as Lloyd George explained to him, would be to reduce the cost of administering these distant and largely desert regions. First and foremost, Britain must find ways of cheaper administration. With regard to Palestine there was a second aim – no less important in the British Government's eyes – to carry out the terms of the Balfour Declaration and facilitate the establishment of a Jewish National Home.

Britain had been awarded a Mandate for Palestine by the San Remo Conference of former wartime Allies in April 1920, whereupon the existing British military administration – for which Churchill had been responsible at the War Office – was replaced by a civil administration, headed by Sir Herbert Samuel as High Commissioner. It was Samuel who, in 1915, when a Cabinet Minister and a Jew, had urged his Cabinet colleagues to establish a Jewish homeland in Palestine once Turkey had been defeated. He was proud of his Jewish heritage, but equally of his Britishness, and was determined to ensure that British interests were upheld in Palestine: for this reason, he was quick to criticise and even punish anything that he regarded as excessive in Zionist demands and actions.

To enable Churchill to focus on the Middle East, and on its twin needs of economy and political evolution, a Middle East Department was set up in the Colonial Office. Its civil service head was John Shuckburgh, who for twenty-one years had served in the India Office political department and was familiar with Muslim attitudes and aspirations. Churchill also asked Colonel T. E. Lawrence, better known as Lawrence of Arabia, to be his Arab affairs adviser. Lawrence had been one of the British officers attached to the Arab Revolt against the Turks in 1917–18, helping Sherif Hussein of Mecca and his sons to drive the Turks from the Arabian peninsula. Hussein had then declared himself King of the Arab Countries.

On 11 January, a month before formally going to the Colonial Office, Churchill was in Paris, where he discussed his new Middle Eastern responsibilities with Alexandre Millerand, the French President, who criticised Britain's support for a Jewish National Home. According to Churchill's account, in a letter to Lloyd George, Lord Curzon – the Foreign Secretary – and two senior government officials, Millerand 'instanced Zionism in Palestine as a cause of disturbing the Arab world,' telling Churchill that 'he feared that the Jews would be very high-handed when they got together there.' Churchill defended British policy towards the Jews, telling Lloyd George, 'I expatiated on the virtues and experience of Sir Herbert Samuel and pointed out how evenly he was holding the balance between Arabs and Jews and how effectively he was restraining his own people, as perhaps only a Jewish administrator could do.'[1]

Negotiations with the Arab leaders beyond Palestine were being carried out by T. E. Lawrence, who informed Churchill on 17 January that he had concluded an agreement with Hussein's eldest son, Emir Feisal, under which, in return for Arab sovereignty in Baghdad, Amman and Damascus, Feisal 'agreed to abandon all claims of his father to Palestine.'[2]

The Lawrence–Feisal agreement, with its Arab acceptance of the Jewish position in Palestine, was welcome news for Churchill. Since the French were installed in Damascus and were not to be dislodged,

---

1 Letter of 12 January 1921 (to Lloyd George, Lord Curzon, Lord D'Abernon and Lord Hardinge): Churchill papers, 16/71.

2 Letter from T. E. Lawrence to Churchill's Private Secretary, 17 January 1921: Churchill papers, 17/14.

Churchill favoured a scheme whereby Feisal would accept the throne of Iraq, and his brother Abdullah the throne of Transjordan, in return for Western Palestine – from the Mediterranean Sea to the River Jordan – becoming the location of the Jewish National Home, under British control.

The first decision Churchill was called upon to make with regard to Palestine concerned the application, by Pinhas Rutenberg – a former Russian revolutionary who had been one of the defenders of the Winter Palace against the Bolsheviks in 1917 – for a concession to harness the waters of the Jordan and Yarkon rivers for electrical power. The concession would give employment to eight hundred people, both Jews and Arabs. The proposal was put to Churchill on 23 February. He agreed on the following day.[3] It was his first commitment to practical Zionist enterprise in Palestine, enabling the Jews to begin to plan for substantial urban and rural development.

In April 1921, Churchill prepared to set off from London for Cairo and Jerusalem. His object was to determine the nature of British rule in both the Palestine and Iraq Mandates. He had set aside four weeks for the task, which, in Palestine, would include visits to Jewish towns and villages. Before he left London, his three senior Middle East Department advisers, Lawrence, Shuckburgh, and Major Hubert Young – who like Lawrence had helped the Arab forces during the revolt against the Turks – informed him that there was no conflict between Britain's wartime pledges to the Arabs and to the Jews. In 1915 the Arabs had been promised 'British recognition and support for their independence' in the Turkish districts of Damascus, Hama, Homs and Aleppo – each of which was mentioned in the promise – but which did not include Palestine or Jerusalem.[4] Two years later Britain had promised a national home for the Jewish people in Palestine, but with no mention of specific borders. If,

3 Minute of 24 February 1921: Colonial Office papers, 733/1.

4 Letter from Sir Henry McMahon to Sherif Hussein, 24 October 1915: *Report of a Committee set up to consider certain correspondence between Sir Henry McMahon and the Sharif of Mecca in 1915 and 1916*: Command Paper 5974 of 1939.

therefore, the land east of the Jordan became an Arab State, and the land west of the Jordan up to the Mediterranean Sea became the area of the Jewish National Home, Britain's two pledges would be fulfilled.

To ensure that Britain had not promised the same area to both the Jews and the Arabs, Churchill's senior adviser at the Middle East Department, Sir John Shuckburgh, asked Sir Henry McMahon why neither Palestine nor Jerusalem had been specifically mentioned in his letters as part of the future Arab sovereignty. McMahon replied that his reasons for 'restricting myself' to specific mention of Damascus, Hama, Homs and Aleppo were '(1) that these were places to which the Arabs attached vital importance and (2) that there was no place I could think of at the time of sufficient importance for purposes of definition further south of the above.' McMahon added, 'It was as fully my intention to exclude Palestine as it was to exclude the more northern coastal tracts of Syria.' The reason he had not mentioned the River Jordan as the most westerly limit of Arab control was that he thought it might be 'desirable' at some later stage of the negotiations to find 'some suitable frontier line' between the Jordan and the Hedjaz railway.[5] This was the area that Weizmann and the Zionist leaders hoped to include within the Jewish National Home.

During 1 March the Political Committee of the Zionist Organisation met in London to discuss Churchill's forthcoming visit. According to the minutes of the meeting, Weizmann was worried about the delay in ratifying the Palestine Mandate. 'There were indications,' he said, 'that Mr Churchill might possibly desire certain changes in the Mandate. He was of a highly impressionable temperament and it was to be expected that the Arabs would organise an agitation to greet him on his arrival in the East.' But, Weizmann added, Churchill had 'a low opinion of the Arab generally.'[6]

Hoping to influence Churchill about the future boundaries of Palestine, Weizmann sent him a thousand-word appeal, asking him

---

5 Letter of 12 March 1922: Foreign Office papers, 371/7797.
6 Meeting of 1 March 1921: Central Zionist Archives.

to extend the eastern boundary of Palestine across the Jordan river to the line of the Hedjaz Railway, or even beyond, deep into Transjordan. The British, Weizmann wrote, could provide 'special safeguards for the Moslem interests in the Hedjaz Railway' in such a way as to allow the whole of Transjordan to become a part of the Jewish National Home. 'It is upon these fields, now that the rich plains to the north have been taken away from Palestine and given to France, that the success of the Jewish National Home must largely rest. Trans-Jordania has from the earliest time been an integral and vital part of Palestine.'

It was east of the Jordan, Weizmann added, that the Israelite tribes of Reuben, Gad and Manasseh 'first pitched their tents and pastured their flocks.' Although 'Eastern Palestine' would never have the same religious or historic significance for the Jews as Palestine west of the Jordan, it might, he felt, 'bulk larger in the economic future of the Jewish National Home.'

Weizmann elaborated his argument in lyrical terms. 'The climate of Trans-Jordania is invigorating; the soil is rich; irrigation would be easy; and the hills are covered with forests. There Jewish settlement could proceed on a large scale without friction with the local population. The economic progress of Cis-Jordania itself is dependent upon the development of these Trans-Jordania plains, for they form the natural granary of all Palestine and without them Palestine can never become a self-sustaining, economic unit and a real National Home.'

In asserting the Zionist claim to the western, fertile areas of Transjordan, Weizmann raised the question of Arab national aspirations. It was clear, he told Churchill, that apart from 'a small corridor' along the Hedjaz Railway, there was 'no concession north of Ma'an, short of Damascus, to which Arab nationalism, would attach any real or permanent value.' The aspirations of Arab nationalism, Weizmann asserted, 'centre around Damascus and Baghdad, and do not lie in Trans-Jordania.[7]

---

7 See map on page 317.

Weizmann did not ask for Transjordan alone to be included in the Palestine Mandate. He also pressed Churchill to take the southern boundary of Palestine down to the Gulf of Akaba, asking for this area as well as Transjordan as compensation for Britain's agreement with France, which fixed the northern boundary in such a way as to 'cut Palestine off' from the Litani River, whose waters the Zionists had hoped to harness for electrical and industrial purposes. The area between Beersheba and the Gulf of Akaba, which Weizmann claimed as part of the area of the Jewish National Home, was 'derelict, but potentially rich in resources essential to Palestine's future,' and ought not to be 'allotted to Egypt.' This area, known as the Negev, was largely waste and of 'no value to any country but Palestine.'[8]

Churchill was not influenced by Weizmann's arguments. He had already decided to separate Transjordan from Palestine. But he had also decided to allow the Negev to form part of the Palestine Mandate, and therefore to be open to eventual Jewish settlement.

Churchill left London on the evening of 1 March, travelling by train to Marseille where he was joined by his wife Clementine, and then continuing by steamship to Egypt, which they reached on 9 March. The Cairo Conference began three days later. Among those present was Sir Herbert Samuel, Britain's first High Commissioner to Palestine, and T. E. Lawrence. The first decision made on Palestine, on 17 March, was that Transjordan should be separated from Palestine, as proposed by the Middle East Department and supported by Churchill, thus enabling Britain to fulfil its wartime pledges to both the Arabs and the Jews. Weizmann's territorial demands had been rejected, but the Jews would be able to settle the land from the Mediterranean to the Jordan, and from the upper Galilee to the Negev desert. This comprised the area of both Israel and the West Bank today.

While in Cairo, Churchill explained that the presence of an Arab

8 Weizmann papers.

ruler under British overall control east of the Jordan would enable Britain to prevent anti-Zionist agitation from the Arab side of the river. Lawrence shared this view, stressing that pressure could be brought on the proposed ruler in Amman, Emir Abdullah, 'to check anti-Zionism.' Lawrence also 'trusted' that after four or five years, 'under the influence of a just policy,' Arab opposition to Zionism 'would have decreased, if it had not entirely disappeared.'[9]

The presence of Lawrence of Arabia was of inestimable benefit to Churchill in his desire to help the Jews of Palestine. Lawrence, like Churchill, saw virtue in the Zionist enterprise. His friendship with the Arab leaders with whom he had fought during the Arab Revolt was paralleled by his understanding of Zionist aspirations, and his keenness to see the Zionists help the Arabs forward in Palestine – and elsewhere in the Middle East – to modernity and prosperity. Two years earlier Lawrence had brought Weizmann to a conference with Emir Feisal, held at the port of Akaba. Lawrence's hope for this meeting was to ensure what he termed 'the lines of Arab and Zionist policy converging in the not distant future.'[10] On the first anniversary of the Balfour Declaration in November 1918, Lawrence had told a British Jewish newspaper: 'Speaking entirely as a non-Jew, I look on the Jews as the natural importers of western leaven so necessary for countries of the Near East.'[11]

9 Colonial Office papers, 935/1/1.
10 T. E. Lawrence papers.
11 Message to the *Jewish Guardian*, 28 November 1918.

CHAPTER SIX

PLEDGES IN JERUSALEM

At midnight on 23 March 1921, Churchill left Egypt for Palestine by overnight train. Sir Herbert Samuel and T. E. Lawrence accompanied him. At that time 83,000 Jews and 600,000 Arabs lived between the Mediterranean Sea and the River Jordan, in what was known as Western Palestine. No Jews lived east of the river. Churchill's principal object in going to Jerusalem was to explain to Emir Abdullah the decision of the Cairo Conference, and of the British Government, that Britain would support him as ruler of the area of the Mandate lying east of the River Jordan – hence its name, Transjordan – provided that Abdullah would accept a Jewish National Home within Western Palestine, and do his utmost to prevent anti-Zionist agitation among his people east of the Jordan.

Lawrence had already secured a pledge from Feisal, Abdullah's brother, that 'all necessary measures' would be taken 'to encourage and stimulate immigration of Jews into Palestine on a large scale, and as quickly as possible upon the land through close settlement and intensive cultivation of the soil.'[1]

On the morning of 24 March, Churchill's train reached Gaza, the first large town within the southwestern boundaries of the Palestine Mandate. Gaza had a population of more than 15,000 Arabs, and fewer than a hundred Jews. A British police guard of honour met him at the railway crossing, and a mounted escort took him to the town. Captain Maxwell Coote, a Royal Air Force officer who had served as Churchill's Orderly Officer in Cairo, later recalled

1 T. E. Lawrence papers.

that there was 'a tremendous reception by a howling mob, all shouting in Arabic "Cheers for the Minister" and also for Great Britain, but their chief cry over which they waxed quite frenzied was "Down with the Jews", "Cut their throats". Mr Churchill and Sir Herbert were delighted with the enthusiasm of their reception, being not in the least aware of what was being shouted. Lawrence of course, understood it all and told me, but we kept very quiet. He was obviously gravely anxious about the whole situation. We toured the town surrounded by this almost fanatical mob which was becoming more and more worked up by its shouting. No one appeared to have bargained for this, but all went off without incident.'[2]

It was twenty-two years since Churchill had last been in a Muslim setting, when he had been part of the British Army fighting the Sudanese Islamic khalif. His views on Islam had been formed then, and were not favourable. In his book *The River War*, first published in 1899, he had written: 'How dreadful are the curses which Mohammedanism lays on its votaries! Besides the fanatical frenzy, which is as dangerous in a man as hydrophobia in a dog, there is this fearful fatalistic apathy. The effects are apparent in many countries. Improvident habits, slovenly systems of agriculture, sluggish methods of commerce, and insecurity of property exist wherever the followers of the Prophet rule or live. A degraded sensualism deprives this life of its grace and refinement; the next of its dignity and sanctity.'

Churchill had gone on to write: 'The fact that in Mohammedan law every woman must belong to some man as his absolute property, either as a child, a wife, or a concubine, must delay the final extinction of slavery until the faith of Islam has ceased to be a great power among men. Individual Moslems may show splendid qualities – but the influence of the religion paralyses the social development of those who follow it. No stronger retrograde force exists in the world. Far from being moribund, Mohammedanism is a militant and

2 Recollections of Captain Maxwell H. Coote, in A. W. Lawrence (editor), *T. E. Lawrence by His Friends*, page 236.

proselytising faith. It has already spread throughout Central Africa, raising fearless warriors at every step; and were it not that Christianity is sheltered in the strong arms of science, the science against which it had vainly struggled, the civilisation of modern Europe might fall, as fell the civilisation of ancient Rome.'[3]

Before Churchill rejoined the train in Gaza, he was presented with a petition signed by the leading Muslims of the town, setting out their aspirations for Arab statehood in Palestine, and protesting against Jewish immigration. The Arab reaction to Churchill's arrival in Palestine did not bode well for fulfilling Lloyd George's instructions for a cheap – and a tranquil – administration. On 25 March there were Arab demonstrations in Haifa to protest against any further Jewish immigration. The British Mandate authorities, who had announced a ban on all public meetings during Churchill's visit, tried to break up the demonstrations. Violence followed, and the police opened fire. A thirteen-year-old Christian boy and a Muslim Arab woman were killed. Following this police action, anti-Jewish riots broke out in Haifa, during which ten Jews and five policemen were injured by knives and stones.

Taking up residence in Government House – the former German hospice on the crest of Mount Scopus, the Augusta Victoria, modelled on the castle of Hohenstaufen in the Rhineland – Churchill worked for three days on the task ahead of him: to listen to both Arab and Jewish representatives, and to give them his answer to their respective requests. He also set up his easel and, as a keen amateur painter, painted the sunset over the city.

On Sunday 27 March Churchill went to the British Military Cemetery on the Mount of Olives, to attend a service of dedication. After the service he made a short speech. 'It was a company of many people and diverse faiths,' he said, 'which had met to commemorate the victorious dead, who had given their lives to liberate the land and to bring about peace and amity amongst its inhabitants, but there

3 Winston S. Churchill, *The River War*, Volume Two, pages 248–50.

remained the duty and responsibility on those who were present to see that the task was completed.'

The cemetery, established after the conquest of Jerusalem at the end of 1917, contained the graves of 2,180 British soldiers, 143 Australians, fifty South Africans, forty British West Indians and thirty-four New Zealanders, as well as sixty men whose bodies it had not been possible to identify, and the graves of sixteen German, five Italian and three Turkish soldiers. 'These veteran soldiers,' Churchill said, 'lie here where rests the dust of the Khalifs and Crusaders and the Maccabees. Peace to their ashes, honour to their memory and may we not fail to complete the work which they have begun.'[4]

The ceremony ended with three volleys fired by a guard of honour, and the sounding of the Last Post.

On 28 March Churchill welcomed Abdullah to Government House in Jerusalem. Abdullah insisted that an Arab Emir in Palestine was the best solution 'to reconcile the Arabs and the Jews.' He expressed his fears to Churchill, asking him: 'Did His Majesty's Government mean to establish a Jewish kingdom west of the Jordan and to turn out the non-Jewish population? If so, it would be better to tell the Arabs at once and not to keep them in suspense . . . The Allies appeared to think that men could be cut down and transplanted in the same way as trees.'

Churchill sought to put Abdullah's mind at rest, telling him that there was 'in his opinion, a great deal of groundless apprehension among the Arabs in Palestine. They appeared to anticipate that hundreds and thousands of Jews were going to pour into the country in a very short time and dominate the existing population. This was not only not contemplated, but quite impossible.' There were then more than 600,000 Arabs in Palestine and 80,000 Jews. 'Jewish immigration would be a very slow process and the rights of the existing non-Jewish population would be strictly preserved.'

'A very slow process' was not what the Zionists had envisaged. But Churchill assured Abdullah that if the Emir promised not to

---

4 *Egyptian Gazette*, 28 March 1921.

interfere with Zionist activity in Western Palestine, the British Government would promise that the Zionist clauses of the Mandate 'would not apply' in Transjordan, and that the Transjordan Government 'would not be expected to adopt any measures to promote Jewish immigration and colonization.'[5] This promise effectively destroyed Weizmann's appeal for Jewish economic development east of the Jordan, and ended Zionist hopes of being able to extend the area of their settlement into the biblical lands of Bashan and Gilead.

As a result of his meetings with Abdullah, Churchill was able to report back to London that Transjordan would become an Arab kingdom ruled by Abdullah, and that Western Palestine, from the Mediterranean to the River Jordan, would be ruled by Britain, with a commitment to continued Jewish immigration.

On 29 March Abdullah visited the Mosque of Omar, the seventh-century Muslim shrine built on Jerusalem's Temple Mount. Just outside the Mosque – where three decades later he was to be assassinated by a Palestinian gunman – he tried to speak to the Arabs who had gathered to see him, but was interrupted by shouts of 'Palestine for the Arabs' and 'Down with the Zionists'. The crowd then marched to the General Post Office to demonstrate against the Balfour Declaration. They were dispersed by armed British police.[6]

That afternoon, in Jerusalem, Churchill visited the building site on Mount Scopus of the future Hebrew University, which opened four years later. Churchill's visit to the site was an important landmark in the university's progress. Before planting a tree, he spoke words of encouragement that thrilled his listeners. 'Personally, my heart is full of sympathy for Zionism,' he told them. 'This sympathy has existed for a long time, since twelve years ago, when I was in contact with the Manchester Jews. I believe that the establishment of a Jewish National Home in Palestine will be a blessing to the whole

---

5 Colonial Office papers, 935/1/1.
6 *Palestine Post*, 30 March 1921.

world, a blessing to the Jewish race scattered all over the world, and a blessing to Great Britain. I firmly believe that it will be a blessing also to all the inhabitants of this country without distinction of race and religion. This last blessing depends greatly upon you.'

Churchill pointed out that Britain's promise 'was a double one. On the one hand, we promised to give our help to Zionism, and on the other, we assured the non-Jewish inhabitants that they should not suffer in consequence. Every step you take should therefore be also for moral and material benefit of all Palestinians. If you do this, Palestine will be happy and prosperous, and peace and concord will always reign; it will turn into a paradise, and will become, as is written in the scriptures you have just presented to me, a land flowing with milk and honey, in which sufferers of all races and religions will find a rest from their sufferings. You Jews of Palestine have a very great responsibility; you are the representatives of the Jewish nation all over the world, and your conduct should provide an example for, and do honour to, Jews in all countries.'

Churchill continued: 'The hope of your race for so many centuries will be gradually realised here, not only for your own good, but for the good of all the world.'[7]

Churchill's speech made a profound impression on the Zionists, who felt that they had found a friend. More than that: James de Rothschild, a leading British Jew and Member of Parliament, understood that by removing Abdullah from any control over Western Palestine, and giving him the eastern part of Mandated Palestine, Churchill had ensured the survival of the Jewish National Home. Thirty-four years later, Rothschild wrote to Churchill, thanking him for the fact that in Jerusalem in 1921 'you laid the foundation of the Jewish State by separating Abdullah's Kingdom from the rest of Palestine. Without this much-opposed prophetic foresight there would not have been an Israel today.'[8]

*

7 Remarks of 29 March 1921: Central Zionist Archives.
8 Letter of 1 February 1955: Churchill papers, 2/197.

On the morning of 30 March the Executive Committee of the Haifa Congress of Palestinian Arabs went to see Churchill at Government House in Jerusalem, and received his answer to their thirty-five page protest against Zionist activity in Palestine. It contained arguments that, while in places contradictory, were an amalgamation of long-held prejudices against the Jews, prejudices that were to remain an integral part of the Arab indictment in the years ahead. In the words of the memorandum: 'The Arab is noble and large-hearted; he is also vengeful, and never forgets an ill-deed. If England does not take up the cause of the Arabs, other Powers will.' It was not only the Muslims of Palestine to whom Britain would have to listen. 'From India, Mesopotamia, the Hedjaz and Palestine the cry goes up to England now. If she does not listen, then perhaps Russia will take up their call some day, or perhaps even Germany.' The voice of Russia, the Palestinian Arabs warned, 'is not heard in the councils of the nations, yet the time must come when it will assert itself.'

In their memorandum, the Arabs sought to prove 'that Palestine belongs to the Arabs, and that the Balfour Declaration is a gross injustice.' As for the Jewish National Home, and the very concept of Jewish nationalism, they informed Churchill: 'For thousands of years Jews have been scattered over the earth, and have become nationals of the various nations amongst whom they settled. They have no separate political or lingual existence. In Germany they are Germans, in France Frenchmen, and in England Englishmen. Religion and language are their only tie. But Hebrew is a dead language and might be discarded. How then could England conclude a treaty with a religion and register it in the League of Nations?'

The Arab memorandum continued: 'Jews have been amongst the most active advocates of destruction in many lands, especially where their influential positions have enabled them to do more harm. It is well known that the disintegration of Russia was wholly or in great part brought about by the Jews, and a large proportion of the defeat of Germany and Austria must also be put at their door. When the star of the Central Powers was in the ascendant Jews flattered them, but the moment the scale turned in favour of the Allies

Jews withdrew their support from Germany, opened their coffers to the Allies, and received in return that most uncommon promise,' – the Balfour Declaration.

'The Jew, moreover,' Churchill was told, 'is clannish and unneighbourly, and cannot mix with those who live about him. He will enjoy the privileges and benefits of a country, but will give nothing in return. The Jew is a Jew all the world over. He amasses the wealth of a country and then leads its people, whom he has already impoverished, where he chooses. He encourages wars when self-interest dictates, and thus uses the armies of the nations to do his bidding.'

The memorandum concluded by asking Churchill to agree to five specific Palestinian Arab requests, 'in the name of justice and right.' These were: 'First: The principle of a National Home for the Jews be abolished. Second: A National Government be created, which shall be responsible to a Parliament elected by the Palestinian people who existed in Palestine before the war. Third: A stop be put to Jewish immigration until such a time as a National Government is formed. Fourth: Laws and regulations before the war be still carried out and all others framed after the British occupation be annulled, and no new laws be created until a National Government comes into being. Fifth: Palestine should not be separated from her sister States.'[9] These States were Syria – then under French rule – and Egypt, under British rule but on the path to independence.

Churchill replied at once, speaking to the deputation in blunt terms. 'You have asked me in the first place to repudiate the Balfour Declaration and to veto immigration of Jews into Palestine,' he said. 'It is not in my power to do so nor, if it were in my power, would it be my wish. The British Government have passed their word, by the mouth of Mr Balfour, that they will view with favour the establishment of a National Home for Jews in Palestine, and that inevitably involves the immigration of Jews into the country. This declaration

9 Haifa Congress of Palestinian Arabs, Memorandum, 14 March 1921: Central Zionist Archives.

of Mr Balfour and of the British Government has been ratified by the Allied Powers who have been victorious in the Great War; and it was a declaration made while the war was still in progress, while victory and defeat hung in the balance. It must therefore be regarded as one of the facts definitely established by the triumphant conclusion of the Great War.'

'Moreover,' Churchill told the Palestinian Arab delegation, 'it is manifestly right that the Jews, who are scattered all over the world, should have a national centre and a National Home where some of them may be reunited. And where else could that be but in this land of Palestine, with which for more than 3,000 years they have been intimately and profoundly associated? We think it will be good for the world, good for the Jews and good for the British Empire. But we also think it will be good for the Arabs who dwell in Palestine, and we intend that it shall be good for them, and that they shall not be sufferers or supplanted in the country in which they dwell or denied their share in all that makes for its progress and prosperity. And here I would draw your attention to the second part of the Balfour Declaration, which solemnly and explicitly promises to the inhabitants of Palestine the fullest protection of their civil and political rights.'

The British Government was determined, Churchill said, to give the Zionist movement 'a fair chance' in Palestine. 'If a National Home for the Jews is to be established in Palestine, as we hope to see it established, it can only be by a process which at every stage wins its way on its merits and carries with it increasing benefits and prosperity and happiness to the people of the country as a whole. And why should this not be so? Why should this not be possible? You can see with your own eyes in many parts of this country the work which has already been done by Jewish colonies, how sandy wastes have been reclaimed and thriving farms and orangeries planted in their stead. It is quite true that they have been helped by money from outside, whereas your people have not had a similar advantage, but surely these funds of money largely coming from outside and being devoted to the increase of the general prosperity of Palestine is one of the very reasons which should lead you to take a wise and tolerant view of the Zionist movement.'

There was no reason, Churchill told the Palestinian Arabs, why Palestine 'should not support a larger number of people than it does at present, and all of those in a higher condition of prosperity.' The task before the Zionists, Churchill added, was one of 'extraordinary difficulty'. The present form of government would continue for many years, and step by step Britain would develop representative institutions leading up to full self-government. 'All of us here to-day will have passed away from the earth and also our children and our children's children before it is fully achieved.' Meanwhile, the Jews would need the help of the Arabs at every stage, 'and I think you would be wise to give them your help and your aid and encourage them in their difficulties. They may fail. If they are not guided by wisdom and goodwill, if they do not tread the path of justice and tolerance and neighbourliness, if the class of men who come in are not worthy of the Jewish race, then they will fail and there will be an end of the experiment. But on the other hand, if they succeed, and in proportion as they do succeed year by year, such success can only be accompanied by a general diffusion of wealth and well-being among all the dwellers in Palestine and by an advance in the social, scientific and cultural life of the people as a whole.'

Churchill concluded his remarks to the Arab deputation by urging them to grasp the positive prospects: 'If instead of sharing miseries through quarrels you will share blessings through cooperation,' he told them, 'a bright and tranquil future lies before your country. The earth is a generous mother. She will produce in plentiful abundance for all her children if they will but cultivate her soil in justice and in peace.'[10]

The Arab deputation withdrew, its appeal rejected, its arguments rebutted. A Jewish deputation followed in its place. They too presented a memorandum, which expressed gratitude to the British for helping to rebuild 'the National Home of Israel', and pointed out

10 Churchill papers, 9/64.

that the Zionist programme 'lays special stress on the establishing of sincere friendship between ourselves and the Arabs.' The Jewish people, it added, 'returning after 2,000 years of exile and persecution to its own homeland, cannot suffer the suspicion that it wishes to deny to another nation its rights.'

The Jewish memorandum sought to assure Churchill that 'The Jewish people have full understanding of the aspirations of the Arabs with regard to a national revival, but we know that by our efforts to rebuild the Jewish National Home in Palestine, which is but a small area in comparison with all the Arab lands, we do not deprive them of their legitimate rights. On the contrary, we are convinced that a Jewish renaissance in this country can only have a strong and invigorating influence upon the Arab nation. Our kinship in language, race, character and history give the assurance that we shall in due course come to a complete understanding with them.'[11]

Churchill did not need convincing, telling the Jews: 'I am myself perfectly convinced that the cause of Zionism is one which carries with it much that is good for the whole world, and not only for the Jewish people, but that it will also bring with it prosperity and contentment and advancement to the Arab population of this country.'

Churchill then spoke to the Jewish deputation about Arab fears; fear of being dispossessed of their lands and property, of being 'supplanted from their rights', and of being put 'under the rule of those who are now in a minority, but who will be reinforced by large numbers of strangers coming from over the seas.'

The Arabs had also expressed alarm, Churchill said, at the character of some of the new Jewish immigrants, 'whom they accuse of bringing Bolshevik doctrines.' It was the duty of the Jews, Churchill added, 'to dispel' these fears. He continued: 'When I go back to London, I have no doubt I shall be told that but for the Zionist movement there would be no need to keep up such a large British garrison, at so great an expense, in this country. You must provide

---

11 Churchill papers, 17/20.

me with the means, and the Jewish community all over the world must provide me with the means, of answering all adverse criticism. I wish to be able to say that a great event is taking place here, a great event in the world's destiny.'

Churchill wished to be able to say on his return to Britain that the 'great event' was taking place 'without injury or injustice to anyone; it is transforming waste places into fertile; it is planting trees and developing agriculture in desert lands; it is making for an increase in wealth and of cultivation; it is making two blades of grass grow where one grew before, and the people of the country who are in a majority are deriving great benefit, sharing in the general improvement and advancement. There is co-operation and fraternity between the religions and the races; the Jews who are being brought from Europe and elsewhere are worthy representatives of Jewry and of the cause of Zionism, and the Zionists are taking every step to secure that that shall be so.'

Concerned about Bolshevik activity and influence among the Jewish immigrants from Russia, Churchill urged that the pioneers 'must be picked men, worthy in every way of the greatness of the ideal and of the cause for which they are striving and in that way you will give me the means of answering effectively those who wish to prevent this experiment and cause from having its fair chance.'

'I earnestly hope that your cause may be carried to success,' Churchill concluded. 'I know how great the energy is and how serious are the difficulties at every stage and you have my warmest sympathy in the efforts you are making to overcome them. If I did not believe that you were animated by the very highest spirit of justice and idealism, and that your work would in fact confer blessings upon the whole country, I should not have the high hopes which I have that eventually your work will be accomplished.'[12]

This was a powerful endorsement of the Zionist enterprise. One of the Jewish delegation, Dr Arthur Ruppin, the founder of the kibbutz movement, wrote in his diary that Churchill's remarks 'made a

---

12 Churchill papers, 9/64.

great impression on all present, as we had been afraid that he had been influenced against us by the Arabs.'[13]

Churchill's appeal in his remarks for 'picked men' struck a deep chord. In farms throughout Europe, including in Soviet Russia, groups of Jews were being trained to become farmers. Only after they had mastered the art of tilling the soil, animal husbandry and other creative rural pursuits, were they sent on to Palestine to start new farming communities. This process was known in modern Hebrew as *hachshara*: preparation.

Churchill left Jerusalem at midday on 30 March. Before catching the evening train from Lydda to Egypt he had time to see two of the most impressive Jewish achievements in Palestine. One was the twelve-year-old Jewish town of Tel-Aviv, next to the ancient and predominantly Arab town of Jaffa. The second was the thirty-nine-year-old agricultural colony of Rishon le-Zion. In his speech to the people of Tel Aviv, in the presence of its mayor, Meir Dizengoff, who had presided over the growth of the city since its foundation two decades earlier, Churchill spoke of how glad he was to have seen 'the result of the initiative of its inhabitants in so short a period during which, too, the war had intervened.'[14]

Churchill also stopped briefly at Sarafend, where a group of new immigrants from Russia were working at road building, the first large public works undertaking by the Mandate authorities using Jewish labour. Weizmann had arranged for Pinhas Rutenberg, the former Russian revolutionary – and later a leading anti-Bolshevik – who was bringing modern irrigation and electrification techniques to Palestine, to accompany Churchill and interpret for him.

Through Rutenberg Churchill asked the new arrivals if they were Bolsheviks. 'This was much on his mind,' Rutenberg later recalled, adding that Churchill 'convinced himself' that the pioneers were not Bolsheviks, but men 'dedicated to the ideal of labour' – the Labour

13 Alex Bein (editor), *Arthur Ruppin: Memoirs, Diaries, Letters*, page 190.
14 Churchill papers, 17/20.

Zionist ideal of redeeming the land by physical work, in the fields, on the roads, in stone quarries and on building sites.[15]

From Sarafend, Churchill was driven ten miles to Rishon le-Zion – Hebrew for 'the first in Zion' – one of the oldest Jewish agricultural villages in Palestine, established four decades earlier during the Turkish period. Before his visit, the inhabitants of Rishon had been divided as to how to receive him. The old-timers wanted to stress the hardships and dangers, including the hostility of some of the nearby Arab villages. The young people wanted to show him what had been achieved, even deciding to greet him on horseback.[16]

The youngsters prevailed. Churchill was met at the entrance by an enthusiastic display of horsemanship. He was then welcomed by the colony's council, and handed a letter of greeting. 'Your kind words we were happy to hear yesterday in Jerusalem,' it stated, 'gave us a clear idea of your opinion and they serve us as a good guarantee to enable us to reach our aim.'[17]

Founded in 1882 with only ten inhabitants, by the time of Churchill's visit to Rishon there were two thousand Jews living there. He was so impressed by their enthusiasm and achievements that ten weeks later he told the House of Commons: 'Anyone who has seen the work of the Jewish colonies which have been established during the last twenty or thirty years in Palestine will be struck by the enormous productive results which they have achieved.' From 'the most inhospitable soil, surrounded on every side by barrenness and the most miserable form of cultivation,' he had been driven 'into a fertile and thriving country estate, where the scanty soil gave place to good crops and good cultivation, and then to vineyards and finally to the most beautiful, luxurious orange groves, all created in twenty or thirty years by the exertions of the Jewish community who live there.'

Churchill recalled how, on approaching Rishon, 'we were surrounded by fifty or sixty young Jews, galloping on their horses, and

15 Y. Ya'ari Poleskin, *Pinhas Rutenberg* (in Hebrew), pages 208–9.
16 Rishon le-Zion Municipal Archive.
17 Churchill papers, 17/20.

with farmers from the estate who took part in the work,' and how, when they reached the centre of the town, 'there were drawn up three hundred or four hundred of the most admirable children, of all sizes and sexes, and about an equal number of white-clothed damsels. We were invited to sample the excellent wines which the establishment produced, and to inspect the many beauties of the groves.'

What Churchill had seen and heard at Rishon impressed on him how precarious the work of the farmers could be, and how essential it was for Britain to protect them. 'I defy anybody, after seeing work of this kind, achieved by so much labour, effort and skill, to say that the British Government, having taken up the position it has, could cast it all aside and leave it to be rudely and brutally overturned by the incursion of a fanatical attack by the Arab population from outside,' he told the House of Commons on his return to Britain. It would be 'disgraceful if we allowed anything of the kind to take place. I am talking of what I saw with my own eyes. All round the Jewish colony, the Arab houses were tiled instead of being built of mud, so that the culture from this centre has spread out into the surrounding district.'[18]

Churchill had been in Palestine for eight days. In that short time he had been struck by the enthusiasm of the Jews and the intensity of Arab hostility against them. The Zionists were optimistic that his visit boded well. According to the May issue of the leading Zionist journal in Britain, Churchill's visit marked 'a turning point in our movement: it indicates the passing from discussion to real practical work. He has detailed our difficulties in no uncertain manner, but with the sympathy and understanding of a friend. He has stated that his Zionism is based upon his faith in the Jewish people to make good in Palestine – it is only left to us to justify that faith.'[19]

---

18 Parliamentary Debates, *Hansard*, 14 June 1921.
19 *Zionist Review*, May 1921.

CHAPTER SEVEN

BUILDING ON THE BALFOUR DECLARATION

At the very moment that Churchill was being impressed by Zionist idealism in Palestine, he was forming a negative view of Islamic extremism as it was then emerging in Saudi Arabia. On 14 June 1921, shortly after his return to Britain, he explained to the House of Commons that a large number of the followers of the new Saudi King, Abdul Aziz al-Saud, known as Ibn Saud, 'belong to the Wahabi sect, a form of Mohammedanism which bears, roughly speaking, the same relationship to orthodox Islam as the most militant form of Calvinism would have borne to Rome in the fiercest times of religious wars' in Europe. The Wahabis, Churchill noted, 'profess a life of exceeding austerity, and what they practice themselves they rigorously enforce on others. They hold it as an article of duty, as well as of faith, to kill all who do not share their opinions and to make slaves of their wives and children. Women have been put to death in Wahabi villages for simply appearing in the streets. It is a penal offence to wear a silk garment. Men have been killed for smoking a cigarette and, as for the crime of alcohol, the most energetic supporter of the temperance cause in this country falls far behind them. Austere, intolerant, well-armed, and blood-thirsty, in their own regions the Wahabis are a distinct factor which must be taken into account, and they have been, and still are, very dangerous to the holy cities of Mecca and Medina.'[1]

Churchill's visit to Palestine had sparked a renewed upsurge of

1 Parliamentary Debates, *Hansard*, 14 June 1921.

Palestinian Arab protests in several towns in Palestine against Jewish immigration. On 18 June 1921 Churchill informed his officials at the Colonial Office that he believed it was impossible for Britain to grant any form of representation to the Arabs that would give them the power to halt Jewish immigration. There was great folly, he warned, in 'going out of our way to procure a hungry lion and then walking up to him with a plate of raw beef to see how much he would like to take.'

The Arabs were insistent that no other solution than representative government, based on an elected assembly, would satisfy them. It was essential, Churchill wrote to his officials, to say to the Arabs: 'We want to give you some elective institutions at once so that you do not feel yourselves left out at the present time. But before we can do this we must have an understanding with your Committee as to what is going to happen about Jewish immigration. We insist upon continuing Jewish immigration within the narrow limits now defined as resources becoming available.' Churchill also wanted to ask the Arabs how they would 'safeguard' the British commitment to Jewish immigration 'from not being interfered with' by any future Arab 'elective body.'[2]

In Cabinet on 31 May, discussing the long-term future of the Palestine Mandate and Arab demands for the immediate establishment of an elected assembly, Churchill had explained that he had decided to suspend the development of representative institutions in Palestine 'owing to the fact that any elected body would undoubtedly prohibit further immigration of Jews.'[3] At the same time, in an attempt to calm Arab fears, he approved a proposal from Sir Herbert Samuel that Jewish immigration would henceforth be limited by the 'economic capacity' of Palestine to absorb newcomers.[4]

This was a blow to the Zionists, yet it was not to prevent more than 400,000 new Jewish immigrants entering Palestine legally

2 Minute of 18 June 1921: Colonial Office papers, 733/14.
3 Cabinet meeting, 31 May 1921: Cabinet papers, 23/25.
4 Letter of 24 March 1922: Colonial Office papers, 733/34.

between 1922 and 1939. For two of those years, economic conditions were so hard that more Jews left Palestine than entered it.

Meeting in London on 22 June, four Dominion Prime Ministers – from Canada, Newfoundland, Australia and New Zealand – shared Arab suspicions of an eventual Jewish majority. Churchill explained to them the British position on Zionism. 'The Zionist ideal,' Churchill told them, 'is a very great ideal, and I confess, for myself, it is one that claims my keen personal sympathy.' But the Balfour Declaration, he added, was more than an ideal. It was also an obligation, made in wartime 'to enlist the aid of Jews all over the world,' and Britain must be 'very careful and punctilious' he explained, 'to discharge our obligations.'

Churchill then outlined his policy as far as Jewish immigration was concerned: 'We must insist on the door to immigration being kept open, insist that immigrants are not brought in beyond the numbers which the new wealth of the country, which was created by public works and better agriculture, can sustain.'

The Canadian Prime Minister, Arthur Meighen, questioned Churchill about the meaning of the words 'National Home'. Did they mean, he asked, giving the Jews 'control of the Government'? To this Churchill replied, 'If, in the course of many, many years, they become a majority in the country, they naturally would take it over.'[5]

Churchill's attitude was widely known, and much disliked. Six days after Churchill's meeting with the Dominion Prime Ministers, the Archbishop of Canterbury, Randall Davidson, Britain's senior Anglican churchman, wrote to him in protest: 'I think I ought to tell you that I have received from a good many quarters requests that I should remonstrate against what is thought to be the undue development of a Zionist policy in Palestine, especially with regard to the purchase of land by or on behalf of Jews and their apparent anticipation that in what are called State lands the development will be entrusted to Jews. Even more important is the possible buying out of

5 Imperial Cabinet, Minutes, 22 June 1921: Lloyd George papers.

reluctant sellers if they are non-Jews with a view to giving the lands to Jews.'[6]

Land purchase by Jews was central to the development of the Jewish National Home, and accepted as such by Churchill. It continued, whenever land and money were available, for almost twenty years, before the British Government brought it effectively to a close, over Churchill's protests.

A Palestinian Arab delegation had arrived in Britain in July, led by Musa Kazem Pasha al-Husseini, the head of one of the leading Palestinian Arab families, and had taken up residence in London for the purpose of lobbying against any further Jewish immigration. 'They do undoubtedly represent a large body of opinion in Palestine,' Samuel was reported as saying.[7] Just as the Arab delegation reached London, Weizmann was summoned by Churchill to the Colonial Office. On 15 July he wrote to a Zionist colleague: 'I had a very long argument with Mr Churchill which lasted one hour and a half. As a matter of fact when Mr Churchill first called me, I refused to go, on the ground that I could not discuss with him profitably the situation, because I knew the sort of declaration he would give. Unless Mr Churchill is prepared to grant us definite concessions, it is of no use discussing academic declarations of sympathy. Mr Churchill then called me again, and I went to him and in quite clear terms pointed out to him the vicious circle into which the attitude of the Palestine administration, and of the Government, is placing us. On the one hand they complain about Zionism being the burden of the British tax-payer, and when we desire to lighten this burden by developing Palestine and so increasing the wealth and productiveness of the country, they refuse to let us go on with our work because they are fearing an Arab outburst.' Weizmann thought that Churchill 'saw the strength of this argument and after a long discussion agreed with my demand' that a conference

6 Letter of 28 July 1921: Churchill papers.
7 As reported by Sir John Shuckburgh to Weizmann: Central Zionist Archives.

should be called at which Balfour, Lloyd George and Churchill would take part.[8]

On 22 July Churchill, Lloyd George and Balfour met Weizmann, at Balfour's house in London, to try to reassure Weizmann that British policy had not changed. At this meeting Weizmann protested that the Balfour Declaration was being whittled away, and that Samuel himself was undermining it. Weizmann pointed out that on 3 June Samuel had declared, in an official speech, that 'the conditions of Palestine are such as not to permit anything in the nature of mass immigration.' Such a statement, Weizmann pointed out, was 'a negation of the Balfour Declaration.' Churchill asked him to explain why this was so, to which Weizmann explained that the Balfour Declaration 'meant an ultimate Jewish majority' whereas Samuel's speech 'would never permit such a majority to eventuate.' According to the minutes of the meeting, Churchill 'demurred at this interpretation' of Samuel's speech, while Lloyd George and Balfour both agreed 'that by the Declaration they had always meant an eventual Jewish State.'[9]

On 5 August one of the principal Middle East advisers at the Colonial Office, Major Young, sent Churchill a forceful minute in which he stressed that both he and the head of the Middle East Department, John Shuckburgh, felt that Herbert Samuel had been pressed 'not only by Arabs, but also by British officials who are not in sympathy with Zionist policy' into taking action 'which was not altogether justified' in restricting Jewish immigration.[10] Samuel saw the other side of the coin, writing to Weizmann five days later in stern tones: 'It is essential to face the facts of the case. Those facts in my opinion are that a very large number of Arabs, including a large number of the educated classes, have come to believe that Zionism means the overwhelming of themselves and their people by immigrant Jews, with the consequence that in the course of time they will

8 Letter of 15 July 1921: Weizmann Archive.
9 Meeting of 21 July 1921: Weizmann Archive.
10 Colonial Office papers, 733/10.

lose not only their political predominance but also their lands and their Holy Places.' The Arabs, Samuel insisted, 'will not accept the fate which they think is in store for them without a fight.' Zionist policy was not based 'upon such stable foundations in Great Britain that it can afford to see those foundations shaken.'[11]

When Churchill received the Palestinian Arab delegation on 22 August, its members were in an uncompromising mood, asking him without prevarication to repudiate the Balfour Declaration and to halt all further Jewish immigration to Palestine. Churchill refused to do either, setting out for the delegation his understanding of the nature of Zionism and telling them in no uncertain terms: 'The Jews are a very numerous people, and they are scattered all over the world. This is a country where they have great historic traditions, and you cannot brush that aside as though it was absolutely nothing. They were there many hundreds of years ago. They have always tried to be there. They have done a great deal for the country. They have started most thriving colonies, and many of them wish to go and live there. It is to them a sacred place. Many of them go there to be buried in the city which they regard as sacred – as you regard it as sacred.'

Churchill then expressed his view of the difference between the Jewish and Arab positions in Palestine. 'The Jews have a far more difficult task than you. You only have to enjoy your own possession; but they have to try to create out of the wilderness, out of the barren places, a livelihood for the people they bring in. They have to bring them in under conditions which make for the general good of the population, and which supplant no one, and deprive no one of their rights and liberties. There may be from time to time instances of oppression, but we will create a machine of government where these matters can be thrashed out and exposed publicly, where it shall not be a government of autocracy but of free speech, and of frank and friendly discussion.'[12]

---

11 Letter of 10 August 1921: Central Zionist Archives.
12 Discussion of 22 August 1921, Minutes: Central Zionist Archives.

The Palestinian Arabs were deeply disappointed, feeling that their attempt to bring an end to Jewish immigration had failed. Violence broke out in Palestine. Twice that November the Arabs of Jaffa and the surrounding villages attacked Jews in the streets and damaged Jewish property. In response, the British administration imposed a collective fine on the Arabs of Jaffa, and on the Arab villages from which some of the attackers had come. On 17 November Churchill wrote to his officials: 'Sir Herbert Samuel should be held stiffly up to the enforcement of the fines on Jaffa.'[13]

Five days later, Churchill rejected Samuel's representations that the political effects of imposing fines should be taken into account. 'It is, in my opinion, essential,' Churchill informed Samuel, 'that Jaffa as well as villages should be made to realise responsibilities with least possible delay. We cannot allow expediency to govern the administration of justice.' Were Samuel to find it difficult to enforce the collection of fines, Churchill added, he would be willing to arrange for a warship to help uphold the High Commissioner's authority.[14]

Churchill was surprised and shocked when Samuel informed him that the Arabs had been provoked to riot by a hard core of Jewish Communists. It was Samuel's responsibility, Churchill replied, to 'purge the Jewish Colonies and newcomers of Communist elements, and without hesitation or delay have all those who are guilty of subversive agitation expelled from the country.' Whatever part Jewish Communists had played in the Jaffa riots, Churchill told Samuel, he was even more angered by the Arab attempt to use violence throughout Palestine 'in the hope of frightening us out of our Zionist policy.' Churchill's attitude was clear. Britain, he instructed Samuel, 'must firmly maintain law and order, and make concessions on their merits and not under duress.'[15]

*

13 Minute of 17 November 1921: Churchill papers, 17/15.
14 Minute of 23 November 1921: Colonial Office papers, 733/7.
15 Colonial Office papers, 733/3.

By the beginning of February 1922 Churchill's officials had drafted a constitution for Palestine that would ensure that no Arab majority could stand in the way of continued Jewish immigration and investment. The Palestinian Arab Delegation continued to lead the campaign against the Balfour Declaration. At Question Time in the House of Commons on 15 February Sir William Joynson-Hicks, a Conservative Member of Parliament, asked the Prime Minister, David Lloyd George, to explain the reason why the Government had promised the Jewish people a national home 'in a country which is already the national home of the Arabs.'[16]

The Middle East Department began its defence of the Balfour Declaration on 1 March, when, on Churchill's instructions, John Shuckburgh sent a letter to the Arab delegation reiterating the government's determination not to go back on its pledge to the Jews. This letter, sent with Churchill's full ministerial authority, stated emphatically that when it was asked 'what is meant by the development of the Jewish National Home in Palestine, it may be answered that it is not the imposition of a Jewish nationality upon the inhabitants of Palestine as a whole, but the further development of the existing Jewish community, with the assistance of Jews in other parts of the world, in order that it may become a centre in which the Jewish people as a whole may take, on grounds of religion and race, an interest and a pride.' In order that this community should have 'the best prospect of free development and provide a full opportunity for the Jewish people to display its capacities, it is essential that it should know that it is in Palestine as of right and not on sufferance.' That was the reason why it was necessary 'that the existence of a Jewish National Home in Palestine should be internationally guaranteed.'[17]

On 3 March the Arab delegation held a meeting of its supporters at the Hyde Park Hotel in London to denounce Britain's 'Zionist policy'. Churchill was later sent an account of how the principal

16 Parliamentary Debates, *Hansard*, 15 February 1922.
17 Letter of 1 March 1922: Central Zionist Archives.

Arab speaker, Shibly al-Jamal, a Protestant Arab who was the secretary to the delegation, was reported to have used language 'about the necessity of killing Jews if the Arabs did not get their way.'[18]

Churchill's promised declaration of policy came on 9 March. In his speech he stressed that the control of Jewish immigration was an essential feature of his Palestine policy, and reiterated his ever-present fears of Bolshevik penetration into the Zionist movement. 'Every effort has been made,' he assured the House, 'to secure only good citizens who will build up the country. We cannot have a country inundated by Bolshevist riffraff, who would seek to subvert institutions in Palestine as they have done with success in the land from which they came.' The immigrants who did arrive, he said, 'bring with them the means of their own livelihood, the Zionist Association expending nearly a million a year in the country.'

Churchill then spoke of the Arab demand for self-determination and representative government, based on a majority vote. This was unacceptable, he said. He could, he declared, do nothing which would involve 'falling into a position where I could not fulfil those pledges to which we are committed by the Zionist policy. I am bound to retain in the hands of the Imperial Government the power to carry out those pledges.'[19]

A month after Churchill's statement, the Jewish industrial chemist and Liberal politician Sir Alfred Mond, who was then Minister of Health, warned Sir Herbert Samuel that the Arab delegation had become 'a focus and a tool of the general anti-Semitic movement.'[20]

For more than a year, Churchill's response to Arab opposition to both Jewish immigration and Zionist enterprise had been to find the means to give the Jews a politically secure, economically viable stake in Palestine. It was for this reason that he favoured Pinhas

18 Letter of 30 March 1922: Colonial Office papers, 733/37.
19 Parliamentary Debates, *Hansard*, 9 March 1922.
20 Letter of 4 April 1922: Viscount Samuel papers.

Rutenberg's scheme to bring electricity to Palestine by harnessing the water power of the Jordan and Yarkon rivers. But when Churchill learned that Rutenberg intended to buy machinery from German firms, he wrote to his Political Secretary, Sir Archibald Sinclair: 'You had better make it clear to Mr Rutenberg and to the Zionists generally that a policy of placing orders in Germany, while unemployment is so serious in this country, will be used as an additional argument against our providing two millions a year to keep a British garrison to support the Zionist policy.'[21]

Rutenberg took the point, and placed his orders for machinery in Britain. By the beginning of June his scheme was accepted by the Colonial Office and received Churchill's personal support. The repercussions were swift. The whole Mandate was under attack. On 21 June a Liberal Peer, Lord Islington, introduced a motion in the House of Lords that the Palestine Mandate was 'inacceptable to this House' because it was 'opposed to the sentiments and wishes of the great majority of the people of Palestine,' and went on to warn that the Rutenberg scheme would invest the Jewish minority with wide powers over the Arab majority.

Lord Islington went on to declare, 'Zionism runs counter to the whole human psychology of the age.' It involved bringing into Palestine 'extraneous and alien Jews from other parts of the world' in order to ensure a Jewish predominance. Jewish immigration, he added, would be a burden on the British taxpayer and a grave threat to Arab rights and development. 'The Zionist Home must, and does, mean the predominance of political power on the part of the Jewish community in a country where the population is predominantly non-Jewish.'

Another Peer, Lord Sydenham, declared that the Palestinian Arabs 'would never have objected to the establishment of more colonies of well-selected Jews; but, instead of that, we have dumped down 25,000 promiscuous people on the shores of Palestine, many of them quite unsuited for colonising purposes, and some of them

21 Letter of 21 March 1922: Colonial Office papers, 733/33.

Bolsheviks, who have already shown the most sinister activity. The Arabs would have kept the Holy Land clear from Bolshevism.'

During his speech, Lord Sydenham warned that the Mandate as being presented by Churchill to the League of Nations, 'will undoubtedly, in time, transfer the control of the Holy Land to New York, Berlin, London, Frankfurt and other places. The strings will not be pulled from Palestine; they will be pulled from foreign capitals; and for everything that happens during this transference of power, we shall be responsible.'[22]

When the vote was taken, the views of the anti-Zionist Lords prevailed, with sixty voting against the Balfour Declaration, and only twenty-nine for it. On the following day, Major Hubert Young, a senior official in the Middle East Department of the Colonial Office, who in 1918 had participated in the Arab Revolt against the Turks, warned Churchill that the anti-Zionist vote 'will have encouraged the Arab Delegation to persist in their obstinate attitude.' Unless the vote in the Lords could be 'signally overruled' by the Commons, Britain's pledges to the Jews would not be able to be fulfilled.[23]

It fell to Churchill to attempt to reverse the House of Lords vote in the House of Commons, and to ensure that the Zionist enterprise could go ahead under British stewardship. Before trying to do so, he made enquiries that would free the Zionists from a particularly damaging complaint being stressed by the Palestinian Arab Delegation in London. The complaint was that the Jewish Colonisation Association had evicted Arabs from their lands in order to settle Jewish immigrants in their place. On 3 July, the day before the crucial debate, Shuckburgh informed Churchill's Private Secretary that 'Mr Churchill may like to know, for the purposes of tomorrow's debate, that this lie has been nailed to the counter.' The land in question was 'mainly swamps and sand dunes.'[24]

22 Parliamentary Debates, *Hansard*, 21 June 1922.
23 Letter of 22 June 1922: Colonial Office papers, 733/22.
24 Letter of 3 July 1922: Colonial Office papers, 733/22.

The House of Commons debate on the Palestine Mandate, and on the Rutenberg concession, took place on the evening of 4 July 1922. Churchill had to try to win support for an increasingly unpopular pro-Zionist policy. Sir William Joynson-Hicks led the attack, opening his speech by deploring the fact that the Rutenberg concession contracts had never been submitted to Parliament. It was his wish, he said, to set out 'the Arab as against the Zionist intentions.' The Arabs felt that Palestine was 'within the territories which were to be handed over to the Arab dominions' once Turkey had been defeated. The 'real trouble' was not the Balfour Declaration, but 'the way in which the Zionists have been permitted by the Government practically to control the whole of the Government of Palestine.'

Arabs who had sought economic concessions had, Joynson-Hicks alleged, been turned away. Rutenberg's scheme was 'grandiose but impracticable,' yet the Colonial Office contract 'gives over the development of the whole country to Mr Rutenberg.' Nor was there any provision in the contract 'for any benefit for the manufacturers of Great Britain. There is no clause providing that any orders should be placed in Great Britain at all.' Britain had spent 'millions of money in Palestine, and sacrificed thousands of lives, and after all this no benefit is to come to England.'

Another Conservative, Sir John Butcher, bitterly attacked Churchill for the powers that the concession gave to Samuel and Rutenberg. 'Is that fair,' he asked, 'to the inhabitants of Palestine, or to the interests of the Arabs?' A year earlier, in the debate on 14 June 1921, Lord Winterton had warned Churchill that once 'you begin to buy land for the purpose of settling Jewish cultivators you will find yourself up against the hereditary antipathy which exists all over the world to the Jewish race.'

Churchill's speech of 4 July was a sustained defence of Britain's pledge to Jewish national aspirations. Dealing first with the Balfour Declaration, he pointed out that there had never been 'any serious challenge' in Parliament to that policy. 'Pledges and promises were made during the War, and they were made not only on the merits, though I think the merits are considerable. They were made because it was considered they would be of value to us in our struggle to win the War. It was considered that the support which the Jews could give us all over the world, and particularly in the United States, and also in Russia, would be a definite palpable advantage.'

In November 1917 almost 'every public man in this country', Churchill pointed out, had supported the Balfour Declaration. Churchill then quoted twelve statements, all supporting it, some of which had been made by the very people who were attacking the policies they had earlier supported. Sir John Butcher, who, Churchill pointed out, 'has just addressed us in terms of such biting indignation' had earlier been 'almost lyrical on the subject.' Churchill then quoted Butcher's words of 1917: 'I trust the day is not far distant when the Jewish people may be free to return to the sacred birthplace of their race, and to establish in the ancient home of their fathers a great, free, industrial community where, safe from all external aggression, they may attain their ideals, and fulfil their destiny.'

Churchill told those critics whom he had quoted: 'You have no right to say this kind of thing as individuals; you have no right to support public declarations made in the name of your country in the crisis and heat of War, and then afterwards, when all is cold and prosaic, to turn round and attack the Minister or the Department which is faithfully and laboriously endeavouring to translate these perfervid enthusiasms into the sober, concrete facts of day-to-day administration. I say, in all consistency and reasonable fair play, that does not justify the House of Commons at this stage in repudiating the general Zionist policy.'

In defending Britain's Palestine responsibilities, Churchill told the House: 'We cannot after what we have said and done leave the Jews in Palestine to be maltreated by the Arabs who have been inflamed against them.' Arab fears of being pushed off the land were 'illusory'. No Jew would be brought in 'beyond the number who can be provided for by the expanding wealth and development of the resources of the country. There is no doubt whatever that at the present time the country is greatly under-populated.'

As for the Rutenberg concession, Churchill explained, it would safeguard the Arabs against being dispossessed, for it enabled the Jews 'by their industry, by their brains and by their money' to create 'new sources of wealth on which they could live without detriment to or subtraction from the well-being of the Arab population.' Jewish wealth, he believed, would enrich the whole country, all classes and all races: 'Anyone who has visited Palestine recently must have seen how parts of the desert have been converted into gardens, and how material improvement has been effected in every respect by the Arab population dwelling around.'

There was 'no doubt whatever' Churchill insisted, that there was in Palestine 'room for still further energy and development if capital and other forces be allowed to play their part.' There was no doubt that there was room 'for a far larger number of people, and this far larger number of people will be able to lead far more decent and prosperous lives.' Apart from this agricultural work – this 'reclamation work' he called it – 'there are services which science, assisted by outside capital, can render, and of all the enterprises of importance which would have the effect of greatly enriching the land, none was greater than the scientific storage and regulation of the waters of the Jordan for the provision of cheap power and light needed for the industry of Palestine, as well as water for the irrigation of new lands now desolate.'

The granting of the Rutenberg concession, Churchill insisted, offered to all the inhabitants of Palestine, Arabs and Jews alike, 'the assurance of a greater prosperity and the means of a higher economic and social life.' He then asked the House of Commons, 'Was not this a good gift which the Zionists could bring with them, the consequences of which spreading as years went by in general easement and amelioration – was not this a good gift which would impress more than anything else on the Arab population that the Zionists were their friends and helpers, not their expellers and expropriators, and that the earth was a generous mother, that Palestine had before it a bright future, and that there was enough for all? Were we wrong in carrying out the policy of the nation and of Parliament in fixing upon this development of the waterways and the water power of Palestine as the main and principal means by which we could fulfil our undertaking?'

Critics of the Rutenberg concession had insisted that it was for the Arab majority to develop the economic wealth of Palestine. Churchill sought to rebut this argument: 'I am told that the Arabs would have done it themselves. Who is going to believe that? Left to themselves, the Arabs of Palestine would not in a thousand years have taken effective steps towards the irrigation and electrification of Palestine. They would have been quite content to dwell – a handful of philosophic people – in the wasted sun-scorched plains, letting the waters of the Jordan continue to flow unbridled and unharnessed into the Dead Sea.'

Churchill proceeded to explain to the House that there would be 'strict Government control' of the prices charged to the consumers for electricity produced under the scheme, and a 'severe limitation on profits' which would, after the company had earned ten per cent of its initial investment, be divided equally between it and the Palestine Government. Once fifteen per cent had been received, 'the whole profit' would revert to the Palestine Government, which, after thirty-seven years, would have the 'full right' to buy the whole scheme.

Several members of both Houses of Parliament had been critical of the concession because it had not been granted to an Arab company. To this, Churchill replied that before he became Colonial Secretary there had been an application from two inhabitants of Bethlehem, 'one an Arab and one a non-Arab', but that they had furnished 'no plans, no estimates, no scheme at all', asking only 'that if there were any concessions going, they would very much like to have them.' For his part, Rutenberg had produced a scheme, in July 1921, 'in the utmost detail, and with considerable backing' and no other application had been received.

Before Churchill spoke, almost every speaker had been critical of Rutenberg himself, and of granting so important an economic benefit to a Russian Jew. Churchill sought to answer these criticisms, telling the House of Commons about Rutenberg and his financial backing: 'He is a man of exceptional ability and personal force. He is a Zionist. His application was supported by the influence of Zionist organisations . . . He produced plans, diagrams, estimates – all worked out in the utmost detail. He asserted, and his assertion has been justified, that he had behind him all the principal Zionist societies in Europe and America, who would support his plans on a non-commercial basis.'

It was the non-commercial aspect of the Rutenberg concession that Churchill wished to stress. The offer of a major concession in Palestine, he pointed out, had 'fallen extremely flat outside the circles of the Zionist followers. Nearly all the money got up to the present time has come from associations of a Jewish character, which are almost entirely on a non-profit-making basis.' There was something deeper in Zionism than cash and profits. 'I have no doubt whatever, and, after all, do not let us be too ready to doubt people's ideals, that profit-making, in the ordinary sense, has played no part at all in the driving force on which we must rely to carry through this irrigation scheme in Palestine. I do not believe it has been so with Mr Rutenberg, nor do I believe that this concession would secure the necessary funds were it not supported by sentimental and quasi-religious emotions.' Churchill continued his speech with a defence of Rutenberg himself: 'He is a Jew. I cannot deny that. I do not see why that should be a cause of reproach.'

Churchill, who had spent the previous months deep in negotiations for the Irish Treaty, then told his parliamentary critics in mocking terms: 'It is hard enough, in all conscience, to make a New Zion, but if, over the portals of the new Jerusalem, you are going to inscribe the legend, "No Israelite need apply", then I hope the House will permit me to confine my attention exclusively to Irish matters.' This elicited much laughter.

One argument used against granting the Rutenberg concession was that Rutenberg was a Bolshevik. 'Nothing is more untrue,' Churchill declared, and went on to give the House of Commons an account of Rutenberg's career: 'He is a Russian, but he is not a Bolshevist. He was turned out of Russia by the Bolshevists.'

Rutenberg, Churchill explained, was 'one of those social revolutionaries who combated that tyranny of the then-despotic Tsarist Government, and who, after the revolution, did their best to combat the still worse tyranny of the Bolshevist rulers who succeeded to the power of the Tsar. His attitude has been perfectly consistent.'

Churchill held all enemies of Bolshevism in high regard. Since November 1917 the Bolsheviks had not only established totalitarian rule and State terror throughout Russia, but had sought to export their system. For several weeks in 1919 it had looked as if Berlin would become a Communist base. In Bavaria and Hungary, Communist regimes had briefly seized power, imposing the worst excesses of the Soviet system.

For his participation in anti-Tsarist revolutionary circles, Churchill told the House of Commons, Rutenberg had been imprisoned several times. He was said to have been the organiser of the execution of the popular leader and police spy Father Gapon. If it was true, Churchill said, that Rutenberg had taken part in the murder of Father Gapon, 'who was an agent provocateur, an agent for the Russian police to obtain the secrets of the revolutionaries with whom he was working', it was also true that in 1917, when he was Deputy Governor of Petrograd, he had recommended to Kerensky to hang Lenin and Trotsky.

After being driven out of Northern Russia, where he had been advising the anti-Bolshevik Russian forces, Rutenberg had gone to the Russian Black Sea port of Odessa. There, Churchill explained, he had been employed by the French authorities during the time of their occupation of the port as part of the Allied attempt to protect it from Bolshevik attack. While in Odessa he had 'rendered good service in securing the escape of large numbers of persons who were committed to the anti-Bolshevist cause,' Churchill told the House, and was considered 'a remarkable man, and very good reports about him have been received. At the same time, I have no doubt that his record is one which would not in every respect compare with that of those who have been fortunate enough to live their lives in this settled and ordered country.'

Churchill then appealed to the House of Commons not to prevent the Mandate authorities 'to use Jews, and use Jews freely, within limits that are proper, to develop new sources of wealth in Palestine.' It was also imperative, if the Balfour Declaration 'pledges to the Zionists' were to be carried out, for the House of Commons to reverse the vote of the House of Lords. 'This vote', Churchill warned, 'might have a serious result in Palestine. It might lead to violent disturbances . . . to distress and bloodshed.' Above all, Britain must keep the pledge that she had given 'before all the nations of the world.'[25]

Churchill's appeal was successful. Only thirty-five votes were cast against the government's Palestine policy, and two hundred and ninety-two in favour. His speech was a personal triumph: 'a brilliant speech,' his Cabinet colleague H. A. L. Fisher wrote in his diary.[26] But there was more work to be done, and to be done immediately. For Churchill had next to submit Britain's Palestine Mandate governing principles for the approval of the League of Nations, under whose authority the Mandates lay. These principles were first presented to Parliament as a White Paper known as the Churchill White Paper.

Serving as the basis of the British Mandate, the White Paper was emphatic in its support for Zionism, pointing out that already by 1922 the Jews had 'recreated in Palestine a community, now numbering 80,000, of whom about one-fourth are farmers or workers upon the land.' The White Paper also reiterated the Colonial Office letter of 1 March to the Palestinian Arab delegation in London, that stated: 'the development of the Jewish National Home in Palestine is not the imposition of a Jewish nationality upon the inhabitants of Palestine as a whole, but the further development of the existing Jewish community, with the assistance of Jews in other parts of the world, in order that it may become a centre in which the Jewish

25 Parliamentary Debates, *Hansard*, 4 July 1922. This speech was published in Berlin by Siegfried Scholem as a 16-page pamphlet in German, *Britische Politik in Palästina*, for the Zionist fundraising organisation Keren Hayesod.
26 Diary entry, 4 July 1922: H. A. L. Fisher papers.

people as a whole may take, on grounds of religion and race, an interest and a pride.' The White Paper, like the letter of 1 March, stressed that in order for the Jewish community in Palestine to have 'the best prospect of free development and provide a full opportunity for the Jewish people to display its capacities, it is essential that it should know that it is in Palestine as of right and not on sufferance.' That was the reason why it was necessary 'that the existence of a Jewish National Home in Palestine should be internationally guaranteed, and that it should be formally recognised to rest upon ancient historic connection.'[27]

The Churchill White Paper was submitted to the League of Nations in Geneva, and approved on 22 July. The Zionists understood that what Churchill had devised gave them the opportunity to move – albeit with a long period of continuous Jewish immigration – towards statehood. On 26 July, four days after the Mandate was approved, Chaim Weizmann wrote to Churchill to congratulate him. 'To you personally,' Weizmann wrote, 'as well as to those who have been associated with you at the Colonial Office, we tender our most grateful thanks. Zionists throughout the world deeply appreciate the unfailing sympathy you have consistently shown towards their legitimate aspirations and the great part you have played in securing for the Jewish people the opportunity of rebuilding its national home in peaceful co-operation with all sections of the inhabitants of Palestine.'[28]

With Churchill's active and persistent support, the establishment of a Jewish National Home in Palestine had become a reality.

27 *Statement of British Policy in Palestine,* the Churchill White Paper: Command Paper 1700 of 1922.
28 Letter of 26 July 1922: Weizmann papers.

CHAPTER EIGHT

AN ANTI-SEMITIC LIBEL, PALESTINE, AND MOSES

In the General Election of 1922 the Lloyd George government was defeated, and an entirely Conservative administration was formed in which Churchill had no place. He had also lost his parliamentary seat at Dundee, and needed to find a new one if he was to return to the House of Commons, in which he had sat for more than two decades. His first attempt, when he stood for the West Leicester constituency in 1923, was unsuccessful. Whenever he spoke in public during his attempts to return to Parliament he was met by the accusation that during the war he had done the bidding of wealthy Jews for illegal gain. This charge, at a time of considerable anti-Jewish feeling in Britain, especially in Conservative circles, was given widespread publicity.

The accusation arose from a lecture given throughout Britain by Lord Alfred Douglas, the poet and former lover of Oscar Wilde. Douglas alleged that immediately after the Battle of Jutland in 1916, as part of a plot engineered by wealthy British Jews headed by Sir Ernest Cassel, an official communiqué was issued by the Admiralty – then headed by Arthur Balfour – to report that the battle had been a heavy setback for Britain. As a result of the dispiriting tone of this communiqué, British stocks had plummeted on the New York Stock Exchange. The Jewish conspirators then bought these stocks at the knock-down price, whereupon Churchill, in return for money from these same Jews, and in connivance with Balfour, issued a second Jutland communiqué. This stated that the battle had been much more favourable to Britain than had earlier been realised. The stocks rose to new heights. The conspirators then sold, making enormous profits.

According to Douglas, the Jewish financiers had rewarded Churchill with £40,000, the equivalent of more than a million pounds in 2006. Cassel, he added, had also paid for the furnishing of Churchill's house in London after Jutland. Neither allegation was true, although Cassel had furnished a small library for Churchill ten years before the outbreak of the war.

Such were Douglas's allegations. When the *Morning Post* called them 'vile insults against the Jews' Douglas sued the newspaper. The trial against the newspaper began on 17 July 1923. During cross-examination, the newspaper's barrister, Patrick Hastings, asked Douglas: 'Do you mean to say that Mr Churchill was financially indebted to the Jews?' 'Yes certainly,' replied Douglas. 'Do you want to persist in that now,' Hastings continued. 'Of course I do,' Douglas replied.

Questioned about the second Jutland communiqué, Churchill was asked: 'Had it anything to do with any manipulation of stocks in any market of the world.' Churchill answered: 'Such an idea never entered my mind.' He was then asked: 'Did you make a penny piece of money in any way out of it,' to which he replied: 'No.'

The *Morning Post* was found guilty of having libeled Douglas, but was only fined a farthing – a quarter of a penny – a derisory amount. Douglas was also ordered to pay Churchill's costs. Furious at this, Douglas published the text of his accusatory lecture as a pamphlet, of which at least 30,000 copies were distributed in London. He sent Churchill a copy with a covering note: 'I challenge you to show your face in the witness box, and answer the questions I shall put to you.'

It was the British Government that decided to take action, bringing a criminal libel case against Douglas. Being a criminal libel brought by the government, and not a regular libel brought by a private individual, the case for the prosecution was conducted by the Attorney General. Both Churchill and Balfour were called as witnesses. When Churchill was asked directly: 'Is there a shadow of truth in any of the accusations made against you?' he replied: 'Not the slightest. From beginning to end it is a monstrous and malicious invention.'

The jury took only eight minutes to reach their verdict. Douglas was found guilty and sentenced to six months in prison.[1] 'I cannot recall the case of any public man who has suffered such abuse and misrepresentation,' Churchill's former Admiralty Secretary wrote to him when the verdict was known. 'It is not possible to hope that your enemies will cease to deprecate your actions and motives, but at any rate this particular outrageous falsehood cannot be publicly repeated. It is largely due to such unjustifiable attacks that you lost your seat at Dundee and failed at Leicester.'[2]

During his almost two-year absence from Parliament, Churchill was asked by a leading member of the Jewish community in Britain, Sir Robert Waley Cohen, to act as an intermediary with the government over the merging of two companies, of which Waley Cohen was managing director, with the Anglo-Persian Oil Company, in which the British Government held a majority of the voting shares. It was Churchill who had negotiated the purchase of the Anglo-Persian Oil Company for the government ten years earlier, on the eve of the First World War, to ensure the supply of oil needed for the Royal Navy, which was then changing rapidly from coal-burning to oil-burning ships.

Churchill agreed to represent Waley Cohen's two companies in the merger plans, which had been rejected by the government the previous year. For his representation he was paid £5,000 – twenty-five times that amount in modern values, and equivalent to the annual salary of a Cabinet Minister. Churchill told his wife that when he asked his former Principal Private Secretary at the Admiralty, Sir James Masterton-Smith, about the propriety of acting as the intermediary, Masterton-Smith was 'very shy of it on large political grounds.' But Churchill, who had recently bought a home in the

---

1 Harford Montgomery Hyde, *Lord Alfred Douglas: A Biography.*

2 Sir William Graham Greene, letter of 14 December 1923: Churchill papers, 2/127.

country, Chartwell, in Kent, needed money for an ambitious rebuilding plan. He therefore approached the Prime Minister, Stanley Baldwin, about the merger, seeking his goodwill and, if possible, assistance. This was not something Churchill wished to be known, writing to Clementine: 'I entered Downing Street by the Treasury entrance to avoid comment. This much amused Baldwin.'

All went well. 'My interview with the PM was most agreeable,' Churchill told Clementine. 'I found him thoroughly in favour of the Oil Settlement on the lines proposed. Indeed he might have been Waley Cohen from the way he talked. I am sure it will come off.'[3] In memorandum on his merger activities, Churchill recalled how, at this meeting, Baldwin told him that he was 'disquieted at the position of the Anglo-Persian company and at the impending decline of the Government holding. He was also on general grounds averse from the continued participation of the British Government in the Oil business. He expressed the opinion that a sum of twenty millions would be a very good price for the Government to obtain for their shares.'

For Churchill, this was a green light. 'I went further into the matter with all the companies concerned,' he noted, 'and at the end of August I had a second interview with the Prime Minister. I told him that I believed that a scheme could be framed which would satisfy the various requirements he had in mind and that subject to his approval I was willing to take part in formulating such a scheme.'

Churchill made it clear to Baldwin that he would have a personal interest in the scheme. 'The Prime Minister expressed his entire approval, and informed me that he thought it desirable the questions should be re-examined.' During September, under Churchill's guidance, an outline scheme was prepared by Waley Cohen's companies and submitted to the government. 'This scheme can be published,' Churchill wrote, 'and I believe that it will be found to be of advantage both to the State and to the special interests of the Admiralty. That however is a matter of opinion.'

3 Letter of 15 August 1923: Spencer-Churchill papers.

Before the merger scheme could be examined by the government departments concerned, Baldwin made a public declaration in favour of Protection. Churchill, a veteran Free Trader, felt it his duty to re-enter public life to oppose the government and publicly attack this policy, and did not want 'to be hampered in my full freedom of opposition to the Government by association with any special interests however legitimate;' for that reason, he informed the companies, before making his first speech attacking the government, 'I must withdraw from the negotiation and renounce any personal interest.'[4]

On 14 November Churchill told Waley Cohen that he would have to withdraw from his work on the merger as he wished to 're-enter public life.'[5] This he did. Although, in March 1924, he lost his attempt to return to Parliament for the Abbey Division of Westminster by a mere forty-three votes, eight months later he was returned as the member for Epping, a constituency just outside London, whereupon Baldwin appointed him Chancellor of the Exchequer.

While Churchill was Chancellor of the Exchequer, the Cabinet was asked to consider a request from Weizmann for a British Government guarantee towards a loan for Zionist economic development in Palestine. Jewish enterprise was in need of financial support; economic hardship in Palestine had led to a decline in the number of Jewish immigrants, and in the previous year – to a small net emigration for 1928 – the British population statistics showed just under 150,000 Jews and more than 700,000 Arabs. The loan, Weizmann explained, would be 'for the sole purpose of promoting and expediting close settlement by Jews on the land, as contemplated by the Mandate.'[6]

Lord Balfour, the architect of the Balfour Declaration, who as

---

4 Memorandum of 20 November 1923: Churchill papers, 2/128.
5 Letter of 15 November 1923: Churchill papers, 2/128.
6 Note of 21 January 1928: Churchill papers, 22/194.

Lord President of the Council was a senior member of the Cabinet, supported the loan. Before the Cabinet was to discuss it, he brought Churchill and Weizmann together at his London home. During the Cabinet discussion, Churchill, who understood from his experiences in 1922 the relative precariousness of the Zionist enterprise when faced by parliamentary hostility, warned his colleagues that such a loan could stimulate anti-Semitic feeling in the House of Commons. He nevertheless supported the loan, as did Balfour. The Cabinet as a whole, however, rejected it.[7]

In 1929 the Conservatives were defeated by Labour at the General Election and Churchill, while remaining a Member of Parliament, was out of office. That summer he embarked on a three-month journey through Canada and the United States. While he was travelling, there was an upsurge of Arab attacks on Jews throughout Palestine. There were then 156,000 Jews in Palestine – almost twice the number as in 1922 – and 794,000 Arabs. The Arab population had itself grown by 130,000 during those years, as much due to immigration as to natural increase.

During the attacks, by armed Arabs against unarmed Jews, 133 Jews were killed. In Jerusalem four thousand Jews were driven from their homes, many of which were then looted. Reaching San Francisco, Churchill was asked by the journalists who met him, how – as a recent member of the British Government and a former Colonial Secretary – the Arab killing of Jews and destruction of Jewish property in Palestine would affect Britain's pledge to allow continued Jewish immigration. The Arabs had no reason to be against the Jews, he said at a luncheon on 11 September, and went on to explain: 'The Jews have developed the country, grown orchards and grain fields out of the desert, built schools and great buildings, constructed irrigation projects and water power houses and have made Palestine a much better place in which to live than it was before they came a few years ago. The Arabs are much better off now than before the Jews came,

7 Cabinet of 13 March 1928: Cabinet papers, 23/57.

and it will be a short time only before they realise it.'[8] This was indeed the case: Arab villages that were near Jewish villages benefited considerably from the installation of water and electricity, as well as from a greater outlet for their produce.

To 'Jewish enterprise,' Churchill stressed, 'the Arab owes nearly everything he has. Fanaticism and a sort of envy have driven the Arab to violence, and for the present the problem is one of proper policing until harmony has been restored.'[9]

Churchill made the same points in an article in the *New York American* magazine. Praising the work of the Zionists in Palestine, he wrote of Rishon le-Zion, the wine-making town he had visited eight years earlier, that out of 'the blistering desert, patience, industry, and civilised intelligence have created green, smiling fields and vineyards and delicious shady groves, the home of thriving, happy, simple communities who, even if there had been no Balfour Declaration, would deserve the strong protection and the sympathies of free and enlightened people in every quarter of the globe.'

As for the Arabs of Palestine, Churchill wrote, they had been brought, as a result of the Jewish presence there, 'nothing but good gifts, more wealth, more trade, more civilisation, new sources of revenue, more employment, a higher rate of wages, larger cultivated areas, a better water supply – in a word, the fruits of reason and modern science.'

Churchill's article ended with a reference to his undiminished fear of Jewish Bolshevism, but on a positive, enthusiastic note: 'So long as the Zionist leaders keep their ranks vigilantly purged of the vicious type of Russian subversive they will have it in their power to revive the life and fame of their native land. They are entitled to a full and fair chance. All the great victorious Powers are committed in their behalf and Great Britain, which has accepted a common

---

8 'Arab Atrocities in Holy Land Ended for All Time, Asserts Statesman in Interview Here', *San Francisco Chronicle*, 12 September 1929.

9 'Churchill Says Arabs Owe Much to Jews': *New York Times*, 13 September 1929.

responsibility in a direct and definite form, must not, and will not, weary of its lawful discharge.'[10]

The British Ambassador in Washington, Sir Ronald Lindsay, was not pleased, writing testily to the Foreign Office: 'The effect of this article can only be to induce Jews in America who might wish to take a moderate view, to refrain from doing so. They will expect a purely Zionist policy from the Conservatives when they come into office again and will hamper any move towards settlement till then, and then the chickens will come home to roost with Mr Winston Churchill.'[11]

While still in San Francisco, Churchill telegraphed the text of his article to London, where it was published in the *Sunday Times* on 22 September 1929. Thus his views on Palestine were widely read on both sides of the Atlantic.

Soon after Churchill returned to Britain, the Labour Government, headed by Ramsay MacDonald, took what Churchill considered a retrograde step with regard to Palestine. In October 1930, the Colonial Secretary, Lord Passfield – the social reformer Sidney Webb – issued a new Palestine White Paper, in which he sought to appease the unremitting Arab hostility to the idea of a Jewish National Home. The Passfield White Paper stated that Britain's obligation under the Mandate was an equal one with regard to the Arab and Jewish communities in Palestine.

Churchill begged to differ. On 2 November 1930, Balfour Day, in an article headed 'Fair Play to the Jews', he explained that the Colonial Secretary had 'overlooked, or ignored, the fact that the obligations are totally different in character.' Churchill then stressed that the 'frequent use' in the new White Paper of the mandatory obligations 'to the inhabitants of Palestine, both Arabs and Jews' diverged fundamentally from his 1922 White Paper – which, following upon the Balfour Declaration and the Mandate, 'recognised

---

10 Winston S. Churchill, 'The Palestine Crisis,' *Sunday Times*, 22 September 1929.
11 Letter of 6 November 1930: Foreign Office papers, 371/14494.

an obligation not only to the inhabitants of Palestine – Arab or Jew – but to the Zionist Movement all over the world, to whom the original promise was made.'

Churchill was emphatic that the British obligation 'was to Jews wherever they might live, to have the right to become part of the Jewish National Home,' and he added, 'No similar obligation had been made to the Arabs outside Palestine.' It was the Jews alone to whom Britain was pledged with regard to building a homeland in Palestine by immigration. As to whether the obligations which Great Britain had contracted by the Balfour Declaration and the Palestine Mandate were wise or unwise, Churchill wrote: 'There is no use answering this at this stage. The sole question is whether they are being fulfilled.'

Churchill noted in his article that the British Government, being 'face to face with the inherent, though not insuperable, difficulties of the problem, have to set limits, both of speed and method, to the practical, year-to-year progress of the Zionist scheme. They have to offer to the Arab population definite and concrete assurances as to the sphere within which their civil and religious rights will be safeguarded.'[12] This approach put obligations on the Zionists, but it did not inhibit their ongoing immigration and economic development, including land purchase.

In the new Parliament of 1931, in which he was excluded from government office, Churchill joined an informal but strong committee of members of both Houses who spoke in favour of Zionist enterprise in Palestine. Among its members were a Labour stalwart Josiah Wedgwood, a former Conservative Foreign Secretary, Sir Austen Chamberlain, and a recently elected Jewish member of the Liberal Party, James de Rothschild. A young Jewish Labour MP, Barnett Janner, the secretary of the committee, later wrote that its members 'made Zionism one of their parliamentary duties.'[13]

*

12 'Fair Play to the Jews', *Sunday Chronicle*, 2 November 1930.
13 Elsie Janner, *Barnett Janner: A Personal Portrait*, page 41.

Randolph Churchill, like his father, supported Zionist aspirations. Many years later he recalled a visit by Weizmann to Churchill's home at Chartwell at the time of the 1929 White Paper discussions, when Randolph was eighteen. His father, he said, had been fascinated by Weizmann's talk and appearance: 'Just like an Old Testament prophet,' he told his son when Weizmann had left.[14]

Churchill had long been fascinated by Jewish history, by the Jewish involvement with the events of the time, and above all by the Jews' monotheism and ethics. These seemed to him a central factor in the evolution and maintenance of modern civilisation. He published his thoughts about this on 8 November 1931, in an article in the *Sunday Chronicle* about Moses.

Noting that the Biblical story had often been portrayed as myth, Churchill declared: 'We reject, however, with scorn all those learned and laboured myths that Moses was but a legendary figure upon whom the priesthood and the people hung their essential social, moral and religious ordinances. We believe that the most scientific view, the most up-to-date and rationalistic conception, will find its fullest satisfaction in taking the Bible story literally, and in identifying one of the greatest of human beings with the most decisive leap-forward ever discernible in the human story.'

Turning to the central theme of Judaism, that of one God whose code of human conduct Moses had received at Mount Sinai, Churchill wrote: 'This wandering tribe, in many respects indistinguishable from numberless nomadic communities, grasped and proclaimed an idea of which all the genius of Greece and all the power of Rome were incapable.'

Moses himself, Churchill wrote, 'was the greatest of the prophets, who spoke in person to the God of Israel; he was the national hero who led the Chosen people out of the land of bondage, through the perils of the wilderness, and brought them to the very threshold of the Promised Land; he was the supreme law-giver, who received from God that remarkable code upon which the religious, moral, and

14 Randolph Churchill recollections, in conversation with the author.

social life of the nation was so securely fastened. Tradition lastly ascribed to him the authorship of the whole Pentateuch, and the mystery that surrounded his death added to his prestige.'[15]

Thirty years later, Churchill gave a copy of this essay to the Israeli Prime Minister, David Ben-Gurion.

15 Winston S. Churchill, 'Moses', *Sunday Chronicle*, 8 November 1930. The article appeared in a series entitled 'Great Bible Stories retold by the World's Best Writers'.

CHAPTER NINE

THE RISE OF HITLER

In Germany, at the election held on 31 July 1932, Adolf Hitler, head of the opposition Nazi Party, won 230 seats, as against 133 for the Social Democrats, and 78 for the Communists. With more than thirteen million votes, the Nazi Party was the largest Party in the State. But they had won only 37.1 per cent of the total poll. The German Chancellor, Franz von Papen, refused to invite them to join his Cabinet. Hitler's immediate reaction to his exclusion from power was to intensify terror in the streets, using his Brownshirt thugs to beat up political opponents and Jews. On 29 August 1932, bowing to the force of terror, von Papen offered Hitler the post of Vice-Chancellor. Hitler refused. His aim was to be offered the Chancellorship itself.

At that moment Churchill left England for Germany with his wife and two of their children, Sarah and Randolph. Churchill was writing a biography of his illustrious military ancestor, John Churchill, Duke of Marlborough, for which he had received valuable constructive criticism from a leading British Jewish historian, Polish-born Professor Lewis Namier. At one point Churchill even contemplated asking Namier to be his principal collaborator.[1]

Churchill's work took him to the scenes of Marlborough's battles, including Blenheim, in Bavaria. It was a Jew, Solomon de Medina, the first practising Jew in England to receive a knighthood, who was Marlborough's chief army contractor during the War of the Spanish Succession (1701–14) supplying Marlborough with money,

1 Julia Namier, *Lewis Namier: A Biography*, page 231.

provisions and military intelligence. Medina later gave evidence against Marlborough for having received six thousand pounds a year from him for his personal use, in return for the supply contract. This was no more, Marlborough explained to the Commissioners of Accounts, than what had earlier been 'allowed as a perquisite' to generals and commanders-in-chief. Churchill was convinced that although the charge was true, Medina had framed it 'in an injurious and misleading form.'[2]

While in Munich, Randolph wanted to introduce his father to Hitler, and asked one of Hitler's friends, Ernst Hanfstaengel, to arrange a meeting. Churchill and Hanfstaengel dined together at Churchill's hotel in Munich. Fifteen years later Churchill recalled how, during dinner, Hanfstaengel 'gave a most interesting account of Hitler's activities and outlook. He spoke as one under the spell.'[3]

Hanfstaengel told Churchill that, as Hitler came each afternoon to that same hotel, 'nothing would be easier' than for the two men to meet. Hanfstaengel hoped that Hitler would join Churchill after dinner. 'I turned up at the appointed hour,' Hanfstaengel recalled. 'Mr Churchill taxed me about Hitler's anti-Semitic views. I tried to give as mild an account of the subject as I could, saying that the real problem was the influx of eastern European Jews and the excessive representation of their co-religionaries in the professions, to which Churchill listened very carefully, commenting, "Tell your boss from me that anti-Semitism may be a good starter, but it is a bad sticker."'

On the following day Hanfstaengel made one further effort to persuade Hitler to meet Churchill, but in vain. Two days later the Churchills left Munich. Hitler, Hanfstaengel noted, 'kept away until they had gone.'[4]

Churchill later recalled, of his near meeting with Hitler: 'In the course of conversation with Hanfstaengl, I happened to say "Why is

---

2 Winston S. Churchill, *Marlborough: His Life and Times*, Volume Four, page 483.
3 Winston S. Churchill, *The Second World War*, Volume One, page 75.
4 Ernst Hanfstaengel, *Hitler – The Missing Years*, pages 447–8.

your chief so violent about the Jews? I can quite understand being angry with Jews who have done wrong or are against the country, and I understand resisting them if they try to monopolise power in any walk of life; but what is the sense of being against a man simply because of his birth? How can any man help how he is born?" He must have repeated this to Hitler, because about noon the next day he came round with rather a serious air and said that the appointment he had made with me to meet Hitler could not take place as the Fuehrer would not be coming to the hotel that afternoon. This was the last I saw of "Putzi" – for such was his pet name – although we stayed several more days at the hotel.'[5]

During his stay in Munich, Churchill saw a procession of uniformed Brownshirts; they were unarmed, but their fanaticism was intense. Within three months, on 30 January 1933, Hitler was appointed Chancellor of Germany. During the last week of March a Nazi manifesto instructed local organisations throughout Germany 'to carry on anti-Jewish propaganda among the people.' On 13 April, a law came into effect barring all Jews from national, local and municipal office. That day, during a debate in the House of Commons, Churchill warned the government of the dangers involved in a militarised Germany, telling the House of Commons that 'one of the things which we were told after the Great War would be a security for us was that Germany would be a democracy with Parliamentary institutions. All that has been swept away. You have dictatorship – most grim dictatorship.'

In his speech to the House of Commons, Churchill stressed several aspects of the German dictatorship: the militarism, appeals 'to every form of fighting spirit', the reintroduction of duelling in the universities, and the persecution of the Jews. Given these things, he commented, 'I cannot help rejoicing that the Germans have not got the heavy cannon, the thousands of military aeroplanes and the tanks of various sizes for which they have been pressing in order that their status may be equal to that of other countries.'

5 Winston S. Churchill, *The Second World War*, Volume One, page 76.

Churchill then warned the House of the folly of continuing British disarmament. This was the policy to which the government, headed by the Labour leader Ramsay MacDonald, but with predominantly Conservative support, was firmly committed. 'When we read about Germany,' Churchill said, 'when we watch with surprise and distress the tumultuous insurgence of ferocity and war spirit, the pitiless ill-treatment of minorities, the denial of the normal protections of civilised society to large numbers of individuals solely on the ground of race – when we see that occurring in one of the most gifted, learned, scientific and formidable nations in the world, one cannot help feeling glad that the fierce passions that are raging in Germany have not found, as yet, any other outlet but upon Germans.'

There were not only 'martial or pugnacious manifestations' in Germany, Churchill pointed out, but also 'this persecution of the Jews, of which so many Hon. Members have spoken, and which appeals to everyone who feels that men and women have a right to live in the world where they were born, and have a right to pursue a livelihood which has hitherto been guaranteed them under the public laws of the land of their birth.'

With extraordinary prescience, Churchill then made another point, full of foreboding. 'There is a danger,' he warned, 'of the odious conditions now ruling in Germany being extended by conquest to Poland, and another persecution and pogrom of Jews being begun in this new area.'[6] There were six hundred thousand Jews in Germany in 1933, and more than three million in Poland. At a time when most British politicians doubted Germany's aggressive intentions, Churchill's forecast seemed far-fetched. Within ten years it had come to pass.

The Nazis, who were assiduously courting Western opinion, were angered by Churchill's speech, especially his censure of their anti-Jewish measures. On 19 April a correspondent of the *Birmingham Post* reported from Berlin: 'Today newspapers are full with "sharp

6 Parliamentary Debates, *Hansard*, 13 April 1933.

warnings" for England.' One headline referred to 'Mr Winston Churchill's "impudence"'.[7]

Among Churchill's visitors in the spring of 1933 was German-born Albert Einstein, who had been in the United States when Hitler came to power. Being Jewish, neither his fame nor his Nobel Prize could help him. In Nazi eyes, as a Jew he was an outcast. Einstein, who was five years younger than Churchill, visited him at Chartwell, where he asked Churchill's help in bringing Jewish scientists from Germany. Churchill responded at once, encouraging his friend Professor Frederick Lindemann – who was at Chartwell during Einstein's visit – to travel to Germany and seek out Jewish scientists who could be found places at British universities.[8] Lindemann did so. As part of a nationwide British university effort, he was able to offer university places to German Jewish scientists who, as a result of these invitations, were able to leave Germany.

It was not always easy, even for a man of Churchill's stature, to persuade others to help. Since 1929 he had been Chancellor of Bristol University, an honorary but respected position. When he approached the Vice-Chancellor of the university, Thomas Loveday, on behalf of one of his parliamentary constituents, to give a place to a twenty-two-year-old German-Jewish medical student, thus enabling the student to leave Germany, the Vice-Chancellor replied that he would ask the Dean of the Faculty of Medicine to look at the application, but added, 'We have of course to limit the number of these unfortunate people from Germany whom we can accept for training as doctors in this country.'[9] Three months later, Loveday wrote again. There had been 'a heavy rush' on entry to the Faculty of Medicine that year 'and we have had to refuse applications for entry from all foreign countries and even from some of the Dominions.'[10]

*

7 *Birmingham Post*, 19 April 1933.
8 Albert Einstein papers.
9 Letter of 15 August 1934: Churchill papers, 2/231.
10 Letter of 19 December 1934: Churchill papers, 2/231.

In the autumn of 1934, Churchill and his wife left England on board the yacht of their friend Lord Moyne, for a holiday in Lebanon, Syria – both under French rule – Palestine, Transjordan and Egypt. They began in Beirut, from where they drove to Palmyra and Damascus and then, on 9 October, across the French-ruled Golan Heights and into British Mandate Palestine, to Nazareth. On the following day they drove through Nablus to Jerusalem, staying at the recently opened King David Hotel, where Lord Moyne joined them. After a night at the hotel, all three left Jerusalem by car for Jericho, then flew east to Amman and south over Transjordan to the ancient city of Petra, from where they flew westward across the Negev and Sinai deserts and the Suez Canal to Cairo.[11]

Churchill's brief holiday visit to Palestine coincided with a spate of night-time Arab attacks on Jewish villages, which often culminated in the destruction of orchards and crops. For ten years the Palestinian Arabs had been incited to violence against the Jews by their spiritual leader, Haj Amin al-Husseini, the Mufti of Jerusalem, whose aim was to bring an end to Jewish immigration and the prospect of a Jewish majority, and to see Arab rule throughout the area of the Mandate.

British policy was to deter the Arab attackers by the collective punishment – in the form of fines – of the Arab villages from which the attacks came. Churchill supported this. Having returned to Britain he wrote to the High Commissioner, Sir Arthur Wauchope: 'I am very much obliged to you for your kindness in writing to me about the effects of collective fining. The results are most encouraging, and thoroughly justify the course you adopted in dealing with the singularly cruel offence of destroying fruit trees in a thirsty land. Thank you also for telling me about the level of the Sea of Galilee. I hope indeed this will cure itself with more rains. I greatly enjoyed my flying visit to Palestine, and was struck by the unanimity with which your praises were sung.'[12]

---

11 See map on page 320.
12 Letter of 21 December 1934: Churchill papers, 2/211.

For the second time in thirteen years Churchill saw the efforts that the Jews were making to develop a thriving agricultural economy in Palestine, and the obstacles that were being put in their way by their Arab neighbours.

In Britain, a General Election was called for 14 November 1935. As the day drew near, it was rumoured that Churchill would be brought back into government. On 24 October he spoke publicly of the dangers to Britain and Europe of German rearmament and of the German population being 'trained from childhood for war.'[13] On the following day the British Ambassador in Berlin, Sir Eric Phipps, sent the Foreign Office an article by the London correspondent of the official Nazi *Völkischer Beobachter*, stating 'that as soon as Mr Churchill opens his mouth, it is safe to bet that an attack on Germany will emerge. He is one of the most unscrupulous political intriguers in England. His friendship with the American Jewish millionaire Baruch leads him to expend all his remaining force and authority in directing England's action against Germany. This is the man whom the government are apparently thinking of including in the Cabinet.'[14]

In an article in the *Strand*, a widely circulated monthly magazine published in both Britain and the United States, Churchill described in uncompromising language the militaristic and racist aspects of the Nazi regime. His sources of information were wide-ranging. He had read Hitler's own book, *Mein Kampf* (My Struggle), and followed the often detailed British newspaper accounts of Nazi rule. Friends in the Foreign Office and the Intelligence Service had brought him first-hand information about the severity of Nazi rule. 'Hitler's triumphant career has been borne onwards,' he wrote in his *Strand* article, 'not only by a passionate love of Germany, but by currents of hatred so intense as to sear the souls of those who swim upon them. Hatred of the French is the first of these currents, and we have only to read Hitler's book, *Mein Kampf*, to see that the French are not the

13 Parliamentary Debates, *Hansard*, 24 October 1935.
14 Telegram of 25 October 1935: Foreign Office papers, 371/18878.

only foreign nation against whom the anger of rearmed Germany may be turned. But the internal stresses are even more striking. The Jews, supposed to have contributed, by a disloyal and pacifist influence, to the collapse of Germany at the end of the Great War, were also deemed to be the main prop of communism and the authors of defeatist doctrines in every form. Therefore, the Jews of Germany, a community numbered by many hundreds of thousands, were to be stripped of all power, driven from every position in public and social life, expelled from the professions, silenced in the Press, and declared a foul and odious race.'

The twentieth century, Churchill wrote, had witnessed 'with surprise, not merely the promulgation of these ferocious doctrines, but their enforcement with brutal vigour by the Government and by the populace.' The Jews were the chief victims of these doctrines. 'No past services, no proved patriotism, even wounds sustained in war, could procure immunity for persons whose only crime was that their parents had brought them into the world. Every kind of persecution, grave or petty, upon the world-famous scientists, writers, and composers at the top down to the wretched little Jewish children in the national schools, was practised, was glorified, and is still being practised and glorified.'

A 'similar proscription', Churchill noted, had fallen on socialists and communists, the trade unionists and the liberal intelligentsia. The slightest criticism was an offence against the State. The courts of justice 'though allowed to function in ordinary cases, are superseded for every form of political offence by so-called people's courts composed of ardent Nazis. Side by side with the training grounds of the new armies and the great aerodromes, the concentration camps pock-mark the German soil.' In those camps, 'thousands of Germans coerced and cowed into submission to the irresistible power of the Totalitarian State.'

In a question that went to the heart of the debate about whether Nazism might moderate its extremism, Churchill asked his readers whether Hitler, 'in the full sunlight of worldly triumph, at the head of the great nation he has raised from the dust, still feels racked by the hatreds and antagonisms of his desperate struggle,' or would those hatreds and antagonisms be discarded like the armour and the cruel weapons of strife under the mellowing influences of success?' Churchill noted that those foreign visitors who had met Hitler had found him 'a highly competent, cool, well-informed functionary with an agreeable manner . . .' The world still hoped that the worst might be over, 'and that we may yet live to see Hitler a gentler figure in a happier age.' Yet while Hitler himself had begun to speak 'words of reassurance' in public, in Germany itself 'the great wheels revolve, the rifles, the cannon, the tanks, the shot and shell, the air-bombs, the poison-gas cylinders, the aeroplanes, the submarines, and now the beginnings of a fleet flow in ever-broadening streams from the already largely war-mobilised arsenals and factories of Germany.'[15]

The Nazis were outraged by Churchill's article. On 29 October, Sir Eric Phipps telegraphed to the Foreign Office from Berlin that the German Foreign Ministry had instructed the German ambassador in London 'to lodge a strong protest against the personal attack on the Head of the German State made in an article by Mr Winston Churchill in the *Strand* magazine. The tone of his article is much resented here. The magazine will be prohibited and the press will probably be allowed to publish no more than a bald statement to the effect that a protest has been lodged.'[16]

Despite German protests, Churchill reiterated his fears of German methods and intentions in each of his election speeches. His worry was that people would not fully recognise the dangers. Churchill also did his utmost to keep himself well informed about the situation of the Jews in Germany. At the end of November 1935 he met Baroness von Goldschmidt Rothschild. The Baroness was the only daughter of a German coal magnate, Herr von Friedländer-Fuld, of Berlin, who had died in 1916 leaving her valuable coal mines. In January 1914 the Baroness had married a cousin of Clementine Churchill, but the marriage was annulled later in the

---

15 Winston S. Churchill, 'The Truth About Hitler', *Strand* magazine, November 1935.
16 Telegram of 29 October 1935: Foreign Office papers, 371/18880.

year. She subsequently married a cousin of Churchill's friend, the Liberal Member of Parliament James de Rothschild. Churchill was shocked by what she told him about the new anti-Jewish legislation, the Nuremberg Laws, that decreed the Jews to be second class citizens.

It was through Leonard Montefiore, a member of the Central British Fund set up to help German Jews after 1933, that Churchill received the reply to a query he had made of the Baroness. On 9 December 1935, Montefiore wrote to Churchill: 'I had a message from the Baroness von Goldschmidt Rothschild that you would like to see a translation of the recent Nuremberg laws affecting the Jews in Germany. I therefore enclose a translation of the laws which appeared in the *Manchester Guardian* together with a commentary and also one from *The Times*. I also enclose a translation of the administrative regulations. I also venture to send a small pamphlet of my own, which attempts to give a description of the situation as it was just before the laws were passed.'[17]

The *Manchester Guardian* cutting, dated 16 September 1935, set out the text of the Nuremberg Laws, which forbade, among other things, 'Marriage between Jews and citizens of the nation of German or kindred blood.' The newspaper noted that 'Another section of this law forbids Jews to employ female citizens of German or kindred blood in their households. Jews are also forbidden to hoist the Reich or national flag or to display the Reich colours. On the other hand they are permitted to display the Jewish colours. The execution of this right is under State protection.' The *Manchester Guardian* noted that 'The principal burden of the Law was to deprive German Jews (many of whose ancestors had come to Germany more than a thousand years before, and many of whom had fought in the German Army in the First World War) of German citizenship.'[18]

Churchill absorbed these harsh facts, and recognised yet more clearly how central and how implacable were Nazi anti-Jewish policies, both on paper and in practice. Further evidence reached him in May

---

17 Letter of 9 December 1935: Churchill papers, 2/238.
18 *Manchester Guardian*, 16 December 1935.

1936, when Harold Laski, the son of his Manchester Jewish friend Nathan Laski, sent Churchill a 287-page book, published by Victor Gollancz, *The Yellow Spot: The Extermination of the Jews in Germany*. The book described in graphic detail 'the outlawing of half a million human beings: a collection of facts and documents relating to three years' persecution of German Jews, derived chiefly from National Socialist sources, very carefully assembled by a group of investigators.'[19]

'I have not yet had time to read the terrible book you have sent me,' Churchill wrote to Laski, and went on to urge the leading Labour Party thinker to 'think a little meanwhile of how to preserve the strength of England, the hope of freedom.'[20] This was a reference to the Labour Party's determined opposition to British rearmament – not to follow the Labour Party's policy of disarmament. For Churchill, the only way to halt the onward march of Nazism was for all the threatened nations to arm, and to join together under the collective security clauses of the Covenant of the League of Nations. 'Arms and the Covenant' was Churchill's call. But even some of those most concerned about the persecution of the Jews in Germany failed to see, for it was not the policy either of the Labour or the Conservative Parties, that a robust British foreign policy might serve as a deterrent to German expansion.

---

19 *The Yellow Spot: The Extermination of the Jews in Germany*. London: Victor Gollancz, 1936.

20 Letter of 17 March 1936: Churchill papers, 2/252.

CHAPTER TEN

DEFENDER OF ZIONISM

In 1935 and 1936, during the last years of Stanley Baldwin's second premiership, the British Government began to limit the number of Jews who could enter Palestine. Between Hitler's coming to power and the end of 1935, more than 120,000 Jews – predominantly from Germany and Poland – had entered Palestine, bringing the Jewish population to 355,000. By far the largest Jewish immigration since the start of the Mandate had taken place in 1935, mostly from Germany – 66,476 Jews in all. The Arab population, also enhanced by immigration from Arab regions as far west as Morocco and as far east as Afghanistan, was more than 1,300,000.

On 24 March 1936 the House of Commons discussed a proposal for setting up a Legislative Council in Palestine on which the Arabs, given the disparity of populations at that moment, would have a substantial majority, and thus a decisive veto on any further Jewish immigration. Electorally the Jews, who at that time constituted twenty-seven per cent of the population, would be powerless.

Churchill's speech was the 'great speech' of the debate, recalled the British Zionist leader Selig Brodetsky.[1] Churchill spoke as the defender of the Mandate pledge that the Jews would in due course be able to form an administration, reminding the House of Commons of the indisputable fact that Arab majority rule 'would be a very great obstruction to the development of Jewish immigration into Palestine and to the development of the national home of the Jews there.' He had 'no hostility for the Arabs,' he insisted. 'I think

1 Professor Selig Brodetsky, *Memoirs: from Ghetto to Israel*, page 171.

I made most of the settlements over fourteen years ago governing the Palestine situation. The Emir Abdullah is in Transjordania, where I put him one Sunday afternoon at Jerusalem . . . But I cannot conceive that you will be able to reconcile, at this juncture and at this time, the development of the policy of the Balfour Declaration with an Arab majority on the Legislative Council. I do not feel a bit convinced of it.'

Churchill then spoke of the situation of the Jews in Germany, and its relevance to the government's Palestine policy. 'There is in our minds,' he said, 'an added emphasis upon this question of Jewish migration which comes from other quarters, at a time when the Jewish race in a great country is being subjected to most horrible, cold, scientific persecution, brutal persecution, a "cold" pogrom as it has been called – people reduced from affluence to ruin, and then, even in that position, denied the opportunity of earning their daily bread, and cut out even from relief by grants to tide the destitute through the winter; their little children pilloried in the schools to which they have to go; their blood and race declared defiling and accursed; every form of concentrated human wickedness cast upon these people by overwhelming power, by vile tyranny.'

Given the persecution of the Jews in Germany, 'Surely,' Churchill asked, 'the House of Commons will not allow the one door which is open, the one door which allows some relief, some escape from these conditions, to be summarily closed, nor even allow it to be suggested that it may be obstructed by the course which we take now.'[2] But the mood of the Cabinet and the control of the Conservative Party managers over the large Conservative majority in the House of Commons meant that no move was made to open the gates of Palestine more widely.

The links between Palestinian Arab extremism and Nazism in their ideas with regard to Jews were becoming widely known. Both German and Italian radio propaganda, which were intensifying, fomented Arab agitation against both the Jews of Palestine and the

2 Parliamentary Debates, *Hansard*, 24 March 1936.

British. These links were proof to Churchill both that many of the Arab demands were being inflamed, and of the danger of allowing representative institutions in Palestine while the Arabs were still in the majority, which they would be for many years.

A month after the Legislative Council debate, Churchill received first-hand information of the extent and nature of Palestinian Arab hostility to the Jews from Major Tulloch, a former army friend who was living in Jericho. Anti-Jewish riots that had broken out in 1936 had been followed by a general strike of all Arabs, Tulloch told him, 'and though the vast majority of them are opposed to it they have been terrorised by a few youths and boys acting under the Strike Committee . . . The crowning stupidity is the case of the students at the Kadoorie Agricultural School in Tulkarm, an establishment built and endowed by a Jew for Arabs in the hope of helping them to improve the Arab method of cultivation and so get better yields and more income. At the orders of these iniquitous "Arab Leaders" the students were ordered to strike as a protest against the Balfour Declaration and the immigration of Jews at all into Palestine.'

Tulloch stressed in his letter that the 'vast majority' of poorer Arabs were only too willing to work with the Jews 'were it not for the way they are terrorised by the "leaders" and lied to in the Arab papers.'[3] With this information from a British eye-witness in Palestine, Churchill was under no illusions as to the intensity or nature of the Arab protests.

On 12 March 1937 Churchill was called to give evidence to the Palestine Royal Commission – widely known as the Peel Commission – headed by Lord Peel, a former Secretary of State for India. The purpose of its enquiries was to examine the nature of Britain's pledge to the Jews and Arabs, and to give suggestions for the future of the Palestine Mandate. Among the members of the commission was Sir Horace Rumbold, who had been British Ambassador in Berlin when Hitler came to power.

3 Letter of 29 April 1936: Churchill papers, 2/253.

Churchill's evidence was of the utmost importance. When he had issued his White Paper in 1922 there were 80,000 Jews and half a million Arabs in Palestine. By 1936, as a result of his White Paper having established the right of Jews to emigrate to Palestine with no other restraint than the economic absorptive capacity of the country, the number of Jewish inhabitants had risen to more than 380,000, of whom almost 30,000 had arrived in 1936. The Arab population had also risen, almost as dramatically, to more than a million and a quarter, many of the Arab immigrants attracted by the prosperity that the Jews were creating throughout the country.

Churchill was asked more than a hundred questions. His answers, recorded by stenographers, and kept secret by the commissioners, provided an intimate insight into his thinking about what the Jewish National Home was intended to be, how it had evolved, and how he envisaged its future.

The first question, asked by Lord Peel, concerned the principle of the economic absorptive capacity with regard to the limits imposed on Jewish immigration. Churchill told the commissioners that 'it was not intended to make it the sole test, still less the foundation; certainly not. Of course, it is always governed on the other side – I must point out – by the fact that we are trying to bring in as many as we possibly can in accordance with the original Balfour Declaration.'

Peel then pointed out to Churchill that on the matter of the economic absorptive capacity of Palestine, 'the Jews claim that yours is the authoritative interpretation issued before the Mandate, which really governs the whole thing, and that it would be a breach of faith if anything was suggested contrary to that.' In reply Churchill stressed that Britain 'undertook to try to bring them in as quickly as we could without upsetting the economic life of the country or throwing it into political confusion. I certainly never considered they were entitled, no matter what other consequences arose, to bring in up to the limit of the economic absorptive capacity. That was not intended. On the other hand, it must be made clear our loyalty is on the side of bringing in as many as we can.'

Peel responded sternly: 'But as you know, the Jews insist very much upon the letter of the bond and it is purely for that reason we put that question to you.' Churchill disagreed. His answer to Peel was emphatic. 'I insist', he said, 'upon loyalty and upon the good faith of England to the Jews, to which I attach the most enormous importance, because we gained great advantages in the War. We did not adopt Zionism entirely out of altruistic love of starting a Zionist colony: it was a matter of great importance to this country. It was a potent factor on public opinion in America and we are bound by honour, and I think upon the merits, to push this thing as far as we can, but we are not bound to any particular detail, nor has anybody a right to say, "You have said at a certain date there must be so many."'

Asked by Professor Reginald Coupland, a distinguished historian of the Commonwealth and the Colonies, about the power of the Mufti of Jerusalem, Haj Amin al-Husseini – the leading Palestinian Arab voice against Jewish immigration – to determine the rate of immigration by his protests, Churchill replied, 'I hope to see the British Government so strong it will not be swayed by them.'

Peel then raised one of the most contentious questions in the Palestine debate, the meaning and aim of the Jewish National Home. Churchill had no doubt as to what the aim had been. 'The conception undoubtedly was', he said, 'that, if the absorptive capacity over a number of years and the breeding over a number of years, all guided by the British Government, gave an increasing Jewish population, that population should not in any way be restricted from reaching a majority position. Certainly not. On the contrary, I think in the main that would be the spirit of the Balfour Declaration.'

As to what arrangement would be made to safeguard the rights 'of the new minority' – the Arabs – Churchill told the commissioners, 'that obviously remains open, but certainly we committed ourselves to the idea that some day, somehow, far off in the future, subject to justice and economic convenience, there might well be a great Jewish State there, numbered by millions, far exceeding the present inhabitants of the country and to cut them off from that would be a wrong.'

'. . . a great Jewish State there, numbered by millions'. These were strong words. Churchill continued, 'We never committed ourselves to making Palestine a Jewish Home. We said there should be a Jewish Home in Palestine, but if more and more Jews gather to that Home and all is worked from age to age, from generation to generation, with justice and fair consideration to those displaced and so forth, certainly it was contemplated and intended that they might in the course of time become an overwhelmingly Jewish State.'

'Over the centuries?' Churchill was asked. 'Over the generations or the centuries,' he replied. 'No one has ever said what is to be the rate at which it is to be done. The British Government is the judge and should keep the power to be the judge.'

Sir Horace Rumbold, who had been the British Ambassador in Berlin when Hitler came to power, pointed out that in the White Paper Churchill had written: 'When it is asked what is meant by the development of a Jewish National Home in Palestine,' it was 'in order that it may become a centre in which the Jewish people may take a pride.' What, Rumbold asked, had Churchill meant by 'may become a centre.' Churchill replied: 'If more Jews rally to this Home, the Home will become all Palestine eventually, provided that at each stage there is no harsh injustice done to the other residents.'

As to whether this would constitute an injustice to the Palestinian Arabs, Churchill was confident that it would not. 'Why is there harsh injustice done,' he asked, 'if people come in and make a livelihood for more and make the desert into palm groves and orange groves? Why is it injustice because there is more work and wealth for everybody? There is no injustice. The injustice is when those who live in the country leave it to be a desert for thousands of years.'

Rumbold, with his personal experience of Berlin in 1933, then asked: 'All that has been strengthened by things like the policy of the Nazi Government in Germany and the economic pressure on the Jews in Poland?' to which Churchill replied: 'That makes it more poignant, but it does not oblige us to do any active injustice to Arabs because of the injustice done to Jews in Europe. We have to see that they do not come in in such numbers that they upset the country and create unfair conditions and we are the judges of that, and the sole judges in my opinion.'

Rumbold was not satisfied, asking if Churchill maintained that Jewish immigration could continue even if 'this policy results in periodical disturbances, costing us the lives of our men and so on?' Churchill had no doubt as to the answer. In his opinion, 'All questions of self-government in Palestine are subordinate to the discharge of the Balfour Declaration – the idea of creating a National Home for the Jews and facing all the consequences which may ultimately in the slow passage of time result from that. That is the prime and dominating pledge upon which Britain must act.'

Had he contemplated the possibility of a Jewish majority, Churchill was asked. He replied emphatically: 'I am sure it would be contrary to the whole spirit of the Balfour Declaration if we were to declare that in no circumstances, however naturally it might arise, would we contemplate a Jewish majority.' As to the local Arabs: 'If we displace so-and-so from this place and so-and-so from that place and he and his family are subject to harsh usage, we cannot have that'; but he insisted that for Britain to say 'this great idea of a Jewish National Home in Palestine was to have a limit put on it and say it is not to be a Jewish National Home if more people get to it than the Arab population, that would not be right.'

Rumbold had another question, about Jewish land purchase and the fact that Jews were not then employing Arabs on the land they had bought. 'I think the Mandatory Power should talk to the Jewish people about it,' Churchill replied, 'and say how foolish they are to do it and how wrong.' The British should say to the Jews: 'If you cannot ease the situation in the way of employing more Arabs, if you cannot get on better terms with these Arabs, that is a reason for our reducing immigration in any given year.'

Churchill then re-iterated strongly: 'We are always aiming at the fact that, if enough Jews come, eventually it may be a great Palestinian State, in which the large majority of the inhabitants would be Jews.' As to when this Jewish majority State would come into being, Churchill commented, 'It is not a thing which will happen for a century or more.' These words would not have pleased the Zionists, had they heard them, but they would have pleased the Arabs even less, for Churchill did envisage a Jewish majority in the end.

Professor Coupland had a strong objection to Churchill's concept of continuing Jewish immigration, calling it 'a creeping invasion and conquest of Palestine spread over half a century, which is a thing unheard of in history?' Churchill was indignant. 'It is not a creeping conquest,' he said. In 1918 the Arabs were beaten 'and at our disposition.' They were defeated 'in the open field. It is not a question of creeping conquest. They were beaten out of the place. Not a dog could bark. And then we decided in the process of the conquest of these people to make certain pledges to the Jews. Now the question is how to administer in a humane and enlightened fashion and certain facts have emerged.'

Coupland then referred to the riots, questioning Churchill – about the use of British troops in Palestine – that 'every few years you go on shooting Arabs down because they dislike the Jews coming in?' to which Churchill replied, accurately: 'Have there not been many more Jews murdered than Arabs?' When Coupland noted that Arabs were killed 'in the end' – mostly shot by British troops – Churchill, again indignant, told his interlocutor: 'You cannot say we go on shooting down the Arabs.' If more Arabs were killed than Jews, they were being killed by the British 'because we are the stronger power.'

Returning to the British conquest of Palestine in the First World War, Rumbold remarked: 'You conquer a nation and you have given certain pledges the result of which has been that the indigenous population is subject to the invasion of a foreign race.' Churchill did not accept that the Jews were a 'foreign race'. 'Not at all,' he said. It was the Arabs who had been the outsiders, the conquerors. 'In the time of Christ,' Churchill pointed out, 'the population of Palestine was much greater, when it was a Roman province.' That was when Palestine was a Jewish province of Rome. 'When the Mohammedan upset occurred in world history,' Churchill continued, 'and the great hordes of Islam swept over these places they broke it all up, smashed it all up. You have seen the terraces on the hills which used to be cultivated, which under Arab rule have remained a desert.'

Rumbold suggested that it would be 'more just' for Churchill to have said 'under Turkish rule', to which Churchill replied, 'I do not know about that. I have a great regard for Arabs, but at the same time you find where the Arab goes it is often desert.' The discussion turned to the question of Arab life in the past. When Rumbold said that the Arabs had created 'a good deal of civilisation in Spain,' Churchill answered: 'I am glad they were thrown out.' Rumbold was indignant: 'They were there six or seven hundred years and they did a great deal there,' he said. Things had 'gone back' since the Arabs left Cordova. To which Churchill remarked, 'It is a lower manifestation, the Arab.' Churchill was not prepared to accept that the Arabs were capable of creating a vibrant culture. What he had seen in Egypt as a soldier thirty-five years earlier, and what he had seen in Palestine on his two visits, in 1921 and 1934, had not impressed him.

Peel then addressed the rise in Palestinian Arab nationalism, and its hostility to the whole Zionist enterprise. Churchill was not deterred in his vision of an eventual Jewish State and Britain's constructive part in its evolution, far off though statehood might be. 'You might have to soft pedal a bit,' he told Peel, 'but you will not alter your purpose. Your purpose is declared. You may go a little bit slower. I regard it as being a thing for England. If she cannot do it she had better give it up.' But Britain could 'perfectly well mark time' for five or ten years. This might also affect the rate of Jewish immigration. The Jews had 'no right' to say to the British, 'You have promised us we can have a further million immigrants.' England, Churchill insisted, 'is the judge.'

When the commissioners turned to Jewish immigration, Churchill produced a note of caution, one that was to disappoint the Zionists when it became known, but one that was to be his view for the rest of the Palestine Mandate, even after the Second World War. 'Are we going too fast?' he asked, and went on to suggest a limit on the pace of Jewish immigration: 'We want these races to live together and to minister to their well-being. Their well-being would be greatly enhanced if they did not quarrel. Where there is now a desert would become a really lovely place, and the Arabs would reap the benefit. We want them to; but if you go too fast and you have these furious outbreaks, then you must go a bit slower. But you must not give in to the furious outbreaks; you must quell them. You may go a bit slower, but do not be diverted from your purpose, which is that you will preserve a nucleus in Palestine round which as many Jews as can get a living will be gathered, without regard to the racial balance of population in the country. That is my view.'

Here was the key to Churchill's continuing support for what the Zionists were trying to do in Palestine: create a viable Jewish life, without threat from the demographic superiority of the Arabs. However qualified or circumscribed, he said, his advice was 'Do not be diverted from your purpose.'

Peel then turned to that article of the Mandate that stated: 'The Mandatory shall be responsible for placing the country under such administrative, political and economic conditions as will secure the establishment of a Jewish national home,' and to facilitate 'the development of self-governing institutions' while at the same time 'safeguarding the civil and religious rights of all the inhabitants of Palestine irrespective of race and religion.' Do you consider these as two parallel duties? he asked Churchill. If the Jews became a majority, Britain might establish self-governing institutions, because it would not then conflict with the establishment of a Jewish National Home. But the Arabs say, 'That is very odd self-government: it is only when the Jews are in a majority that we can have it.'

When Churchill was asked if the Arabs were right in saying 'that it is the entry of the Jews and the Jewish Home' that prevented them from having self-governing institutions, he replied that the Mandate limited the development of Arab self-governing institutions 'as long as they do not accept the spirit of the Balfour Declaration. The moment they accept that spirit, with all the pledges of their civil liberties, the question falls to the ground.' But the Arabs 'resist and they do not want it.' Churchill added, 'If I were an Arab I should not like it, but it is for the good of the world that the place should be cultivated, and it never will be cultivated by the Arabs.'

When Coupland noted that 'Arab nationalism sees it cannot get the self-government which Iraq, Syria, Trans-Jordan and Egypt have all got, for one reason only, because the Jewish National Home is there,' Churchill answered, 'Because England entered into obligations.' Coupland pressed his point. 'It would be a great relief I should have thought to the average Englishman,' he told Churchill, 'to find he had not got to go on denying self-government to these Arabs, had not got to go on shooting the Arabs down because of keeping his promise to the Jews. It is a most disagreeable position to be in.'

Churchill did not see this as an obstacle. He told the commissioners: 'My view is that you should go on and persevere with the task, holding the balance in accordance with the declaration, allowing the influx of new immigrants to take place as fast as can be, but having the right to slow it down when you like and having power and force of the right kind to support you, but if you cannot do that, give it up and let Mussolini take it on, which he would be very anxious to do. Someone else might come in. You would have to face that. A power like Italy would have no trouble. There are powers in the world which are the rising powers which are unmoral powers; they admit no morals at all.'

Rumbold then asked Churchill how, in the existing circumstances, he could apply the article of the Mandate, which said that 'Jewish immigration shall be facilitated under suitable conditions.' What did 'suitable conditions' mean? Rumbold asked. 'At present the atmosphere is one of unconcealed hostility. That is not a proper atmosphere for doing anything in. If you take a plant or any organism it will not flourish in certain conditions.'

Churchill's answer touched on the pace of immigration, but did not suggest that it should be seriously curtailed. 'That means you must not push too hard,' he said. Perhaps the Jews had, with the Germans treating them so badly, 'pushed in too many. There has been an extra drive and that drive started up the Arabs. I should have thought the Jews would have been clever enough to have conciliated the Arabs. Money helps things. When land is bought, perhaps the Arab might be given land more suitable to him. That is how they should go on.'

Churchill did have a criticism of the Zionists in the earlier years of the Mandate. 'They made a mistake,' he told the commissioners, 'in saying they would only employ their own people on their own work. It was never intended that that should happen. It was intended that the two races should intermingle.'

Coupland then complained that the Jewish Agency – set up in 1930 as liaison between the Jews of Palestine and the British Mandate, and headed by David Ben-Gurion – had its representatives in London 'and they can speak to the Colonial Office and the Arabs feel on their side they are rather left in the cold. They have not the great engine the Jews have.' Churchill replied brusquely, not hiding his preference: 'It is a question of which civilisation you prefer.'

Sir Horace Rumbold then asked Churchill, 'When do you consider the Jewish Home to be established? You have no ideas of numbers? When would you say we have implemented our undertaking and the Jewish National Home is established? At what point?' Churchill's answer was unequivocal. Britain's undertaking would be implemented 'when it was quite clear the Jewish preponderance in Palestine was very marked, decisive, and when we were satisfied that we had no further duties to discharge to the Arab population, the Arab minority.'

When Sir Laurie Hammond asked Churchill if, until there was a Jewish majority, 'we have to go on as the Mandatory Power, governing the country against the wishes of the majority of the people in the country?' Churchill replied: 'Certainly, against the wishes of both of them, because the Jews will not be satisfied with your soft-pedalling of immigration,' and the Arabs will hate the fact that Britain was saying, 'We are going to work up to this goal,' the goal of a Jewish majority. If the Peel Commission felt that Britain had to give up the Mandate, Churchill told the commissioners, a great many people would say, 'All right, give it up.' But not a single person would say, 'Hold the Mandate and abandon the pledge to the Jews.'

Peel broke in at this point to say that Britain 'might have some compunction if she felt she was downing the Arabs year after year when they wanted to remain in their own country.' Churchill rejected this line of reasoning, and allowed himself to be drawn into a more contentious discussion. 'I do not admit that the dog in the manger has the final right to the manger,' he told the commissioners, 'even though he may have lain there for a very long time. I do not admit that right. I do not admit, for instance, that a great wrong has been done to the Red Indians of America, or the black people of Australia. I do not admit that a wrong has been done to those people by the fact that a stronger race, a higher grade race, or, at any rate, a more worldly-wise race, to put it that way, has come in and taken their place.'[4]

When the Peel Commission report was published in April 1937 it did not quote from Churchill's evidence or make it public. It did however cite his 1922 White Paper declaration that the development of the Jewish National Home 'is not the imposition of a Jewish nationality upon the inhabitants of Palestine as a whole, but the further development of the existing Jewish community . . . in order that it may become a centre in which the Jewish people as a whole may take, on grounds of religion and race, an interest and a pride.'[5]

'This definition of the National Home,' the commissioners wrote, 'has sometimes been taken to preclude the establishment of a Jewish State. But, though the phraseology was clearly intended to conciliate, as far as might be, Arab antagonism to the National Home, there is nothing in it to prohibit the ultimate establishment of a Jewish State, and Mr Churchill himself has told us in evidence that no such prohibition was intended.'[6]

---

4 Peel Commission Report, proof copy of Churchill's evidence: Churchill papers, 2/317.

5 *Statement of British Policy in Palestine* (the Churchill White Paper): Command Paper 1700 of 1922.

6 *Palestine Royal Commission Report*: Command Paper 5479 of 1937.

CHAPTER ELEVEN

THE PARTITION DEBATE: 'A COUNSEL OF DESPAIR'

It was widely assumed that the Peel Commission would recommend the partition of Palestine into two separate sovereign States, one Jewish and one Arab. Partition was favoured by Dr Weizmann, who preferred a small State at once rather than the prospect – always open to potential setback – of a larger State in the relatively distant future. On 8 June 1937, Weizmann presented his reasoning at a private dinner given by Sir Archibald Sinclair at which Churchill was present, as well as James de Rothschild and several parliamentary supporters of Zionism: Leo Amery, Clement Attlee, Colonel Josiah Wedgwood and Captain Victor Cazalet. 'You know, you are our masters,' Churchill told Weizmann, and he added, pointing to those present, 'If you ask us to fight, we shall fight like tigers.'

Weizmann, in pressing for Partition as the best he felt the Jews could hope for – 'frontiers so drawn as to be adequate as well as defensible' – also asked for an annual Jewish immigration of between 50,000 and 60,000, slightly lower than the highest rate – 66,472 in 1935 – since the start of the Mandate.

At the dinner, Churchill spoke emphatically against Partition. The British Government were 'untrustworthy; they would chip off a piece here, and chip off a piece there; and Dr Weizmann's dream of an annual immigration of 60,000 or so would be smashed from the outset.' The 'only thing' that the Jews could do was 'persevere, persevere, persevere!' Partition would be appeasement to Arab pressure, he warned. But even with Partition a Jewish State would not come into being, as the Arabs would immediately start trouble and the British Government would back down.

Churchill told Weizmann that he 'quite realised' that the British Government 'had let the Jews down in the past, and felt it was shameful that they should wake up only now, when the Jews came to them in dire distress. The Jews should wait until the whole of Western Palestine was theirs, as envisaged by the 1922 White Paper. 'The time would come' when Britain was strong again, 'and the Jews must hang on.' Meanwhile, the government should be warned 'that there would be no walk-over for their proposals' of Partition.[1]

On the following morning, 9 June, Weizmann gave an account of this meeting to a number of leading Zionists then in London, including Ben-Gurion, who sent an account of it to the Jewish Agency in Jerusalem. While not contradicting Weizmann's first version, it added some light and colour – and apparently also some Churchillian profanities against the British Government leaders, made, Weizmann reported, under the influence of drink. While the meal was in progress Churchill had exclaimed 'Let's eat less, I want to hear what Chaim has to say.' When Weizmann said that he would accept Partition if the British Government would agree to allowing 50,000 to 60,000 immigrants a year Churchill had 'jumped up and interrupted him' with the words: 'You're wrong, Weizmann. Your State is a mirage' – the partitioned state, that is. 'They won't let you bring in 60,000. The Arabs will toss bombs, they'll receive help from Iraq, and the Government will back out.'

Churchill added that in 1922 Rutenberg had told him about the geographic needs of the Jewish National Home. 'Rutenberg spoke to me about all this, demanded that I promise this mountain and that mountain – I have no idea where these mountains are located. I haven't seen the map, and I won't. But all these the Mandate will fulfil.' After Sinclair and Wedgwood had opposed Partition, and Cazalet and James de Rothschild supported it, and thus supported Weizmann, Churchill again 'jumped up' and denounced Partition

1 Notes of a conversation, 8 June 1937: Central Zionist Archives.

as 'a fraud'. The members of the Baldwin government were 'idiots, talentless . . . If England depends on them it will be destroyed . . . However, this situation will not continue much longer – England will wake up and defeat Mussolini and Hitler, and then your time will come too.'[2]

On 14 June Weizmann wrote to Churchill that he had spoken to the Colonial Secretary, William Ormsby-Gore, and 'gathered that you have pressed very strongly the idea that the Southern part of Palestine should not be incorporated into the Arab State – if and when such a State comes to be set up. This is a point which worries us a great deal, for obvious reasons, and I would like to express to you my heartiest thanks, both for the advice you gave me last Tuesday, and for all you have done with Mr Ormsby-Gore to endeavour to make that project (if such a project comes off) as acceptable as possible in the circumstances.'[3]

The Peel Commission published its report on 7 July 1937. As anticipated, it proposed the division of Palestine into a Jewish State and an Arab State in separate geographic areas within Western Palestine. Jerusalem and Bethlehem – including the Holy Places – were to be a separate entity governed by Britain, together with a British-controlled corridor from Jerusalem to the sea, through Ramleh and Jaffa, both of which towns would also be retained by Britain. The corridor would give Britain access to the sea.[4]

Partition was to be debated in the House of Commons on 21 July 1937. For several weeks beforehand, debate raged among the Zionists as to whether or not to accept a truncated, incomplete Palestine, without even the substantial Jewish areas of Jerusalem. Ten days before the debate, Weizmann, who continued to favour Partition, again saw Churchill in London. Churchill reiterated that he did not favour Partition: that the Mandate intended that the

2 Report of 9 June 1937: Ben-Gurion Archive.

3 Letter of 14 June 1937: Weizmann Archive. The 'Southern part of Palestine' in Weizmann's letter was the Negev Desert from Beersheba southwards.

4 See map on page 321.

Jewish State, when eventually it came into being, should constitute the whole of Palestine from the Mediterranean to the River Jordan.[5]

Recognising that Partition might nevertheless be the actual outcome, Churchill saw William Ormsby-Gore, the Secretary of State for the Colonies, who in 1918 had been an Assistant Political Officer in Palestine. Churchill asked him to include in the proposed Jewish State the northern Negev desert, which the Peel Commission had allocated in its entirety to the Arab State, but which Weizmann and the Zionists were keen to cultivate.[6]

Two weekends before the Partition debate, Churchill was a guest of James and Dorothy de Rothschild at Waddesdon Manor, where he was unexpectedly approached by the Zionist Revisionist leader, Vladimir Jabotinsky. It was Lady Violet Bonham Carter (the daughter of the former Prime Minister, H.H. Asquith) who had encouraged Jabotinsky to seek Churchill out – even if it meant gate-crashing a weekend house party. She also wrote to Churchill that in her view Partition 'should not be rushed through in a fortnight. People are so ignorant of the geographical proportions and strategic position of the tiny corner now allotted to the Jews.'[7] Lady Violet underlined the word 'tiny'.[8]

Jabotinsky and Churchill had not met before. Churchill was inevitably intrigued by his interlocutor, despite – or even because of – the unorthodox method of their meeting. While Weizmann was the long-established, diplomatic, determined leader of mainstream Zionism, Jabotinsky was the charismatic head of the impatient, visionary, militaristically inclined wing, the Revisionists, with its Betar youth wing.

In London at the outbreak of the First World War, Jabotinsky

5 Notes of a conversation, 11 July 1937: Weizmann Archive.
6 As reported by William Ormsby-Gore to Weizmann: Weizmann Archive.
7 Letter of 16 July 1937: Churchill papers, 2/316.
8 Lord Balfour was wont to describe Palestine as 'only the size of Wales.' The whole Mandate area from the Mediterranean to the River Jordan, and from the Upper Galilee to the Negev desert, would fit into Vermont – one of the smallest of the United States – or Canada's Vancouver Island, off the coast of British Columbia.

had urged the formation of a Jewish Legion to fight the Turks. While in Cairo, he had been instrumental in forming the Zion Mule Corps that fought at Gallipoli. In 1918, in battle against the Turks, he led a unit of Jewish soldiers across the River Jordan. In 1920, when Churchill was Secretary of State for War, he had been sentenced to fifteen years in prison by a British military court in Palestine for confronting an Arab mob in Jerusalem during the Passover riots that year. Amnestied within a few months, he formed a breakaway Zionist movement, the World Union of Zionist Revisionists. In 1930 the British banned Jabotinsky from Palestine. He went to Eastern Europe, electrifying the Jewish multitudes by his demand for the establishment of a Jewish State on both sides of the Jordan, and calling on them to emigrate en masse: he hoped for a million and a half immigrants.

Writing to Churchill on 16 July, Jabotinsky apologised for his 'informal approach, and for disturbing whatever there may be of repose in your week-end seclusion.' Lady Violet Bonham Carter had told him that Churchill was not sure whether he would speak in the Partition debate. Jabotinsky then explained: 'This letter is an attempt to urge you to intervene. To me as a Jew – and even opponents never deny that I do represent the feelings of the Jewish masses – you are one of the very limited inner circle of British statesmen responsible for the birth of the Jewish Commonwealth idea between 1917 and 1922; and we expect you to defend it now that it is so dangerously threatened, and would be grievously disappointed if your voice were not heard.'

What the Jews wanted, above all, Jabotinsky wrote, was 'room for colonisation.' As the Jews gradually realised that Partition 'kills all their hopes, their opposition crystallises.' The 'worst feature of the whole business,' Jabotinsky added, 'is that we shall have no time even to state our case. I hope it will be stated by friends, in the first place by you.' In his memorandum Jabotinsky stressed that a partitioned Palestine would create a Jewish State too small in area to be defendable from sustained Arab attack from outside it. The Partition scheme 'is to be rejected', he wrote, even if the area of the proposed

Jewish State could be increased, since even if it were to include the northern Negev it offered 'no room for any considerable Jewish immigration.'

Once 'prematurely formed', Jabotinsky believed, the Jewish State 'could never expand either by peaceful penetration or by conquest. On the contrary, such a Jewish State would be destined to be eventually captured by the neighbouring Arab States, the conquest being probably accompanied by destruction and massacre.' So tightly hemmed in was the area designated for the Jewish State that the density of its population was already equal to that of Germany and almost double that of France. In addition, more than half of the 645,000 inhabitants occupying the area allocated to the Jewish State were not Jews but Arabs. The hope expressed in the Peel Report that the Arabs could be induced to 'trek' away eastward was 'a fallacy'. The Jewish State 'would be a rich and busy place, and people do not, as a rule, voluntarily emigrate from rich into poor districts. Nor would there be any room for them to go to in the Arab State deprived of Jewish energy and capital.' The addition of Jerusalem to the Jewish State – 'whether the modern city only or the whole of it' – would be of no account as a significant geographic area. As to the northern Negev, this was 'an area where no water has so far been found, an area destined at best for dry or semi-dry farming,' able to sustain no more than 125,000 Jewish settlers.

Jabotinsky then wrote about the Jewish populations of Poland, Lithuania, Latvia, Romania and Czechoslovakia. 'The homeless Jewish masses in Eastern and Central Europe,' he told Churchill, 'constitute a reservoir of distress numbering eight to nine millions.' In some of these Eastern countries, 'the only argument against anti-Semitism is the hope that Palestine will some day be able to absorb large masses of Jewish emigrants. The moment this prospect becomes obviously impossible, an unprecedented outburst of anti-Jewish feeling is to be expected, and governments will be powerfully urged to follow the Nazi example in placing anti-Semitism on the Statute book.'

Jabotinsky then made a plea for the wider Revisionist aim of a Jewish State on both sides of the Jordan: 'It would mean a refuge for several million Jews, without any need to displace the million Arabs who live there now, or their progeny.' But the moment the Balfour Declaration was abolished outside the narrow limits of the proposed Jewish State, 'immigration of Jews into the Arab State will only be possible within limits which the Arab government will tolerate. Even if such immigration will be allowed at all (it may even be encouraged, in small numbers bringing in big capital), it will never be suffered to reach such a size as to change the predominantly Arab character of any district. The Jews may be allowed to form new ghettos in Arab territory, but not to form new Jewish majorities with the consent of an Arab government.'

Any hope of using the area proposed for the Jewish State for organising a Jewish army that would eventually conquer the rest of Palestine by force was 'utterly absurd,' Jabotinsky wrote. 'The Jewish army will be unable even to defend the "Jewish State" if, or rather when, it will be attacked by the Arab countries: the "Jewish State" consists essentially of plains dominated by hills which will belong to the Arabs, Tel Aviv being within fifteen miles from the nearest Arab mountain gun and Haifa within eighteen miles.'

This being so, the capture of the small Jewish State by its Arab neighbours, Jabotinsky warned, would be inevitable. 'A dwarfish area, whose defenders can never grow to more than a handful, but full of riches and culture, will be surrounded not by the Arab Palestine only, but by an Arab Federation from Aleppo to Basra and Sanaa (for the Report openly invites the proposed "Arab State" to join such a Federation). It will inevitably be coveted, and inevitably attacked at the first opportunity; and the meaning of "opportunity" is – any moment when the British Empire will be in trouble elsewhere.'[9]

Churchill was impressed by these arguments, and saw Jabotinsky again a few days later, for an hour in the House of Commons.[10]

---

9 Vladimir Jabotinsky, 'Note on the Palestine Partition Scheme', 16 July 1937: Churchill papers, 2/316.

10 Joseph B. Schechtman, *The Jabotinsky Story: Fighter and Prophet, The Last Years, 1923–1940*, page 323.

Jabotinsky's points made their mark. When the Commons debated the Peel Report on 21 July, Churchill opposed any final commitment to partition. He first spoke about the Balfour Declaration, insisting, as he had done on so many occasions in the past sixteen years, that it was 'a delusion to suppose that this was a mere act of crusading enthusiasm or quixotic philanthropy.' On the contrary, he stressed, it was a measure taken 'in the dire need of the War with the object of promoting the general victory of the Allies, for which we expected and received valuable and important assistance. We cannot brush that aside and start afresh as though it had never been given, and deal with this matter as if we had no obligations or responsibility.'

Churchill explained that he could not vote for the government motion to approve the principle of Partition. 'Take the military aspect alone,' he said. 'The gravest anxieties arise about that. There are two sovereign States, one a rich and small State more crowded than Germany, with double the population to the kilometre of France, and then in the mountains in the surrounding regions, stretching up to Baghdad with the Assyrians and the desert tribes to the south, the whole of this great Arab area confronting this new Jewish State, and in between the two the British holding a number of extremely important positions with responsibilities at present altogether undefined.'

How could the House of Commons decide at that moment, Churchill asked, 'that we will stand between these two sovereign States and keep the peace between them without knowing at all to what we are committing ourselves?' It was a problem 'where all the world is looking to see whether Great Britain behaves in an honourable manner, in a courageous manner and in a sagacious manner.'[11]

When the debate ended, as a result of Liberal and Labour Party opposition the government agreed not to proceed with Partition, but to keep it as a possibility for the future. Churchill was quick to ensure that his point of view remained vocal and visible. Writing in the *Evening Standard* two days after the debate, he described the

11 Parliamentary Debates, *Hansard*, 21 July 1937.

'plan of cutting Palestine into three parts' as 'a counsel of despair' and he went on to ask: 'One wonders whether, in reality, the difficulties of carrying out the Zionist scheme are so great as they are portrayed, and whether in fact there has not been a very considerable measure of success.' In the sixteen years that had passed since the Mandate, many troubles had been overcome, and 'great developments' had taken place in Palestine. When he made his previous visit three years earlier, he was 'delighted at the aspect of the countryside. The fine roads, the new buildings and plantations, the evidences of prosperity, both among Jews and Arabs, presented on every side, all gave a sense of real encouragement.'

The change that had taken place since his visit in 1934 was due, Churchill explained, 'to outside events' that were not Britain's fault: 'The persecutions of the Jews in Germany, the exploitation of anti-Semitism as a means by which violent and reactionary forces seize, or attempt to seize, despotic power, afflicted the civilised world with a refugee problem similar to that of the Huguenots in the seventeenth century. The brunt of this has fallen upon this very small country and administration of Palestine. Jewish immigration, suddenly raised to 30,000 or 40,000 a year, may not have exceeded the "economic absorptive capacity" of the settled districts, but it naturally confronted the Arabs with the prospect, not of an evolutionary growth of the Jewish population, but of actual flooding and swamping which seemed to bring near to them the prospect of domination.'

Churchill then expressed the immigration conflict in vivid terms. 'Too much current was put on the cables,' he said. 'And the cables have fused. That may be a reason for mending the cables and reducing the current. It is surely no reason for declaring that electricity is a fluid too dangerous for civilisation to handle.' He had the 'strong impression', Churchill concluded, 'that the case for perseverance holds the field.'[12]

---

12 Winston S. Churchill, 'Partition Perils in Palestine', *Evening Standard*, 23 July 1937. This article was later published in book form in Winston S. Churchill, *Step By Step*, with the title 'Partition in Palestine'.

On 28 July, at Chartwell, Churchill had a two-hour talk after dinner with Henry Mond, the second Baron Melchett. A former Member of Parliament, and a director of Imperial Chemical Industries, Melchett was a close friend of Weizmann, and of Churchill. Randolph Churchill was the only other person present. In reporting on the conversation to Weizmann, Melchett expressed his concern at Churchill's insistence that the Mufti of Jerusalem, Haj Amin el-Husseini, the principal fomentor of the Arab revolt, should be arrested, using if necessary 'violent methods'. The main talk was about Partition, which, Churchill insisted, would mean war, as 'long before the Jewish State is able to organise itself, and either get in the necessary men to defend the position, or the necessary arms, they will be attacked by the Arabs and wiped out.' This was Jabotinsky's view.

Churchill warned Melchett that the British officials in Palestine and in the Colonial Office 'are against you, and they will see to it that you do not, in effect, get a sovereign State.' Churchill's suggestion was that the Jews 'insist upon the execution of the Mandate,' even if it meant accepting a reduction in immigration and probable restriction on the sale of land. That situation might last for five, ten or even twenty years. 'But never mind, the principle remained unchanged. Your claim, which is based on moral not physical grounds remains unaltered. The world is going to go through stormy and perilous times. There will probably be wars; no one knows what the outcome of these will be. Through all this period causes will survive: little territories will not. The great cause of Zionism is capable of surviving two or three wars.'

Churchill spoke optimistically of the Zionist future. For as long as Britain was the mandatory power it would preserve Palestine intact and 'to a greater or lesser degree' protect the Zionists' interests. After the period when immigration was restricted and land purchase curtailed, 'things will then get better again: more immigration will be allowed and more land sales will be allowed. The thing will swing backwards and forwards in accordance with the circumstances and the amount of pressure which Zionists are able to bring to bear on British public opinion.' Churchill added: 'Zionism is a great cause and has survived many centuries and will continue to do so. Temporary restrictions of any sort are not incompatible with the great Zionist principles.'

Churchill was emphatic that Partition would be a mistake. The small Jewish State envisaged in the Partition plan, he argued, 'can be ravished by its enemies, defeated in war, annexed to other powers or suffer any of the other incidents that are common to small States in the fortunes and chances of war. Once you have accepted your State, and it has gone, or been destroyed, your great moral claims will have disappeared too.' Churchill then used an expression he had not used before, which struck Melchett forcibly: 'The only reason why the cable has broken down is because you put too much current on it and it has fused. It should be repaired, and is still a good cable. The reason you put too much current on it was due to persecution in Germany, by no means your fault. You are in no way to blame. But the facts must be realised and a more moderate tempo must be used in the future.'

Churchill knew that his advice would be deeply disappointing to the Zionists, whose persistent hope was for a more rapid pace of immigration. But with Arab hostility so intense that Britain was having to send an increasing number of troops to Palestine, Churchill wanted to see that pace reduced. Even so, he did not believe that it would affect the ultimate goal of Zionism: statehood. If the Mandate was 'worked a bit slower, on the lines that had been intended,' he said, eventually he 'considered it to be inevitable that we should have sovereignty over the whole of Palestine, although that might take a century or two centuries.' Jewish civilisation, Churchill told Melchett, was 'the stronger and would ultimately dominate,' but the Jews 'must go slowly and not try to hurry on this thing yet.' He was a friend to Zionism and 'would do everything to help; but he was 'not going to be more Zionist than the Zionists.' Churchill added, in Melchett's words to Weizmann, that: 'Of course, if we are going to arrive at an arrangement satisfactory to ourselves he would be the last person in the world to oppose it.'

As to how the Zionists should conduct themselves during the Partition discussions, Churchill told Melchett that he was 'all for hard bargaining and for taking a great stand on the Balfour Declaration,' telling Melchett that the Zionists must take up 'a fighting position.'[13]

On 3 September 1937, as the Jewish leaders debated for and against Partition, Churchill wrote an article in the *Jewish Chronicle* that came down firmly against. He began, however, with a sympathetic account of Weizmann's desire to accept, reluctantly, the truncated Jewish State. He could 'readily understand', he wrote, Dr Weizmann, and others with him who have borne the burden and heat of the day, and without whose personal effort Zionism would perhaps no longer be a reality, being attracted by the idea of a sovereign Jewish State in Palestine, however small, which would set up for the first time, after ages of dispersion and oppression, a coherent Jewish community and rallying point for Jews in every part of the world.' Instead of constant bickering with British Mandate officials, and annual disputes about the quota of immigrants, there would be 'a responsible Government and independent autonomous State, a member of the League of Nations, to play its part not only in the Holy Land but in world affairs.'

Opposition to Partition came, Churchill noted, from Jews who 'complain that the small part, already thickly populated, to be confided to them is wholly inadequate, and offers no real scope for future immigration and expansion.' But the Arabs, 'who might perhaps be induced to acquiesce in the present proposals, will certainly resist strenuously any modification of them in favour of the Jews.' Under Partition, conflict would be inevitable. He doubted that the Jews would 'rest content with the area assigned to them. Certainly the Arabs will, from the outset, be on the alert against the slightest encroachment.'

The Arabs, 'children of the desert' as Churchill described them, were 'always armed and rapidly improvise a fighting power. The Jews,

13 Letter of 29 July 1937: Central Zionist Archives.

on the other hand, living in settled districts, will require a regularly trained defence drilling on barrack squares. Naturally, they will arm their soldiers with the best weapons they can buy, and very terrible weapons can now be bought.' It was almost certain 'that an electric atmosphere will prevail on both sides.' Every measure the Jewish State took for its defence would look like 'a design for aggression.' A strong Jewish Army, once developed, 'could always be used to extend the Jewish frontiers if opinion changed – as change it might.' The trend of events 'would bc sct towards an armed collision.'

Churchill saw no solution in the much-discussed proposal that Britain should be the policeman of a partitioned Palestine. If the British forces were to stand 'between the rival races and interpose a cordon,' he wrote, they would have to be greatly strengthened, but there were 'already great demands upon our very small army.' It might not be easy to provide the necessary garrisons. Fighting would be inevitable. Partition would 'certainly be attended with friction, and possibly with reprisals by the Arabs upon Jews who wish to dwell in the Arab zonc.'

This was a bleak picture. The hopeful assumption which underlay the Peel Report, Churchill pointed out, that once sovereign States, 'however small and primitive, have become members of the League of Nations, their troubles are ended, they never do any wrong themselves, and will never be molested, is, to say the least of it, premature.' The British Government had hitherto found it difficult to keep order between Jews and Arabs even when only sporadic local riotings and murders occurred. 'Why should it be thought more capable of restraining the organised armies which will certainly be brought into being by both these independent Sovereign States?'

The policy of Partition, Churchill warned, 'will not lead away from violence, but into its very heart; will not end in peace, but in war.' It would be far better to persevere along the old lines. The Jews were steadily being settled in the land of their fathers. The Arabs might well be conciliated from day to day and month to month by the sense of increased well-being in which both races shared. The best course would be if Jews and Arabs would themselves agree 'for a term of years the mode of living and the settlement which, without perhaps solving the problems of the future, would afford to the present generation a measure of peace, prosperity, and happiness.' It is in that direction 'that wise men should look and bold men march.'[14]

It was the Jews and Arabs who were about to be called upon to agree upon a settlement. On 23 December the British Government established a new commission of enquiry, headed by Sir John Woodhead, former Finance Member of the Government of Bengal, who was instructed to assemble the materials on which, when the 'best possible' scheme of Partition had been formulated, they could then 'judge its equity and practicability.'[15]

---

14 Winston S. Churchill, 'Why I Am Against Partition', *Jewish Chronicle*, 3 September 1937.

15 Letter of 23 December 1937 from the Colonial Secretary to the High Commissioner for Palestine: Command Paper 5634 of 1937.

CHAPTER TWELVE

NAZISM RAMPANT: 'ABOMINABLE PERSECUTION'

In 1936, at the height of the Partition debate, Churchill met Eugen Spier, a German-Jewish refugee from Nazism who was living in Britain. Churchill was looking for some means to make the Nazi danger more widely known to the public, with the help of leaders in all walks of public life. Spier later recalled how 19 May 1936 'saw the first luncheon of a new group, later called the Focus, aimed at bringing together representatives of all Parties and groups opposed to Nazism.' Between May 1936 and the summer of 1939, Spier contributed £9,600 towards the organisation of the Focus.[1] Its members gave Churchill an important phalanx of support in his anti-Nazi stance.[2]

While on holiday in France in 1936, Churchill learned more about the Nazi persecution of the Jews. On 13 September 1936 he wrote to his wife from the South of France: 'I dined near Toulon with Frau Friedlander Fuld now Mrs Goldsmith Rothschild. She was pathetic about the treatment of the Jews in Germany. They have a terrible time. She is a remarkable woman.'[3]

Dominant in Churchill's political philosophy was the primacy of open debate, fair play and equal rights. Speaking in Paris on 24 September – the object of this French visit – he set out what he believed to be the basic evils of both the Nazi and Communist

---

1 £250,000 in today's money values.

2 Eugen Spier, *Focus: A Footnote to the History of the Thirties.*

3 Letter of 13 September 1936: Baroness Spencer-Churchill papers.

systems. For him persecution of opinion and of race had no justification. 'Between the doctrines of Herr Goebbels and Comrade Trotsky,' he declared, 'there ought to be room for you and me . . .'[4]

While in France, Churchill spent time with the Prime Minister, Leon Blum – who was soon to visit him at Chartwell – and with one of Blum's senior Cabinet colleagues, Georges Mandel, both Jewish politicians and strong opponents of the appeasement of Germany. In 1940, Mandel was one of the French Cabinet ministers who argued in favour of continuing the war in North Africa. For this patriotic stance, and because he was a Jew, Mandel was murdered by the Vichy French police. Churchill was deeply moved by his fate, and in 1946 sent his son Randolph to represent him at the anniversary ceremony at the site in the forest near Fontainebleau, where the murder had taken place.[5]

On 13 November 1936, Churchill wrote to his son Randolph to explain that the basis of the Anti-Nazi League, which he had recently helped to launch, 'is of course Jewish resentment at their abominable persecution. But we are now taking broader ground rather on the lines of my Paris speech.' A Peace with Freedom committee had been formed. It aimed 'at focusing and concentrating the efforts of all the Peace societies like the New Commonwealth and the League of Nations Union in so far as they are prepared to support genuine military action to resist tyranny or aggression.'[6]

In his letter to Randolph, Churchill referred to the New York lawyer, Louis Levy, who had helped Churchill on a personal matter. This concerned Victor Oliver von Samek, a thirty-eight-year-old, twice divorced, Austrian-born Jewish actor, radio comedian and pianist known by his stage name as Vic Oliver, who had eloped earlier that year with Churchill's twenty-two-year-old daughter Sarah. Churchill had asked Levy to find out the details of Oliver's second marriage,

4 Speech of 24 September 1936: Churchill papers, 9/121.
5 Letter of 7 July 1946: Squerryes Lodge Archive.
6 Letter of 13 November 1936: Churchill papers, 2/283.

to make sure that the divorce had been finalised – Churchill had already obtained details of the first marriage and divorce in Austria – and also to find out if there were 'any more of these marriages besides these two.' Levy was able to put Churchill's mind at ease. Oliver was free to marry Sarah, and Churchill acquired a Jewish son-in-law.

Churchill was supportive of Sarah and her choice. When the couple travelled to the United States on a German liner, he made sure, through his contacts at the Home Office, that no harm would come to an Austrian-born Jew on board a German ship. Two years later, Churchill wrote to Sir Alexander Maxwell, the Permanent Under-Secretary of State at the Home Office, who had served under him twenty-eight years earlier, of Vic Oliver's wish to become a naturalised British subject. 'Although,' he wrote, 'in the first instance, as you may have heard, I opposed his marriage with my daughter, I have come to like and esteem him greatly and I am sure that any assistance you can give to his wish will be well bestowed.'[7]

In the East End of London, Sir Oswald Mosley's fascists and a group of predominantly Communist Jews clashed in 1936 in what was known as the Battle of Cable Street. Churchill's concerns about Communism in Britain led him to write in the *Evening Standard*, three weeks after his Paris speech: 'It is especially important that British Jewry should keep itself absolutely clear from this brawling. In Great Britain the law-abiding Jew need not look to the Communist for protection. He will get that as his right from the Constable.'[8]

Reading these sentences, Churchill's friend Desmond Morton, a devout Roman Catholic, wrote to him: 'I am no anti-Semitist, no more are you. It is a matter I do not remember your having touched upon in public before. The paragraph seemed to me to hint at more than it expressed.'[9] What it did express was Churchill's

7 Letter of 18 June 1938: Churchill papers, 1/326.
8 Winston S. Churchill, 'War Is Not Imminent', *Evening Standard*, 15 October 1936.
9 Letter of 16 October 1936: Churchill papers, 2/259.

fear of any Communist affiliation and activity, whether by Jews or non-Jews.

Churchill continued to issue his warnings about Nazi tyranny. On 5 February 1937, in the *Evening Standard*, he wrote of how the Nazi regime in Germany was imposing its power and ideology. 'The hate-culture continues,' he pointed out, 'fostered by printing press and broadcast – the very instruments, in fact, which philosophers might have hoped would liberate mankind from such perils.'[10]

That spring, Churchill was asked to write an article about an issue then much debated: should the Jews, wherever they lived, find ways to challenge the persecution of German Jewry, or should they leave that task to the governments among whom they lived. In a note that he dictated to his secretary on 26 April, Churchill set out for his literary assistant Adam Marshall Diston, the topics he wanted the article to cover. 'Obviously there are four things,' Churchill wrote. 'The first is to be a good citizen of the country to which he belongs. The second is to avoid too exclusive an association in ordinary matters of business and daily life, and to mingle as much as possible with non-Jews everywhere, apart from race and religion. The third is to keep the Jewish movement free from Communism. The fourth is a perfectly legitimate use of their influence throughout the world to bring pressure, economic and financial, to bear upon the Governments which persecute them.'[11]

Churchill was about to gain a far wider readership for his articles than he could have imagined possible. The cause of this change was a Hungarian Jew, Imre Revesz – later known as Emery Reves. Setting up his literary agency in Berlin in the early 1930s, and syndicating articles by leading European democratic politicians, Reves was forced by the rise of Hitler to move his organisation to Paris. There

---

10 Winston S. Churchill, 'Europe's Peace', *Evening Standard*, 5 February 1937.

11 Churchill papers, 8/546. This article written in its entirety by Marshall Diston, and with some anti-Semitic overtones, was never published. In enclosing his 3,000-word draft, Diston, somewhat crudely, wrote to Churchill that there were 'quite a number of Jews who might, with advantage, reflect on the epigram: "How odd/Of God/To choose/The Jews."'

he began again, extending the number of anti-Nazi writers whose worked he syndicated. On 25 February 1937, in London, Churchill and Reves met for the first time. They met again four days later, when Churchill agreed to give Reves exclusive rights for the publication of all his articles 'of international interest', outside the British Empire and North America.

Reves would arrange for the translations and, where possible, for simultaneous publication in all European countries. Reves would pay Churchill sixty per cent of the proceeds, with a guaranteed minimum of £25 for each article sold: more than £500 in today's values. By the end of the year he had placed Churchill's articles every two weeks in twenty-five different European cities, among them seventeen capitals: Paris, Copenhagen, Stockholm, Brussels, Luxembourg, Oslo, Helsinki, Riga, Tallin, Prague, Vienna, Warsaw, Kaunas, Athens, Belgrade, Bucharest and Budapest. Also among the regular publishers of Churchill's articles were the main Yiddish newspapers in Warsaw, Vilna and Kovno, enabling three large Jewish communities to follow Churchill's warnings. Reves also placed the articles in two Palestine newspapers read mostly by Jews, the Tel Aviv Hebrew-language *Ha'aretz* and the Jerusalem English-language *Palestine Post.*[12]

In an article in the *Evening Standard* on 17 September 1937, which Reves placed in newspapers throughout Europe, Churchill appealed to Hitler to become 'the Hitler of peace.' It was, he felt, the last chance for Hitler to halt the massive rearmament that could only mean war. 'We cannot say that we admire your treatment of the Jews or of the Protestants and Catholics of Germany,' Churchill wrote, 'but these matters, so long as they are confined inside Germany, are not our business.' What mattered was for Germany to give up its desire for conquest.[13]

---

12 Martin Gilbert (editor), *Winston Churchill and Emery Reves, Correspondence, 1937–1964*. For all the European cities in which Reves placed Churchill's articles, see map on page 312.

13 Winston S. Churchill, 'Friendship With Germany', *Evening Standard*, 17 September 1937. This article was later published in book form in Winston S. Churchill, *Step By Step*.

In an attempt to seek constructive agreement with Germany, the new British Prime Minister, Neville Chamberlain, sent a senior Conservative, Lord Halifax, to visit Hitler. The visit was discussed – and by some denounced – in the House of Commons on 21 December. Chamberlain expressed his regret that the debate was taking place at all. During the debate, Churchill, turning his back on his placatory appeal to Hitler of three months earlier, spoke critically of the persecution of the Jews in Germany. 'It is a horrible thing,' he said, 'that a race of people should be attempted to be blotted out of the society in which they have been born.'

Churchill went on to express his unease about Lord Halifax's visit to Berlin at a time when Germany was beginning to demand the transfer of the industrially rich German-speaking region of Sudetenland from Czechoslovakia. 'We must remember,' he said, 'how very sharp the European situation is at the present time. If it were thought that we were making terms for ourselves at the expense either of small nations or of large conceptions which are dear, not only to many nations, but to millions of people in every nation, a knell of despair would resound through many parts of Europe.'[14]

The mounting tension in Europe in 1938 and the situation in Palestine were inextricably linked. The continuing flight of Jewish refugees from Germany to Palestine was provoking renewed Arab violence, much of it Arab attacks and ambushes against the British, who built a series of Beau Geste forts throughout the country, with machine gun pillboxes at every entrance to Jerusalem. The Jews were also divided, with a small but active minority – fiercely denounced by Weizmann and Ben-Gurion – turning to acts of terror against both the Arabs and the British. A grim cycle of violence had emerged: Arab acts of terror against Jews, Jewish reprisals against Arabs, British military force against both sets of insurgents, Arab extremists murdering several hundred Arab moderates, and German

14 Parliamentary Debates, *Hansard*, 21 December 1937.

and Italian radio propaganda inflaming Arab intransigence: all threatening the future sanity of a tormented Holy Land.

On 20 October Churchill published his thoughts in an article in the *Daily Telegraph* entitled 'Palestine at the Crossroads'. The article appeared three weeks after the Munich Agreement, of which Churchill was one of the leading opponents. At Munich, to Hitler's surprise, Britain and France had pressed the Czechoslovak government to let him annex its industrially rich Sudetenland region, which was also Czechoslovakia's natural and fortified line of defence. 'Amid world preoccupation,' Churchill wrote, 'the conditions in Palestine have passed into eclipse,' but 'the lull in Europe, while the victorious Nazis are gathering their spoil, forces us to turn our eyes to this distracted country, for which we are responsible.' It was a 'shocking scene' that met the view. 'The whole of this small province is sinking into anarchy. Jews and Arabs carry on hideous vendettas of murder and reprisal. Bombs are thrown among harmless villagers on market days. Women and children are massacred by Arab raiders in the night. The roads are being broken up. The railways have largely ceased to work.'

British control was proving hard to maintain. 'A considerable portion of the British regular army, together with large bodies of armed police, hold the main centres of Government, and sally forth upon foray and patrol.' A 'rival administration' had been set up by the Arab 'rebels' and ruled over considerable areas. In addition, 'the rebels are powerfully aided by arms, explosives, money and propaganda from German and Italian sources.'

Every few days the newspapers reported Arab deaths in action against the British. 'The spectacle is vexatious and discreditable,' Churchill wrote. 'Great Britain is called upon at immense expense and trouble, and some loss of life, to carry on a policy of severe repression, with all its painful features, not for her own sake, but because of the bitter racial feud which has now developed between the Arab and Jew.' Hitler and Mussolini 'mock at the ill-success of our methods,' pointing the moral of British 'inefficiency'. It was a charge, Churchill noted, for which there was 'more than sufficient foundation.'

With the start of the Arab riots in 1936, Churchill pointed out, the British Government had found 'the line of least resistance' in sending out the Peel Commission. After further delays, 'during which the state of the country steadily deteriorated', a second Commission, headed by Sir John Woodhead, had been sent out 'to report upon the methods by which the report of the first Commission should be brought into operation. Meanwhile everything grew worse: murders began and reprisals were taken, reinforcements were brought in driblets, strong measures were taken by halves, and so by an unbroken process of vacillation and weakness the country has degenerated into its present horrible plight; and a blood feud has grown between the Arab and Jew, of which the end cannot be foreseen.'

One solution that had been proposed was 'to throw up our task as insoluble' and return the Mandate to the League of Nations. Britain would have to admit 'that we had tried our best, and that we had found ourselves incapable of discharging our duty.' No doubt Germany and Italy 'would eagerly come forward' to offer to take over the Mandate, 'if only for the strategic advantages which Palestine would offer to them.' But if the Mandate were not to be given up, what, Churchill asked, remained? His answer was clear: 'There remains only the policy of fidelity and perseverance. We must unflinchingly restore order, and suppress the campaign of murder and counter-murder between the two races. We must give protection to the large Jewish community already established in the country; but we should also give to the Arabs a solemn assurance embodied if possible in an agreement to which Arab and Jew should be invited to subscribe, that the annual quota of Jewish immigration should not exceed a certain figure for a period of at least ten years.'

Churchill recognised that proposing any form of restriction on Jewish immigration for the coming ten years would, as he wrote in his article, 'arouse a furious outcry, and involve us in a long and thankless task, but should it seem the only way, we must face it with steadfastness and conviction if we are still to preserve our good name.'[15]

---

15 Winston S. Churchill, 'Palestine at the Crossroads', *Daily Telegraph*, 20 October 1938.

That outcry was not long in coming. On the day after Churchill's article, Lionel Bakstansky, General Secretary of the Zionist Federation of Great Britain, wrote to Sir Archibald Sinclair, Churchill's friend and a friend of the Zionists, that Churchill's statement 'that the large Jewish immigration of 1933/5 was a cause of the upheaval,' overlooked the fact 'that immigration coincided with a period of the greatest prosperity which Palestine has enjoyed.' As for Churchill's suggestion of restricted Jewish immigration for a period of ten years, 'I need not tell you,' Bakstansky wrote, 'how surprising it is that such a suggestion should come from him, who was responsible for the introduction of the economic absorptive capacity principle in 1922, and how unfortunate it is that he should lend his weight and authority to such a proposal at this particular juncture in the history of the Jewish people, when between six and seven million Jews in Europe are for all practical purposes either homeless or devoid of permanent security.'

It was also 'unfortunate', Bakstansky wrote, that Churchill's article should have appeared 'at a moment when we have reason to believe that the British Government itself is contemplating its future policy in Palestine on the basis of a severely restricted Jewish immigration.' Hitherto the Zionists had noticed 'some reluctance' on the British Government's part to proceed with such a policy 'in the light of their knowledge of House of Commons opinion and their belief that such a policy would not command friendly support in Parliamentary circles.' Churchill's article, however, might 'change the whole situation and induce the Government to proceed with a distinctly restrictive policy. We feel that it is most urgent that it should be made known to the Government that Churchill's view is not supported by those who have played a leading part in the Palestine controversy in Parliament.'[16]

Neville Chamberlain and his colleagues were convinced that the Arabs were not to be alienated. They saw the issue in the perspective of Britain's dependence in the Mediterranean and Middle East on Arab and Muslim goodwill. In 1938 Britain was the largest single ruler of Muslims in the world, with twenty million Muslim subjects

16 Letter of 21 October 1938: Central Zionist Archives.

in British India alone. In addition to its own Muslim subjects, Britain was reliant upon two independent Muslim countries, Egypt and Iran: Egypt for the security of the Suez Canal and the imperial route to the East, and Iran for the security of the Anglo-Persian Oil Company's production, essential for Britain's oil-burning warships.

The Cabinet was convinced that a quiescent Arab and Muslim world was essential for Britain, and that if appeasement was required to secure that quiescence, the government's commitments to the Jews in Palestine were an obvious sacrifice. The fate of the Jews in Jerusalem or Tel Aviv had become vulnerable to pressure exerted in Delhi, Karachi, Cairo, Baghdad and Riyadh; pressure that was proving all-too effective.

The worsening situation in Germany had come to dominate Jewish concerns. One weekend in May, Churchill was at a country house in Dorset where the other guests included James de Rothschild and his wife Dorothy. A few days later, James de Rothschild, a member of the Other Club, the private dining club of which Churchill was a founder, wrote to him of how 'you spoke with such sympathy last week' about the Jewish situation in Germany. But Rothschild reminded Churchill that he had mentioned 'that the number of Jews in the various professions and occupations had been, in the days before Hitler, very high in comparison with the proportion which Jews bore to the total population.' This claim, Rothschild pointed out, had been 'fostered by Nazi propaganda, and has been widely accepted.'[17]

With his letter James de Rothschild enclosed an article that had appeared in the *Manchester Guardian* more than two and a half years earlier, on 3 January 1936, 'which disproves this by official German statistics.' The article noted that Nazi propaganda 'speaks of a Jewish monopoly and complains that non-Jewish Germans were unable to find a place in these professions' but that 'a glance at the official statistics proves the contrary.'

17 Letter of 27 May 1938: Churchill papers, 2/329. The country house was Cranborne, in Dorset, the home of Viscount Cranborne, then Parliamentary Under-Secretary of State for Foreign Affairs.

The 564,379 Jews of Germany at the most recent census – that of 1925 – made up 0.9 per cent of the total German population. The highest Jewish percentage before Hitler came to power had been among lawyers – both barristers and solicitors – where it amounted to 16.25 per cent of the German population. The percentage of Jewish doctors was 10.88. In German cultural life, 5.61 per cent of theatre producers were Jews, 5.05 per cent of editors and authors, 3 per cent of actors and dancers, 2.44 per cent of painters and sculptors, and 2.04 per cent of musicians and singers. Among university teachers the percentage was 2.64 per cent. The percentage of Jews among teachers in the elementary and secondary schools was 0.53 per cent. These percentages, commented the *Manchester Guardian*, were 'neither a stranglehold nor a monopoly.'[18]

In the light of these facts, Churchill never repeated his erroneous remarks. He followed closely the developments in Germany, which included increasingly rapid rearmament, and the onward thrust of anti-Jewish legislation and violence.

In March 1938 Germany annexed Austria. The swastika flag was raised over the Austrian parliament building and Hitler entered Vienna in triumph. The persecution of Jews began from the first days of the new regime. Writing in the *Daily Telegraph* on 6 July, Churchill drew attention to events in Austria since its annexation by Germany four months earlier. 'It is easy to ruin and persecute the Jews,' he wrote, 'to steal their property; to drive them out of every profession and employment; to fling a Rothschild into a prison or a sponging house; to compel Jewish ladies to scrub the pavements; and to maroon clusters of helpless refugees on islands in the Danube; and these sports continue to give satisfaction.' It was part of the policy of German Nazism, Churchill added, 'to treat with exemplary rigour all persons of German race who have not identified themselves with Nazi interests and ambitions.'[19]

---

18 *Manchester Guardian*, 3 January 1936.
19 Winston S. Churchill, 'Germany's Discipline for the Old Austria', *Daily Telegraph*, 6 July 1938.

Eight days after Churchill wrote this article, he and Professor Lindemann met Gauleiter Foerster, the leader of the Nazi Party in the Free City of Danzig, which had been separated from Germany under the Treaty of Versailles. Foerster had long demanded the city's re-unification with Germany. The first topic Churchill and Foerster discussed was the Jews of Danzig, numbering 4,000 in all. According to Churchill's memorandum of the conversation, which he sent to Lord Halifax: 'I remarked that I was glad they had not introduced the anti-Jewish laws' in Danzig. To which Foerster replied that the Jewish problem was not acute in Danzig, but that 'he was anxious to know whether this type of legislation in Germany would prevent an understanding with England. I replied that it was a hindrance and an irritation, but probably not a complete obstacle to a working agreement, though it might be to comprehension. He appeared to attach great importance to this point.'[20]

Between the end of 1938 and the outbreak of war a year later, all but 1,600 of Danzig's Jews had been allowed to emigrate. Many of the remainder left in early 1940, and were on board the doomed passenger liner *Patria*, with whose fate Churchill was to be directly concerned. Only six hundred remained in the city when the deportations began in 1942; almost none of them survived.

At Chartwell on 19 August, another of Churchill's German visitors was Major Ewald von Kleist, one of the German General Staff officers opposed to Hitler's expansionist plans, who told Churchill that if they could only receive 'a little encouragement they might refuse to march' against Czechoslovakia.[21] After Kleist's visit, Churchill appealed publicly for the German officer corps to overthrow Hitler. Responding to this in a speech at Weimar on 6 November, Hitler attacked Churchill by name. 'Mr Churchill has declared openly that in his opinion the present régime in Germany should be abolished in cooperation with internal German forces who would put themselves gratefully at his disposal for the purpose.

20 Foreign Office papers, 800/314.

21 Notes of a conversation, 19 August 1938: Foreign Office papers, 800/309.

If Mr Churchill had less to do with émigrés, that is to say, exiled foreign paid traitors, and more to do with Germans, then he would see the whole idiocy and stupidity of what he says. I can only assure this gentleman that there is in Germany no such power as could set itself against the present régime.'[22]

On 28 October the German Government had begun a mass expulsion of all 20,000 Polish Jews resident in Germany. The expulsions, which took place amid scenes of brutality and hardship, provoked Herschel Grynszpan, the seventeen-year-old son of one of the families expelled, to shoot and mortally wound a diplomat in the German Embassy in Paris. The shooting took place on 7 November. Two days later the German newspapers accused Churchill of being linked to the murder plot. The *Angriff* newspaper, the mouthpiece of the Minister of Propaganda, Dr Goebbels, headlined the murder: 'The work of the instigator-international: A straight line from Churchill to Grynszpan.'

The *Angriff* article went on to state: 'While in London the Churchill clique, unmasked by the Führer, was busy with sanctimonious deception, in Paris the murder weapon spat in the hands of a Jewish lout and destroyed the last measurable remnants of credibility in the assertion that agitation for war and murder against the Third Reich has never been carried on or contemplated.'[23]

Despite Hitler's allegations, there had been no international plot, only a desperate act by a despairing individual. But when the German diplomat succumbed to his wounds, it was made the excuse for a violent anti-Jewish pogrom throughout Germany, beginning in the early hours of 10 November. More than a thousand synagogues and places of worship were set on fire, several thousand homes ransacked, hundreds of Jews savagely beaten, and more than ninety murdered. Within a few days, 30,000 Jews were arrested: scholars, doctors, lawyers, engineers, bankers, shopkeepers, teachers, men

22 Reported in *The Times* on 7 November 1938.
23 Reported in *The Times* on 9 November 1938.

who had once played a leading part in German national and civic life, and former front-line soldiers who had fought in the German army in the First World War. All were sent to concentration camps, where most were beaten and tortured, and several thousand were killed. Anti-Jewish measures intensified. On 13 November the Jews were ordered to cease all trading and business activities by the end of the year. A massive fine was then imposed on the whole Jewish community of Germany for the Paris murder.

Churchill's correspondents kept him informed of these developments. From Paris, Emery Reves sent him full reports of what he had learned. In London, Ian Colvin, a British journalist with well-placed contacts in Berlin, sent Churchill notes of a secret speech Hitler had made, just after the pogrom, to 'three or four of the highest functionaries' of the German Foreign Ministry. The notes began: 'He wanted to eliminate from German life the Jews, the Churches, and suppress private industry. After that, he would turn to foreign policy again.'[24]

---

24 Memorandum of 23 November 1938: Churchill papers, 2/340.

CHAPTER THIRTEEN

PALESTINE: THE LEGITIMATE JEWISH HAVEN

Churchill's immediate reaction to the Kristallnacht pogrom in Germany on the night of 9/10 November 1938, when more than a thousand synagogues were destroyed and tens of thousands of Jewish businesses and homes looted, was to press for the re-opening of Palestine for the tens of thousands of German and Austrian Jews who were seeking a safe haven there. On the day before the Palestine debate in the House of Commons he received from Weizmann's secretary, Doris May, a copy of the Palestine Government's estimate of the population. By March 1938, the most recent date for calculations, there were 1,002,406 Arabs and 401,557 Jews in Palestine. In the year 1937, just under 12,000 Jews had been allowed to enter, and in the first three months of 1938, just under 6,000.

In the House of Commons debate on 24 November, Churchill made a forceful speech. The picture he painted with regard to Britain's stewardship of Palestine was dire. 'There is tragedy in Palestine,' he declared. 'Blood is shed, murders are committed, executions are carried out, terror and counter-terror have supervened in the relationship between the Jews and the Arabs, both of whom have a right to dwell in the land which the Lord hath given them. The whole economic revival of Palestine, which was in active progress three years ago, has been cast down. From whatever angle you observe this scene, I say that it is painful. It is even horrible, and mark you, whether we feel it or not, it is humiliating to us in this country.'

With anger born of impotence to influence policy, Churchill told the House – with its large majority of loyal government supporters – 'I accuse His Majesty's Government of having been, for more than three years, incapable of forming a coherent opinion upon the affairs of Palestine. All this time matters in Palestine have been going from bad to worse, and throughout all this period, when the situation was passing continuously out of control, the Government seemed to be constantly seeking the line of least resistance. What is astonishing is that, considering how long they have been looking for the line of least resistance, their patient quest has not been attended with a greater measure of success.' The pattern was this: 'A year passes, six months pass – we have a Debate on Palestine. Do not let it be forgotten that people are dying there, that they are being executed and meeting grisly deaths from day to day and week to week, while here all that can be done is to have from time to time Debates and pay each other compliments, and, above all, run no risks of taking any decision.'

As to the Peel Commission, Churchill was scathing. 'Having sat at the Colonial Office on these sort of matters about Palestine,' he said, 'I can assure the House that there was nothing that the Royal Commission, headed by Lord Peel, could possibly have discovered in Palestine that was not already known to the Middle Eastern Department of the Colonial Office – nothing.' But the formation of a Royal Commission 'with imposing names, the gratifying leading articles in the newspapers, all this was a device to save the Cabinet from making up its mind.'

What had happened, Churchill asked, after the House of Commons persuaded the government not to endorse the Peel Partition plan? The government had said: 'Partition is still the policy and the principle but, of course, nothing is going to happen for quite a long time. Meanwhile, there will be further consultations and inquiries.' Churchill was contemptuous. For more than a year 'no policy was proclaimed by the Mandatory Power. Can we wonder that the position degenerated?'

Another Royal Commission had then been sent out, in order,

Churchill mocked, 'to report upon the first Royal Commission.' It was the second Commission, headed by Sir John Woodhead, that 'brings us to this day's Debate.' That Commission had reported, in Churchill's caustic words, 'that the plan of the first Royal Commission was rubbish, and that Partition was impracticable.'[1] The Colonial Secretary, Malcolm MacDonald, had suggested that the time had come for a conference. Churchill could not contain his scorn. 'After three years of chatter, vain, futile chatter on this subject, he announces that we are to have some discussion. It would be laughable but for the grim background upon which failure to meet this situation manifests itself.'

First, Churchill said, law and order must be restored. Then there should be a ten-year plan, with the assent, if possible, of all parties, 'and let us enforce that plan with resolute conviction and use all our strength to make it successful.' That plan would involve a curb on Jewish immigration. 'I hold, having been somewhat concerned in these matters, that we have obligations to the Palestinian Arabs as well as to the Jews and world Jewry.' It was Britain's duty to make a 'fair offer' to the Palestinian Arabs. If they refused that offer 'we must still endeavour to do justice; but justice unhampered by any special understanding with them.'

Churchill did not speak without having a plan of his own. It was to fix the immigration of the Jews into Palestine for ten years 'at a certain figure', which at the end of the ten-year period 'will not have decisively altered the balance of the population as between Arab and Jew.' But in the first place the British Government must consider the fact of 'the great increase in the Arab population during the time of the Zionist policy.' According to the census figures, this Arab increase had been 'almost as great as that of the Jewish population.'

---

1 In fact, the Woodhead Commission Report supported Partition, and proposed three revised versions of the Peel Commission plan, in one of which Britain would retain not only the Jerusalem area but also Haifa, Tiberias and the whole of Galilee, which Peel had allocated to the Jewish State. This plan gave the Jewish State less than five per cent of the land area of Western Palestine.

According to the figures of the Woodhead Report 'it has been considerably greater.'[2]

A previous speaker, Sir Archibald Sinclair, who had recently become Leader of the Liberal Party, had pointed out, Churchill noted, 'that this great increase in the Arab population disposes at once of the suggestion that they are being driven out by Jewish immigrants. They are, on the contrary, being brought into Palestine, into the sunlight of life by the very process we are pursuing and which we are determined to pursue.' Quoting the annual British Mandate census figures, as submitted to the League of Nations, Churchill noted that in the past fifteen years, between 1923 and 1938, there had been, according to the official figures, an increase of 300,000 in the Arab population and 315,000 in the Jewish population. 'Therefore, it would seem to me, having regard to our war-time pledges, that it would obviously be right for us to decide now that Jewish immigration into Palestine shall not be less in any given period than the growth of the Arab population arising largely from the animating and fertilising influence of the Jews.'

Malcolm MacDonald had indicated that the Arabs expected an increase of up to 1,500,000 in the following twenty years. 'It is perfectly clear, therefore,' Churchill pointed out, 'that Jewish immigration is no inroad on the Arab population as long as it keeps pace with the growth of the Arab population. Indeed, that gave 'the Jews, the Zionists' an interest in stimulating an increase in the Arab population, and 'helping them in their employment and bringing the two into a common interest in the matter.'

It seemed to Churchill 'that we owe it to the Arabs' to make them an offer that Jewish immigration 'shall not be so great in the ten-year period as to derange seriously the existing balance between the Jew or Arab populations.' That, he was confident, would be a 'great assurance' to the Arabs.

---

2 The Woodhead Commission calculated that the Jewish population had increased by 343,000 between 1919 and 1938, the Arab population by 419,000: *Palestine Partition Commission Report*, Command Paper 5854 of 1938, page 23.

Churchill's ten-year plan for a curb on Jewish immigration was a blow to the Zionists, who hoped to bring in sufficient immigrants to secure a Jewish majority within that ten-year period. But Churchill no longer saw this as the way forward. 'I quite agree that you cannot expect Palestine to absorb the whole of the exodus of the Jews from other countries,' he said, 'but the figure of immigration is one which should be settled. There is the crux of the matter; that is the question around which fighting is going on, and I think it should be settled on a ten-year basis. First fix the quota of your immigration, and then give this overriding assurance to the Arabs that in the ten-year period they will not be submerged.' That policy would, Churchill calculated, lead to Jewish immigration of between 30,000 and 35,000 a year. This was a substantial figure, three times the actual number of Jewish immigrants in 1937, which had been just over 10,000, and twice that for 1938, which was to be just under 15,000.

There were those who said that the Arabs might not agree even to the reduced figure of 30,000 to 35,000 Jewish immigrants a year. 'In the event of the Arabs refusing to come to any agreement,' Churchill responded, 'there would be in that case no arbitrary limit upon immigration. We should offer them a limit for their consent, but if their consent is not forthcoming and we have to rely on these other elements to maintain our security, then we must have no upward bar except what is practically possible in that respect.'

Churchill spoke positively of the ability of the Jews to defend themselves in Palestine. 'Although the Jewish colonies have not been protected by the Imperial Government,' he pointed out, 'they have held their own without difficulty and not one of them has been seriously attacked.' The Arabs should be told 'quite plainly that unless they accept within a reasonable period of time a fair offer and cease to wage war upon the Crown of Britain we shall have to carry out our plan, not without regard to their rights but without any sense of special obligation.'[3]

---

3 Parliamentary Debates, *Hansard*, 24 November 1938.

Within a month of Churchill's speech, on 21 December, the British Government's dependence on Arab goodwill had been made clear to those at the Cabinet table. Churchill was never to know that the Secretary of State for Air, Sir Kingsley Wood, told his colleagues that in the view of the Air Staff 'if another crisis should find us with a hostile Arab world behind us in the Middle East, then our military position would be quite untenable.' The Foreign Secretary, Lord Halifax, stressed that the forthcoming conference in London between the British Government, the Zionists and the Arab States 'must be so conducted to ensure that the Arab States would be friendly to us.'[4]

The conference, with Arab and Jewish leaders sitting around the same table, was held at St James's Palace in London in January 1938. Its outcome was indecisive. Churchill's plan to act without Arab consent, and to act in the interest of the Jews if the Arabs rejected the proposed reduction of Jewish immigration, did not find favour with those British politicians who wanted to appease Arab sentiment – not only in Palestine but throughout the Arab world.

One result of this particular appeasement policy was an upsurge in official British pressure against Jewish refugees from Germany and Austria who were trying to reach Palestine without Palestine certificates, the essential documentation without which they would not be allowed to enter. With Lord Halifax's approval, British diplomatic pressure was put on five governments, those of Greece, Yugoslavia, Turkey, Bulgaria and Romania, not to allow 'illegal' immigrants to transit their countries en route for Palestine.

Churchill sought to help the Jews of Germany and Austria by finding some other place of refuge. While on holiday in the South of France in January 1939 he met an Albanian diplomat, Chatin Sarachi, a member of one of Albania's leading Roman Catholic landowning families. Sarachi was sympathetic to the idea of Albania taking in refugees, and after raising the matter in the Albanian capital, wrote to Churchill: 'I have been authorised to negotiate.'[5]

---

4 Cabinet Minutes, 21 December 1938: Cabinet papers, 23/96.
5 Letter of 13 March 1939: Foreign Office papers, 371/24081.

Within a month, Mussolini sent his troops into Albania, its independence was destroyed, and the rescue scheme came to nought.

The more Churchill warned about Hitler's aggressive intentions in Europe and called for accelerated British rearmament, the more Neville Chamberlain and the Conservative Party machine belittled his arguments and his judgment. On 9 December 1938, in a speech to his constituents, Churchill pointed out that four years earlier he had urged that the Royal Air Force should be doubled and then redoubled. In response, Lord Samuel, then a leading advocate of the Liberal Party's call for disarmament, had 'thought my judgment so defective that he likened me to a Malay running amok. It would have been well for him and his persecuted race if my advice had been taken. They would not be where we are now and we would not be where we are now.'[6]

Churchill's bitterness was strong. He had been kept out of the decision-making process for so long. His warnings about Nazism had been clear and detailed, but to no avail. While Chamberlain and his Cabinet did not want Churchill in their inner circle, a larger and larger segment of the British public was calling for him to be given a place. This demand found strong expression in February and March 1939 in the illustrated magazine *Picture Post,* which in two successive issues called for Churchill to be brought back into government. The articles were illustrated with photographs of Churchill at Chartwell, his home and place of virtual exile, where he was seen working, bricklaying, reading – and waiting.

The articles owed much to the vision of the editor and designer of *Picture Post,* Stefan Lorant, a Hungarian Jew who in 1919, at the age of eighteen, had fled the anti-Semitic atmosphere of Admiral Horthy's regime and gone to Germany, where he became a pioneer of illustrated magazines. In 1933 Lorant had been imprisoned by the Nazis in Dachau for six months, before intervention by the Hungarian Government led to his release. His book *I Was Hitler's*

6 Speech of 9 December 1938: Churchill papers, 9/133.

Prisoner, published in 1935, was one of the first accounts in English of the concentration camp system.

Lorant spent a day at Chartwell, with a photographer, talking to Churchill and working out how best to present the call for his return to government. The two issues of *Picture Post* that followed Lorant's visit marked a turning point in the public perception of Churchill as a man whose knowledge and experience were not being used. The first issue was published on 25 February 1939 with text by Henry Wickham Steed, a former editor of *The Times* and a member of the Anti-Nazi League. Its theme: 'The greatest moment of his life is yet to come.'[7]

---

7 *Picture Post*, 25 February 1939.

CHAPTER FOURTEEN

THE BLACK PAPER: 'THIS MORTAL BLOW'

Between the start of the Arab uprising in April 1936 and the spring of 1939, Arab attacks on British troops and military installations had been continuous. According to the British War Office statistics, more than five thousand Palestinian Arabs were killed by British troops during that three-year period. At the same time, at least five hundred Arabs had been killed by their fellow-Arabs because they had advocated good relations with the Jews, and were unwilling to oppose continued Jewish immigration. Churchill had gone to great lengths to warn of the scale and intensity of this conflict, and of the need to resolve it without reneging on Britain's promise to the Jews.

In searching for a means to end Arab violence inside Palestine, Neville Chamberlain and his colleagues bowed to the growing pressure of the independent Arab States beyond Palestine, in particular Saudi Arabia and the recently independent Egypt and Iraq, for an end to any further Jewish immigration. At the Cabinet's Palestine Committee on 20 April 1939, Neville Chamberlain stressed that it was of 'immense importance' with regard to British strategy 'to have the Moslem world with us.' Chamberlain added, 'If we must offend one side. Let us offend the Jews rather than the Arabs.'[1] The result was a British Government decision, reached in May 1939, to devise a policy that would ensure a permanent Arab majority, and a permanent Jewish minority, in Palestine. The policy was to be implemented by

1 Cabinet Palestine Committee, 20 April 1939: Cabinet papers, 24/285.

the Colonial Office under Malcolm MacDonald. The MacDonald White Paper – known to the Jews as the Black Paper – laid down a final limit to Jewish immigration of a total of 75,000 Jews during the coming five years.

The crux of this limit was that after the five-year period had passed, self-governing institutions would be set up, with the Jews still in a minority. At that point in time Arab approval would be needed for any further Jewish immigration. The Arabs would have power to prevent a Jewish majority for all time. That power would come into effect in May 1944. The government figure of a maximum of 75,000 Jewish immigrants included up to 25,000 emergency Palestine certificates. The five-year average of 15,000 a year was half that of the annual 30,000 to 35,000 that Churchill had earlier proposed, and which he had regarded as the lower rate of Jewish immigration needed to calm Arab fears. As well as giving the Arabs the power to prevent for all time a Jewish majority in Palestine, the 1939 White Paper cut off the persecuted Jews of central and eastern Europe from one of the main places of refuge left open to them, and from the possibility of an eventual Jewish State that would serve as a place of unimpeded sanctuary.

The White Paper was made public on 19 May 1939. Before it was debated in the House of Commons, Churchill invited Weizmann to lunch with him at his London apartment. In his memoirs, Weizmann recalled how Churchill 'produced a packet of small cards and read his speech out to us; then he asked me if I had any changes to suggest. I answered that the architecture was so perfect that there were only one or two small points I might want to alter – but they were so unimportant I would not bother him with them.'[2]

During the second day of the debate, on 23 May, Churchill spoke with force and bitterness against what he believed was both a betrayal of the Balfour Declaration, and a shameful act of appeasement. 'I find this a melancholy occasion,' he said; others 'may feel that the burden of keeping faith weighs upon them rather oppressively. Some may be

2 Chaim Weizmann, *Trial and Error: The Autobiography of Chaim Weizmann*, page 411.

pro-Arab and some may be anti-Semite. None of these motives offers me any means of escape because I was from the beginning a sincere advocate of the Balfour Declaration and I have made repeated public statements to that effect.'

As a person 'intimately and responsibly concerned' in the earlier stages of Britain's Palestine policy, Churchill said, 'I could not stand by and see solemn engagements into which Britain has entered before the world set aside for reasons of administrative convenience or – and it will be a vain hope – for the sake of a quiet life.' He would, he said, 'feel personally embarrassed in the most acute manner if I lent myself, by silence or inaction, to what I must regard as an act of repudiation.'

Of the proposed Arab veto on all Jewish immigration after 1944, Churchill declared: 'Now, there is the breach; there is the violation of the pledge; there is the abandonment of the Balfour Declaration; there is the end of the vision, of the hope, of the dream.'

Churchill was particularly concerned about the effect of the White Paper on world opinion in the context of Britain's attempt to rally the democratic and threatened forces of Europe against Nazism and Fascism. 'What will our friends say?' he asked. 'What will be the opinion of the United States of America? Shall we not lose more – and this is a question to be considered maturely – in the growing support and sympathy of the United States than we shall gain in local administrative convenience, if gain at all indeed we do? What will our potential enemies think? What will those who have been stirring up these Arab agitators think?'

Would the Arab agitators themselves not be encouraged, Churchill asked, 'by our confession of recoil? Will they not be tempted to say: "They're on the run again. This is another Munich" and be the more stimulated in their aggression by these very unpleasant reflections which they make?'

Churchill turned to the situation in Europe. In March 1939 Hitler had entered Prague as a conqueror, his first act of military aggression against an independent, non-German State. Czechoslovakia, already emasculated at Munich, was no more. In response, Neville

Chamberlain had given Poland, Romania and Turkey guarantees against outside aggression and, much encouraged by Churchill, was negotiating with the Soviet Union to bring it into the alliance system.

Linking this search for allies with the new Palestine White Paper, Churchill warned: 'Shall we not undo by this very act of abjection some of the good which we have gained by our guarantees to Poland and to Rumania, by our admirable Turkish Alliance and by what we hope and expect will be our Russian Alliance?' These recent foreign developments had to be considered. Might not the new White Paper 'be a contributory factor – and every factor is a contributory factor now – by which our potential enemies may be emboldened to take some irrevocable action and then find out, only after it is all too late, that it is not this Government, with their tired Ministers and flagging purpose, that they have to face, but the might of Britain and all that Britain means?'

It was hoped by the government, Churchill pointed out, 'to obtain five years of easement in Palestine by this proposal,' but he was convinced that the consequences would be 'entirely the opposite.' As he saw it, a 'sense of moral weakness' in the mandatory Power 'will rouse all the violent elements in Palestine to the utmost degree.'

Angered by, and afraid of, the impact on the European situation of the White Paper's appeasement of the Arabs, Churchill warned the Conservative Party: 'The policy which you think is a relief and an easement you will find afterwards you will have to retrieve, in suffering and greater exertions than those we are making.'

He would end his speech, Churchill said, 'upon the land of Palestine', and as he did so he directed his criticisms first against MacDonald and then against Chamberlain. First, he quoted from MacDonald's speech: 'Yesterday the Minister responsible descanted eloquently in glowing passages upon the magnificent work which the Jewish colonists have done. They have made the desert bloom. They have started a score of thriving industries, he said. They have founded a great city on the barren shore. They have harnessed the Jordan and spread its electricity throughout the land.' Angrily,

Churchill told the House: 'So far from being persecuted, the Arabs have crowded into the country and multiplied till their population has increased more than even all world Jewry could lift up the Jewish population. Now we are asked to decree that all this is to stop and all this is to come to an end. We are now asked to submit – and this is what rankles most with me – to an agitation which is fed with foreign money and ceaselessly inflamed by Nazi and by Fascist propaganda.'

Churchill knew the extent to which German and Italian radio broadcasts had been inflaming Arab anti-Jewish and anti-British sentiment in Palestine. He finally turned his criticism against Chamberlain. Twenty years earlier, he pointed out, Chamberlain himself 'used these stirring words' – which Churchill then quoted: 'A great responsibility will rest upon the Zionists, who, before long, will be proceeding, with joy in their hearts, to the ancient seat of their people. Theirs will be the task to build up a new prosperity and a new civilisation in old Palestine, so long neglected and misruled.' Such were Chamberlain's words to the Jews at the time of the Balfour Declaration. 'Well, they have answered his call,' Churchill declared. 'They have fulfilled his hopes. How can he find it in his heart to strike them this mortal blow?'[3]

Churchill's speech, widely publicised in newspapers throughout Britain, and in the English-language *Palestine Post*, gave hope to the Zionists. 'Your magnificent speech may yet destroy this policy,' Dr Weizmann telegraphed to him that day.[4] 'Words fail me to express thanks.' Nathan Laski wrote from Manchester: 'May I congratulate you upon the great and statesmanlike speech you made on the Palestine question last night. I think it is not exaggerating to say that you will get the blessings of millions of Jews all over the world.'[5] So impressed were the Zionist leaders by the speech that it was later published as a pamphlet by the British Association for the National Home in Palestine.[6] And, three years later, during the Second World War, when Churchill

3 Parliamentary Debates, *Hansard*, 23 May 1939.
4 Telegram of 23 May 1939: Weizmann papers.
5 Letter of 24 May 1939: Churchill papers, 2/379.
6 *What Mr Churchill Said in 1939 About the Palestine White Paper.*

was in conflict with his War Cabinet colleagues over the future of Palestine, he circulated the speech to them as a Cabinet paper.

The Palestine White Paper of 1939 was neither destroyed nor modified as a result of Churchill's speech. The government commanded one of the highest majorities in British political history, and the final vote was 268 to 179 in favour of its policy. No amount of argument could change ingrained attitudes. On 30 July Chamberlain commented on the persecution of the Jews of Germany in a letter to one of his sisters: 'I believe the persecution arose out of two motives; A desire to rob the Jews of their money and a jealousy of their superior cleverness.' His letter continued: 'No doubt Jews aren't a lovable people; I don't care about them myself; but that is not sufficient to explain the Pogrom.'[7] Not a 'lovable people': with such an attitude at the highest level of government it was a misfortune for the Jews that Churchill, their most articulate and passionate defender, was out of political office.

On 8 August, in a broadcast to the United States, Churchill spoke to his American listeners of 'a hush' all over Europe. 'It is the hush of suspense, and in many lands, it is the hush of fear,' he said. One could also hear the tramp of armies; the armies of Germany and Italy. 'After all, the dictators must train their soldiers. They could scarcely do less in common prudence, when the Danes, the Dutch, the Swiss, the Albanians – and of course the Jews – may leap out upon them at any moment and rob them of their living space.'[8]

Hitler had long demanded 'living space' for the German people: it was one of his most strident demands, self-serving and threatening at the same time. In search of living space, and of the further spread of Nazi rule and terror, on 25 August 1939 Germany signed a pact with the Soviet Union, whereby the two countries would partition Poland between them. On 1 September 1939 Germany invaded Poland. The Second World War had begun.

---

7 Letter of 30 July 1939: Neville Chamberlain papers.
8 Broadcast of 8 August 1939: Churchill papers, 9/137.

CHAPTER FIFTEEN

THE FIRST NINE MONTHS OF WAR

On 3 September 1939, two days after the German invasion of Poland, Britain and France declared war on Germany. That day, Neville Chamberlain brought Churchill back into the Cabinet after ten years exclusion, appointing him First Lord of the Admiralty, the post he had held on the outbreak of war in 1914. On 19 September, Weizmann dined with him at his official residence, Admiralty House. Brendan Bracken, one of the Conservative rebels who had voted against the Palestine White Paper four months earlier, was present. The Jewish Agency notes of the meeting recorded Churchill's suggestion that Weizmann prepare 'a list of our requirements' with regard to the participation of the Palestinian Jews in the British war effort, and should consult Brendan Bracken with regard to it. Churchill then said 'that he would then see that it was put through.'

During their talk, Weizmann gave Churchill an indication of 'the spirit of the Jews of Palestine', pointing out that 75,000 young Jewish men and women there had registered for national service, to fight as part of the British armed forces wherever they might be needed. Churchill asked if they were armed, 'and on receiving a negative reply said that he would arm them.' If the Jews were armed, Churchill said, it would be possible to take British troops away from Palestine.

When Churchill said that 'presumably we would not need first-class arms for these people,' Weizmann replied that what was important 'was to create cadres and establish a military organisation.' Churchill asked that Bracken and Weizmann 'prepare something definite.' He added that he believed that once the Jews were armed 'the Arabs would come to terms with them.'[1] Encouraging words, sincerely meant, but Churchill was unable to persuade the Cabinet.

To the annoyance of his Cabinet colleagues, Churchill continued to challenge the White Paper, and to speak in Cabinet against draconian restrictions on future Jewish land purchase. These restrictions, unlike the immigration restrictions, had yet to be finalised. On 15 December Churchill wrote to Malcolm MacDonald: 'I should be obliged to you if you would let me know whether, and if so when, the question of applying the new Land Ordinance to Palestine will come before the Cabinet, and also to ask that it would be brought before the Cabinet before being put into execution.' He noted: 'It will be the cause of very great friction with the Jews and with Dr Weizmann, and will raise political issues in the House of Commons. I feel in view of my past association with the Palestine question, that I ought not to let the matter pass without discussion.'

Churchill saw Weizmann again on 17 December. 'Mr Churchill was very cordial,' record the Jewish Agency notes, and deeply interested in Weizmann's forthcoming visit to America. Weizmann thanked Churchill 'for his unceasing interest in Zionist affairs,' telling him, 'You stood at the cradle of this enterprise; I hope that you will see it through.' When Churchill asked Weizmann what he meant by 'seeing it through', Weizmann replied 'that after the war the Zionists would wish to have a State of some three or four million Jews in Palestine.' To this Churchill replied, 'Yes, indeed, I quite agree with that.'[2]

The proposed Land Transfer Regulations forbade further Jewish land purchase throughout the area now known as the West Bank, as well as in most of present-day Galilee: more than four million acres of Mandatory Palestine. Although Jews would be allowed to continue to buy land in areas of existing Jewish settlement along much of the

1 Notes of a meeting of 19 September 1939: Weizmann papers.
2 Notes of a meeting of 17 December 1939: Weizmann papers.

coast and in the hinterland of Haifa, Jewish land purchases would be strictly curtailed in the immediate environs of Jerusalem – a city with a Jewish majority – and in the Jezreel Valley, where there were already more than twenty Jewish farming villages. Jews were also forbidden to extend their land purchases in three other areas of existing Jewish settlement: the Jerusalem corridor, the area around Beersheba, and the area north of Acre.

In a memorandum that he wrote for the War Cabinet on Christmas Day 1939, Churchill was sharply critical of a proposed Foreign Office telegram to the British Ambassador in the United States, Lord Lothian. The telegram was a re-iteration of the 1939 Palestine White Paper and its restrictions on Jewish immigration. Churchill, who less than eight months earlier had been the leading parliamentary critic of the restrictions, was not pleased. The 'trend of American opinion' since the outbreak of the war, he warned, 'has been disappointing, and the movement to interpret neutrality in the strictest manner has gathered unexpected strength.' As American attention was becoming increasingly concentrated upon the following year's Presidential election, 'do we really wish at this juncture to throw what Lord Lothian calls "the powerful factor" of the influence of American Jewry into the scales against us? Can we afford to do so?'

Churchill then reminded his Cabinet colleagues that 'it was not for light or sentimental reasons that Lord Balfour and the Government of 1917 made the promises to the Zionists which have been the cause of so much subsequent discussion. The influence of American Jewry was rated then as a factor of the highest importance, and we did not feel ourselves in such a strong position as to be able to treat it with indifference.' With a Presidential election only a year away, 'and when the future is full of measureless uncertainties, I should have thought it was more necessary, even than in November 1917, to conciliate American Jewry and enlist their aid in combating isolationist and indeed anti-British tendencies in the United States.'

He was 'most reluctant', Churchill wrote, 'to stir pre-war disputes; but I cannot help being struck with the uncompromising tone of the draft telegram just sent to Lord Lothian. It must be remembered that the White Paper gave rise to the sharpest differences of opinion in the House of Commons. The Labour and Liberal Opposition denounced it as a breach of faith. Mr Lloyd George and I, who both were concerned in the giving or interpretation of the original promise, were forced to testify in this sense. Both the Liberal and Labour Parties voted against the White Paper, and a number of Conservatives, of whom I was one, voted with them. The Labour Party spokesman announced that should they obtain power, they could not be bound by the White Paper as an instrument.' Since then the Mandates Commission of the League of Nations 'has pronounced against the validity of the White Paper, having regard to the conditions of the Mandate. In fact it is hardly possible to find a topic more calculated to divide British opinion and to enable those elements who support the war, but do not like the Government, to come together, and to make a powerful case that our war effort is being hampered by undue insistence upon the views of the pre-war Cabinet.'

It would seem, Churchill pointed out, 'that if the war darkens and deepens, we may have increasingly to rely upon the support of the Liberal and Labour Parties to marshal the whole force of the nation. They would certainly regard the White Paper as a grievous obstacle. Moreover it seems to me most unlikely that any future British Government which may take office in the next five years will espouse the theme of the White Paper that all Jewish immigration into Palestine will be closed down at the end of that period, unless the Arab majority is found willing to re-open it.' It was wrong for the draft telegram to Lord Lothian to speak about the White Paper 'as a just, fixed, unalterable settlement.'

Churchill told his War Cabinet colleagues – all of whom had supported the restrictions on Jewish immigration to Palestine—that Weizmann had gone to see him before he left for New York. 'I am sure,' Churchill wrote, 'that it is his whole desire to bring United States opinion as far as he possibly can on to our side, but the line indicated in the draft telegram may well make his task impossible, and he will find himself confronted with the active resentment of American Jewry. Their anger may become public and be readily exploited by all unfavourable elements in the United States. This may do us great harm there; and when the repercussions of this outcry reach this country the Government will have to face a debate in the House of Commons which will be not only embarrassing, but dangerous and damaging to our common interest.'

What Lord Lothian should be told to say, in Churchill's view, was that the White Paper represented the sincere effort of the pre-war Cabinet to hold the scales evenly between Jew and Arab, and to fulfil all the pledges which had been given, 'but that there were admittedly great differences of opinion about this in the House of Commons; and that it was our desire during the war to reduce all domestic controversies to the smallest limits. He could continue that His Majesty's Government were not now prepared to take a new view of the policy announced by the former Cabinet, but that having regard to the attitude adopted by the Mandates Commission of the League of Nations, they felt that the future of Palestine was one of the questions which must find its place in the general peace settlement at the end of the war; and that meanwhile nothing would be done to prejudice the final form which that settlement would take.'

This was to be Churchill's theme throughout the war: that no permanent restriction on Jewish immigration should be imposed, but that the future of Palestine should be determined at a peace conference after the war. 'The one thing he ought not to say,' Churchill told his colleagues, 'is that with the world in flux and the life of every European nation and the British Empire hanging in the balance, the sole fixed, immutable inexorable fact was that Jewish immigration into Palestine would come to an end after five years in accordance with the White Paper.'

Astonished by the continuing intensity of feeling against Jewish immigration among his War Cabinet colleagues, and in the Foreign Office, Churchill ended his Christmas Day memorandum: 'Many people are called upon in these days to make sacrifices, and sacrifices not only of opinion, in order to save the country, and I venture to urge for the sake of our sailors and soldiers, and of all our hopes of victory that we also should allow no minor obstacles to complicate our task.'[3] The Cabinet Ministers were unmoved; most of them had been in the Cabinet seven months earlier when the policy had been decided.

Determined to prevent Churchill having information about the trickle of Jews who were making their way to Palestine by sea illegally, the civil servants concerned decided that he should not be informed that Royal Navy ships, for which he was responsible, were being used to intercept refugee traffic. When he discovered this at the beginning of 1940 he was incensed. On 4 January 1940 he wrote to MacDonald: 'I was somewhat surprised to see that the telegram about intercepting was sent off without being shown to me. These orders cannot be carried out.'[4]

On 12 February 1940 the question of Palestine was on the War Cabinet agenda, when, at the start of the final discussion on the Land Transfer Regulations, Churchill told his colleagues he 'regretted greatly that this policy should be adopted in the interests of one of the two parties to whose welfare the Mandate had enjoined us to pay an equal regard.' He went on to point out that the proposed land transfer restrictions, as first set out in the White Paper, had been condemned by the majority of the Mandates' Commission at Geneva. In his view, 'it was a shortsighted policy' that would 'put a stop to agricultural progress in Palestine.'

After stressing, as he had done several times before in the House of Commons, that the Jewish settlers had made 'tremendous strides in recent years, while there was no prospect that the Arabs would ever abandon their primitive methods of cultivation,' Churchill told his War Cabinet colleagues that it was a 'striking fact' that the Arab population had shown the largest increase in those areas where land had been purchased by Jews. The policy of restricting land sales

3 Winston Churchill, War Cabinet Paper, 25 December 1939: Cabinet papers, 67/3.
4 Letter of 4 January 1940: Admiralty papers, 116/4312.

would almost certainly be followed by a slump in land values, 'from which Arabs and Jews alike would suffer.' In addition, he asked, 'what was the urgency in taking these steps? Our action would cause a great outcry in American Jewry.'

The Secretary of State for War, Oliver Stanley, had a different perspective. 'Looking at the matter from the economic point of view,' he said, 'it might be a good thing for Palestine, Jew and Arab alike, if steps were taken to slow down the movement for the intensive cultivation of the land. There was great danger of overproduction of citrus fruits.' MacDonald, the Secretary of State for the Colonies, said he and his advisers 'were inclined to hold this view,' but that, 'on the other hand, one could not withhold one's tribute of admiration for the work the Jews had carried out in reviving a dead countryside.' It had long been government policy, MacDonald added, to teach the Palestinian Arabs to modernise their agricultural methods, and this might be continued by an offer of financial assistance.

Churchill responded by saying that he 'personally, ascribed to Government encouragement very little of the credit for the great agricultural improvements which had taken place in Palestine. Broadly speaking, they were all the result of private Jewish efforts. So far as the Government of Palestine had played any part in agricultural development, it was with Jewish money wrung from the settlers by taxation.' Nor was Churchill impressed by 'the political grounds on which it was attempted to justify our action in bringing this great agricultural experiment to an end. The political argument, in a word, was that we should not be able to win the war without the help of the Arabs.' Churchill said he did 'not in the least admit the validity of that argument.'

Churchill then told his colleagues that provided 'there was no ambiguity about his position, and that his views were on record in the War Cabinet Minutes, he would not press further this opposition to the Secretary of State's land proposals.'

Turning to the question of arming the Jews, Churchill said that 'it might have been thought a matter for satisfaction that the Jews in

Palestine should possess arms, and be capable of providing for their own defence. They were the only trustworthy friends we had in that country and they were much more under our control than the scattered Arab population.' Churchill thought 'that the sound policy for Great Britain at the beginning of the war would have been to build up, as soon as possible, a strong Jewish armed force in Palestine. In this way we should have been able to use elsewhere the large and costly British Cavalry force, which was now to replace the eleven infantry battalions hitherto locked up in Palestine.'

It was 'an extraordinary position' Churchill concluded, 'that at a time when the war was probably entering its most dangerous phase, we should station in Palestine a garrison one-quarter the size of our garrison in India' – and this for the purpose of forcing through a policy which, in his judgment, was unpopular in Palestine and in Great Britain alike.[5]

Churchill also reiterated at the War Cabinet the need to make use of both Jewish and Arab military manpower 'so as to free for use elsewhere the greater part of the Regular battalions now held there for internal security purposes.' By 'balancing the Arabs against the Jews' in the units that might be formed, 'not only would an outlet be provided for the more adventurous spirits in those peoples, but each community would be enabled to keep watch upon the other.' Despite these arguments, the War Cabinet would not agree to arming the Jews of Palestine, or to a joint Jewish-Arab force. Churchill's opposition to the Jewish land purchase restrictions was likewise unsuccessful. Nor did his circulation to the War Cabinet on 24 February of a telegram that Weizmann had sent him, describing the 'deplorable' results of the restrictions, and not only in Jewish circles, have any influence.[6]

The Land Transfer Regulations were put in place on 28 February.[7] 'The effect of these regulations,' David Ben-Gurion,

5 War Cabinet Minutes, 12 February 1940: Cabinet papers, 65/5.
6 Cabinet papers, 65/5.
7 Command Paper 6180 of 1940.

Chairman of the Executive Committee of the Jewish Agency, declared, 'is that no Jew may acquire in Palestine a plot of land, a building, or a tree, or any right in water, except in towns and a very small part of the country.' The regulations 'not only violate the terms of the Mandate but completely nullify its primary purpose.'[8]

In the first week of May 1940 there was mounting criticism in Parliament of Chamberlain's conduct of the war. The question of who would succeed him dominated political talk. On 8 May Sir Samuel Hoare, the Secretary of State for Air, and one of those closest to the pulse of the Conservative Party, drew up a private list of what he called 'Winston's mistakes' – mistakes that made him an unsuitable candidate to succeed Chamberlain. One of these mistakes read tersely: 'Pro-Zionist row over land settlement in Palestine.'[9]

Fortunately for Britain, and for the Jews in Palestine, Zionist considerations did not determine who would become Prime Minister. When, on 10 May 1940, German forces struck simultaneously at Holland, Belgium, Luxembourg and France, Chamberlain agreed to resign. That evening a young Palestinian Jew, Ben Gale, who was in Tel Aviv, recalled how, in the middle of a lecture, 'the chairman interrupted the speaker to read a note handed to him by a messenger.' The note read: 'Chamberlain has stepped down and Winston Churchill is now Prime Minister.' 'Everyone in the large hall stood up and cheered wildly. With Churchill at the helm there was now hope for the Jews of Palestine!'[10]

At the Jewish Agency's office in London, the historian Lewis Namier, whom Churchill had consulted on his Marlborough biography eight years earlier, 'picked up echoes of afflicted Jewry's deliverance that had rustled through their ranks at Churchill's elevation.'[11]

---

8 *Palestine Post*, 29 February 1940.
9 Viscount Templewood papers.
10 Ben Gale, letter to the author, 20 February 1996.
11 Julia Namier, *Lewis Namier: A Biography*, page 245.

CHAPTER SIXTEEN

PRIME MINISTER: THE PALESTINE DIMENSION

From the first days of Churchill's premiership, as fears of a German invasion of Britain intensified, there was a call for all eleven battalions of British troops in Palestine, and their support troops – twenty thousand soldiers in all – to be brought back to Britain. This would leave the Jews at the mercy of Arab attack. Churchill, with his joint authority as Prime Minister, and also Minister of Defence, suggested that the Jews should be armed for their own protection, but on 23 May he was informed by his Principal Private Secretary, Eric Seal, that the Secretary of State for the Colonies, Lord Lloyd, had 'strong objections', as he feared the 'worst possible repercussions on the Arab world.'[1]

Lord Lloyd was far from alone among British policymakers in fearing that the 'Arab world' – however defined – would turn against Britain if it saw any favours being given to the Jews of Palestine, even arming them in self defence. Eric Seal agreed with Lloyd, writing to Churchill: 'I must confess that I have a strong feeling that he is right about arming the Jews.'[2]

Churchill was not convinced. 'How can you remove all the troops and yet leave the Jews unarmed – and disarmed by us?' he wrote to Seal.[3] He then explained to Lloyd what he had in mind. 'I do not want Jewish forces raised to serve outside Palestine,' he wrote.

---

1 Eric Seal note, 23 May 1940: Premier papers, 3/348.
2 Note of 23 May 1940: Premier papers, 3/348.
3 Churchill note, 23 May 1940: Premier papers, 3/348.

COURTESY OF THE LATE MIRIAM ROTHSCHILD

1. Lord Randolph Churchill (right) with Nathan Meyer Rothschild, 1st Baron Rothschild, known as 'Natty', in Lord Rothschild's garden at Tring.

CHURCHILL COLLEGE ARCHIVE

2. Churchill at a garden party given by his Manchester Jewish constituents, 23 August 1907.

CHURCHILL COLLEGE ARCHIVE

3. Churchill at the Manchester garden party with Dr Joseph Dulberg, one of the leaders of the Jewish community, 1907.

CHURCHILL COLLEGE ARCHIVE

4. Dr Dulberg introducing Churchill to some of his Jewish constituents.

5. Churchill and Sir Ernest Cassel at a weekend party in Biarritz, 1907. In front of them is Mrs George Keppel. King Edward VII was one of the guests.

6. Churchill and his wife Clementine, October 1908, at the opening of a new wing of the Manchester Jewish Hospital. It was the couple's first official public appearance since their marriage.

ILLUSTRATED SUNDAY HERALD

ZIONISM versus BOLSHEVISM.

A STRUGGLE FOR THE SOUL OF THE JEWISH PEOPLE.

By the Rt. Hon. WINSTON S. CHURCHILL.

Mr. Churchill inspecting his old regiment, the 4th Hussars, at Aldershot last week.

Good and Bad Jews.

"National" Jews.

International Jews.

Terrorist Jews.

"Protector of the Jews."

A Home for the Jews.

Duty of Loyal Jews.

7. The first page of Churchill's controversial 'Zionism versus Bolshevism' article in the *Illustrated Sunday Herald*, 8 February 1920. The photograph shows Churchill inspecting troops of his former regiment, the 4th Hussars, in January 1920.

COURTESY OF THE LATE SYBIL,
DOWAGER MARCHIONESS OF CHOLMONDELEY

8. Churchill and A. J. Balfour, 1920.

CENTRAL ZIONIST ARCHIVES

9. Outside Government House, Jerusalem, March 1921. Far left, Lady Samuel; behind her, her son Edwin; next to her, the Emir Abdullah; behind him (head turned away from camera), Dorothy de Rothschild, who is looking at her husband, James de Rothschild. To the Emir's left: Sir Herbert Samuel, Winston Churchill and Clementine Churchill.

10. Churchill greeted by Jewish scouts and guides, Mount Scopus, Jerusalem, on his way to plant a tree at the site of the future Hebrew University, March 1921. Sir Herbert Samuel is on Churchill's right, doffing his hat. Between them, in bowler hat, is the Under-Secretary of State for the Colonies, Leo Amery.

11. Churchill in Tel Aviv, with the city's mayor, Meir Dizengoff, March 1921.

YAD CHAIM WEIZMANN

12. Chaim Weizmann, Churchill's closest and most long-standing contact with the Zionist movement.

CENTRAL ZIONIST ARCHIVES

13. Pinhas Rutenberg, whose scheme to bring electric power to Palestine by harnessing the waters of the River Jordan was supported by Churchill in the House of Commons.

JABOTINSKY ARCHIVE

14. Vladimir Jabotinsky, leader of the Zionist Revisionist movement, who provided Churchill with arguments against the Partition of Palestine, 1937.

COURTESY OF LADY SOAMES

15. Churchill and Albert Einstein at Chartwell, spring 1933.

ASSOCIATED PRESS

16. The former French Prime Minister and leader of the Popular Front, Léon Blum, with Churchill at Chartwell, May 1939.

COURTESY OF WENDY REVES

17. Emery Reves and Churchill in Paris, October 1938.

COURTESY OF THE LATE EUGEN SPIER

18. Eugen Spier, who helped Churchill set up the Anti-Nazi League.

COURTESY OF THE LATE DOROTHY DE ROTHSCHILD

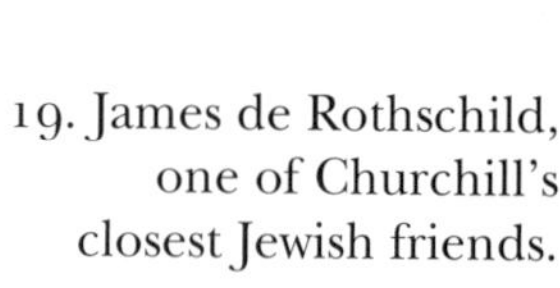

19. James de Rothschild, one of Churchill's closest Jewish friends.

COURTESY OF THE LATE STEFAN LORANT

20. Churchill and Stefan Lorant at Chartwell, February 1939.

STUDIO EDMARK

21. Randolph Churchill, seen here in front of a portrait of Tito, speaking to Yugoslav partisans in German-occupied Yugoslavia, 1944. Randolph proposed a scheme to fly Jewish refugees to safety.

KENNETH ROSE/WEIDENFELD & NICOLSON

22. Victor Rothschild, who was responsible during the Second World War for testing Churchill's gifts of food and cigars to ensure that the Prime Minister was not poisoned.

LIBRARY OF CONGRESS

23. King Ibn Saud of Saudi Arabia and President Roosevelt, meeting on board the USS *Quincy*, off Alexandria, Egypt, as Roosevelt returned from the Yalta Conference to the United States, 14 February 1945.

HMSO/BRITISH MINISTRY OF INFORMATION, MIDDLE EAST

24. King Ibn Saud and Churchill meet at the Fayyum Oasis, Egypt, 17 February 1945. Between them is Ibn Saud's interpreter; to the right, Churchill's wartime ADC, Lieutenant-Commander 'Tommy' Thompson.

REVES COLLECTION, DALLAS MUSEUM OF ART

25. Churchill, his daughter Sarah and Emery Reves, at La Pausa, in the South of France, 1956.

ASSOCIATED PRESS

26. Churchill and Bernard Baruch, the Jewish American financier and friend whom Churchill rebuked for not supporting Zionism.

CHURCHILL COLLEGE ARCHIVE, NEMON COLLECTION

27. The sculptor Oscar Nemon (left), his bust of Churchill (centre), and (far right) Churchill's bust of Nemon, which Churchill did while he was being sculpted. It is the only known sculpture by Churchill.

COURTESY OF LORD WOLFSON OF ST MARYLEBONE

28. The Israeli Ambassador Eliahu Elath (left), and Sir Isaac Wolfson, present Churchill with an award for his support of Zionist endeavour. Behind Churchill is a painting of the Central Synagogue in Hallam Street, London, destroyed during the Blitz.

JEWISH CHRONICLE

29. David Ben-Gurion with Churchill, Hyde Park Gate, 2 June 1961. At the end of their meeting, Churchill gave Ben-Gurion a copy of an article Churchill had written about Moses, thirty years earlier.

COURTESY OF MAJOR EDMUND DE ROTHSCHILD

30. Ben-Gurion and Edmund de Rothschild in London, shortly after Churchill's funeral, 1965.

'The main and almost the sole aim in Palestine at the present time is to liberate the eleven battalions of excellent Regular troops who are now tethered there. For this purpose the Jews should be armed in their own defence, and properly organised as speedily as possible. We can always prevent them from attacking the Arabs by our sea power which cuts them off from the outer world, and by other friendly influences. On the other hand, we cannot leave them unarmed when our troops leave, as leave they must at a very early date.'[4]

Churchill saw Lloyd, and finding him emphatically opposed to arming the Jews, pressed him to talk with Weizmann 'about the protection of Jewish settlements; and try to bring him along with you.' Churchill added: 'You know what I think about the White Paper.'[5] American Jews also expressed their view. At the height of his dispute with Lloyd, Churchill received a telegram from Lord Lothian, the British Ambassador in Washington, stating that the Jews in the United States 'want Jews in Palestine to be organised under British command to defend Palestine from outside attack and to help the Allies. If Palestine were overrun and Jews had not been put in a position to defend their country, there would certainly be a most deplorable effect on American Jews' opinion.'[6]

Lothian's telegram gave Churchill extra ammunition in his debate with Lord Lloyd. 'This is a matter in which I take a great interest,' he wrote to Lloyd on 25 June. 'The cruel penalties imposed by your predecessor upon the Jews in Palestine for arming have made it necessary to tie up needless forces for their protection. Pray let me know exactly what weapons and organisation the Jews have for self-defence.'[7]

Those 'cruel penalties' were the ten-year prison sentences imposed by Malcolm MacDonald on forty-two Jews who had been caught drilling with weapons; a forty-third was sentenced to life

---

4 Letter of 23 May 1940: Churchill papers, 20/13.
5 Letter of 28 May 1940: Premier papers, 3/348.
6 Telegram of 21 June 1940: Premier papers, 3/348.
7 Minute of 25 June 1940: Churchill papers, 20/13.

imprisonment. But when, on 27 June, Churchill reiterated in Cabinet that he wished the Jews in Palestine to be armed, Lloyd spoke against. Churchill had no authority to overrule a Secretary of State. All he could do was write and expostulate, pointing out in a letter to Lloyd on the following day that twenty thousand 'sorely needed' British and Australian troops were tied up in Palestine. 'This is the price we have to pay for the anti-Jewish policy which has been persisted in for some years. Should things go badly in Egypt all these troops will have to be withdrawn. The position of the Jewish Colonists will be one of the gravest danger. It is little less than a scandal at a time when we are fighting for our lives that these very large forces should be immobilised in support of a policy which only commends itself to a section of the Conservative Party.'[8]

One of those in London in the autumn of 1940 was the Chairman of the Jewish Agency Executive, David Ben-Gurion, who had reached Britain from Palestine ten days before Churchill became Prime Minister. The impression that Churchill's leadership made on Ben-Gurion was profound. On 7 June, after the evacuation of the British Expeditionary Force from Dunkirk, he wrote to his wife about Churchill's radio broadcast after the evacuation: 'I know that you cannot stand against Hitler with speeches. Without planes and tank and bombs and cannons we will not destroy the "Mechanized Attila" . . . But Churchill's speech was undoubtedly the steadfast and stubborn persistence of the English nation to stand and fight to the end.'

The phrase 'Mechanized Attila' had been coined by the Jewish former French Prime Minister, Léon Blum, with whom Churchill had been much impressed in their meetings before the war.

Ben-Gurion understood the nature and the impact of Churchill's oratory, telling his wife in this same letter: 'Churchill did not find reassurance in false consolations. He did not hide the severity of the blow that befell the Allies in Flanders: ". . . our thankfulness for

---

8 Minute of 28 June 1940: Premier papers, 3/348.

the escape of our Army – must not blind us to the fact that what happened in France and Belgium is a colossal military disaster." Only a great man who believes in his strength can allow himself to say such bitter words – and before the entire nation. And it was this brave statement that gave meaning and importance to the things he said immediately afterwards – that England would fight until it wins, would fight for years, would fight alone – if it needs to! And the words with which he finished his speech will ring in the ears of the world for years to come.'

Ben-Gurion then quoted those words, which were indeed to be among the most memorable of Churchill's war utterances, that the British Empire and the French Republic, 'linked together in their cause and in their needs, will defend to the death their native soil, aiding each other like good comrades to the utmost of their strength. We shall fight on the seas and oceans, we shall fight with growing confidence and growing strength in the air, we shall defend our island whatever the cost may be, we shall fight on the beaches, we shall fight on the landing grounds, we shall fight in the fields and in the streets, we shall fight in the hills; we shall never surrender, and even if, which I do not for a moment believe, this island or a large part of it were subjugated and starving, then our Empire beyond the seas, armed and guarded by the British Fleet, would carry on the struggle, until in God's good time, the New World, with all its power and might, steps forth to the rescue and the liberation of the Old.'[9]

These words, Ben-Gurion told his wife, 'were not merely a jest. This is the spirit of the rebellious England, and in it a guarantee for better days – even if not the soonest.'[10]

On 8 August Ben-Gurion wrote to his wife again: 'And how great is this nation that found a suitable leader in this terrible hour – and at the right moment, and one could say that if England – and with it all of humanity, were to survive the Nazi disaster – it would be due only to the rule of democracy and freedom that has taken root so

9 Parliamentary Debates, *Hansard*, 4 June 1940.
10 Letter of 7 June 1940: Ben-Gurion Archive.

deeply. It's hard to describe how much England has changed. Since Churchill inherited Chamberlain's place, the silent and confident bravery beating in every Englishman's heart is the fruit of this exchange.'[11]

The memory of Churchill's leadership in 1940 was to inspire Ben-Gurion himself eight years later, when he led a nation likewise believed by many inside it – and out – to be on the verge of destruction.[12] In a letter to Churchill sixteen years after the end of the war, Ben-Gurion wrote of how, in London, from the beginning of May until September 1940, 'I heard the historic speeches in which you gave utterance to the iron determination of your people and yourself to fight to the end against the Nazi foe. I saw you then not only as the symbol of your people and its greatness, but as the voice of the invincible and uncompromising conscience of the human race at a time of danger to the dignity of man, created in the image of God. It was not only the liberties and the honour of your own people that you saved.'[13]

On 20 August, in the course of one of his most stirring wartime speeches, Churchill declared that from the moment the Germans 'drove the Jews out' – and thereby lowered their 'technical standards' – 'our science is definitely ahead of theirs.'[14] Churchill knew the contribution the German Jewish refugees had made. Some of the first of them had been brought to Britain from Germany following his own meeting with Einstein in the spring of 1933. Churchill also appreciated the Jewish military contribution to the British war effort at this time of grave danger to Britain. In September, fifteen battalions of Palestinian Jews, almost 20,000 men – all volunteers – were incorporated into the British Army and sent to join the defence of Egypt against Italian and German attack.

From the outbreak of the war in September 1939, tens of thousands of 'enemy aliens' had been arrested and interned in Britain.

---

11 Letter of 8 August 1940: Ben-Gurion Archive.
12 David Ben-Gurion, in conversation with the author, 1971.
13 Letter of 2 October 1961: Churchill papers, 2/506.
14 Parliamentary Debates, *Hansard*, 20 August 1940.

Some were German Nazis then resident in Britain, some were German anti-Nazi refugees, and others were German citizens who happened to be in Britain when war broke out, including many German and Austrian Jews, among them Churchill's pre-war supporter Eugen Spier. Fears of a German parachute landing, and of a fifth column that would support the invaders behind the lines, meant that an immediate, all-encompassing, unselective action was needed. At the beginning of August, when the threat of parachute landings had receded, Churchill told the War Cabinet that, with Britain's position 'considerably more secure than in May', it should be possible 'to take a somewhat less rigid attitude in regard to the internment of aliens.'[15] A day later, he authorised the liberation 'of considerable numbers' of the internees, 'now that we are feeling a good deal firmer on our feet,' as he explained on 2 August to the chairman of the Council of Aliens.[16]

Churchill encouraged those internees who were released to join the British Army. Many did so, fighting on the war fronts as they opened up, and volunteering for missions behind German lines, where their fluency in German would be both a protection and a source of intelligence information.

On 15 September, a wave of Italian warplanes bombed Tel Aviv. There were five military deaths: four British and one Australian soldier. Ninety-five Jews, all civilians, were also killed, fifty-eight of them children. As soon as Churchill was told of the raid, he telegraphed to the Mayor of Tel Aviv, the city he had visited two decades earlier: 'Please accept my deep sympathy in losses sustained by Tel Aviv in recent air attack. This act of senseless brutality will only strengthen our united resolve.'[17]

On 20 November 1940 Churchill received details from the Jewish Agency of the situation of those Jews, the 'illegal' immigrants, who

---

15 War Cabinet Minutes, 1 August 1940: Cabinet papers, 65/14.
16 Letter of 2 August 1940, to the Earl of Lytton: Churchill papers, 20/6.
17 Telegram to Israel Rokach, 15 September 1940: Churchill papers, 20/14.

had been deported by the British authorities in Palestine to the British colonial island of Mauritius, in the Indian Ocean, where they were kept in strict confinement. He took immediate steps to make sure that their detention was less onerous, writing that day to the Secretary of State for the Colonies, Lord Lloyd: 'I had never contemplated the Jewish refugees being interned in Mauritius in a camp surrounded by barbed wire and guards. It is very unlikely that these refugees would include enemy agents, and I should expect that the Jewish authorities themselves, as Weizmann can assure you, would be most efficient and vigilant purgers in this respect.'

Churchill added that deportation to Mauritius, on which Lloyd had insisted, 'should be confined to future illegal immigrants', and that those in Palestine, 'after careful vetting, be allowed to stay.'[18] On 22 November Churchill wrote again to Lloyd: 'As the action has been announced, it must proceed, but the conditions in Mauritius must not involve these people being caged-up for the duration of the war. The Cabinet will require to be satisfied about this.'[19]

That autumn, in Germany, a Committee for Sending Jews Overseas, organised by an SS lieutenant, Adolf Eichmann, had chartered three ships in Romania, on which a total of 3,600 Jews, most of them from Germany, Austria and Czechoslovakia, left the Romanian Black Sea port of Tulcia in September 1940 and arrived in Palestine separately, starting on 1 November. The SS aim was to embarrass the British Government by sending Jews to Palestine who did not have the necessary immigration certificates. Following the pre-war policy laid down by Neville Chamberlain's Cabinet, each ship was intercepted by the Royal Navy. Its passengers were then transferred to a fourth ship, the *Patria*, for transport to the British Indian Ocean island of Mauritius, where they would be interned with the other 'illegals' already aboard.

The *Patria* was a pre-First World War French ship that had been seized by the British in Haifa harbour in June 1940, after the

18 Minute of 20 November 1940: Churchill papers, 20/13.
19 Minute of 22 November 1940: Churchill papers, 20/13.

French-German armistice. It was about to leave Haifa, with 1,972 of the recently arrived illegals on board, when it was blown up in Haifa harbour. The explosive charge had been set by the Haganah, the Jewish Agency's military arm, with the aim of preventing the ship from sailing. The charge had proved more devastating than intended. The British Commander-in-Chief in the Middle East, General Wavell, telegraphed to the Secretary of State for War that the survivors of the explosion, which had killed 267 of the refugees, must still be shipped to Mauritius.

In this telegram, Wavell warned that if the survivors of the explosion were allowed to stay in Palestine 'it will be spread all over Arab world that Jews have again successfully challenged decision of British Government and that policy of White Paper is being reversed. This will gravely increase prospect of widespread disorders in Palestine.'[20]

Wavell's telegram was seen by Churchill, who replied to it himself: 'Personally, I hold it would be an act of inhumanity unworthy of British name to force them to re-embark.' In instructing Wavell to let the refugees stay in Palestine, Churchill commented: 'I hope at least that you will believe that the views I have expressed are not dictated by fear of violence.'[21]

As a result of Churchill's intervention, the *Patria* survivors were allowed to remain in Palestine. But the Cabinet was equally insistent that in future all illegals who were intercepted should be sent to Mauritius. Churchill agreed, 'provided', as he had insisted two weeks earlier, 'these refugees are not sent back to the torments from which they have escaped and are decently treated.'[22] When the European war ended, the deportees in Mauritius were allowed to leave: eighty per cent chose to go to Palestine and were admitted without delay.

The issue of illegal immigration was again on the Cabinet agenda on Christmas Eve, when ministers argued in favour of the strictest measures against those illegal immigrants who were caught

20 Telegram of 30 November 1940: Premier papers, 4/51/2.
21 Telegram of 2 December 1940: Premier papers, 4/51/2.
22 Handwritten note, 14 November 1940: Premier papers, 4/51/1.

as they tried to land on the soil of the Jewish National Home. But Churchill informed the Commonwealth Governments that the British Government 'have also to consider their promises to the Zionists, and to be guided by general considerations of humanity towards those fleeing from the cruellest forms of persecution.'[23]

Having received this clear indication of Churchill's attitude, Sir John Shuckburgh, the former head of Churchill's Middle East Department, who had become Permanent Under-Secretary of State at the Colonial Office, took steps to avoid the Prime Minister's scrutiny of his department's actions. He did this by not informing Churchill of the suspension of the quota. On 24 December, Shuckburgh told his departmental colleagues: 'Our object is to keep the business as far as possible on the normal administrative plane and outside the realms of Cabinet policy and so forth.'[24] As a result of this civil service decision, Churchill was not informed when, soon afterwards, the quota for April to September 1941 was also suspended, and no immigration certificates were issued for that period either.

Churchill's Cabinet colleagues looked askance at his contrasting attitude to Jews and Arabs. On 9 January 1941 news reached the Colonial Office from the Governor of Aden that there was jubilation in the colony as a result of a British victory over the Italians at Bardia in North Africa, and that photographs of Churchill as 'the Victorious Vizier' were in great demand.[25] Lord Lloyd asked his officials to write to Churchill's Principal Private Secretary, John Martin: 'Lord Lloyd thinks that the Prime Minister might like to see that some Arabs have virtue in them.'[26] The word 'some' was underlined. Martin showed the note to Churchill, who noted on it: 'I have been one of the best friends the Arabs ever had, and have set up Arab rulers in Transjordania and Iraq which still exist.'[27]

*

23 Telegram of 24 December 1940: Premier papers, 4/51/1.
24 Minute of 24 December 1940: Colonial Office papers, 733/419.
25 Telegram sent on 8 January 1941, received 9 January: Churchill papers, 20/32.
26 Letter of 10 January 1941: Churchill papers, 20/32.
27 Handwritten note, 11 January 1941: Churchill papers, 20/32.

In German-occupied Poland, the Jews were being confined to ghettos and reduced to penury and starvation. From Romania, one of Germany's allies, news of the imminent killing of Jews by members of the fascist Iron Guard reached London at the end of January 1941. Churchill felt that a protest should be made at once to the Romanian dictator, Ion Antonescu, and advised Anthony Eden, the Foreign Secretary: 'Would it not be well to tell General Antonescu that we will hold him and his immediate circle personally responsible in life and limb if such a vile act is perpetrated?' Churchill added, 'Perhaps you may think of something more diplomatic than this.'[28] In fact, the killings had taken place before Churchill had been told that they were imminent: in sadistic fury, the Iron Guard had hunted down and killed several hundred Jews, injuring thousands more, and looting hundreds of shops and homes.

Despite the Palestinian Jewish battalions that had been formed, Dr Weizmann still wanted a specifically Jewish force, with its own insignia and flag, to serve as an integral part of the British Army. Weizmann hoped for a complete division of 12,000 men. Churchill was supportive, but General Wavell was opposed, arguing, as he had when the refugees on the *Patria* were about to be allowed to stay in Palestine, that this would create anger and protest in the Arab world. Churchill was indignant, writing to the new Colonial Secretary, Lord Moyne, on 1 March: 'General Wavell, like most British military officers, is strongly pro-Arab. At the time of the licences to the shipwrecked illegal immigrants being permitted, he sent a telegram not less strong than this, predicting widespread disaster in the Arab world, together with the loss of the Basra-Baghdad-Haifa route. The telegram should be looked up, and also my answer, in which I overruled the General and explained to him the reason for the Cabinet decision. All went well and not a dog barked. It follows from the above that I am not in the least convinced by all this stuff': Wavell's fears that any favour shown to the Jews in Palestine would lead to the whole Arab world turning against Britain.' Churchill

28 Minute of 1 February 1941: Premier papers, 3/374/13A.

added that the Arabs, under the impression of recent British victories, 'will not make trouble now.'

With Wavell about to oversee a desperately risky British military commitment to Greece, Churchill did not feel able to overrule him. The Jewish army project was put off for six months, but, Churchill wrote, it 'may be reconsidered again in four months.'[29] For the War Office and the Colonial Office, however, this postponement provided an excuse for a far longer delay.

When Churchill saw Weizmann on 12 March, he told the Zionist leader that there was no need for a long conversation as their thoughts were '99 per cent identical.' Churchill added that whenever he saw him it gave him 'a twist in his heart'. He would have to postpone the Jewish military force, he said, but stressed that he would not let Weizmann down.

One of those 'other matters' was the post-war future of the Jewish community in Palestine. Churchill believed he could persuade the existing independent Arab States to accept a Jewish State in their midst, once Germany and Italy – the persistent stimulators of Arab unrest – had been defeated. 'At the end of our conversation,' Weizmann noted, 'the PM said that he was thinking of a settlement between us and the Arabs after the war. The man with whom we should come to an agreement is Ibn Saud. He said the PM would see to it and would use his good offices.' Ibn Saud 'would be made the Lord of the Arab countries', the 'Boss of the Bosses' was how Churchill expressed it. But Churchill added, as Weizmann noted, that Ibn Saud 'would have to agree with Weizmann (he put it that way) with regard to Palestine.'[30]

The issue of arming the Jews inside Palestine arose again as German and Italian forces advanced deep into Egypt, threatening to reach the Suez Canal. At the same time, Churchill knew from his most secret sources that Germany was putting pressure on Turkey to allow the passage of German troops through Turkey, thus threatening

29 Letter of 1 March 1941: Churchill papers, 20/36.

30 'Note of a conversation', 12 March 1941: Yad Chaim Weizmann, Weizmann Archive.

Palestine from the north. On 10 May, a year to the day after he had become Prime Minister, Churchill wrote to Moyne's successor as Colonial Secretary, Viscount Cranborne – 'I have always been most strongly in favour of making sure that the Jews have proper means of self-defence for their Colonies in Palestine. The more you can get done in this line, the safer we shall be.'[31]

With the danger of German forces moving south through neutral Turkey and north from Egypt in a pincer attack on Palestine, the Jewish community was encouraged by the British to prepare a plan of self-defence, and to build fortifications on the crest of Mount Carmel, high above Haifa, to face the attackers whether they came from the north or the south.

Three years before the 1939 White Paper's intended permanent Arab majority in Palestine was due to take effect, Churchill began his plans to prevent it coming to pass. On 19 May 1941 he dictated a note for the War Cabinet that at the time of giving 'very great advancements to the Arab world' – postwar independence for both Syria and Lebanon – 'we should, of course, negotiate with Ibn Saud a satisfactory settlement of the Jewish problem; and, if such a basis were reached, it is possible that the Jewish State of Western Palestine might form an independent Federal Unit in the Arab Caliphate.' Churchill added: 'This Jewish State would have to have the fullest rights of self-government, including immigration and development, and provision for expansion in the desert regions to the southward, which they would gradually reclaim.'[32]

The southward desert region was the largely uninhabited Negev, home to small numbers of Bedouin nomads, an area Churchill had long believed ought to be developed by the Jews, and about which Weizmann had first written to him more than twenty years earlier.

The future of the Jewish community in Palestine was again in Churchill's mind during his first wartime meeting with President

31 Letter of 10 May 1941: Churchill papers, 20/36.
32 Cabinet memorandum, 19 May 1941: Cabinet papers, 120/10.

Roosevelt in August 1941. On 20 August, the President presented Churchill with the Atlantic Charter, his vision of the postwar world. Under this, Britain and the United States would pledge themselves 'to respect the right of all peoples to choose the form of government under which they will live.'[33] Churchill supported such a promise, but not with regard to the Arabs of Palestine, explaining to Roosevelt that 'the Arabs might claim by majority that they could expel the Jews from Palestine, or at any rate forbid all future immigration.' Churchill added, by way of explanation of his concern: 'I am strongly wedded to the Zionist policy, of which I was one of the authors.'[34]

Roosevelt was not swayed, but Churchill persevered. At a meeting of the War Cabinet on 2 October he insisted that if Britain and the United States 'emerged victorious from the war, the creation of a great Jewish State in Palestine would inevitably be one of the matters to be discussed at the Peace Conference.' Not all Churchill's Cabinet colleagues shared his vision. During this meeting the Colonial Secretary Lord Moyne reported that Weizmann and other members of the Zionist Organisation, 'were making increasingly large claims as to the possibilities of Jewish immigration after the war.' Weizmann had recently suggested 'that at least three million Jews should be absorbed comparatively quickly into Palestine.' This, Moyne told the War Cabinet, was 'impracticable, and he thought that the time had come when we should say something to prevent our silence being taken as evidence of assent to these increasing claims.'

In response to Moyne's remarks, Churchill told the War Cabinet that he was 'disposed to doubt the need for a public reply to these claims, but thought that perhaps a private warning might be given.' In a remark that was to be at variance with his own hostile policy towards Jewish immigration after the war, Ernest Bevin, Minister of Labour and National Service, said that 'if an autonomous Jewish

---

33 'Joint Declaration by the President and the Prime Minister', 12 August 1941: Premier papers, 3/485/7; widely reproduced in the British and American newspapers.

34 Prime Minister's Personal Minute, 20 August 1941: Churchill papers, 20/36.

State could be set up, the question of regulating the flow of immigration thereto would be a matter to be settled by the authorities of that State. This would greatly ease our difficulties in the matter.'[35] For a brief moment, Churchill, and one of his future opponents on the question of future Jewish statehood, were in agreement.

35 War Cabinet Minutes, 2 October 1941: Cabinet papers, 65/19.

CHAPTER SEVENTEEN

'THESE VILE CRIMES'

On 21 June 1941 the armed might of Germany turned against the Soviet Union. As the German Army advanced, SS killing squads began the systematic mass murder of Jews in every captured town and village. Top-secret German police radio messages about this, and about the mass murder of non-Jewish Soviet citizens, were intercepted by British Intelligence, and shown to Churchill. He had to be careful not to reveal his source, for fear of alerting the Germans to the fact that their most secret communications – including many of their daily military, naval and air force instructions – were being read by the code-breakers at Bletchley Park. Although he could not therefore mention Jews directly, Churchill, in his broadcast on 24 August when speaking about German atrocities in Russia, stated without prevarication that 'whole districts are being exterminated.' He added, 'We are in the presence of a crime without a name.'[1]

That crime continued. On 27 August Churchill was shown a German police decrypt reporting the execution of 367 Jews in South Russia; on 1 September a report of the shooting of 1,246 Jews; on 6 September of the shooting of 3,000 Jews; on 11 September, more than five thousand Jews near Kamenets-Podolsk. Churchill was informed that day by Bletchley Park: 'The fact that the Police are killing all Jews that fall into their hands should by now be sufficiently well appreciated. It is not therefore proposed to continue reporting these butcheries specially, unless so requested.'[2] In fact, the murder

---

1 Broadcast of 24 August 1941: Churchill papers, 9/152.
2 National Archives records, HW1/30, 35, 40 and 51.

later that month of more than 33,000 Jews at Babi Yar near Kiev was not known at Bletchley Park, as the German police units in Russia had been warned from Berlin not to compromise their ciphers. But within two months of Churchill's broadcast, sufficient details of the mass killing of Jews had become known through sources other than Germany's own top-secret radio signals. Churchill took advantage of this on 14 November, when he sent a personal and signed message to the *Jewish Chronicle*, which the weekly newspaper printed in full.

'None has suffered more cruelly than the Jew,' Churchill wrote, 'the unspeakable evils wrought on the bodies and spirits of men by Hitler and his vile regime. The Jew bore the brunt of the Nazi's first onslaught upon the citadels of freedom and human dignity. He has borne and continues to bear a burden that might have seemed to be beyond endurance. He has not allowed it to break his spirit; he has never lost the will to resist. Assuredly in the day of victory the Jew's sufferings and his part in the struggle will not be forgotten. Once again, at the appointed time, he will see vindicated those principles of righteousness which it was the glory of his fathers to proclaim to the world.'[3]

On 7 December 1941 the Japanese attacked both United States and British possessions in the Far East and the Pacific Ocean. Four days later, as the United States faced formidable setbacks in the Pacific, Hitler declared war on her: the country that had tenaciously declined to declare war on him for more than two years, despite his conquests and wide-ranging destruction. Churchill, travelling by sea to Washington, secured an American commitment to seek the defeat of Hitler before that of the Japanese. The 'swell of victory and liberation,' he told the House of Commons on his return from Washington, was 'bearing us and all the tortured peoples onwards safely towards the final goal.'[4]

Then, as in the months and years ahead, as the Allies struggled

3 *Jewish Chronicle*, 14 November 1941.
4 Parliamentary Debates, *Hansard*, 27 January 1942.

to come to grips with a determined, relentless enemy, the fate of those 'tortured peoples', including the Jews, but also Poles, Czechs, Serbs and Greeks, was first and foremost dependent on the ability of the Allies – principally the British, Americans and Soviets – to halt the onward march of German power, and then, at great cost to themselves in the lives of their soldiers, sailors and airmen, to drive the invader back from his mastery of Europe – mastery which, in December 1941, extended from the Atlantic coast of France to the Baltic Sea and the Black Sea.

On 11 February 1942, Chaim Weizmann's younger son, twenty-five-year-old Flight Lieutenant Michael Weizmann, Royal Air Force Volunteer Reserve, was shot down over the Bay of Biscay. His body was never found, and Weizmann asked Churchill to try to find out if, by chance, he has managed to get ashore in Spain and had been interned, or been taken prisoner of war. Churchill did what he could, but there was nothing to report.[5]

In Churchill's mind, the Jewish fate in Europe and the Jewish future in Palestine were inextricably linked. Greatly unwelcome to those who had created the 1939 White Paper policy – many of them his wartime colleagues – were his interventions to allow Jewish immigrants to remain in Palestine when their lack of Palestine Certificates made them subject to deportation. When he discovered, on 2 February 1942 – alerted to the fact by his son Randolph – that 793 illegal immigrants who had reached the coast of Palestine on board the *Darien*, and been interned in a camp in Palestine, were about to be deported to Mauritius, he instructed Lord Moyne to release the refugees from internment and allow them to remain in Palestine. Churchill pointed out that up to the time that the decision to deport the *Darien* refugees had been taken: 'It looked as if we should be

5 Today, Michael Weizmann's name is on the Runnymede Memorial to the 20,337 British and Commonwealth airmen lost in the Second World War during operations from the United Kingdom and northern and western Europe, who have no known grave.

subjected to a wave of illegal immigration, but now that the whole of south-eastern Europe is in German hands, there is no further danger of this.'[6]

Lord Moyne was not convinced, writing to Churchill on 7 February: 'Any relaxation of our deterrent measures is likely to encourage further shipments of the same kind.' The fate of the *Darien* passengers, Moyne insisted, would be a test case of the government's determination to adhere to their proclaimed policy, and any concessions would cause great damage to the British Government's 'reputation in the Middle East for trustworthiness and firmness.'[7]

Churchill persevered, and the *Darien* passengers were allowed to remain in Palestine. But at a meeting on 5 March the War Cabinet insisted on laying down, as a basic principle of British policy, that: 'All practicable steps should be taken to discourage illegal immigration into Palestine.'[8] Entrenched policies and prejudices were impossible to dislodge, yet Churchill never gave up in the battle for his Palestine policy. It was still two years before the 1939 White Paper would come into effect, with its automatic Arab majority, putting an end to all Jewish hopes of sovereignty. On 27 April 1942, in a War Cabinet memorandum, he informed his colleagues with stark brevity: 'I cannot in any circumstances, contemplate an absolute cessation of immigration into Palestine at the discretion of the Arab majority.' Churchill suggested not only a future Jewish self-governing regime in Palestine, but, in addition, turning two former Italian colonies, Eritrea on the Red Sea and Tripolitania (part of today's Libya) on the Mediterranean, 'into Jewish colonies, affiliated, if desired, to the National Home in Palestine.'[9]

At no point during his wartime premiership were Churchill's sympathies to Zionist aspirations shared by the majority of his Cabinet. Oliver Harvey, Anthony Eden's Private Secretary, noted in

---

6 Prime Minister's Personal Minute: Premier papers, 1/51/1.
7 Minute of 7 February 1942: Colonial Office papers, 733/446/76021.
8 War Cabinet Minutes, 5 March 1942: Cabinet papers 65/25.
9 Cabinet papers, 66/36.

his diary that year, about the Foreign Secretary: 'Unfortunately AE is immovable on the subject of Palestine. He loves Arabs and hates Jews.'[10]

For two years the main focus of the British war effort was to avoid defeat, invasion, and destruction from the German air bombardment. By mid-1942 the tide was turning. Determined British efforts on land, at sea and in the air, and Churchill's own daily endeavours, searched for every means of weakening the German war machine until such a time as the liberation of Europe could begin. On 5 July, as the fighting raged in North Africa, Churchill wrote to the Colonial Secretary, Lord Cranborne, with regard to the creation of a Jewish militia in Palestine, a scheme still opposed by both the War Office and the Colonial Office: 'Now that these people are in direct danger,' Churchill wrote to Cranborne, 'we should certainly give them a chance to defend themselves.'

On an even more sensitive matter, Churchill went on to warn Cranborne: 'It may be necessary to make an example of these anti-Semite officers and others in high places. If three or four of them were recalled and dismissed, and the reasons given, it would have a salutary effect.'[11] These were strong words, proof to many of Churchill's colleagues that he was, indeed – in the words of General Spears – 'too fond of Jews.' Indeed, Churchill went so far, that September, as to warn Spears himself – then British Minister-Resident in Lebanon – 'against drifting into the usual anti-Zionist and anti-Semitic channel which it is customary for British officers to follow.' Spears had opposed what Churchill described as 'my old idea of four States in a Confederation, of which three were Arab and one Jewish.'[12]

No anti-Semitic officers were dismissed, nor would the Cabinet Ministers concerned withdraw their opposition to a specifically

10 Diary entry, 24 April 1943: *Diaries and Papers of Oliver Harvey (Lord Harvey of Tasburgh)*, page 249.
11 Minute of 5 July 1942: Premier papers, 4/51/9.
12 Prime Minister's Personal Minute, 10 September 1942: Premier papers 4/52/5.

Jewish military force. On 6 August, however, after the British and Commonwealth forces had been forced back deep into Egypt by Rommel's Desert Army, there were calls throughout Palestine for Jewish and Arab volunteers, and a Palestine Regiment was established. Enough volunteers came forward to form three Jewish battalions and one Arab battalion, all wearing British insignia. After several weeks of intense training in Palestine, they were sent across the Suez Canal to the battle zone.

In German-dominated Europe, the deportation of Jews to their deaths in distant camps in German-occupied Poland, deportations that had begun in July 1942, was reaching a crescendo. On 7 September 1942, *The Times* reported the 'unabated ruthlessness' of the round-up of Jews in France by Vichy French police. Women and children, it stated, were 'suddenly notified' that they could visit their relatives in various internment camps, and were then 'forced to accompany the deportees without being given any opportunity to make preparations.' Recently 'a train containing 4,000 Jewish children, unaccompanied, without identification papers or even distinguishing marks, left Lyons for Germany.'[13] The destination in Germany was known, both to *The Times* and to Churchill, only as 'somewhere in Poland'. Their destination was in fact Auschwitz, although this was not known either in France or by the Allied nations.

Churchill reacted immediately. Speaking in the House of Commons on the day after the report in *The Times*, he pointed out that the 'brutal persecutions' in which the Germans had indulged 'in every land into which their armies have broken' had been augmented by 'the most bestial, the most squalid and the most senseless of all their offences, namely, the mass deportation of Jews from France, with the pitiful horrors attendant upon the calculated and final scattering of families.' Churchill added: 'This tragedy fills me with astonishment as well as with indignation, and it illustrates as

---

13 *The Times*, 7 September 1942.

nothing else can the utter degradation of the Nazi nature and theme, and the degradation of all who lend themselves to its unnatural and perverted passions.' Pausing for a moment, Churchill declared: 'When the hour of liberation strikes in Europe, as strike it will, it will also be the hour of retribution.'[14]

Britain redoubled its efforts to drive Hitler from his conquests. In September 1942 the war was being waged in the Atlantic Ocean, in the Western Desert, and in the air above Germany night after night, relentlessly, to the limit of the bombers' range. At the same time, Churchill was determined to find a way to land on European soil and begin the liberation of the continent. It was to involve almost two years of intense planning before the Normandy landings could take place.

In the autumn of 1942 more details reached the West about the mass murder of Jews in camps set up for that purpose on occupied Polish soil – Treblinka, Chelmno, Sobibor and Belzec – camps that lay far beyond the limits of Britain's bombers. On 29 October at the Albert Hall in London, Christian and Jewish leaders led a public protest against the massacres. Churchill, who was then in the United States, sent a letter to be read out by William Temple, the newly appointed Archbishop of Canterbury. 'I cannot refrain,' Churchill wrote, 'from sending, through you, to the audience which is assembling under your Chairmanship at the Albert Hall today to protest against Nazi atrocities inflicted on the Jews, the assurance of my warm sympathy with the objects of the meeting. The systematic cruelties to which the Jewish people – men, women, and children – have been exposed under the Nazi régime are amongst the most terrible events of history, and place an indelible stain upon all who perpetrate and instigate them. Free men and women denounce these vile crimes, and when this world struggle ends with the enthronement of human rights, racial persecution will be ended.'[15]

Three days later, from Washington, on the twenty-fifth anniversary

14 Speech of 8 September 1942: *Hansard.*
15 *Jewish Chronicle,* 6 November 1942.

of the Balfour Declaration, Churchill sent a telegram to Weizmann: 'My thoughts are with you on this anniversary. Better days will surely come for your suffering people and for the great cause for which you have fought so bravely.'[16] That great cause was Zionism. That day, Churchill also sent a message to the *Jewish Chronicle*, re-iterating and adding to his message of a year earlier: 'None has suffered more cruelly than the Jew the unspeakable evils wrought on the bodies and spirits of men by Hitler and his vile regime. The Jew bore the brunt of the Nazis' first onslaught upon the citadels of freedom and human dignity. Assuredly in the day of victory, the Jews' sufferings and his part in the struggle will not be forgotten. Once again, at the appointed time, he will see vindicated those principles of righteousness which it was the glory of his fathers to proclaim to the world. Once again, it will be shown that, though the mills of God grind slowly, yet they grind exceeding small.'[17]

That winter the Jewish Agency in Jerusalem asked that 4,500 Bulgarian Jewish children, with five hundred accompanying adults, should be allowed to leave Bulgaria for Palestine. The new Colonial Secretary, Oliver Stanley, put the request to Churchill, pointing out that British public opinion had been 'much roused by recent reports of the systematic extermination of the Jews in Axis and Axis-controlled countries.'[18] Churchill replied to Stanley's request: 'Bravo!' and he added, 'But why not obtain, as you will, the hearty endorsement of the War Cabinet?' Churchill had already arranged for the rescue effort to be put on the War Cabinet agenda.[19]

Thus encouraged by Churchill, Stanley successfully approached the Turkish Government to allow transit through Turkey. Before the arrangements could be finalised, the British Government offered to take a further 29,000 Jews, children and their adult escorts, from throughout South-Eastern Europe. These would come within the existing 1939 White Paper numbers – including

16 Telegram of 2 November 1942: Weizmann papers.
17 *Jewish Chronicle*, 2 November 1942.
18 Letter of 9 December 1942: Colonial Office papers, 733/438/1.
19 Minute of 11 December 1942: Premier papers, 4/51/2.

the 25,000 emergency certificates – and could thus be justified, in the words of the Foreign Office, to 'Moslem and Arab opinion'. Once more, the Turkish Government agreed to safe passage.[20] It was his 'most urgent desire,' Oliver Stanley wrote to a Member of Parliament as the project seemed to falter, 'that everything possible should be done to give effect to these immigration schemes with promptitude and alacrity.'[21] But a telegram from Clifford Norton, the senior British diplomat in Switzerland, a key neutral listening post, stated that the rescue plans had 'come to the ears of the Germans who are successfully insisting on a stiffer line.'[22]

German intervention had been stimulated by the Mufti of Jerusalem, Haj Amin al-Husseini, who, having fled from Palestine in 1938 to avoid arrest by the British for his part in the Arab revolt, was then in Berlin. Determined to keep Jews from Palestine, on 12 May Haj Amin asked Hitler to press the Bulgarian Government not to allow the children to leave. His intervention was effective. On 27 May Clifford Norton reported from Berne that the Bulgarian Government 'have now decided, clearly under German pressure,' to close the Bulgarian-Turkish frontier 'to all Jews.'[23]

In December 1942, Churchill was shown a report from a Polish courier, Jan Karski, a Roman Catholic member of the Resistance, who had made his way to Britain. Karski described how he had seen several thousand Jews being forced with great brutality by heavily armed SS men into the cattle cars of a train for an unknown but clearly horrendous destination: in fact to the death camp at Belzec. Karski's account, widely publicised, and broadcast over the BBC, was recognised as a culminating truth towards which, since the summer, many fragmentary pieces reaching the West, had contributed.

---

20 Foreign Office telegram of 2 February 1943: Colonial Office papers, 733/438/1.
21 Letter of 29 March 1943: Colonial Office papers, 733/438/2.
22 Telegram of 7 May 1943: Colonial Office papers, 733/438/2.
23 Telegram of 27 May 1943: Colonial Office papers, 733/438/3. Haj Amin's request to Hitler is in the Nuremberg Trial documents, NG 2757.

Jewish and Christian leaders in Britain pressed for a public statement by the Allies that would tell the world that the fate of the Jews was something beyond the normal cruelties of war; that it was a deliberate attempt not only to destroy Jews in vast numbers, but to kill every Jew in Europe within SS grasp. In the War Cabinet, Anthony Eden supported a public declaration. 'It was known,' he said, reporting the most recent information to reach London, 'that Jews were being transferred to Poland from enemy-occupied countries, for example Norway; and it might be that these transfers were being made with a view to wholesale extermination of Jews.'[24]

When issued on 17 December 1942 from London, Washington and Moscow simultaneously, and widely broadcast, the impact of the Allied Declaration was, as Churchill wished, considerable. Its central paragraph united not only Britain, the Soviet Union and the United States, but also the eight Governments-in-Exile – those of Belgium, Czechoslovakia, Greece, Luxembourg, Holland, Norway, Poland and Yugoslavia – as well as General de Gaulle's French National Committee, in condemnation 'in the strongest possible terms' of what it described as 'this bestial policy of cold-blooded extermination.'

In describing the deportations the declaration was graphic: 'None of those taken away are ever heard of again,' it stated. 'The infirm are left to die of exposure and starvation or are deliberately massacred in mass executions.' The number of victims 'of these bloody cruelties' were 'reckoned in many hundreds of thousands of innocent men, women and children.'

One focus of the declaration was Churchill's call for retribution. Despite initial hesitation from Washington, which would have preferred the word 'alleged' to be placed before the word 'crimes', Churchill had insisted that the declaration make clear, not only that the Germans were pursuing a 'bestial policy of cold-blooded extermination', but that those committing these crimes against the Jews would be hunted down after the war and brought to trial.[25]

---

24 War Cabinet Minutes, 14 December 1942: Cabinet papers, 65/28.
25 Declaration of 17 December 1942, final text: Premier papers, 4/100/3.

After Eden read out the declaration in the House of Commons, James de Rothschild, speaking as a British Jew, said he hoped that, as broadcast by the BBC, the declaration might 'percolate throughout the German-infected countries,' and that, in doing so, it would give 'some faint hope and courage to the unfortunate victims of torment and insult and degradation.' Rothschild also hoped that when news of the declaration reached the Jews inside Europe, they would feel 'that they are supported and strengthened by the British government and by the other United Nations,' and that the Allies would 'continue to signify that they still uphold the dignity of man.'[26]

On the day of the Allied Declaration, the Women's International Zionist Organization (WIZO), founded in 1925, held a mass protest meeting at the Wigmore Hall, London. During the meeting a message was read out from Churchill's wife, Clementine, in which she wrote of Hitler's 'satanic design to exterminate the Jewish people in Europe,' and informed the assembled ladies: 'I wish to associate with you in all your grief, and I pray your meeting may help to keep the attention of the British people focused upon the terrible events which have occurred and are impending in Nazi Europe.'[27]

Amid all the pressing concerns of the war on land, at sea and in the air, and the desperate struggle to find the means to challenge the continuing Nazi domination of Europe, Churchill always made time to deal with Jewish issues. Only two weeks after the Allied Declaration, which gave such encouragement to the Jews that their fate was not forgotten, he supported a request by the Polish Government in London for air raids on Germany, with leaflets to be dropped at the same time as the bombs, 'warning the Germans,' Churchill informed his Chiefs of Staff Committee, 'that our attacks were reprisals for the persecution of the Poles and the Jews.' At their meeting on the evening of 31 December, he asked if it would be possible for the Royal Air Force to undertake 'two or three heavy raids' on Berlin during the first period of favourable weather in January.

---

26 Parliamentary Debates, *Hansard*, 17 December 1942.
27 Report in the *Palcor Bulletin*, 17 December 1942.

The Chief of the Air Staff, Sir Charles Portal, warned that any such raids 'avowedly conducted on account of the Jews would be an asset to enemy propaganda.'[28]

Churchill had no power to overrule his air chief on operational matters, but he continued to keep a vigilant eye on all Jewish issues. On 6 February 1943, after a five-hour flight to Algiers, from where the Vichy French authorities had been ejected three months earlier, he discovered that the Vichy laws against the Jews of Algeria were still in force there. He insisted they be repealed at once. This was done.[29]

Back in London from North Africa, at lunch with the Spanish Ambassador on 7 April, Churchill protested at the Spanish Government's closure of the Franco-Spanish frontier in the Pyrenees to Jewish refugees. Churchill told the Ambassador 'that if his Government went to the length of preventing these unfortunate people seeking safety from the horrors of Nazi domination, and if they went farther and committed the offence of actually handing them back to the German authorities, that was a thing which would never be forgotten and would poison the relations between the Spanish and British peoples.'[30]

Churchill was able to see, from intercepted diplomatic telegrams from the Spanish Ambassador in London to his government in Madrid, that the message was passed on. He also learned within a few days that the Spanish authorities had re-opened the border for Jewish refugees.

In April 1943 the Jews of Warsaw, faced with a renewal of the deportations that had begun the previous summer, rose up against the German occupation forces. The revolt, which took place far beyond the range of any possible Allied help, was crushed with the utmost severity and cruelty. Fifty years later, Churchill's grandson Winston – Randolph Churchill's son – was invited to London

28 Air Ministry papers, 8/433.
29 Churchill War Papers archive.
30 Interview of 7 April 1943: Cabinet papers, 66/36.

University to address an anniversary commemoration of the revolt. Following his speech a woman in the audience had approached him. At the time of the uprising, she said, 'I was a girl of just twelve. We had all been herded into the Ghetto – supposedly for our safety. But then people all around us started to disappear, we knew not where – we were all very frightened. We had one of the few radios in the Ghetto and, whenever your grandfather was due to broadcast on the BBC, my family and our friends would gather round. I could not understand English, but I knew that if I and my family had any hope of coming through this war alive, it depended upon that one, strong, unseen voice . . . I was the only member of my family to survive. I was liberated by British forces in 1945.'[31]

There were many calls in the British Parliament, and from Jews and their friends elsewhere, including the United States, for more to be done to give sanctuary to Jews who managed to escape the Nazis. The result of these calls was a conference held in Bermuda in May 1943. Taking the lead, Britain agreed to allow all Jewish refugees who had reached neutral Spain to cross the Straits of Gibraltar and be given sanctuary in Allied-controlled North Africa. When the United States Government opposed this, Churchill intervened directly with Roosevelt, telegraphing to the President that the 'need for assistance to refugees, in particular Jewish refugees, has not grown less since we discussed the question.' Churchill added: 'Our immediate facilities for helping the victims of Hitler's anti-Jewish drive are so limited at present that the opening of the small camp proposed for the purpose of removing some of them to safety seems all the more incumbent on us.'[32]

Churchill's initiative was successful; many hundreds of Jewish refugees from Nazism, who were being held in detention camps in Spain, made their way to a safe haven. But the number of refugees

---

31 Winston Churchill (Churchill's grandson), talk at London University on the fiftieth anniversary of the Warsaw Ghetto uprising, April 1993: Winston Churchill papers.
32 Telegram of 30 June 1943: Premier papers, 4/51/4.

able to escape Nazi-dominated Europe was minimal. If more had been able to leave, there were still 33,000 unused Palestine Certificates within the 1939 White Paper quota. From 1 April 1939 to 31 March 1943 the total number of Jews reaching Palestine both legally and illegally had been 41,169. This left 33,831 certificates still unused.[33]

At the end of June 1943 the distinguished Socialist thinker, Harold Laski – the son of Churchill's Manchester friend Nathan Laski – sent a letter to Churchill, complaining that in a recent speech Churchill had made no reference to the Jews. 'Although in my speech at the Guildhall,' Churchill replied, 'I referred only to the wrongs inflicted by Hitler on the Sovereign States of Europe, I have never forgotten the terrible sufferings inflicted on the Jews; and I am constantly thinking by what means it may lie in our power to alleviate them, both during the war and in the permanent settlement which must follow it.'[34]

By the summer of 1943 as many as two and a half million of Poland's three and a half million Jews had been killed. A further million Jews in western Russia and the Baltic States had likewise been murdered. The deportations from Western Europe to death camps in the East continued. On 24 July at the Prime Minister's country residence, Chequers, Churchill gave supper to the British air ace, Guy Gibson, and his wife Eve.

Gibson was about to embark on a goodwill mission to Canada and the United States. 'We were shown a film, captured from the Germans,' Eve Gibson later wrote, 'depicting the atrocities inflicted on the Jews and the inhabitants of occupied countries. It was quite ghastly and the Prime Minister was very, very moved. He told me that it was shown to every American serviceman arriving in this country.'[35] Some of these were airmen who would be bombing Germany

---

33 Statistical summary: Colonial Office papers, 733/436.
34 Letter of 5 July 1943: Premier papers, 4/51/8.
35 Letter to the author from Eve Gibson, 17 May 1980. Guy Gibson was killed in action in September 1944.

day after day without respite. Others were soldiers who had begun training for the cross-Channel landings, less than a year away.

Churchill cast about for whatever means were possible to impede or halt the German atrocities. It might, he told the War Cabinet, have a 'salutary effect' on the Germans if Britain, the United States and the Soviet Union were to make an immediate declaration 'to the effect that a number of German officers or members of the Nazi Party, equal to those put to death by the Germans in the various countries, would be returned to those countries after the war for judgement.'[36]

With War Cabinet approval, Churchill drafted a declaration that he then sent to Roosevelt and Stalin. As the Allied armies were advancing, it read, 'the recoiling Hitlerites and Huns are redoubling their ruthless cruelties.' All those responsible for, or having taken a consenting part 'in atrocities, massacres and executions' were to be sent back to the countries 'in which their abominable deeds were done in order that they may be judged and punished according to the laws of those liberated countries.'

Churchill's draft declaration continued: 'Let those who have hitherto not imbued their hands with innocent blood beware lest they join the ranks of the guilty, for most assuredly the three allied powers will pursue them to the uttermost ends of the earth, and will deliver them to their accusers in order that justice may be done.' Such a declaration, Churchill believed, would make at least 'some of these villains shy of being mixed up in butcheries now that they know they are going to be beat.'[37]

Eden did not want so explicit a declaration, writing to Churchill on 9 October: 'Broadly, I am most anxious not to get into a position of breathing fire and slaughter against War Criminals, and promising condign punishments, and a year or two hence having to find a pretext for doing nothing.'[38] Churchill persevered, and prevailed.

---

36 Premier papers, 4/100/9.
37 Premier papers, 4/100/9.
38 Premier papers, 4/100/9.

On 1 November 1943 the Allies issued the Moscow Declaration, which followed almost exactly the wording of Churchill's draft. The Allies would compile a list of the 'abominable deeds . . . in all possible detail' from throughout Nazi-controlled Europe. They would then pursue those who had joined 'the ranks of the guilty . . . to the uttermost ends of the earth', and would deliver them to their accusers 'in order that justice may be done.'[39]

The hope was twofold: to deter the killers, and to assure the Jews of the world that, when Germany was defeated, justice would be done. As a result of the Moscow Declaration and Churchill's persistence, German war criminals captured by the Allies were sent for trial to the countries where they had committed their crimes. Some of the most notorious, 5,000 in all, were executed in Warsaw, Cracow, Prague and Bratislava, the scenes of their worst excesses.

39 Premier papers, 4/100/9.

CHAPTER EIGHTEEN

PALESTINE: A VIGILANT EYE

In the summer of 1943, after discussion with Weizmann, Churchill put forward a plan whereby Britain would offer King Ibn Saud of Saudi Arabia the leadership of an Arab Federation throughout the Middle East, and pay him £20 million a year, in exchange for his support for a Jewish State in Palestine.[1] But Anthony Eden was outraged when he heard from the British Embassy in Washington that Weizmann, in conversation with Roosevelt's foreign policy adviser Sumner Welles, had referred to the project as 'the PM's plan', as if it were a fact.

Indignantly, Eden wrote to Churchill that such a move would be the opposite of British official policy. 'I do not know how far Dr Weizmann has authority to speak in your name,' Eden wrote, 'but I am a little worried about the danger of confusion arising in Washington. Our present Palestine policy has been accepted by Parliament. I know well your personal feeling on this but there has been no discussion suggesting that the US government should be approached as regards the possibility of modifying it.' Eden went on to remind Churchill – who knew this all too well – that the 1939 Palestine White Paper, voted for by a large parliamentary majority, was unequivocally against letting Palestine become a Jewish State.[2] Churchill replied, without withdrawing from his position: 'Dr Weizmann has no authority to speak in my name. At the same time, I expressed these views to him when we met some time ago and you have often heard them from me yourself.'[3]

---

1 In the money values of today, £20 million is in excess of £300 million.
2 Premier papers, 4/52/3.
3 Premier papers, 4/52/3.

In his continuing opposition to the 1939 Palestine White Paper, Churchill was under pressure to accept that one of the few Cabinet supporters of Jewish statehood, Leo Amery, Secretary of State for India, should not be a member of the Cabinet committee set up to discuss the issue. On 11 July Churchill wrote to Eden: 'I have decided not to remove the Secretary of State for India's name from the Cabinet Committee on Palestine and the Jews. It is quite true he has my way of thinking on this point, which no doubt is to be deplored, but he has great knowledge and mental energy.'[4]

Churchill knew that Amery, as an Under Secretary in Lloyd George's government, had been a strong supporter of the Balfour Declaration when it was under discussion in 1917. What he did not know was that Amery was of Hungarian Jewish descent on his mother's side: that did not become known until many years after Churchill's death.

A further element entered into the Palestine debate when Roosevelt, under pressure from his State Department, suggested arming the Arabs of Palestine in order to gain their support for the Allied war effort, and hopefully their participation in the wider struggle. On 6 October Churchill wrote to Sir Alexander Cadogan, Permanent Under-Secretary of State at the Foreign Office: 'I could, of course, point out to the President the dangers of arming the Arabs while leaving the Jews practically disarmed, and the serious consequences this may have on the fulfilment of our policies towards the Jews at the end of the war. This, I think, would be decisive. The whole matter should be watched with the greatest vigilance.'[5]

On 25 October Weizmann was one of Churchill's luncheon guests at Chequers. Churchill's brother Jack and his son Randolph were also there, as was Clement Attlee, Deputy Prime Minister and Leader of the Labour Party. Weizmann's notes give a vivid account of the discussion, during which Churchill told those present that 'after they had crushed Hitler they would have to establish the Jews

4 Prime Minister's Personal Minute, 11 July 1943: Churchill papers, 20/104.
5 Churchill's War Papers archive.

in the position where they belonged. He had had an inheritance left to him by Lord Balfour, and he was not going to change.' Weizmann commented that he did not think Churchill would change, but that 'there were dark forces working against them which might force the Cabinet's hand.' Churchill told Weizmann, 'You have some very good friends: for instance, Mr Attlee and the Labour Party are committed on this matter.'

Attlee interjected that he certainly was committed, adding that he thought 'something should be done' about allowing the Jews to settle in Transjordan. Churchill commented he had been thinking about Partition, but that Transjordan as an extra outlet for the Jews 'was a good idea', thus echoing Weizmann's argument two decades earlier that Transjordan should be part of the Jewish National Home. Churchill added: 'He knew the terrible situation of the Jews. They would get compensation, and they would also be able to judge the criminals.'

Attlee then told Weizmann that 'some of his people were overplaying their hand,' a reference to Jewish demands for statehood immediately after the war, and that the British 'were sometimes threatened.' Churchill said 'they should not do that. He personally would prefer one good row. He would advise them not to have a series of rows. What they had to do was to watch the timing. He could not say publicly what he was telling Dr Weizmann now: there would be questions, and he would have to lose time explaining. They could quote his public utterances, and say that he would not budge from them.'

Churchill told Weizmann that he understood that there were some Jews in America who opposed Zionism. To combat this attitude, he suggested that Weizmann should 'try and win over' Bernard Baruch. Churchill then informed Weizmann that he had told Baruch he was wrong to be against Zionism 'but had not succeeded in persuading him.' Churchill then assured Weizmann that he was 'not going to change his views; he would bite deeply into the problem, and it was going to be "the biggest plum of the war."'

When Churchill mentioned Partition, both Randolph Churchill

and Weizmann demurred. Churchill replied 'that he had been against it originally, but now they had to produce something new instead of the White Paper. He had not meant Partition in the literal sense – he then mentioned something about the Negev and Transjordan' – both of which might be part of the future Jewish State.

Speaking of the Arabs, Churchill remarked that 'they had done very little, and in some instances had made things difficult for us. He would remember this when the day of reckoning came.' When the Palestine issue came up he would speak out, he said, and he then gave his listeners the headings of his speech. He ended by saying that Weizmann 'need not worry,' the Jews had 'a wonderful case.'[6]

Two years earlier, in Baghdad, Rashid Ali al-Gailani, the leader of the Iraqi nationalist movement with links to Nazi Germany, had led a military revolt against the British. As he seized power in Baghdad, Rashid Ali assured Germany that his country's natural resources would be made available to the Axis in return for German recognition of the right of the Arab States to independence and political unity, as well as the right to 'deal with' the hundreds of thousands of Jews who were then living in Arab lands.

Rashid Ali had been defeated, but his rebellion, at a time of British military weakness throughout the Middle East and in Greece, had rankled: 'The Arabs have done nothing for us during this war, except for the rebellion in Iraq,' Churchill wrote to the Chiefs of Staff Committee in late September. 'Obviously we shall not proceed with any plan of partition which the Jews do not support.' Churchill knew well the hostility of British officials in the Middle East to every aspect of Zionism. 'Of every fifty officers who came back from the Middle East' he told the Chiefs of Staff Committee, 'only one spoke favourably of the Jews – but that has merely gone to convince him that he was right.'[7]

*

6 Weizmann Archive.

7 Churchill War Papers archive.

In January 1944 Churchill was in Washington to discuss war policy during the coming year, when the Allies were to land on the Normandy beaches, take the war to northern Europe, and in time to Germany itself. But the future of the half million Jews in Palestine was never far from his mind. In a telegram from Washington on 12 January 1944 he had harsh words for those Cabinet Ministers who were pressing him to implement the 1939 Palestine White Paper, whereby it had been proposed, as of May 1944, to create an Arab majority government in Palestine, thus making even a partitioned Jewish State impossible. 'Surely we are not going to make trouble for ourselves in America,' he telegraphed to Attlee and Eden, and, looking ahead to the Presidential election in November 1944, 'hamper the President's chances of re-election for the sake of this low-grade gasp of a defeatist hour.'[8]

On 15 February 1944 Churchill invited Weizmann to dinner. After the meeting Weizmann was asked by his Zionist colleagues whether Churchill's response to the idea of a Jewish 'commonwealth' in Palestine after the war had been positive. 'Yes, his attitude is usually encouraging,' Weizmann reported. 'We don't have reason to worry, because we have a good response indeed.'[9]

Six months had passed since Churchill had written to Roosevelt about how 'Our immediate facilities for helping the victims of Hitler's anti-Jewish drive are so limited.' An opportunity to do more came in the first months of 1944, as an increasing number of Jews from Romania and Bessarabia began to make their way by ship across the Black Sea to Istanbul. Their aim was to get to Palestine. On 30 March 1944 Moshe Shertok, the head of the international department of the Jewish Agency, asked Oliver Stanley, the Colonial Secretary, to allow any Jew reaching Istanbul from Nazi-occupied Europe to be admitted to Palestine. The precedent was a Colonial Office arrangement to this end, agreed in 1942, but overlaid with tight bureaucratic strings and

8 Telegram of 12 January 1944: Churchill papers, 20/179.
9 Notes of a meeting held on 15 February 1944: Israel Defence Force archive.

tape. 'Eventually,' Shertok telegraphed to Jerusalem, 'Stanley agreed liberal interpretation' – one that would be based on individual applications that the Jewish Agency should itself recommend.

It was a breakthrough in the search for a safe haven. On 3 April Shertok reported to Jerusalem that Stanley had also agreed to 'keep matters elastic, reviewing policy in light of actual escape from Nazi lands,' and to make an official British approach to the Turkish Government 'for liberal transit.'[10] The result was quickly seen. On 8 April the Jewish Agency telegraphed from Istanbul to Jerusalem that the steamship *Maritza*, carrying 244 Jewish refugees from Romania, had arrived that day in Istanbul, and that the passengers would be leaving the city in two days' time by train for Palestine.

Henceforth, any Jew who reached Istanbul could continue on to Palestine irrespective of Palestine Certificates and quotas – in effect of the 1939 White Paper. Each time a boat with refugees reached Istanbul, the refugees – mostly survivors of the concentration camps in Romania – were sent to Palestine by rail within forty-eight hours. To expedite matters, if there were a hundred Jews on the ship, they were given a single British passport, in its familiar dark blue cover, with each of the names typed on a single sheet of paper and pasted onto the inside cover. With that single passport, every one of the refugees reached Palestine. More than six thousand Jews made that journey of liberation.

On 15 April 1944, at Chequers, Churchill pondered the question of who should succeed Sir Harold MacMichael, whose term as British High Commissioner in Palestine was coming to an end. The half million Jews of Palestine feared a High Commissioner unsympathetic towards their hopes of statehood. Churchill therefore suggested that Weizmann himself should succeed MacMichael, or, failing Weizmann, that another British Jew, Lord Melchett, the son of the former Sir Alfred Mond, a distinguished industrialist and former Minister of Health, should be chosen.

---

10 Telegram of 3 April 1944: Central Zionist Archives.

Churchill saw many benefits of having Weizmann as High Commissioner, the first Jew to hold that office since Sir Herbert Samuel twenty years earlier. When the Colonial Secretary, Oliver Stanley, expressed scepticism, Churchill resorted to a double tactic: stalling, and putting more arguments to make his case. 'We have plenty of time in which to settle this appointment,' he wrote, and continued, 'I do not think it should be of a departmental character. It should certainly be one to give satisfaction to the Jews and, at the same time, do justice to the Arabs. I wonder if Dr Weizmann would take it? He had rendered great service by his science to the Allied cause. He would certainly take a world-wide view. It might ruin him with the Jews, but it would, in the first instance, quell a good deal of the trouble in the United States.'

Churchill added: 'You can depend on Weizmann. He would not take on a job if he did not mean to stick to the conditions which would have to be imposed. The present Lord Samuel, when Governor of Palestine, held the scales there evenly, and got much abused by fellow Jews. Another possibility would be Lord Melchett, if his health were good enough to stand it, but Weizmann would be better. I believe both of them would be ready to work towards your partition scheme.' In addition, Churchill wrote, 'I do not believe at all in Colonial Office officials or military men in this particular task so full of world politics.'[11]

On 19 April Churchill presided at a meeting of the Defence Committee. General Sir Alan Brooke, Chief of the Imperial General Staff, warned of the repercussions in Palestine that might follow the political crisis in Egypt, where King Farouk wished to dismiss his Prime Minister and appoint someone more amenable to the royal wishes. The Jews, warned Brooke, 'who we knew were forming a secret army in Palestine, might well seize on such a moment to create trouble.' Churchill was sceptical. He did not believe there would be 'any general trouble with the Jews,' he said, telling the Defence Committee that there were 'a small number of extremists

11 Colonial Office papers, 967/89.

who were likely to cause trouble and there might be some murders,' but a general uprising was most unlikely. It might be advisable, he added, 'to tell Dr Weizmann that if such murders continued and the campaign of abuse of the British in the American papers did not stop, we might well lose interest in Jewish welfare.'[12]

Churchill never did 'lose interest' either in Jewish welfare or in the Jewish future in Palestine. Having consistently supported the Jewish majority interpretation of the 1922 White Paper, he refused to allow the 1939 White Paper, despite its passage into law by an overwhelming majority of Members of Parliament, to come into effect. This was certainly unconstitutional. But it ensured that the Jews would not be subjected to the rule of those whose one aim was to deny them statehood in any form.

Early in 1944, Randolph Churchill, who had parachuted behind German lines in Yugoslavia to serve as a liaison officer with the Yugoslav communist partisans led by Marshal Tito, also acted as a conduit for a Jewish Agency request that Palestinian Jews should be parachuted into Nazi-dominated Europe. The Agency hope was that they could contact the surviving Jewish communities, mainly in Hungary and Slovakia, and help organise rescue efforts both for Jews and for escaped Allied prisoners-of-war and aircrew who had been shot down. These Jewish parachutists, trained by the Royal Air Force and parachuted behind German lines, were an integral part of Britain's war against Hitler. Of the thirty-two volunteers, seven were caught and killed, two of them women, the Hungarian-born Hanna Senesh and the Slovak-born Havivah Reik.[13]

Following the German occupation of Hungary in mid-March 1944, Weizmann also asked Churchill to approach Marshal Tito. Weizmann wanted Tito to help any Jews who managed to escape from German-occupied Hungary into the Communist-controlled

---

12 Defence Committee (Operations), 19 April 1944: Cabinet papers, 69/6.

13 Randolph Churchill's contact in Cairo was Reuven Zaslani (later Shiloah), a senior Haganah representative. In 1951 he became the first director of the Mossad.

areas of Yugoslavia to be sent on to Allied-controlled southern Italy. Randolph Churchill suggested to his father one way that this might be done: the small aircraft that flew men and supplies into the partisan-held air strips near Topusko in Yugoslavia, would return to their Allied bases at Foggia in southern Italy, with Jewish refugees. Churchill sent Tito a message along these lines, asking him to receive the Jews who managed to flee southward from Hungary. On 21 June Churchill was informed by the Foreign Office: 'Marshal Tito has consented to facilitate the escape of Jewish refugees through his lines from Hungary, with the idea that they should reach southern Italy, via Dalmatia.'[14]

A year later, in London, Randolph Churchill informed Weizmann that he 'had tried to save 115 Jews in Yugoslavia; he has saved 112 but 3 had perished.'[15]

14 Premier papers, 4/51/10.
15 Notes of a meeting held in London on 14 June 1945: Weizmann Archive.

CHAPTER NINETEEN

SEEKING TO SAVE JEWS

On 4 July 1944 a short but graphic report reached the Foreign Office in London, revealing that the 'unknown destination in the East' to which there had been so many reports of Jewish deportations, was the SS-run camp of Auschwitz-Birkenau. The report was a telegraphic summary of a much larger one that was still on its way, detailing the nature and extent of mass murder at Auschwitz since the summer of 1942. The report also revealed that the Jews of Hungary, who for the previous three months had been deported to an 'unknown destination' on a daily basis, were being gassed at Auschwitz at a previously unheard of rate of 12,000 a day.

This horrific news reached the West as a result of the escape from Auschwitz of four Jews who, on reaching Slovakia, compiled an eyewitness report of what they had seen at Auschwitz. These reports were then smuggled to Switzerland, from where they were telegraphed to London, Washington and Jerusalem.[1] As soon as Weizmann learned the true nature of Auschwitz, and that deportations there were still taking place in Hungary, he went to the Foreign Office to see Anthony Eden, together with Moshe Shertok, the Jewish Agency official in charge of diplomatic contacts and initiatives. The meeting took place on 6 July 1944. Eden immediately passed on their news, and their urgent requests, to Churchill.

Among their requests, Weizmann and Shertok appealed to the Allies to bomb the railway lines leading from Budapest to Auschwitz,

1 There is a full account of the escapes and their aftermath in Martin Gilbert, *Auschwitz and the Allies.*

along which it was suddenly clear that several hundred thousand Hungarian Jews had been, and were still being, transported to their deaths. Churchill's response was immediate, and positive: 'Get anything out of the Air Force you can,' he wrote to Eden, 'and invoke me if necessary.'[2]

Churchill's emphatic instruction did not need to be carried out. Three days after he endorsed the bombing of railway lines leading from Hungary to Auschwitz, the deportation of Jews from Hungary to Auschwitz was halted. Churchill later learned, from a decrypted message from the Turkish Ambassador in Budapest to the Turkish Foreign Minister in Ankara, that it was the Hungarian Regent, Admiral Horthy, who had called for an end to the deportations.[3]

When Horthy told the German Minister to Hungary, SS General Veesenmayer, that the deportations must stop, Veesenmayer was indignant, but had neither the men nor the political power to continue the deportations without Hungarian Government support. The immediate cause of Horthy's intervention was an American daylight bombing raid on Budapest on 2 July. This raid had nothing to do with the appeal to bomb the railway lines to Auschwitz; it was part of a long-established pattern of bombing German fuel depots and railway marshalling yards. But the raid had gone wrong, as many did, and several government buildings in Budapest, as well as the private homes of several senior Hungarian Government officials, had been hit.

These buildings and homes included some that had been listed in a telegram sent from Switzerland to the Foreign Office in London by a British diplomat, Elizabeth Wiskemann, who – deliberately without using a code – had suggested bombing specific buildings in Budapest in order to force the Hungarian Government to stop the deportation of Jews to Auschwitz. In her open telegram – read, as she

2 Note of 7 July 1944: Premier papers, 4/51/10.
3 Telegram of 7 July 1944, decrypted and seen by Churchill on 18 July 1944: National Archives records: HW1/3084.

had intended, by the Hungarian intelligence service – she gave the location of government buildings involved in organising the deportations, including the police and railway ministries without whom the deportations could not take place, and also the home addresses of Hungarian Government officials involved.

When the Hungarian intelligence services read this telegram they concluded that the American air raid of 2 July was a deliberate answer to it, and a warning – which clearly could be repeated – to halt the deportations. Neither General Wiessenmayer, nor Lieutenant-Colonel Adolf Eichmann, who was in Budapest about to begin the deportation of all 120,000 Jews there – the last surviving Hungarian Jewish community – had any option but to defer to the Hungarian Government's demand, and the deportations ceased.

Before news of this decision became known, the Jewish Agency asked the British Government for broadcasts over the BBC in order to give publicity to the deportations. Churchill's response was emphatic. 'I am entirely in accord,' he informed Eden, 'with making the biggest outcry possible.'[4] This was done, with radio broadcasts from London not only describing the truth about Auschwitz, but also warning Hungarian railway workers, in their native tongue, that if they participated in the deportations – which could not be carried out without them – they would be branded as war criminals and brought to justice when the war was over. On 5 July Eden told the House of Commons that 'there are unfortunately no signs that the repeated declarations made by His Majesty's Government in association with the other United Nations of their intention to punish the instigators and perpetrators of these frightful crimes have moved the German Government and their Hungarian accomplices either to allow the departure of even a small proportion of their victims or to abate the fury of their persecution. The principal hope of terminating this tragic state of affairs must remain the speedy victory of the Allied nations.'[5]

---

4 Premier papers, 4/51/10.
5 Parliamentary Debates, *Hansard*, 5 July 1944.

Churchill knew that the war could only be brought to an end by an Allied victory; by continuing and often uncertain exertions, incurring heavy losses on land, at sea and in the air. Even as the Hungarian Jewish fate hung in the balance, British, American, Canadian and Polish troops were engaged in battle in Normandy, confronting a German force far more tenacious than they had anticipated, and suffering heavy losses. By the first week of July, after a month of fighting, the Allies had yet to break out of the Normandy beachhead. It was to take them more than six months to fight their way eastward to Germany.

In the second week of July, Churchill was told of an Anglo-American dispute about thirty-two Hungarian Jews who managed to buy their freedom by handing the SS their factories and properties, and had been flown from Hungary to neutral Lisbon. On 8 July a telegram from the British Ambassador in Lisbon warned of the American State Department's fear that the arrival of these Hungarian Jews 'is a German move to plant suspicion in Soviet minds' – suspicion concerning a separate peace between Germany and the western Allies.

Churchill dismissed the State Department's apprehension out of hand, writing to Eden on 10 July: 'Surely this only means that these poor devils have, at the cost of ninety per cent of their worldly possessions handed over in useful condition, procured an opportunity to escape from the butcheries to which their fellow-countrymen are doomed.' Churchill added that, with regard to the ambassador's fears that the Soviet Union would be suspicious of a possible peace feeler, 'the only suspicion planted in my mind is that some of these German murderers have lined their pockets well with a view to their future. I presume you will discount any far-fetched Russian suspicions by telling them all about it, and even possibly mentioning the kind of interpretation I put upon this action. It is a naked piece of blackmail on threats of murder.'[6]

The State Department still feared a Soviet accusation of separate

6 Minute of 10 July 1944: Premier papers, 4/51/10.

peace negotiations between Britain, the United States and Germany, and continued to oppose any help for the rescue effort. Churchill urged Eden to ignore this fear, writing to him on 6 August: 'It seems to be a rather doubtful business. These unhappy families, mainly women and children, have purchased their lives with probably nine-tenths of their wealth. I should not like England to seem to be wanting to hunt them down. By all means tell the Russians anything that is necessary, but please do not let us prevent them from escaping.' Churchill added: 'I cannot see how any suspicion of peace negotiations could be fixed on this miserable affair.'[7]

On 11 July, five days after the halting of the deportations from Hungary, Churchill was asked whether Britain should open negotiations, as the Jewish Agency wished it to do, with the SS. The Jewish Agency wanted to follow up what we now know to have been an SS deception plan, giving the SS goods and money for the release of Hungarian Jews who had, in fact, already been murdered. In rejecting any such negotiations, even through a neutral power, Churchill's reaction to the escapees' report of the mass murders at Auschwitz was emphatic and unequivocal. 'There is no doubt,' he wrote to Eden, 'that this is probably the greatest and most horrible crime ever committed in the whole history of the world, and it has been done by scientific machinery by nominally civilised men in the name of a great State and one of the leading races in Europe.'

Churchill did not limit his reaction to outrage. His comment continued: 'It is quite clear that all concerned in this crime who may fall into our hands, including the people who only obeyed orders by carrying out the butcheries, should be put to death after their association with the murders has been proved. Public declarations should be made,' Churchill instructed, so that everyone connected with the murders 'will be hunted down and put to death.'[8]

*

7 Minute of 6 August 1944. Premier papers, 4/51/10.
8 Minute of 11 July 1944. Foreign Office papers, 371/42809.

The Archbishop of Canterbury, William Temple, and the Jewish industrialist Lord Melchett, had both written to Churchill in the first week of July about the deportation of Hungarian Jews and German plans to kill all the deportees. On 13 July Churchill replied to both men, in similar terms, telling Melchett that he could add nothing to Eden's statement of 5 July and adding: 'There is no doubt in my mind that we are in the presence of one of the greatest and most horrible crimes ever committed. It has been done by scientific machinery by nominally civilised men in the name of a great state and one of the leading races of Europe. I need not assure you that the situation has received and will receive the most earnest consideration from my colleagues and myself but, as the Foreign Secretary said, the principal hope of terminating it must remain the speedy victory of the Allied Nations.'[9] In his letter to the Archbishop of Canterbury, Churchill re-iterated the sentence: 'I fear we are the witnesses of one of the greatest and most horrible crimes ever committed in the whole history of the world.'[10]

On 3 July the War Cabinet discussed another Jewish Agency request, for a Jewish military force to fight alongside the Allied forces in Italy. Churchill was still much in favour of such a force, but the Secretary of State for War, Sir James Grigg, objected to a Jewish Division – 12,000 men – as 'quite impracticable for quantative reasons,' and expressed his 'grave doubts' as to the 'practicability' even of a Brigade Group half that number, for the formation of which 'he was averse.' In response, Churchill told the War Cabinet that he felt 'that in view of the sufferings which the Jewish people were at present enduring there was a strong case for sympathetic consideration of projects in relation to them.' He would accept the objections to a full Division, but felt that 'we should not refuse to examine the possibility of a Brigade Group.'[11]

9 Letter of 13 July 1944: Churchill papers, 20/138A.
10 Letter of 13 July 1944: Churchill papers, 20/138A.
11 War Cabinet conclusions, 3 July 1944: Cabinet papers, 65/43.

The War Office remained hesitant, even hostile, stating only that the idea of a Jewish force would be 'carefully examined.' Churchill was not impressed. 'When the War Office say they will "carefully examine" a thing,' he wrote to the Cabinet Secretary on 10 July, 'they mean they will do it in.'[12] But he continued to press for the formation of a Jewish Brigade Group, writing to Grigg on 26 July: 'I like the idea of the Jews trying to get at the murderers of their fellow-countrymen in Central Europe, and I think it would give a great deal of satisfaction to the United States.' During the earlier discussion, the War Office had also opposed a special flag for the Jewish Brigade Group. Churchill was not convinced. 'I cannot conceive,' he wrote in his letter of 26 July, 'why this martyred race, scattered about the world, and suffering as no other race has done at this juncture, should be denied the satisfaction of having a flag.'[13]

In explaining to Roosevelt what he wanted done, Churchill telegraphed to Washington on 23 August that after 'much pressure' from Weizmann he had arranged that the War Office would raise a Jewish military force 'in what you would call a regimental combat team.' Churchill commented: 'This will give great satisfaction to the Jews when it is published and surely they of all other races have the right to strike at the Germans as a recognisable body.' Churchill added: 'They wish to have their own flag which is the Star of David on a white background with two light blue bars. I cannot see why this should not be done. Indeed I think that the flying of this flag at the head of a combat unit would be a message to go all over the world.' If the 'usual silly objections' were raised, Churchill added, 'I can overcome them.'[14]

The War Office finally deferred to Churchill's persistence, announcing on 19 September the formation of a Jewish Brigade Group to take part in active operations. At last the Jews could

---

12 Minute of 10 July 1944: Premier papers, 4/51/9.
13 Minute of 26 July 1944: Premier papers, 4/51/9.
14 Telegram of 23 August 1944: Roosevelt papers. Published in Warren Kimball (editor), *Churchill and Roosevelt, the Complete Correspondence*, Volume Three, pages 286–7.

participate, as Churchill wished, as a specifically Jewish force, with their own flag, in the Allied fight against Nazism. The first five thousand Jewish volunteers were organised into three infantry battalions and sent to the war front in Italy, where they formed an integral – and proud – part of Field Marshal Alexander's forces. They were the only Jewish formation in the Second World War, in any army, that fought under the Jewish flag. In Palestine, those who had not enlisted earlier in the Palestinian Jewish battalions in 1940, or in the Palestine Regiment in 1942, were eager to face the German enemy.

The Jewish community in Palestine had listened to Churchill's radio speeches since 1940, and seen him many times on the cinema newsreels. The slogan that had first appeared under his portrait in the public streets – 'Winning Winnie' – intended by the officials to exert an optimistic influence, had no resonance with the Hebrew and Yiddish-speaking population. The slogan was therefore changed to the similar, up-beat call of 'Win We Will', printed in its Hebrew version in bold biblical-style letters. In the words of one young man then in Palestine, Igo Feldblum, 'Confident in this prophecy, many enlisted in the Jewish Brigade and fought alongside the Allies.'[15]

In all, 30,000 Palestinian Jews fought in the British forces in the Second World War. More than seven hundred were killed in action.

Throughout the summer of 1944, Greek Communist insurgents, who were fighting the German occupation forces, hoped to take power in Greece when the Germans were driven out. Churchill was warned by the British Foreign Office that money – provided through clandestine channels by the United States – was being paid to Greek Communists to protect Jews fleeing imminent arrest and deportation. These Jews were refugees from Hungary who had been fortunate to have had enough money to bribe the Hungarian authorities to allow them to travel to Greece. But following the German occupation of Hungary, the Germans had begun to hunt down Hungarian Jews in Greece for deportation.

---

15 Igo Feldblum, letter to the author, 26 June 2005.

British policy was to boycott the Greek Communists in every way, but Churchill felt that saving Jews had priority over any such consideration. Asked to press the United States to halt the flow of money, he declined. 'It is quite possible,' he wrote, 'that rich Jews will pay large sums of money to escape being murdered by the Huns.' It was 'tiresome' that this money should get into the hands of the Communists, 'but why on earth we should go and argue with the United States about it I cannot conceive.'

Churchill's chief argument was a moral one. 'We should take a great responsibility if we prevented the escape of Jews, even if they should be rich Jews,' he wrote, and added, in scathing tones: 'I know it is the modern view that rich people should be put to death wherever found, but it is a pity that we should take up that attitude at the present time. After all, they have no doubt paid for their liberation so high that they will only be poor Jews, and therefore have the ordinary rights of human beings.'[16]

On 26 August 1944, Randolph Churchill took his father a copy of the full report of the four escapees from Auschwitz. This had been issued a month and a half earlier as an official document by the War Refugee Board in Washington, but never sent to Churchill, who had only been shown the summary version telegraphed to London at the beginning of July. Not for the first time, Randolph had alerted his father to an aspect of the Jewish fate that had not reached the Prime Minister through official channels.

Among the letters Churchill received in September 1944 was one from Harold Laski, then a senior member of the Labour Party executive. Laski wanted the nation to erect a statue in Churchill's honour after the war. 'As I look at the Europe Hitler has devastated,' he wrote, 'I know very intimately that, as an Englishman of Jewish origin, I owe you the gift of life itself.'[17] Churchill replied, 'I value the thought which inspired you to send it.'[18] But he felt a park in

16 Letter of 14 July 1944: Foreign Office papers, 371/43689.
17 Letter of 2 September 1944: Churchill papers, 20/143.
18 Letter of 21 September 1944: Churchill papers, 20/138.

one of the heavily bombed areas of south London would be a more fitting memorial than a statue.

That October, when Churchill was in Moscow for negotiations with Stalin about the future of Poland, the Jewish Agency learned that the Jews of Budapest, who had been saved from deportation in July, were again in danger. On 16 October Weizmann wrote to Churchill's Principal Private Secretary, John Martin, asking that, as a precondition of Allied peace negotiations with Hungary, 'all steps be taken by Hungary to protect Jews from German attempts to exterminate them.' Churchill's Private Office decided not to forward the appeal to him, and he never saw it.[19]

Shortly after Churchill's return from a visit to Moscow, the Jewish Agency learned that renewed deportations to Auschwitz were taking place in Poland, and asked for a public Allied protest. The Foreign Office was sceptical, but Churchill was not, writing to Eden: 'Surely publicity given about this might have a chance of saving the multitudes concerned.'[20] At Churchill's suggestion, the British Government consulted both the United States and the Soviet Government. The Americans replied that they wished to issue a warning. The Soviet Government made no reply. Britain and the United States acted without the Soviets, broadcasting a denunciation of the deportations from Washington and London on 10 October. As Churchill wished, the wording was unambiguous: 'If these plans are carried out, those guilty of such murderous acts will be brought to justice and will pay the penalty for their heinous crimes.'[21]

This warning brought an immediate response from Berlin, denouncing the reports on which it was based as 'false from beginning to end.' At the Foreign Office, Frank Roberts noted: 'A satisfactory reaction. Our declaration may for once have been worth while.'[22]

---

19 Premier papers, 4/51/10.
20 Premier papers, 3/352/4.
21 Foreign Office papers, 371/39454.
22 Foreign Office papers, 371/39454.

CHAPTER TWENTY

'IF OUR DREAMS OF ZIONISM ARE TO END . . .'

In Palestine, two underground Jewish organisations, the Irgun and the Stern Gang – the former led by a future Prime Minister of Israel, Menachem Begin – had begun to pursue a campaign of assassination against British Mandate officials and soldiers, hoping thereby to drive the British out of Palestine. They also killed fellow Jews who sought actively to oppose them. Of the forty-two people assassinated by the Stern Gang, more than half were Jews. In February, two British police officers were killed in Haifa. In March, three British policemen were killed in Tel Aviv and three more in Haifa. In August 1944 the Stern Gang made a failed attempt to kill Sir Harold MacMichael, the British High Commissioner; during the attack both his aide-de-camp and his police driver were wounded.

The Jewish Agency rejected terror as a means of advancing the Zionist cause. Within a few days of the assassination attempt on MacMichael, Churchill was informed that, at the insistence of Weizmann and Ben-Gurion, the Agency was co-operating closely with the Mandate authorities to find the would-be killers, their organisers and their weapons.

On 27 September an Irgun force estimated at 150 attacked four British police stations. Two days later, a senior British police officer of the Criminal Intelligence Department was assassinated while walking to his office in Jerusalem. The Jewish Agency and the British authorities worked closely to end these acts of terror. During the course of this co-operation, known to the Jews of Palestine as the

'Season' – the hunting season – the Jewish Agency's defence force, the Haganah, helped the British to secure the arrest of three hundred Irgun and Stern Gang members; 251 of them were deported to detention camps in British-controlled Eritrea and Sudan.

Weizmann knew that each act of Jewish terrorism would strike a blow at his attempts to persuade the British Government, by argument and negotiation, to secure a Jewish State in Palestine once the war was ended. Churchill accepted Weizmann's assurances that terrorism was not the path chosen by the Jews of Palestine or by the Zionist movement in their search for statehood.

In October 1944, while in Cairo, Churchill attended a conference on the post-war future of the Middle East. On 20 October he told the conference that, while 'the Arabs have done nothing for us except to revolt in Iraq,' he did not want to upset the Arabs in Syria, who were seeking independence from France, 'because of the pill – Zionism – which he knew they would have to swallow in Palestine.'[1]

On 4 November 1944, after Churchill had returned to London, Weizmann was invited to Chequers to discuss the future of Palestine over lunch. The meeting marked a decisive moment in the direction that Zionist diplomacy would take. When Weizmann asked Churchill to make a public statement about setting up a Jewish State in Palestine after the war, Churchill replied that he could make 'no pronouncement just now,' nor would he be able to say anything 'until the end of the German war, which might take from three to six months.' He then warned Weizmann that, as Prime Minister, he had 'little support in the Conservative Party' for the idea of a Jewish State.

When Weizmann replied that he had heard that opinion in the Conservative Party was 'veering round' on Palestine, Churchill replied that it might be so, but it was a slow process, and he would have to 'speak to them on the subject.' Churchill then told Weizmann that he had been rather struck by the opposition to Zionism among certain Jews in the United States, and mentioned

---

1 Oliver Harvey, diary, 20 October 1944: John Harvey (editor), *Diaries and Papers of Oliver Harvey (Lord Harvey of Tasburgh)*, pages 363–4.

the name of Bernard Baruch. In reply, Weizmann said that there might be a few rich and powerful Jews who were still against Zionism, but that these Jews 'did not know very much about the subject.' He would like to repeat to Churchill what he had once said to Balfour, that Balfour 'met the wrong type of Jews.' Smiling at this, Churchill reiterated that still there were some Jews who were opposed to Zionism, and again mentioned Baruch. Those Jews who were against Zionism, Weizmann replied, had also been those who were against Roosevelt and Churchill. Churchill commented that Weizmann was right, and that he, Churchill, knew it.

Churchill told Weizmann that if opponents of Zionism in the Conservative Party started talking in the same way as the military, 'it only hardened his heart.' But he would still like to have as much support as he could get. Weizmann then asked what truth there was in the rumours he had heard about a Partition scheme for Palestine that would give the Jews 'merely a beach-head – or a bathing beach – in Tel Aviv.' Such rumours, Churchill said, were 'a pack of lies.' He had seen Field Marshal Lord Gort, the distinguished soldier who would succeed Sir Harold MacMichael as High Commissioner for Palestine, and had told Gort how he felt about the matter.

As to the details of any partition, Churchill commented, he, too, was for the inclusion of the Negev in any Jewish State, as was Weizmann. If the Jews could get the 'whole of Palestine,' Churchill added, 'it would be a good thing.' But if it came to a choice between no State at all, and Partition, then they should take Partition.

American Jews, Churchill told Weizmann, must give active support, and not merely criticism. If he and Roosevelt were to meet at the conference table, they would 'get what they wanted' for the Jews of Palestine.

Weizmann then indicated the kind of speech he thought Churchill might make to the Arabs. Churchill replied that he had already spoken in that way, but that Roosevelt and he would do it again. Churchill then referred to Jewish terrorism in Palestine, in particular the recent murder of British soldiers, but, as Weizmann's record of the discussion noted, Churchill 'had not laboured the point.'

Churchill also promised Weizmann that in everything concerning the future of Palestine, the Zionist leader would be consulted, and he asked Weizmann whether it was the Zionists' intention 'to bring in large numbers of Jews into Palestine?' Weizmann replied in the affirmative, telling Churchill that they had in mind something like 100,000 or more Jews a year for some fifteen years. Churchill asked whether that meant something like one-and-a-half million Jews, to which Weizmann replied that this was so 'in the beginning.'

Weizmann also spoke of the large numbers of Jewish children in Europe who would have to be brought to Palestine after the war, to which Churchill replied 'that it would be for the Governments to worry about the children.' He then mentioned financial aid, whereupon Weizmann told him that 'if the political field were clear then the financial problem would become one of secondary importance.'

The luncheon was over. It had been, Weizmann noted, 'a long and most friendly conversation.' Churchill took Weizmann to his study, and repeated his three themes: nothing would happen until the end of the war; he was in close touch with the Americans on the subject; and Weizmann would be consulted. Churchill seemed worried, Weizmann noted, that America 'was more or less academic' in its attitude, and that he, Churchill, was not supported in the Conservative Party. Nor, Weizmann noted, did Churchill 'think much of the Arabs and their attitude to the war.'

Weizmann wanted to show Churchill a map in order to make his points against Partition, but Churchill, who was confident of his own grasp of the geographic aspects and did not want just then to be drawn into such details, countered, to Weizmann's disappointment, by saying 'that he did not want to study maps with Dr Weizmann.' At one stage in the conversation Churchill mentioned that he had a committee sitting on the Palestine problem, on which were 'all their friends': Sir Archibald Sinclair, and 'the Labour people.'

During their luncheon Churchill had told Weizmann that Lord Moyne, then Minister Resident in Cairo – a man believed by the Zionists to be totally opposed to their aspirations for statehood – had come round to Churchill's way of thinking with regard to the establishment of a Jewish State in Palestine after the war. Churchill was emphatic that Moyne had 'changed and developed in the past two years', and advised Weizmann to go to Cairo as soon as possible to see Moyne and discuss the future of Palestine with him.[2] The British Government would arrange air transport.

Weizmann, relieved to learn of Moyne's change of heart, readily agreed to go. But twenty-four hours after Weizmann left Chequers, and before he could set off for Cairo, two Jewish terrorists, Eliahu Bet-Zouri and Eliahu Hakim, members of the Stern Gang, attacked Moyne's car outside his home in Cairo, killing Moyne and his driver.

Churchill was deeply distressed by the murder of one of his close friends. As Walter Guinness, Lord Moyne had been his Financial Secretary at the Treasury twenty years earlier. In reporting Moyne's murder to the War Cabinet on 6 November, Churchill suggested that the Colonial Secretary, Oliver Stanley, should see Weizmann 'and impress upon him that it was incumbent on the Jewish Agency to do all in their power to suppress these terrorist activities.'[3] Speaking in the House of Commons of his grief, Churchill noted that during the past year Moyne had 'devoted himself to the solution of the Zionist problem,' and he added, 'I can assure the House that the Jews in Palestine have rarely lost a better or more well-informed friend.'[4]

As Churchill prepared a formal statement for Parliament on Moyne's murder, he was pressed by Oliver Stanley either to suspend Jewish immigration to Palestine altogether, or to threaten to suspend it unless all terrorism ceased. Churchill was reluctant to take either course, writing to Stanley a few hours before he was due to speak in the House of Commons: 'Will not suspension of immigration or a threat of suspension simply play into the hands of the extremists? At present, the Jews generally seem to have been shocked by Lord Moyne's death into a mood in which they are more likely to listen to Dr Weizmann's counsels of moderation. The proposed announcement would come as

---

2 Discussion of 4 November 1944: Weizmann Archive.
3 War Cabinet Minutes, 6 November 1944: Cabinet papers, 65/44.
4 Parliamentary Debates, *Hansard*, 7 November 1944.

a shock of a different kind and, so far from increasing their penitence, may well provide a not unwelcome diversion and excite bitter outcry against the Government.'

If immigration were suspended, Churchill pointed out, 'Dr Weizmann will no doubt join in the protests (saying that the whole community are being punished for the acts of a small minority), but the initiative in such a situation will pass to the extremists. Thus those responsible for the murder will be themselves the gainers. It may well unite the whole forces of Zionism and even Jewry throughout the world against us instead of against the terrorist bands.'

The situation certainly called for 'signal action', Churchill told Stanley, 'but should it not be more clearly directed against that section of the community with whom the responsibility lies – e.g. by enforcing even more drastic penalties in the case of those found in possession of firearms or belonging to proscribed societies? In particular, might not action be taken against the nominally respectable leaders of the party, whose extremist wing are the authors of these political crimes? If their national status is non-Palestinian, they might be deported: if Palestinian they should be banished.'[5]

As Churchill wished, the rules on immigration remained unchanged; indeed, an increasing number of Jewish survivors of the atrocities in eastern Romania were at that very moment being allowed to proceed by train from Istanbul to Palestine. Although Churchill would allow no punitive measures against the Jewish community, he spoke strongly in a statement in the House of Commons on 17 November of the impact of 'a shameful crime which has shocked the world and has affected none more strongly than those like myself who, in the past, have been consistent friends of the Jews and constant architects of their future. If our dreams for Zionism are to end in the smoke of assassins' pistols, and our labours for its future to produce only a new set of gangsters worthy of Nazi Germany, many like myself would have to reconsider the position we have maintained so consistently and so long in the past.'

---

5 Churchill to Oliver Stanley, 17 November 1944: Churchill papers, 20/153.

There were cheers from many members. Churchill continued: 'If there is to be any hope of a peaceful and successful future for Zionism these wicked activities must cease, and those responsible for them must be destroyed, root and branch.' There were further cheers. Churchill then told the House: 'I have received a letter from Dr Weizmann, President of the World Zionist Organization – a very old friend of mine – who has arrived in Palestine, in which he assures me that Palestine Jewry will go to the utmost limit of its power to cut out this evil from its midst. In Palestine, the Executive of the Jewish Agency has called upon the Jewish community – and I quote his actual words – "to cast out the members of this destructive band, deprive them of all refuge and shelter, to resist their threats, and render all necessary assistance to the authorities in the prevention of terrorist acts and in the eradication of the terrorist organisation". These are strong words, but we must wait for these words to be translated into deeds. We must wait to see that not only the leaders but every man, woman, and child of the Jewish community does his or her best to bring this terrorism to a speedy end.'

These remarks were met by what the parliamentary record noted as 'Loud cheers.' The primary responsibility for destroying the terrorists, Churchill stressed, lay with the British authorities in Palestine, who had already, two weeks before Moyne's murder, arrested and deported 251 Jews suspected of terrorist activities. But even though the primary responsibility was that of the government, Churchill added, full success depended upon the 'wholehearted' co-operation of the entire Jewish community, a co-operation the British Government was entitled to demand and to receive.[6]

Unknown to Churchill, on 16 December Eliahu Golomb, the head of the underground forces of the Haganah, which had denounced the murder of Lord Moyne and was working closely with the British to halt Jewish terrorism, met secretly with Nathan Friedman-Yellin, a member of the Stern Gang's ruling triumvirate. Two Stern Gang members were then on trial for Moyne's murder,

6 Parliamentary Debates, *Hansard*, 17 November 1944.

and the triumvirate wanted to carry out some spectacular act of warning and reprisal. One possibility being discussed was to assassinate Churchill himself. After a stormy discussion, Friedman-Yellin promised Golomb that the Stern Gang would not make any attempts on Churchill's life.[7]

The continuing acts of Jewish terror inside Palestine, not only against the British but also in a mounting spiral of violence against the Arabs, could not completely be curbed by the Jewish Agency. Churchill was under pressure to send British reinforcements to Palestine, and also to Syria where local Arabs were fighting the French. But with British troops engaged in trying to prevent a Communist takeover in Greece, he declined to do so, writing to the head of his Defence staff, General Ismay, on 28 January 1945: 'As long as we keep our troops well concentrated, a certain amount of local faction fighting can be tolerated and we can march in strength against the evil-doers. I am therefore not admitting the need of great reinforcements. Suppose a lot of Arabs kill a lot of Jews or a lot of Jews kill a lot of Arabs, or a lot of Syrians kill a lot of French or vice versa, this is probably because they have a great desire to vent their spite upon each other. Our attitude should be one of concentration and reserve. We really cannot undertake to stop all these bloodthirsty people slaying each other if that is their idea of democracy and the New World. The great thing is to hold on to the important strategic places and utter wise words in sonorous tones. I should like to think it very likely that there would be civil wars in these countries unless they are stopped by a series of decrees from the three victorious Great Powers. We are getting uncommonly little out of our Middle East encumbrances and paying an undue price for that little.' Having vented his frustration, Churchill told Ismay: 'The above obiter dicta are not to go beyond you.'[8]

The assassins of Lord Moyne were brought to trial in Egypt. Churchill followed the case closely. 'Everyone would be in favour of

7 Haganah archives.
8 Minute dated 28 January 1945: Premier papers, 3/296/9.

these two assassins having a fair trial,' he wrote to Eden, 'but if they are found guilty of having murdered Walter Moyne and are not put to death with all proper despatch by the Egyptian Government, I cannot measure the storm that will arise.'[9]

Moyne's murderers were found guilty. When, almost two months later, Churchill learned they had not yet been executed, he telegraphed to the British Ambassador to Egypt: 'I hope you will realise that unless the sentences duly passed upon the assassins of Lord Moyne are executed, it will cause a marked breach between Great Britain and the Egyptian Government. Such a gross interference with the course of justice will not be compatible with the friendly relations we have established. As they may be under pressure from Zionist and American Jewry, I think it right to let you know my personal views on the matter. You will no doubt use the utmost discretion and propriety in anything you may do. I have no reason of course to believe that the law will not be allowed to take its course and only send you this for greater assurance.'[10]

'It is of the utmost importance,' Churchill telegraphed to the ambassador again, from the Crimea, on 12 February, 'that both assassins should be executed,' and he instructed the ambassador to make 'an instant complaint' at the delay.[11] The executions duly took place.

Angered and dismayed though Churchill was by Lord Moyne's murder, he refused to allow it to deflect him from his Zionist sympathies. When the question of Moyne's successor arose, it was Churchill who personally turned down two Colonial Office nominees, Lord Selborne and Lord Winterton, senior Conservatives with long experience of government and administration, both of whom, he soon found out, were hostile to the idea of a Jewish State in Palestine.

In December 1944 Churchill flew from Britain to Greece, seeking to halt a Moscow-inspired Communist insurgency, and to persuade the

9 Letter of 3 December 1944: Churchill papers, 20/153.
10 Telegram of 28 January 1945: Churchill papers, 20/211.
11 Telegram of 12 February 1945: Churchill papers, 20/223.

Greek Communists to join a national government. To give his arguments the backing of force, he proposed moving a complete division of British troops, twelve thousand men, from Palestine to Greece. 'This of course would mean,' he pointed out to the War Office, 'that no violent action could be taken in Palestine, irritating the Jews, such as the search for arms on a large scale, until the situation is easier all round.'[12]

Conscious of the strong Conservative opposition to any future Jewish State in Palestine, and aware that his own views carried almost no weight with the Party of which he had been the leader since the autumn of 1940, Churchill advised Weizmann to go to the United States to win the support of the President and Congress. In a top-secret report, dated December 1944, the London office of the Washington-based Office of Strategic Services (OSS) noted that when Weizmann reached the United States he intended to see Roosevelt and representatives of the government 'with a view to seeking their aid for the prosecution of his plans. Mr Churchill himself, he said, had recommended him to adopt this course.'[13]

Churchill's instinct was right: Weizmann did indeed find more support in political circles in the United States than he had found in Britain, but despite Churchill's assurance to Weizmann that if Churchill and Roosevelt were to meet at the conference table 'they would get what they wanted' for the Jews of Palestine, even Roosevelt – unknown to Churchill – was about to change his mind about supporting the Zionist hopes of statehood.

---

12 Telegram of 28 December 1944: Churchill papers, 20/182.
13 Office of Strategic Services (OSS) papers: State Department Archives.

CHAPTER TWENTY-ONE

THE SAUDI ARABIAN DIMENSION

As 1945 began, three independent Arab States – Saudi Arabia, Egypt and Iraq – wanted to know what Britain and the United States intended with regard to the Jewish future in Palestine. Churchill continued to seek a Zionist solution whereby the 517,000 Jews then in Palestine, just under a third of the Arab population, would have their own State in which they would not be at the mercy of a hostile Arab majority, but able to govern themselves, albeit in only about a third of the area they had hoped for.

In February, off the coast of Egypt, Churchill called on Roosevelt on board the American warship *Quincy*. Roosevelt was gravely ill; Churchill had already been shocked at his pallor at the Yalta Conference a week earlier, and felt that he did not have long to live. He had in fact only two months. Shortly before Churchill called on him on *Quincy*, Roosevelt had spent several hours with the Saudi monarch, Ibn Saud. It was Churchill who had urged Ibn Saud to meet Roosevelt, who, Churchill told the Saudi monarch 'is also one of my most cherished friends.'[1]

The President's meeting with Ibn Saud on 14 February was not encouraging for Churchill's hopes of a future Jewish State in Palestine. According to the secret American account of the President's meeting with Ibn Saud, a copy of which was sent to Churchill, Roosevelt began the discussion by asking the King for his advice regarding 'Jewish refugees driven from their homes in Europe.' The King replied, 'The Jews should return to live in the

1 Telegram of 9 February 1945: Premier papers, 4/77/1A.

lands from which they were driven.' The Jews whose homes had been 'completely destroyed and who have no chance of livelihood in their homelands should be given living space in the Axis countries which oppressed them.'[2]

Colonel William A. Eddy, who had accompanied Ibn Saud by sea from Jeddah, noted that Ibn Saud had remarked about the Jewish survivors: 'Give them and their descendants the choicest lands and homes of the Germans who had oppressed them.'[3]

Roosevelt replied that the Jews were 'reluctant to go back to Germany,' and that they nurtured a 'sentimental' desire to go to Palestine. Ibn Saud countered by telling Roosevelt: 'Make the enemy and the oppressor pay; that is how we Arabs wage war. Amends should be made by the criminal, not by the innocent bystander. What injury have Arabs done to the Jews of Europe? It is the "Christian" Germans who stole their homes and lives. Let the Germans pay.'

Arabs and Jews 'could never cooperate' Ibn Saud told Roosevelt, 'neither in Palestine nor in any other country,' and he warned of 'the increasing threat to the existence of the Arabs' as a result of continued Jewish immigration and Jewish land purchase. The Arabs 'would choose to die,' the King told the President, 'rather than yield their land to the Jews.'[4] It was the Arab custom, Ibn Saud explained, 'to distribute survivors and victims of battle among the victorious tribes in accordance with their numbers and their supplies of food and water. In the Allied camp there are fifty countries, among whom Palestine is small, land-poor, and has already been assigned more than its quota of European refugees.'[5]

Charles Bohlen, an American diplomat on board *Quincy*, wrote in his memoirs that Ibn Saud also told Roosevelt that in the past there

---

2 'Memorandum of Conversation between His Majesty Abdul Aziz al Saud, King of Saudi Arabia, and President Roosevelt, 14th February 1945, aboard USS *Quincy*': Premier papers, 4/77/1A.
3 William A. Eddy, *FDR Meets Ibn Saud*, page 32.
4 'Memorandum of Conversation between His Majesty Abdul Aziz al Saud, King of Saudi Arabia, and President Roosevelt, 14th February 1945, aboard USS *Quincy*': Premier papers, 4/77/1A.
5 William A. Eddy, *FDR Meets Ibn Saud*, page 33.

had never been 'any conflict between the two branches of the Semitic race in the Middle East.' What had 'changed the whole picture was the immigration from Eastern Europe of people who were technically and culturally on a higher level than the Arabs.' As a result, the Arabs 'had greater difficulty in surviving economically.' The fact that these 'energetic Europeans were Jewish' was not the cause of the trouble, the King said, 'it was their superior skills and culture.'[6]

The President then, according to the secret record, told the King he had heard from Churchill that the Jews might be settled in Libya, 'which was far larger than Palestine and thinly populated.' Ibn Saud rejected this at once, telling Roosevelt that 'it would be unfair to the Muslims of North Africa.' He went on to tell Roosevelt that 'the hope of the Arabs is based upon the word of honour of the Allies and upon the well-known love of justice of the United States, and upon the expectation the United States will support them.'

Roosevelt assured Ibn Saud that 'he would do nothing to assist the Jews against the Arabs and would make no move hostile to the Arab people,' nor would his government change in its policy in Palestine 'without full and prior consultation with both Jews and Arabs.' Roosevelt suggested that the King support an Arab mission to Britain and the United States to press the argument against Zionist aspirations, because, said the President, 'many people in America and England are misinformed.' The King replied that such a mission might be useful, but 'more important to him was what the President had just told him concerning his own policy toward the Arab people.'[7]

After the meeting with Ibn Saud, Roosevelt told his senior advisers that Arabs and Jews were on a 'collision course' toward war in Palestine, and that on his return to Washington he planned to meet with congressional leaders to seek 'some new policy that would head

6 Charles E. Bohlen, *Witness of History*, page 203.

7 'Memorandum of Conversation between His Majesty Abdul Aziz al Saud, King of Saudi Arabia, and President Roosevelt, 14th February 1945, aboard USS *Quincy*': Premier papers, 4/77/1A.

it off.'[8] On 5 April, only a week before his death, Roosevelt wrote to Ibn Saud from Washington, reaffirming his promise made on board *Quincy* that he would 'take no action, in my capacity as Chief of the Executive Branch of this Government, which might prove hostile to the Arab people.'[9]

This commitment was at complete variance with what Churchill believed to be Roosevelt's – and his own – support for a Jewish State in Palestine. In describing his meeting with Ibn Saud, Roosevelt told Congress how his change of mind had come to pass: 'On the problem of Arabia,' he said, 'I learned more about that whole problem – the Moslem problem, the Jewish problem – by talking with Ibn Saud for five minutes than I could have learned in the exchange of two or three dozen letters.'[10] On hearing this, one of Roosevelt's senior aides remarked sarcastically, 'The only thing he learned was what everyone already knew, that the Arabs didn't want any more Jews in Palestine.'[11]

Churchill understood the meaning of Roosevelt's unexpected commitment to the Arab point of view with regard to Palestine – whether based on whim or oil. Roosevelt had no sense or sensitivity, as Churchill did, for the idealism and enterprise of Zionism, something Churchill had seen first hand fourteen years earlier. Churchill recognised Ibn Saud's inflexibility with regard to the Jews, but he was committed to trying to persuade the King to adopt a positive position towards a future Jewish State in Palestine, quite apart from the possibility of an additional Jewish presence in Libya.

Leaving *Quincy*, Churchill was driven to Cairo, from where, on 17 February, he travelled through the desert to the Hotel du Lac on Lake Fayyum, where Ibn Saud was staying. One of those British officials present at Fayyum, Laurence Grafftey Smith, the newly

8 Thomas W. Lippman, 'The Day FDR met Saudi Arabia's Ibn Saud', *The Link*, Volume 38, Issue 2.

9 This letter was the only part of Roosevelt's discussions with Ibn Saud that was published: the full text appeared in the *New York Times* on 19 October 1945.

10 Charles E. Bohlen, *Witness to History*, page 204.

11 Thomas W. Lippman, 'The Day FDR met Saudi Arabia's Ibn Saud'.

appointed Minister to Saudi Arabia, who was on his way to Riyadh. He later recalled that Churchill had told him before the meeting with Ibn Saud, 'that in deference to the view of Eden and the Foreign Office, he was not going to mention Palestine to the King.'[12] The oil-rich kingdom was not to be pushed into the arms of the United States. Grafftey Smith later reflected with pride that he had succeeded in persuading Churchill not to mention Palestine.[13]

Grafftey Smith was wrong. During Churchill's conversation with Ibn Saud, as Churchill himself reported to the War Cabinet two days later, he had raised the Palestine issue without prevarication. As the War Cabinet noted, Churchill 'had pleaded the case of the Jews with His Majesty but without, he thought, making a great deal of impression, Ibn Saud quoting the Koran on the other side, but he had not failed to impress upon the King the importance which we attached to this question.'[14]

The official account of what Churchill and Ibn Saud discussed was to remain secret until 2006, when I requested access to it while writing this book. It shows that at the start of the discussion, Ibn Saud explained to Churchill that 'his position was very difficult. The Jews in Palestine were continuously increasing in number; they were even forming a sort of Government of their own, with a Prime Minister, a Foreign Minister and a Minister of Defence. They also had formed a military force of 30,000 men with modern arms and equipment. They had thus become a great danger to the Arabs.' If it was 'only a question of Jews and Arabs,' the King explained, 'the Arabs would fight the Jews, and, even if they were not victorious, they would not mind because they would go to Paradise.' He had continually advised moderation to the Arabs with regard to Palestine, 'but he feared that a clash might come and then he would be in a great difficulty.' He did not wish to get involved in such a conflict, which would also bring Saudi Arabia into conflict with Britain.

---

12 Sir Laurence Grafftey Smith, letter to the author, 11 February 1985.
13 Sir Laurence Grafftey Smith, in conversation with the author, 1970.
14 War Cabinet Minutes, 19 February 1945: Cabinet papers, 65/51.

Churchill sought to assure Ibn Saud that Britain would not allow the Jews to attack the Arabs with armed forces. 'We had control of the seas and could easily deprive them of supplies. At the same time the Jews must have a place to live in – that is to say, in Palestine. He had never been in favour of Palestine being a National Home, but of a National Home in Palestine.' Churchill pointed out that the work done by the Jews in cultivating desert areas in Palestine 'was advantageous to the Arabs, whose population and welfare were increased thereby.' He hoped that he might count on the King's assistance to promote 'a definite and lasting settlement' between the Jews and the Arabs.

Ibn Saud said that he 'counted on British friendship with the Arabs and on British justice.' In response, Churchill assured him 'of our friendship with the Arabs and pointed out that we had done a lot for the Arabs since the last war in establishing Arab States in Iraq and Transjordan.' But, as the account of the discussion noted, he felt 'that he could not altogether satisfy' Ibn Saud regarding Palestine.[15]

The OSS wanted to know what Churchill had discussed in Cairo. In a top secret report on 21 February, its Middle East agency informed Washington that it had learned that at a series of meetings in Egypt between Churchill, Eden, King Farouk of Egypt, President Kuwatli of Syria, and Ibn Saud, 'discussions centered on the question of the partitioning of Palestine to an independent coastal Jewish State and to an Arab State which would be "fused" with Greater Syria. It is reported that the plan, including the creation of Greater Syria, was accepted by all parties at the meetings, but that Churchill made it clear that the plan must have the approval of the British Parliament before it could be put into effect. Under this plan Lebanon is said to have been promised complete autonomy, but as part of Greater Syria.'[16]

15 'Cairo Conversations, February 1945': Premier papers, 4/77/1A.
16 Office of Strategic Services (OSS) papers: State Department Archives.

Greater Syria was considered by Arab nationalists to include Syria, Lebanon and Palestine. It was not in fact to the British Parliament, as the OSS believed, but to a post-war Middle East peace conference that Churchill looked to secure an independent Jewish State in Palestine. Churchill was under no illusions as to the difficulties of his task. On 25 March he was shown a letter from Emir Abdullah of Transjordan warning him unequivocally: 'The inhabitants of the Arab world are in a ferment over the future of Palestine.' One reason, Abdullah explained, was that 'The Arabs believe at present that the Jews want to have Palestine only as a means of their future domination of the whole Arab world economically as well as politically.'[17] Six weeks later Churchill was shown an equally long and emphatic letter from Ibn Saud, insisting that the formation of a Jewish State in Palestine 'will be a deadly blow to the Arabs and a constant threat to peace.' The 'ambitions of the Jews,' the King insisted, 'are not confined to Palestine alone. The preparations they have made show that they intend to take hostile action against neighbouring Arab countries.' The Jews were preparing in Palestine 'to create a form of Nazi-Fascism within sight of the democracies and in the midst of the Arab countries . . .'

Part of the King's letter was an historical complaint. The Biblical Joshua had captured the land of the Canaanites – 'an Arab tribe' – 'with great cruelty and barbarity.' The Arabs had been in Palestine since 3,500 years before Christ. They had ruled it 'alone or with the Turks' for 1,300 years. The 'disjointed rule of the Jews did not exceed 380 confused and sporadic years,' ending in 332 BC. For 2,200 years 'there have been few Jews there and they have had no influence . . . The Jews were merely aliens who had come to Palestine at intervals and had then been turned out over two thousand years ago.'[18]

Churchill knew these arguments well. He had first heard them, and variants of them, and had sought to rebut them, twenty-four

17 Letter dated 10 March 1945: Premier papers 4/52/2.
18 Undated letter, shown to Churchill on 2 May 1945: Premier papers, 4/52/2.

years earlier in Jerusalem. He had heard Ibn Saud reiterate them at Fayyum. He was nevertheless convinced that the establishment of a Jewish State in Palestine would be one of his main post-war tasks, and challenges, and that he had the historical justification as well as the determination and skill to bring that State into being. Churchill's plans were never to be discussed, however, either in the British Parliament, as the OSS had imagined, or at a post-war peace conference on the Middle East that Churchill had envisaged, and where he hoped Ibn Saud could be persuaded to support a sovereign independent Jewish State as part of an Arab Federation of which Ibn Saud would be the head. 'It is my earnest hope that our deliberations will produce a result that will be just to the rights and interests of all concerned,' Churchill replied to Ibn Saud's complaints.[19]

Within five months of the meetings on board *Quincy* and at Fayyum, the Conservative Party was defeated at the British General Election, and a new Prime Minister, Clement Attlee, found himself in charge of Britain – and of Palestine. Churchill, who became Leader of the Opposition, could only watch in frustration, disbelief and anger as the final act of the Mandate drama unfolded.

---

19 Telegram of 21 May 1945: Foreign Office papers, 954/15.

CHAPTER TWENTY-TWO

FROM WAR TO PEACE: 'I SHALL CONTINUE TO DO MY BEST'

In March 1945 the Second World War was still being fought with great ferocity in northern Europe, on the Eastern Front, in the Balkans and in Italy. The Allied armies in Italy, commanded by Field Marshal Sir Harold Alexander, included the Jewish Brigade Group, with its Star of David insignia on which Churchill had insisted. On learning of Alexander's successes on the battlefield, Churchill telegraphed, 'Never, I suppose, have so many nations advanced and manoeuvred in one line victoriously,' and he went on to note: 'The British, Americans, New Zealanders, South Africans, British-Indians, Poles, Jews, Brazilians, and strong forces of liberated Italians have all marched together in that high comradeship and unity of men fighting for freedom and for the deliverance of mankind.'[1]

On 18 April, as Allied forces penetrated deep into Germany, the Supreme Commander of the Allied Expeditionary Forces, General Dwight D. Eisenhower, telephoned Churchill about the entry of his troops into a concentration camp at Ohrdruf, near Gotha. The sight that met the American troops there was overwhelming in its horror: four thousand emaciated bodies dumped in ditches – Russian prisoners-of-war, Polish slave labourers, and Jews of a dozen nationalities, all of whom had died of starvation and disease, or who had been shot in mass executions as the Allied armies drew near. On the following morning, after American troops had reached Ohrdruf,

1 Churchill to Field Marshal Alexander, 29 April 1945: Churchill papers, 20/216.

Eisenhower's Chief of Staff, General Bedell Smith, telephoned a further message for Churchill about yet more camps that had been overrun, including Buchenwald. These, he explained, 'are even indescribably more horrible than those about which General Eisenhower spoke to you yesterday and of which photographs have appeared in the press today.' Buchenwald, near Weimar, was 'the acme of atrocity.'

An American delegation, Eisenhower told Churchill, 'might be too late to see the full horrors, whereas an English delegation, being so much closer, could get there in time.'[2] Churchill agreed at once. Eisenhower's hope, Churchill told Eden, was that the Members of Parliament and journalists 'should be sent out at the earliest possible moment to inspect the indescribable horrors, far beyond any hitherto exposed, which are coming to light as the various torture camps are examined.' Especially in the neighbourhood of Weimar, Churchill explained, 'the atrocities have surpassed all example or indeed imagination.'[3]

That afternoon Churchill spoke to the House of Commons about the horror felt by the government at the proofs 'of these frightful crimes now coming into view.' Eisenhower had invited him, he explained, to send a group of Members of Parliament at once to his headquarters in order that they may themselves have visual and first-hand proof of these atrocities. The matter was of urgency, 'as it is not possible to arrest the processes of decay in many cases.' In view of this urgency, Churchill had come to the conclusion that eight members of the House of Commons and two members of the Lords should form a parliamentary delegation, and travel at once to the Supreme Headquarters, where Eisenhower would make all the necessary arrangements for their inspection of the scenes, whether in the American or British sectors of the front.

Churchill asked for volunteers for 'this extremely unpleasant but none the less necessary duty.' They must be chosen that afternoon, so that they could start the next day. 'I hope,' Churchill said,

---

2 Premier papers, 4/100/11.
3 Telegram of 19 April 1945: Churchill papers, 20/215.

'the House will approve of the somewhat rapid decision I have taken.'[4] The House of Commons did approve. 'People are profoundly shocked here,' Churchill telegraphed to Eisenhower that evening.[5] And on the following morning he telegraphed to his wife Clementine, who was then visiting hospitals in the Soviet Union: 'Here we are all shocked by the most horrible revelations of German cruelty in the concentration camps. General Eisenhower has invited me to send Parliamentary Delegation. I accepted at once and it will start tomorrow. They will go to the spot and see the horrors for themselves – a gruesome duty.'[6]

The British parliamentary delegation reached Buchenwald on 27 April. 'One half-naked skeleton,' they wrote in their report, 'tottering painfully along the passage as though on stilts, drew himself up when he saw our party, smiled, and saluted.' Ten days had passed since liberation. The number of daily deaths in the first days after the liberation of the camp had been a hundred or more. On the day before the visit of the parliamentarians, thirty-five inmates had died, 'being already beyond the power of medicine to save.'[7]

On 7 May 1945 the German armies surrendered unconditionally. The German war was over. The murder of six million Jews, and of more than ten million other captive peoples – Russians, Poles, Greeks and Serbs among them – was at an end. Churchill had been a central figure in the destruction of the German war machine and Nazi tyranny, driving forward the British war effort on land, at sea and in the air for five years. Simon Hass, a Polish Jew who survived the war in a Soviet labour camp, later recalled a fellow-prisoner's comment as the war raged: 'We have no bread, but we have Churchill.'[8]

Almost twenty years after the end of the war – and three days after

---

4 *Hansard*, 19 April 1945.
5 Telegram of 19 April 1945: Churchill papers, 4/100/11.
6 Telegram of 20 April 1945: Spencer-Churchill papers.
7 *Buchenwald Camp: The Report of a Parliamentary Delegation*: Command Paper No. 6626 of 1945. Churchill's copy is in Premier papers, 4/100/11.
8 The Reverend Simon Hass, in conversation with the author, 30 November 2006.

Churchill's death – Halina Neuman, a survivor of the Warsaw Ghetto, wrote to the *New York Times* from her home in Newark, New Jersey: 'May I have the privilege of telling your readers what Winston Churchill meant to us, the hunted, the persecuted, in hiding from the Nazis? When all the lights went out in Europe, in the black of the nights for months and months to come, his voice, his speeches kept us alive. He and his voice gave us the only hope that the evil would pass, and that the world was not coming to an end. God bless his memory.'[9]

The war against Germany was over, but the future of Palestine remained obscure. So too was the future of more than a hundred thousand Jews who had been liberated in the concentration camps or emerged from hiding, and were being gathered in Displaced Persons camps in Germany. Only a few of those in the DP camps wanted to go back to their homes in Central and Eastern Europe, homes that had been taken over by local people who did not want the few surviving Jews to return. For most survivors, Europe was the blood-soaked graveyard of their families, friends and communities. For many, it was Palestine that beckoned.

On 22 May 1945, two weeks after the German surrender, Chaim Weizmann wrote to Churchill, enclosing an appeal by the Jewish Agency for an end to all restrictions on Jewish entry into Palestine. 'The Jewish people have waited till the end of the German war,' Weizmann wrote, 'not only for their deliverance from Hitler, but also from the injustice of the White Paper of 1939, which has so intensely aggravated both their sufferings and the loss of human life. We remember with gratitude how the voice of British conscience spoke through you.'

Perceptively, Weizmann told Churchill: 'We have noted how, during the years of war, you have never let yourself be drawn into saying anything which could be interpreted as an acceptance of the White Paper. This has enabled me to urge upon my people patience. But now the German war is over. Under your leadership victory has

---

9 *New York Times*, 28 January 1965.

come. Your word could never carry greater weight than it does now. The White Paper still stands. It is prolonging the agony of the Jewish survivors. Will you not say the word which is to right wrongs and set the people free?' Weizmann added, in anguish: 'The position of the Jews in the liberated countries is desperate, the political position in Palestine is becoming untenable, and so is my personal position as President of the Jewish Agency. The arguments I have been using cease to apply. What victory does not give us now, when is it to come? Every passing week, every reply in Parliament which treats the White Paper as law, increases the prescriptive interest of our opponents in that fatal document. This is the hour to eliminate the White Paper, to open the doors of Palestine, and to proclaim the Jewish State. It is my solemn duty to make to you this appeal for action, and for immediate action.'[10]

Churchill was sympathetic to Weizmann's appeal, but he knew that his power to act was running out. On 23 May, the day after Weizmann's letter, and two days after the Labour Party decided to leave Churchill's all-Party coalition, the coalition was dissolved. The new 'caretaker' administration, headed by Churchill, was an entirely Conservative one. A large percentage of Conservative Members of Parliament were unsympathetic to the Zionist cause and supported the White Paper restrictions, for which they had voted six years earlier. Nor was this new administration more than a stopgap one; it would be in place only until the General Election gave voters the chance to replace it with Labour. The election results would be known in July.

On 9 June Churchill sent Weizmann a short answer to his letter of 22 May. 'There can I fear be no possibility,' he wrote, 'of the question being effectively considered until the victorious Allies are definitely seated at the Peace table.'[11] This had been Churchill's stated plan for Palestine for more than a year.

There was considerable distress in Zionist circles at this reply. When it was discussed at the Zionist Political Committee in London

10 Letter of 22 May 1945: Churchill papers, 20/234.
11 Letter of 9 June 1945: Churchill papers. 20/234.

on 13 June, Weizmann decried Churchill's letter as 'an insult to their intelligence.' But he had discussed it with Churchill's Principal Private Secretary, John Martin, who was about to leave Downing Street for the Colonial Office, and Martin had told him that 'it was absurd to think' that Churchill had changed his opinion. He suggested that Weizmann propose to Churchill that they meet after the General Election. Ben-Gurion thought this was mere words, warning Weizmann that using the Election was the 'only excuse' Britain could give the Jews for telling them to wait.

For Ben-Gurion, Churchill's letter was 'the greatest blow they had received.' Although Churchill had 'no bad intentions towards them' and still considered himself 'as a friend of Zionism,' the Jewish people were 'absolutely powerless and helpless' and it was 'most evil to deceive people.' Weizmann was also bitter. If Churchill 'had wanted to settle things,' he said, 'he would have done so.' As to the late President Roosevelt's alleged remarks to Dr Stephen Wise, one of the leaders of American Jewry, that he favoured a Jewish State, Weizmann wondered whether that 'was just moonshine – merely something to keep the wolf from the door.'[12]

That evening, 13 June, Weizmann saw Randolph Churchill. On the following morning Weizmann told his colleagues, including Ben-Gurion, that he had shown Randolph his father's letter, at which Randolph had said, 'Do not pay too much attention to what my father writes. He is tired and weary and worn.' Weizmann told his colleagues that it was 'all very well' for Randolph to say that, but that he, Weizmann, 'was left with a letter postponing an important decision to a very indefinite date.'[13]

On 15 June Weizmann wrote directly to Churchill, and straightforwardly: 'My dear Mr Prime Minister: I would like to thank you for your note of June 9th, though I confess that its contents come as a great shock to me. I had always understood from our conversations that our problem would be considered as soon as the German war was

12 Notes of a meeting held in London on 13 June 1945: Central Zionist Archives.
13 Notes of a meeting held in London on 14 June 1945: Central Zionist Archives.

over: but your phrase "until the victorious Allies are definitely seated at the Peace table" substitutes some indefinite date in the future. I can hardly believe this to have been your intention, because I am sure you realise what the continuance of the White Paper of 1939 is involving for the Jewish people. It bars the doors of Palestine against the surviving remnant of European Jewry, and many refugees have to wander or die, unable as they are to go to Palestine. As regards the 600,000 Jews in Palestine, the continuation of the White Paper means confinement to a territorial ghetto consisting of five per cent of the area of Western Palestine. They could hardly put up with this during the war; now it becomes unbearable. Every week in which Palestine continues to be administered under the White Paper renders the tragedy more acute. I most earnestly beg of you to bear all this in mind.'[14]

When no reply had reached Weizmann by 27 June, he vented his deep disappointment at a further meeting of the Zionist Political Committee. The Jews, he told his colleagues, 'were only a small people.' He could not fight Churchill, or Roosevelt's successor as President, Harry S. Truman, but he could 'keep his conscience clear' by telling the leaders of the Western world, 'You have done what you have done, but you cannot expect me to swallow it.' Weizmann went on to tell his colleagues that he felt 'very bitter; he had reached the end of a long road. They had tried their best. He had no confidence in the meeting of the Big Three. Nobody cared what happened to the Jews. Nobody had raised a finger to stop them being slaughtered. They did not even bother about the remnant which had survived.'[15]

Churchill had been still struggling to answer Weizmann's letter of 15 June. His first reaction, in sending a copy of it to the Colonial Secretary, was: 'I think it better to leave Dr Weizmann's letter unanswered. But these notes may help you to put forward some ideas for a reply.'[16] In the event, Churchill sent his own reply, dated 29 June.

14 Letter of 15 June 1945: Churchill papers, 20/234.
15 Notes of a meeting held in London on 27 June 1945: Central Zionist Archives.
16 Letter of 29 June 1945: Churchill papers, 20/234.

It was a serious attempt to set out the situation as he saw it. 'My dear Weizmann,' Churchill wrote, 'I am afraid I can add nothing to my letter of June 9 except to explain that the Peace table means the Peace table for the settlement of problems arising out of the end of the war in Europe. I do not know what course the Great Powers will take about this. But I trust that after the July Conference, before the end of the year, there will be some coherent attempt on the part of the major Allies to settle the various outstanding territorial questions, and that would be the time when the Jewish position in Palestine would rightly fall to be considered.'

Churchill then explained to Weizmann his growing conviction that it was to the United States that the Jews of Palestine should look for satisfaction – and for statehood. 'It has occurred to me for some time,' Churchill wrote, 'reading all the attacks in the American papers on the way Britain has behaved in handling the Zionist question, that it might be a solution of your difficulties if the Mandate were transferred from Britain to the United States who, with her great wealth and strength and strong Jewish elements, might be able to do more for the Zionist cause than Great Britain. I need scarcely say I shall continue to do my best for it. But, as you will know, it has very few supporters in the Conservative Party, and even the Labour Party now seem to have lost all zeal.'[17]

Churchill was both right and realistic; Weizmann was near despair. Yet Churchill's intention remained to discuss Palestine at a special Middle East peace conference: the 'Peace table' Churchill called it. This, he hoped, would be held after the Potsdam conference – code name Terminal – that was to begin on 15 July, presided over by the Big Three: Churchill, Stalin and Truman, to discuss the future of Europe, and the continuing war against Japan.

Seeking to put Weizmann's mind at ease, Churchill wrote to John Martin on 15 June, for transmission to Weizmann: 'I said till the Peace Table, which means the peace table in Europe unless the Japanese

---

17 Letter of 29 June 1945: Churchill papers, 20/234.

war comes to an end beforehand.'[18] Weizmann was not assuaged, telling his closest confidants on 27 June, at Zionist headquarters in London, that Churchill and Roosevelt had 'let them down, maybe not intentionally, but inadvertently. They made promises which they did not carry out or mean to carry out. They were only a small people; he could not fight Churchill or Truman but he could keep his conscience clear by telling them "You have done what you have done, but you cannot expect me to swallow it." He did not think the Agency would swallow it. He knew his resignation might lead to a dangerous state of affairs, and that the consequences for them might be serious. He felt very bitter; he had reached the end of a long road. They had tried their best. He had absolute confidence in Mr Churchill and Gen. Smuts but both their letters were great disappointments.'[19]

On 20 July Randolph Churchill wrote to his father: 'I had a talk with Weizmann yesterday. As you probably know the World Zionist Organization are meeting on July 31 for the first time for six years. Weizmann appears genuinely concerned at the possibility of being thrown out by the Extremists unless he can hold out some hope for the future. Immigration is of course the burning topic. He fears that, unless the present ban can be mitigated in some way, there are bound to be a lot of illegal immigrants, many of whom will be caught and ejected, possibly with bloodshed.'

Weizmann had told Randolph that President Truman was 'fully informed on the position and very sympathetic.' Randolph told his father: 'I am sorry to trouble you with this now, when you must have so many other much more important things in mind. But it occurred to me that, whether or not you discuss Palestine with Truman, and whether or not any useful results are reached, somebody ought to see Weizmann before the 31st and brief him on the line he ought to take.'[20] Churchill suggested Oliver Stanley, who saw Weizmann; but

---

18 Note of 17 June 1945: Churchill papers, 20/234.

19 Notes of a meeting held on 27 June 1945: Central Zionist Archives. Smuts had taken Churchill's view, that any settlement must wait until the proposed Middle East peace conference.

20 Letter of 20 July 1945: Churchill papers, 20/234.

the Middle East Peace conference would have to wait until after Potsdam.

On 5 July the British electors cast their votes. The results would not be known for another three weeks until the soldiers' votes, including those who were still on active service in the Far East, had been counted. On 6 July, the day before leaving England for a nine-day respite, painting in the French Pyrenees, Churchill wrote to the Colonial Secretary Oliver Stanley and the Chiefs of Staff, with a copy to Eden: 'The whole question of Palestine must be settled at the Peace table, though it may be touched upon at Terminal. I do not think we should take the responsibility upon ourselves of managing this very difficult place while the Americans sit back and criticise. Have you ever addressed yourself to the idea that we should ask them to take it over? I believe we should be the stronger the more they are drawn into the Mediterranean. At any rate the fact that we show no desire to keep the Mandate will be a great help. I am not aware of the slightest advantage which has ever accrued to Great Britain from this painful and thankless task. Somebody else should have their turn now.'[21]

At Potsdam the Big Three did not discuss the future of Palestine. Churchill had not been averse to doing so prior to the Middle East 'Peace table', but Oliver Stanley told Churchill on 13 July that he and Eden felt that 'in the absence of any Government decision either on short term or long term policy it would be best' – at Potsdam – 'not to raise the question ourselves.'[22] Churchill knew that there was no way that the Conservative caretaker government would come round to his point of view.

At Potsdam the future of Poland – on which the Soviet liberators were imposing Communist rule – dominated the discussions. Palestine did come up briefly and tangentially during a discussion about what was to become of the former Italian colonies, in particular Tripolitania

21 Letter of 6 July 1945: Churchill papers, 20/234.
22 Letter of 13 July 1945: Churchill papers, 20/234.

and Cyrenaica – which were later joined together to form Libya. Churchill raised the possibility of transferring Tripolitania and Cyrenaica, then under British military occupation, to Jewish rule and future settlement. Britain had 'wondered if any of these countries would do for the Jews,' Churchill told Truman and Stalin, 'but it appeared that the Jews were not very smitten with this suggestion.'[23] As Churchill knew, the half million Jews of Palestine, builders of towns, tillers of the soil, creators of its national and educational institutions, had no intention of even discussing an alternative National Home.

Churchill broke off the Potsdam talks to return to Britain to learn the election results. The Conservative Party had been defeated at the polls and Labour was returned to power for the first time in fourteen years. The British people, Churchill told Captain Pim, the head of his wartime Map Room, 'are perfectly entitled to vote as they please. This is democracy. This is what we have been fighting for.'[24]

As Churchill had warned Weizmann a few weeks before the election results were known, the Labour Party had lost its zeal for Zionism. The new Prime Minister, Clement Attlee, appointed Ernest Bevin as Foreign Secretary. In 1929 Bevin had attributed the Arab riots in Palestine to Arab peasant indignation against the power of Jewish money – a cruel mischaracterisation at a time when the Zionist movement had been struggling with lack of funds and with the burden of defending Jewish towns and villages against unprovoked Arab attack.

On taking charge of British foreign policy on 27 July 1945, Bevin set himself against allowing into Palestine the 100,000 survivors of the Holocaust who were then being gathered in Displaced Persons camps in the British and American zones of Germany. He also set himself against Churchill's assurances to the Peel Commission eight years earlier that the British Government contemplated, in due

---

23 Potsdam protocol: 'P (Terminal) 6th Meeting', 5 p.m., 22 July 1945: Cabinet papers, 99/38.
24 Sir Richard Pim, in conversation with the author, 1975.

course, a Jewish majority and a Jewish State in Palestine. These were severe blows to the half million Jews of Palestine, and to those Jews waiting in DP camps in Europe to be given refuge there.

In the spring of 1946 Churchill was in the United States. On 18 March he was the guest of honour at a dinner given by Bernard Baruch in New York. One of the guests present, Elisha Friedman, a leading economist, wrote to Churchill the following day to compliment him on having spoken with 'the assured touch of a master.' Churchill had moved him 'most deeply,' Friedman wrote, 'when you said you were a Zionist.' Indeed, Friedman continued, Baruch had told him 'that you were trying to convert him to Zionism. This was heartening to me, for I have not succeeded in doing so, after thirty years of effort.'[25]

The British Government not only refused to allow the 100,000 survivors to emigrate to Palestine, it also sent to detention in camps in Cyprus those who were caught trying to arrive by sea. This led to an upsurge in conflict in Palestine, with Jewish terrorists carrying out violent attacks on British troops and police. Faced by unrest and violence that it did not have the troops or will power to challenge, the Cabinet in London set up an Anglo-American Commission to make recommendations about the future of Palestine, with a view to ending the Mandate. The Commission concluded that the British Mandate should be replaced by two sovereign nations, one Jewish, the other Arab, in a partitioned Palestine.

Churchill had come to see Partition as the only realistic solution. On 1 May 1946 he wrote, as part of a draft letter to Clement Attlee: 'I strongly favour putting all possible pressure upon the United States to share with us the responsibility and burden of bringing about a good solution on the lines now proposed by the Anglo-American Commission. If adequate American assistance is not forthcoming, and we are plainly unable either to carry out our pledge to the Jews of building up a national Jewish home in Palestine,

25 Letter of 19 March 1946: Churchill papers, 2/6.

allowing immigration according to absorptive capacity, or if we feel ourselves unable to bear single-handed all the burdens cast upon us by the new Commission's report we have an undoubted right to ask to be relieved of the Mandate.'[26]

In the event, Churchill decided not to send this paragraph, but it reflected a view he had held and expressed on several occasions in the past.

In Palestine acts of Jewish terror continued: on 16 June there was a countrywide sabotage of bridges, and two days later, five British officers were kidnapped from the Officers' Club in Tel Aviv. But such actions were still the method of a minority that believed violence was the way to drive out the British. 'Yielding to terrorism would be a disaster,' Churchill wrote to Attlee on 2 July 1946, but he added: 'At the same time I hold myself bound by our national pledges, into which I personally and you also and your Party have entered, namely the establishment of a Jewish National Home in Palestine, with immigration up to the limit of "absorptive capacity", of which Britain, as the Mandatory Power, was the judge.' Churchill went on to tell Attlee: 'Several of my friends are far from abandoning Partition, and I am very much inclined to think this may be the sole solution.'[27] 'We shall not accept any solution,' Attlee replied, 'which represents abandonment of our pledges to the Jews or our obligations to the Arabs.'[28]

In Poland, those survivors of the Holocaust who wanted to return to their pre-war homes and rebuild their shattered lives were attacked and even murdered by Poles who did not want them to return to the homes that were being lived in since the deportations of 1942 by neighbours and strangers. In Kielce on 4 July 1946, forty-two Jews were killed by an anti-Semitic Polish mob. Two of those killed were young children. Four were teenagers who had

26 Draft letter of 1 May 1946: Churchill papers, 2/42.
27 Letter of 2 July 1946: Churchill papers, 2/237.
28 Letter of 4 July 1946: Churchill papers, 2/237.

reached the city a few days earlier and were on their way to Palestine. Within twenty-four hours of the killings becoming known, more than five thousand Polish Jews fled westward, determined to make their way to Palestine. Tens of thousands more followed in the months ahead.

CHAPTER TWENTY-THREE

THE KING DAVID HOTEL BOMB: 'WE ARE TO BE AT WAR WITH THE JEWS OF PALESTINE'

In Palestine, Jewish terrorism reached a climax on 22 July 1946 with the blowing up of the British Secretariat wing of the King David Hotel in Jerusalem by the Irgun, commanded by Menachem Begin. Ninety-one people were killed, most of them civilians: among them forty-one Arabs, seventeen Jews, and fifteen Britons working in the Mandate administration. During the debate in the House of Commons on 1 August, speaker after speaker expressed outrage at this act of Jewish terror. By contrast, Churchill sought to balance his sense of outrage with his understanding of the whole history of the Mandate, of which he had been an integral part from its outset twenty-four years earlier. His speech was among his most important parliamentary efforts, seeking to coax a hostile House towards a more balanced position.

'The years during which we have accepted the Mandate,' Churchill told the House, 'have been the brightest that Palestine has known and were full of hope. Of course, there was always friction, because the Jew was, in many cases, allowed to go far beyond the strict limits of the interpretation which was placed upon the Mandate.' These 'strict limits' had been laid down in the Churchill White Paper of 1922: that there should be no Jewish immigration beyond the 'economic absorptive capacity' of Palestine. That was the phrase, Churchill pointed out, 'which I coined in those days and which seems to remain convenient – the Mandatory Power being, it was presumed, the final judge of what that capacity was. During the greater part of a quarter of a century which has passed, this policy was carefully carried out by us.'

Churchill then spoke warmly about the Jewish achievements in Palestine. The Jewish population multiplied from about 80,000 to nearly 600,000, he said. Tel Aviv 'expanded into the great city it is, a city which, I must say, during this war and before it, welcomed and nourished waifs and orphans flying from Nazi persecution.' Many refugees 'found a shelter and a sanctuary there, so that this land, not largely productive of the means of life, became a fountain of charity and hospitality to people in great distress. Land reclamation and cultivation and great electrical enterprises progressed. Trade made notable progress, and not only did the Jewish population increase but the Arab population, dwelling in the areas colonised and enriched by the Jews, also increased in almost equal numbers. The Jews multiplied six-fold and the Arabs developed 500,000, thus showing that both races gained a marked advantage from the Zionist policy which we pursued and which we were developing over this period.'

Churchill then spoke of the 1939 White Paper, and of the changes wrought by the coming of war less than four months later. 'I have never altered my opinion,' he said, 'that the White Paper constituted a negation of Zionist policy which, the House must remember, was an integral and indispensable condition of the Mandate. That is the view which I hold today.' The 1939 White Paper, he pointed out, 'was violently resented by the Jews in Palestine, and by world Jewry, a large majority of whom – although there are notable exceptions – regard Zionism as a great ideal, and as the cherished hope of their race, scattered throughout the world.'

Churchill pointed out that in 1941, at a 'most critical time' of the war, the situation in the Middle East 'was aggravated by the revolt of the pro-German Arab elements in Iraq. No doubt our Zionist policy may have led, in part, to that divergence of Arab sentiment. But the revolt was quelled.' There were two facts to be borne in mind, Churchill said, with regard to the war: 'First that Zionists and the Palestine Jews were vehemently and undividedly on our side in the struggle and, secondly, that they no longer need our assistance to maintain themselves in their national home against local Arab hostility. A general attack upon them by all surrounding Arab States would be a different matter, and that would clearly be one which would have to be settled by the United Nations organisation.' It was almost universally assumed in 1946 that the United Nations – then made up of those countries that had defeated Germany and Japan – would act in unison against any aggressor.

Churchill turned to British policy towards the Arabs. 'How did we treat the Arabs?' he asked. His answer was clear. 'We have treated them very well. The House of Hussein reigns in Iraq. Feisal was placed on the throne, his grandson is there today. The Emir Abdullah, whom I remember appointing at Jerusalem, in 1921, to be in charge of Transjordania, is there today. He has survived the shocks, strains and stresses which have altered almost every institution in the world. He has never broken his faith and loyalty to this country. Syria and the Lebanon owe their independence to the great exertions made by the British Government to make sure that the pledges made by them, at the time when we were weak, but, nevertheless, were forced to take action by entering the country to drive out the Vichy French, were honoured. We have insisted on those pledges being made good.'

Churchill rejected claims that Britain had not been a friend of the Arabs. ' I cannot admit that we have not done our utmost to treat the Arabs in a way which so great a race deserves and requires.' The 1922 territorial settlement had been much to their advantage. 'I will not have it said that the way we treated this matter was inconsiderate to the Arabs. On the contrary, I think that they have had a very fair deal from Great Britain. With all those countries which are given to their power and control, in every way they have had a very fair deal. It was little enough, indeed, that we had asked for the Jews – a natural home in their historic Holy Land, on which they have the power and virtue to confer many blessings for enjoyment, both of Jew and Arab.'

Churchill sought to show the change in Britain's treatment of the Jews of Palestine after the Labour victory in 1945. 'At the

General Election which followed the victorious ending of the German war,' he said, 'the Labour Party, which was believed to champion the Zionist cause in the terms I have defined, and not only in those terms, but going, in many cases, far beyond – to set up a Jewish State in Palestine' – had, during the General Election campaign, made 'most strenuous pro-Zionist speeches and declarations. Many of their most important leaders,' Churchill pointed out, 'were known to be ardent supporters of the Zionist cause, and their success was, naturally, regarded by the Jewish community in Palestine as a prelude to the fulfilment of the pledges which had been made to them, and indeed opening the way to further ambitions. This was certainly the least which everybody expected.'

In fact, Churchill stressed, 'all sorts of hopes were raised among the Jews of Palestine, just as other hopes were raised elsewhere. However, when the months slipped by and no decided policy or declaration was made by the present Government, a deep and bitter resentment spread throughout the Palestine Jewish community, and violent protests were made by the Zionist supporters in the United States. The disappointment and disillusionment of the Jews at the procrastination and indecision of the British Labour Government are no excuse, as we have repeatedly affirmed here, for the dark and deadly crimes which have been committed by the fanatical extremists, and these miscreants and murderers should be rooted out, and punished with the full severity of the law. We are all agreed about that.' But, Churchill insisted, the expectations that had been aroused by the Labour Party, and 'the resultant revulsion of feeling, are facts, none the less, to be held constantly before our minds. They cannot say all these things, and then let a whole year pass away and do nothing about it, and then be surprised if these pledges come home to roost in a most unpleasant manner.'

The Jews in Palestine scrutinised Churchill's words for every sign of encouragement. 'Had I had the opportunity of guiding the course of events after the war was won a year ago,' he said, 'I should have faithfully pursued the Zionist cause as I have defined it; and I have not abandoned it today, although this is not a very popular moment to espouse it; but there are two things to say about it.' Churchill then spoke words that cast a sudden dampener, telling the House of Commons that he entirely agreed with what a leading member of the Labour Government, the President of the Board of Trade, Sir Stafford Cripps, had said earlier, that 'no one can imagine that there is room in Palestine for the great masses of Jews who wish to leave Europe, or that they could be absorbed in any period which it is now useful to contemplate.' Churchill commented: 'The idea that the Jewish problem could be solved or even helped by a vast dumping of the Jews of Europe into Palestine is really too silly to consume our time in the House this afternoon. I am not absolutely sure that we should be in too great a hurry to give up the idea that European Jews may live in the countries where they belong. I must say that I had no idea, when the war came to an end, of the horrible massacres which had occurred; the millions and millions that have been slaughtered. That dawned on us gradually after the struggle was over.'

But 'if all these immense millions have been killed and slaughtered,' Churchill continued, 'there must be a certain amount of living room for the survivors, and there must be inheritances and properties to which they can lay claim. Are we not to hope that some tolerance will be established in racial matters in Europe, and that there will be some law reigning by which, at any rate, a portion of the property of these great numbers will not be taken away from them. It is quite clear, however, that this crude idea of letting all the Jews of Europe go into Palestine has no relation either to the problem of Europe or to the problem which arises in Palestine.'

At this point a Jewish Member of Parliament, Sidney Silverman, rose to ask: 'The Right Hon. Gentleman is not suggesting, is he, that any Jew who regarded a country in Europe as nothing but the graveyard and cemetery of all his relatives, friends and hopes should be compelled to stay there if he did not want to do so?'

To this Churchill replied: 'I am against preventing Jews from doing anything which other people are allowed to do. I am against that, and I have the strongest abhorrence of the idea of anti-Semitic lines of prejudice.'

Churchill then spoke of what he called 'the crux of the argument I am venturing to submit to the House,' that in his view 'an unfair burden was being thrown upon Great Britain by our having to bear the whole weight of the Zionist policy, while Arabs and Moslems, then so important to our Empire, were alarmed and estranged, and while the United States, for the Government and people of which I have the greatest regard and friendship, and other countries, sat on the sidelines and criticised our shortcomings with all the freedom of perfect detachment and irresponsibility.' He had therefore 'always intended to put it to our friends in America, from the very beginning of the postwar discussions, that either they should come in and help us in this Zionist problem, about which they feel so strongly, and as I think rightly, on even terms, share and share alike, or that we should resign our Mandate, as we have, of course, a perfect right to do.'

Churchill told the House of Commons that he was convinced 'that from the moment when we feel ourselves unable to carry out properly and honestly the Zionist policy as we have all these years defined it and accepted it, and which is the condition on which we received the Mandate for Palestine, it is our duty at any rate to offer to lay down the Mandate.' Britain had 'never sought or got anything out of Palestine. We have discharged a thankless, painful, costly, laborious, inconvenient task for more than a quarter of a century with a very great measure of success.'

Many people 'have made fine speeches about the Zionist question,' Churchill continued. 'Many have subscribed generously in money, but it is Great Britain, and Great Britain alone, which has steadfastly carried that cause forward across a whole generation to its present actual position, and the Jews all over the world ought not to be in a hurry to forget that.' If, he warned, 'in the Jewish movement or in the Jewish Agency there are elements of murder and outrage which they cannot control, and if these strike not only at their best but at their only effective friends, they and the Zionist cause must inevitably suffer from the grave and lasting reproach of the atrocious crimes which have been committed. It is perfectly clear that Jewish warfare directed against the British in Palestine will, if protracted, automatically release us from all obligations to persevere, as well as destroy the inclination to make further efforts in British hearts. Indeed, there are many people who are very near that now.'

Churchill was right. Jewish terrorism in Palestine had created a backlash of anger in Britain that permeated the whole country. Members of Parliament, never collectively supporters of Zionism, had become far more hostile to it even than at the time of the Rutenberg debate twenty-four years earlier, when Churchill had argued the case in favour of Zionist and Jewish enterprise.

Despite his warning, Churchill refused to succumb to the prevailing mood, telling the House: 'We must not be in a hurry to turn aside from large causes which we have carried far.' And he went on to speak of Weizmann, 'that dynamic Jew whom I have known so long, the ablest and wisest leader of the cause of Zionism, his whole life devoted to the cause, his son killed in the battle for our common freedom. I ardently hope his authority will be respected by Zionists in this dark hour, and that the Government will keep in touch with him, and make every one of his compatriots feel how much he is respected here. It is perfectly clear that in that case we shall have the best opportunities of carrying this matter further forward.'

Churchill contrasted British Government policy in Palestine with that in India and Egypt. The government, he said, 'are, apparently, ready to leave the 400 million Indians to fall into all the horrors of sanguinary civil war – civil war compared to which anything that could happen in Palestine would be microscopic; wars of elephants compared with wars of mice . . . We scuttle from Egypt . . . we abandon the Canal Zone about which our treaty rights were and still are indefeasible; but now, apparently, the one place where we are at all costs and at all inconvenience to hold on and fight it out to the death is Palestine, and we are to be at war with the Jews of Palestine, and, if necessary, with the Arabs of Palestine.'

If the United States were not willing to 'come and share the burden of the Zionist cause,' Churchill reiterated, then Britain should give immediate notice 'that we will return our Mandate to the United Nations Organisation and that we will evacuate Palestine within a specified period.'[1] 'I wish indeed,' Weizmann wrote to Churchill on the following day, 'that Fate had allowed you to handle our problem; by now it would probably all have been settled, and we would all have been spared a good deal of misery.'[2]

1 Parliamentary Debates, *Handsard,* 1 August 1946.
2 Letter of 2 August 1946: Churchill papers, 2/8.

CHAPTER TWENTY-FOUR

'A SENSELESS, SQUALID WAR WITH THE JEWS'

Learning in late August 1946 of British plans to disarm the Jews of Palestine, in an attempt to end the continuing Jewish terrorist attacks on both British and Arab targets, Churchill sent a message to Attlee, through Attlee's Principal Private Secretary, Leslie Rowan, noting that the disarmament of the Jews 'carries with it the obligation to protect them from the Arabs.'[1]

Acts of Jewish terror continued. On 9 September, during an attack on the Area Security Office in Jaffa, a British officer was killed. On 17 October a British police inspector was shot dead in the main street in Jerusalem. On 30 October a British constable was killed during a sabotage action at Jerusalem railway station. On 9 November four British policemen were killed when a booby-trap bomb exploded while they were searching a house for hidden explosives. On 13 November two British policemen were killed while patrolling the Jerusalem-Jaffa railway line. Four days later four policemen were killed when their truck was blown up outside Tel Aviv. On 29 December a British officer and three army sergeants were kidnapped and flogged.

The New Year brought no abatement of Jewish terrorist activity. On 3 January 1947, five British soldiers were injured when their jeeps were blown up by mines. That same day an Arab constable, badly hurt in an earlier attack, died of his injuries. On 12 January four people were killed when a bomb was exploded at the District

1 Letter of 21 August 1946: Churchill papers, 2/46.

Police Headquarters in Haifa.[2] On 27 January a British judge, Ralph Windham, was kidnapped by six armed Jewish terrorists from his court in Tel Aviv; he was released two days later.

Shortly before Churchill spoke in the Palestine debate of 31 January, the government announced that during the previous year Jewish terrorists had killed forty-five British soldiers, twenty-nine members of the British-manned Palestine Police Force, sixty-three Jewish civilians, sixty Arab civilians, and fourteen British civilians, including two British Jews serving in the Mandate administration.

During the debate of 31 January, Churchill spoke unequivocally of 'this series of detestable outrages', but he also cautioned his fellow Members of Parliament – with all his authority as Leader of the Opposition – not to support reprisals against the Jews, and even to be wary of making war on the terrorists. In Churchill's words: 'The idea that general reprisals upon the civil population and vicarious examples would be consonant with our whole outlook upon the world of affairs and with our name, reputation and principles, is, of course, one which should never be accepted in any way. We have, therefore, very great difficulties in conducting squalid warfare with terrorists. That is why I would venture to submit to the House that every effort should be made to avoid getting into warfare with terrorists; and if a warfare with terrorists has broken out, every effort should be made – I exclude no reasonable proposal – to bring it to an end.'

Churchill also urged the House, as he had done in his previous speech on Palestine, not to turn its back on a Jewish National Home in Palestine. His friends on the Conservative benches, he pointed out, 'do not agree with the views which I held for so many years about the Zionist cause. But promises were made far beyond those to which responsible Governments should have committed themselves. What has been the performance? The performance has been a vacuum, a gaping void, a senseless, dumb abyss – nothing.' The

---

2 'Main terrorist incidents', 1 June 1946–6 March 1947: Colonial Office papers, 733/477/3.

'outrageous' acts of Jewish terror in Palestine, Churchill pointed out, were being committed by a 'small, fanatical desperate minority.'

Churchill then spoke about one of that 'fanatical minority', Dov Gruner, who was under sentence of death. While awaiting execution, Gruner had been asked – following British pressure on the Jewish Agency – to appeal against execution, so that the British Mandate authorities could accept his appeal, and thereby secure the release of Judge Windham, who had been seized as a hostage by Gruner's terrorist group. In return for not hanging Gruner, the judge would be freed. But Gruner refused to appeal, insisting that the sentence be carried out. While insisting that a sentence once pronounced must be carried out, Churchill spoke with admiration of Gruner's stand, telling his fellow parliamentarians: 'The fortitude of this man, criminal though he be, must not escape the notice of the House.'

Churchill turned to the financial aspect of British rule in Palestine. 'We are told that there are a handful of terrorists on one side and 100,000 British troops on the other.' The cost to Britain was between £30 million and £40 million a year, 'which is being poured out and which would do much to help to find employment in these islands, or could be allowed to return to fructify in the pockets of the people.'[3] One hundred thousand men was 'a very definite proportion of our Army for one and a half years. How much longer are they to stay here? And stay for what? In order that on a threat to kill hostages we show ourselves unable to execute a sentence duly pronounced by a competent tribunal. It is not good enough. I never saw anything less recompensive for the efforts now employed than what is going on in Palestine.'

Churchill was convinced that Britain no longer had the means, the will, or the moral right to continue to hold the Mandate. He saw 'absolutely no reason' why 'poor, overburdened and heavily injured' Britain should continue to suffer 'all this pain, toil, injury and suffering.' Unless the United States was prepared to 'come in with us shoulder to shoulder on a fifty per cent basis on an agreed policy, to

3 In the money values of today, £30 million is in excess of £450 million.

take a half and half share of the bloodshed, odium, trouble, expense and worry,' Britain should lay its Mandate at the feet of the United Nations: 'Whereas, six months ago, I suggested that we should do that in twelve months I suggest now that the period should be shortened to six months. One is more and more worried and one's anxiety deepens and grows as hopes are falsified and the difficulties of the aftermath of war, which I do not underrate, lie still heavily upon us in a divided nation, cutting deeply across our lives and feelings.'

Churchill's conclusion was forthright: 'I earnestly trust that the Government will, if they have to fight this squalid war, make perfectly certain that the will power of the British State is not conquered by brigands and bandits, and unless we are to have the aid of the United States, they will, at the earliest possible moment, give due notice to divest us of a responsibility which we are failing to discharge and which in the process is covering us with blood and shame.'[4]

Following the debate of 31 January 1947, the British Labour Government decided to return the Palestine Mandate to the United Nations. This Cabinet decision was made public two weeks later. Britain would leave Palestine as soon as the process of transferring the Mandate to the United Nations could be completed. Meanwhile, despite this decision, Jewish terrorists continued to attack British military targets. On 1 March a bomb was exploded inside the Officers' Club in Jerusalem. Fourteen officers were killed, the highest single death toll by terrorist action thus far. On 12 March Churchill spoke again in the House of Commons of the cost of the continuing struggle, telling his fellow members: '£82 million since the Socialist Government came into power squandered in Palestine, and 100,000 Englishmen now kept away from their homes and work, for the sake of a senseless, squalid war with the Jews, in order to give Palestine to the Arab, or God knows who.'

'Scuttle everywhere,' Churchill taunted, 'is the order of the day – Egypt, India, Burma. One thing at all costs we must preserve: the

4 Parliamentary Debates, *Hansard*, 31 January 1947.

right to get ourselves world-mocked and world-hated over Palestine, at a cost of £82 million.'[5]

British hostility to Zionist enterprise, so often a mask for anti-Semitism, was anathema to Churchill, who challenged it wherever he found it, including among his friends. The fact that Harold Laski, who had recently been appointed head of the Labour Party Secretariat, was Jewish, was a cause of derisive comment by some senior Conservatives. To one of Laski's detractors, Brigadier General Lord Croft, who had been Parliamentary Under Secretary of State for War in Churchill's wartime coalition, Churchill wrote words of warning: 'My Dear Henry, I see you used an expression in your speech the other day about Laski that he was "a fine representative of the old British working-class", or words to that effect. Pray be careful, whatever the temptation, not to be drawn into any campaign that might be represented as anti-Semitism.'[6]

Churchill did not know that anti-Jewish sentiments were also being expressed by President Truman, in the privacy of his diary. On 21 July 1947, Truman received a telephone call from Henry Morgenthau Jr, the Secretary of the Treasury, who was much concerned about the ship *Empire Rival*, on which, on the orders of the British Foreign Secretary Ernest Bevin, the Royal Navy was deporting illegal Jewish refugees back to Europe, where they had been living in Displaced Persons camps since the end of the war two years earlier. 'He'd no business whatever to call me,' Truman wrote in his diary. 'The Jews have no sense of proportion nor do they have any judgement on world affairs.'

Truman then noted that, shortly after the war, Morgenthau had brought a thousand Jews from Europe to New York 'on a supposedly temporary basis and they stayed.' Truman added: 'The Jews, I find, are very, very selfish. They care not how many Estonians, Latvians,

---

5 Parliamentary Debates, *Hansard*, 21 March 1947. In the money values of today, £82 million is in excess of £12,000 million.
6 Churchill to Lord Croft, 20 June 1945: Churchill papers, 20/194B.

Finns, Poles, Yugoslavs or Greeks get murdered or mistreated as DPs as long as the Jews get special treatment. Yet when they have power, physical, financial or political, neither Hitler nor Stalin has anything on them for cruelty or mistreatment to the underdog.'

Truman's cruel comments were not limited to Jews. 'Put an underdog on top,' he wrote in his diary, 'and it makes no difference whether his name is Russian, Jewish, Negro, Management, Labor, Mormon, Baptist he goes haywire. I've found very, very few who remember their past condition when prosperity comes.'[7]

Churchill had a different perspective; in the sixth and final volume of his war memoirs, first published in 1953, he reflected on two peoples, the Jews and the Greeks. 'The Greeks rival the Jews in being the most politically-minded race in the world,' Churchill wrote. 'No matter how forlorn their circumstances or how great the peril of their country, they are always divided into many parties, with many leaders who fight among themselves with desperate vigour. It has been well said that wherever there are three Jews it will be found that there are two Prime Ministers and one leader of the Opposition. The same is true of this other famous ancient race, whose stormy and endless struggle for life stretches back to the fountain springs of human thought.'

Churchill's reflections on the Greeks and the Jews continued: 'No two races have set such a mark upon the world. Both have shown a capacity for survival, in spite of unending perils and sufferings from external oppressors, matched only by their own ceaseless feuds, quarrels, and convulsions. The passage of several thousand years sees no change in their characteristics and no diminution of their trials or their vitality. They have survived in spite of all that the world could do against them, and all they could do against themselves, and each of them from angles so different have left us the inheritance of their genius and wisdom. No two cities have counted more with mankind than Athens and Jerusalem. Their messages in religion, philosophy, and art have been the main guiding lights of modern faith and

7 Diary entry, 21 July 1947: Truman papers.

culture. Centuries of foreign rule and indescribable, endless oppression leave them still living, active communities and forces in the modern world, quarrelling amongst themselves with insatiable vivacity. Personally I have always been on the side of both, and believed in their invincible power to survive internal strife and the world tides threatening their extinction.'[8]

8 Winston S. Churchill, *The Second World War,* Volume Five, page 654.

CHAPTER TWENTY-FIVE

THE STATE OF ISRAEL ESTABLISHED: 'AN EVENT IN WORLD HISTORY'

Britain's Palestine Mandate came to an end on 14 May 1948. That day, David Ben-Gurion proclaimed the independence and name of the State of Israel. The Soviet Union and the United States both recognised Israel at once. Britain declined to do so. Within a few hours of Israel's declaration of independence, five Arab armies invaded, from Lebanon, Syria, Transjordan and Egypt, with Iraqi troops in support, seeking to bring a rapid end to the Jewish State. Among those forces was the Arab Legion. Raised and trained in Transjordan, and led by British officers, the Arab Legion opened artillery fire on the Jewish quarter of the Old City of Jerusalem. Several hundred Jews were killed in the fighting before the Jewish Quarter was overrun.

Perturbed that British officers were involved in the attack, Churchill drafted a press statement that he intended to telephone to the BBC and the Press Association. 'As Parliament is not sitting,' he wrote, 'I think it necessary to place on record the deep anxiety that is felt about the policy of the British Government in Palestine.' Giving up the Mandate was 'a most grave decision. I never conceived it possible that the Government, in carrying it out, would not show the strictest impartiality between Jew and Arab. Instead of this it appears that the Arab Legion, led by forty British officers, armed with British equipment and financed by British subsidy, has fired on the Jewish quarter of Jerusalem.'

Churchill pointed out that opening fire was 'a violation of the impartiality which at the least we were bound to observe.' Article One of the Treaty of Alliance between Britain and Transjordan, 'signed as recently as March this year,' prescribed that 'each of the high contracting parties undertakes not to adopt in regard to foreign countries an attitude which is inconsistent with the Alliance or might create difficulties for the other party thereto.' By failing to invoke this Article, Churchill wrote, 'we become in marked degree responsible for the military action of the Arab Legion.'[1]

To the United States Ambassador in London, Lewis Douglas, Churchill wrote on 26 May: 'I am deeply disturbed about the situation which has arisen in Palestine, and at the policy of His Majesty's Government and am proposing to raise the matter in the House of Commons.'[2] Churchill's concern was assuaged, however, two days later when he learned that all British officers in the Arab Legion had been withdrawn from active participation in the attack on Jerusalem. 'It would be amazing in any Government but this,' he told a meeting at Perth in Scotland on 28 May, 'that the danger of allowing British officers to be compromised in this way was not seen beforehand.'[3]

On 2 June there was a lunch at the Savoy in Churchill's honour, given by the Conservative Party. Henry Channon, a Conservative Member of Parliament, noted that Churchill's reception, although not unfriendly, was 'tepid' and he went on to explain: 'I think that the Party resents both his unimpaired criticism of Munich, recently published, and his alleged pro-Zionist leanings.'[4] Churchill's own frustrations at being unable to influence events in the Middle East from a position of authority were considerable. 'I do not think events would have taken this particular course,' he wrote to Lord Melchett on 7 June, 'if they had not been wrested from my hands in the moment of our general victory. Then there was a chance of a good

1 Draft Press Statement: Churchill papers, 2/46.
2 Letter of 26 May 1948: Churchill papers, 4/57.
3 Speech of 28 May 1948: Randolph S. Churchill (editor), *Europe United: Speeches 1947 and 1948 by Winston S. Churchill*, pages 342–3.
4 Henry Channon diary, 2 June 1948: Robert Rhodes James (editor), *Chips*, page 426.

solution, now I can do no more.'[5] Asked by his friend and wartime colleague Brendan Bracken to intervene again in debate, Churchill replied: 'I cannot do any more on Palestine. Events must take their course.'[6]

In September 1948 Churchill was in the South of France, partly on holiday, partly writing his war memoirs. Among those who visited him there was a Conservative Member of Parliament, Robert Boothby, a strong supporter of Zionism, who had written to *The Times* protesting against the Arab Legion shelling of Jerusalem. Boothby later recalled that when the conversation turned to the future of the Jews then fighting for their survival on the battlefield, 'I said that they were going to win hands down in Palestine, and get more than they ever expected.' To Boothby's remark, Churchill replied: 'Of course. The Arabs are no match for them. The Irgun people are the vilest gangsters. But, in backing the Zionists, these Labour people backed the winners; and then ran out on them.' Churchill also told Boothby he was 'quite right' to send his letter to *The Times*.

At that point in the conversation, Churchill's son-in-law Christopher Soames commented – as Boothby recalled – that public opinion in Britain was 'pro-Arab and anti-Jew.' 'Nonsense,' replied Churchill. 'I could put the case for the Jews in ten minutes. We have treated them shamefully. I will never forgive the Irgun terrorists. But we should never have stopped immigration before the war.' Churchill went on to say that he had always been reluctant to meet Weizmann during the war because he found him so fascinating that he would spend too much of his time talking to him. 'Weizmann gives a very different reason,' Boothby said. 'What is that?' Churchill asked. 'Last time I saw him,' Boothby replied, 'he said that the reason you would not see him was because, for you, he was "Conscience."' Churchill was silent.[7]

---

5 Letter of 7 June 1948: Churchill papers, 2/153.
6 Letter of 19 July 1948: Churchill papers, 2/146B.
7 Lord Boothby, *My Yesterday, Your Tomorrow*, pages 211–12.

As Churchill worked in the South of France and at Chartwell on his war memoirs, the negotiations to sell them in the United States were handled in large part by Emery Reves. As well as securing Churchill a substantial American advance, Reves also sold the memoirs to thirteen European publishers for translation, and to an Israeli publisher in Tel Aviv who brought out a Hebrew-language edition. The six volumes, entitled *The Second World War*, focused on British policy, the struggle of the armed forces, and the story of Churchill's war leadership. The volumes were concerned with Britain at war: the Home Front when it faced the threat of invasion, the struggle to avoid defeat, and the hard, prolonged efforts to destroy the all-powerful Nazi war machine, as well as the war against Japan.

Important though the fate of the Jews was during Churchill's wartime premiership, and frequent though his wartime interventions were, the Jewish aspect of the war was not a significant part of his volumes. These focused on the Great Powers, and on the battlefields. There were, however, references to Nazi persecution of the Jews in his first volume; to the arming of the Jews in Palestine in volume two; to the Jewish Army in volume three; to Zionist policy in volume four; to the Jews and the future of Palestine in volume five; and to both the Jewish Brigade Group and the persecution of the Jews of Hungary in volume six. This last volume included Churchill's intervention in July 1944 on behalf of Jews trying to escape from Greece, and his forceful wartime description of the Holocaust as 'probably the greatest and most horrible crime ever committed in the whole history of the world.'[8]

As Churchill was writing the memoirs, this view was confirmed when Emery Reves told him of the fate of his own family, shot to death with more than 1,240 Jews on the frozen banks of the Danube by Hungarian troops and police at Novi Sad, in Hungarian-occupied Yugoslavia. Churchill's principal research assistant, Bill Deakin, later recalled how shocked Churchill had been to learn of their fate,

---

8 Winston S. Churchill, *The Second World War*, Volume Six, page 597.

forced out onto the ice of a tributary of the Danube, which was then shelled, so that they all drowned.[9] Reves, who was one of those who read the typescript with a critical eye, never suggested that there should be more mention of the Nazi war against the Jews. Nor did the young Oxford philosopher Isaiah Berlin, who was among those Churchill asked to scrutinise the text of volume one, and who made many proposals as to content; Churchill described him as 'my friend' Isaiah Berlin.[10]

In sending Churchill his points on volume one, Berlin wrote: 'You did, I recollect, order me to be quite candid.'[11] In his notes to Churchill, Berlin praised his handling of the 'tremendous story of the Rise of Hitler.'[12] Nor did Bill Deakin, who had witnessed the plight of Jewish refugees in German-occupied Yugoslavia, present Churchill for inclusion in the wartime volumes with more than a fragment of the documents bearing on Jewish issues that were a part of Churchill's wartime archive – not even the files relating to Churchill's initiative to help bring Jews out of Yugoslavia to safety.

After six months of Jewish statehood, Britain's Labour Government still refused to recognise the State of Israel. On 9 October 1948, during a speech at a Conservative Party rally in North Wales, Churchill declared: 'The Socialists, more than any other Party in the State, have broken their word in Palestine and by indescribable mismanagement have brought us into widespread hatred and disrepute there and in many parts of the world.'[13]

In November 1948 Dorothy de Rothschild sent Churchill a memorandum written by twenty-five-year-old Marcus Sieff, a member of the Marks and Spencer family. Sieff, who had spent several months in Israel working for Ben-Gurion, stressed the danger of

---

9 Sir William Deakin, in conversation with the author, 1972.
10 Letter to Lord Camrose, 4 January 1948: Churchill papers, 1/141.
11 Letter of 14 February 1948: Churchill papers, 1/141.
12 Notes, undated, January–February 1948: Churchill papers, 4/141.
13 Speech of 5 October 1948, gramophone recording: Robert Shillingford papers (Shillingford was the future husband of Churchill's secretary Lettice Marston).

Arab extremism against Israel if Britain continued in its refusal to recognise the new State. In a covering letter of 2 November 1948 – the thirty-first anniversary of the Balfour Declaration – Sieff wrote to Churchill that many Israeli leaders were anxious to see ties with Britain renewed, but that British policy in the United Nations Assembly with regard to Israel and the Arab States 'prevents any such rapprochement.'[14]

Speaking in the House of Commons on 10 December, Churchill raised the question of the British Government's continual refusal to recognise the State of Israel: 'The Jews have driven the Arabs out of a larger area than was contemplated in our partition schemes,' he pointed out, but went on to say: 'They have established a Government which functions effectively. They have a victorious army at their disposal and they have the support both of Soviet Russia and of the United States. These may be unpleasant facts, but can they be in any way disputed? Not as I have stated them. It seems to me that the Government of Israel which has been set up at Tel Aviv cannot be ignored and treated as if it did not exist.'

Churchill pointed out that nineteen countries had already recognised Israel, 'and we, who still have many interests, duties and memories in Palestine and the Middle East and who have played the directing part over so many years, would surely be foolish in the last degree to be left maintaining a sort of sulky boycott.' Britain, he urged, should send an envoy 'without delay' to Tel Aviv.[15] His suggestion was ignored. Attlee and Bevin could not shake off the bitterness of what they saw as their humiliation by a group of Jews who had been determined to force Britain out of Palestine, and had succeeded. Nor did the British Cabinet wish to offend the Arab countries around Israel whose goodwill, and in the case of Saudi Arabia whose oil, was never far from their minds.

*

14 Marcus Sieff, 'Implications of British policy towards Israel', 25 October 1948: Churchill papers, 2/46.

15 Parliamentary Debates, *Hansard*, 10 December 1948.

At the beginning of 1949, armistice negotiations were begun between Israel, Egypt, Jordan and Lebanon. But there was still spasmodic fighting, which threatened a wider conflict on 7 January 1949, when Israeli aircraft shot down three Royal Air Force Spitfires on a reconnaissance mission over Israeli positions just inside the Sinai border of Egypt. One British pilot was killed. To defuse the crisis, Ernest Bevin ordered the immediate release of the remaining 'illegal immigrant' detainees being held by the British in Cyprus. During an emergency debate on 22 January, Churchill spoke with passion of Bevin's 'astounding mishandling of the Palestine problem,' a mishandling, he said, that had been 'gross and glaring.'

Churchill's first criticism was that Britain had still not recognised Israel, nine months after that State had been proclaimed in Tel Aviv and had been recognised by the United States and the Soviet Union, as well as by more than a dozen other States. 'De facto recognition has never depended upon an exact definition of territorial frontiers,' he told Bevin. 'There are half a dozen countries in Europe which are recognised today whose territorial frontiers are not finally settled. Surely, Poland is one. It is only with the general Peace Treaty that a final settlement can be made. Whoever said, "How can we recognise a country whose limits and boundaries are not carefully defined?" I am astonished to find the Right Hon. Gentleman giving any countenance to it.'

Bevin had made reference to the mistakes some countries had made in hastily recognising Indonesia. Churchill agreed that recognition, or hasty recognition, 'would be a bad precedent, but how absurd it is to compare the so-called Republic of Indonesia with the setting-up in Tel Aviv of a Government of the State of Israel, with an effective organisation and a victorious army.'

Churchill then drew Bevin's attention to a longer timetable than the events of the previous months and years: 'Whether the Right Honorable Gentleman likes it or not, and whether we like it or not, the coming into being of a Jewish State in Palestine is an event in world history to be viewed in the perspective, not of a generation or a century, but in the perspective of a thousand, two thousand or even three thousand years. That is a standard of temporal values or time values which seems very much out of accord with the perpetual click-clack of our rapidly-changing moods and of the age in which we live. This is an event in world history. How vain it is to compare it with the recognition, or the claims to recognition, by certain countries, of the Communist banditti, which we are resisting in Malaya, or of the anarchic forces which the Dutch are trying to restrain in Indonesia.'

Many in the Conservative Party including himself, Churchill said, had 'always had in mind' that the Jewish National Home in Palestine 'might some day develop into a Jewish State.' With the Jewish National Home having come into existence, Churchill mocked, 'it is England that refuses to recognise it, and, by our actions, we find ourselves regarded as its most bitter enemies. All this is due, not only to mental inertia or lack of grip on the part of the Ministers concerned, but also, I am afraid, to the very strong and direct streak of bias and prejudice on the part of the Foreign Secretary.'

This was a strong accusation against Bevin. As protests erupted, Churchill declared: 'I do not feel any great confidence that he has not got a prejudice against the Jews in Palestine.'

Churchill pointed out that Bevin had thought in May 1948 that the Arab League, founded in Cairo three years earlier, was stronger 'and that it would win if fighting broke out.' He, Churchill, had taken another view: 'I certainly felt that the spectacle of the Jewish settlements being invaded from all sides – from Syria, Transjordan and Egypt – and with a lot of our tanks and modern tackle was, on the face of it, most formidable, but I believed that that combination would fall to pieces at the first check, and I adhered to the estimate I had formed in the war of the measure of the fighting qualities and the tough fibre of the Zionist community, and the support which it would receive from Zionists all over the world. But the Foreign Secretary was wrong; wrong in his facts, wrong in the mood, wrong in the method and wrong in the result, and we are very sorry about it for his sake and still more sorry about it for our own.'

Churchill noted that in May 1948 Britain had 'arrayed' against itself the United States, the Soviet Union, the Israelis, and supporters of Zionism all over the world, without – and he wanted the Conservative Members of Parliament 'to realise this' – doing the 'slightest service' to the Arab countries to whom Britain had 'very serious obligations.' He continued: 'This is a poor and undeserved result of all that we have created and built up in Palestine by the goodwill and solid work of twenty-five years. We have lost the friendship of the Palestinian Jews for the time being.' He was glad to have read a recent statement by Weizmann 'pleading for friendship between the new Israeli State and the Western world. I believe that will be its destiny. He was an old friend of mine for many years. His son was killed in the war fighting with us. I trust his influence may grow and that we shall do what we can, subject to our other obligations – because we cannot forget those other obligations – to add to this influence. I hope that later on a truer comprehension of the Zionist debt to this country will revive.'

Churchill then spoke of how, after the war, he was sure Britain could have obtained both Arab and Jewish support for a Partition scheme, whereby two separate States, one Jewish and the other Arab, would have been set up in Palestine. As Churchill said this, Attlee rose to ask Churchill 'if he thought that could have been done, why did he not do it after the war? He was in power.' To this Churchill replied caustically: 'No. The world and the nation had the inestimable blessing of the Right Honorable Gentleman's guidance.' Churchill's view was that Britain could have agreed immediately after the war on a Partition scheme that would have been more favourable to the Arabs 'than that which will now follow their unsuccessful recourse to arms.' In their attempt to defeat the newly declared State of Israel in May 1948, after considerable initial success – with Egyptian troops reaching the southernmost suburb of Jerusalem – the Arab forces had been driven back across the borders they had rejected at the time of the United Nations Partition resolution in November 1947.

As Churchill spoke of how, in his view, a Partition scheme acceptable to both the Jews and Arabs could have been agreed before the end of the Mandate, he was interrupted by Thomas Reid, a Labour

Member for Parliament and a former member of the Woodhead Commission, who asked: 'Agreed with whom? Would it not have led to a major war in the Near East if Partition had been pursued?' To which Churchill answered: 'I am sure we could have made better arrangements for the Arabs at that time – I am not talking of the Jews – than will be possible after there has been this unfortunate recourse to arms. Indeed, the scheme of Partition proposed by UNO was better than what they will get now, after their defeat.'

Churchill spoke next of the Royal Air Force reconnaissance mission that had come to such a violent end. 'Curiosity to know what was going on,' he said, 'would certainly not justify doing a thing so improvident as this sortie of aircraft at such a moment. I say it was the quintessence of maladresse' of which Bevin and Attlee, 'who take the responsibility, were guilty. And now poor old Britain – Tories, Socialists, Liberals, Zionists, anti-Zionists, non-Zionists alike – we find ourselves shot down in an air skirmish, snubbed by the Israeli Government, who said, "We understand you do not recognise us," and with a marked lack of support from the international bodies upon which we depend so greatly and whose opinions we value so highly.'

Churchill turned to the question of Jewish immigration between the wars. The 'whole point' of his own White Paper of 1922, he said, had been that Jewish immigration was to be free, 'but not beyond the limits of economic absorptive power.' Britain could not allow it to be said, Churchill explained, 'that newcomers were coming in, pushing out those who had lived there for centuries. But the newcomers who were coming in brought work and employment with them, and the means of sustaining a much larger population than had lived in Palestine and Transjordan. They brought the hope with them of a far larger population than existed in Palestine at the time of Our Lord.' In the twenty-seven years since 1922 and his White Paper, the Jewish population of Palestine 'doubled or more than doubled, but so did the Arab population of the same areas of Palestine. As the Jews continued to reclaim the country, plant the orange groves, develop the water system, electricity and so forth, employment and means of livelihood were found for ever-larger numbers of Arabs – 400,000 or 500,000 more Arabs found their living there – and the relations of the two races in the Jewish areas were tolerable in spite of external distractions and all kinds of disturbances. General prosperity grew.'

The idea 'that only a limited number of people can live in a country,' Churchill pointed out, 'is a profound illusion; it all depends on their co-operative and inventive power. There are more people today living twenty storeys above the ground in New York than were living on the ground in New York a hundred years ago. There is no limit to the ingenuity of man if it is properly and vigorously applied under conditions of peace and justice.'[16]

After listening to Churchill's speech, a leading Jewish businessman and philanthropist, Sir Simon Marks, whom Churchill had met on a number of occasions, wrote to him: 'I know that our mutual friend Dr Weizmann will be thrilled at the news, and particularly at your remark that "this is a great event in world history."'[17]

That 'news' was the Labour Government's announcement at the end of the debate that Britain was about to recognize the State of Israel.

Among those who had listened to Churchill's speech was Sir Simon Marks's nephew, Marcus Sieff, whose earlier notes had given Churchill a picture of Israeli perspective and hopes. 'I know from my experience,' Sieff wrote to him, 'not only here but in the Middle East in the early years of the War, how great was the part you played in the last quarter of the century in constructing the bridges between this country and the Jews of Palestine, and how the name of Britain stood in that community.' The Labour Government's Palestine policy in recent years had 'largely destroyed' those bridges, Sieff wrote, 'but you have again given a lead which, if sincerely followed by the Government, will go a long way to restoring those ties to the advantage of the moderate people, be they Gentile, Arab or Jew, and for which all moderate people must be grateful.'[18]

---

16 Parliamentary Debates, *Hansard*, 22 January 1949.
17 Letter of 31 January 1949: Churchill papers, 2/163.
18 Letter of 31 January 1949: Churchill papers, 2/46.

Nine days after Churchill's speech, Britain formally recognised Israel. In answer to a telegram of thanks from Weizmann, who had been elected Israel's first President, Churchill replied: 'I look back with much pleasure on our long association,' and he added, in his own hand: 'The light grows.'[19]

19 Letter of 9 February 1949: Churchill papers, 2/46.

CHAPTER TWENTY-SIX

'AN OLD ZIONIST LIKE ME'

On 24 February 1949, Israel and Egypt signed an armistice. A month later an armistice was signed between Israel and Lebanon. Armistice negotiations between Israel and Jordan were in their concluding stages. Israel's War of Independence was at an end. That March, Churchill was in the United States. Britain was about to recognise Israel. At a meeting in New York on 29 March with American Zionist leaders to discuss Israel's future, Churchill assured them that he was supportive. 'Remember,' he said, 'that I was for a free and independent Israel all through the dark years when many of my most distinguished countrymen took a different view. So do not imagine for a moment that I have the slightest idea of deserting you now in your hour of glory.'[1]

Almost thirty years had passed since Churchill had planted a tree on the site of the future Hebrew University of Jerusalem. In the last months of the war he had been the co-patron, with the South African leader Jan Smuts, of the appeal to establish a memorial at the university to Orde Wingate, the wartime commando leader killed in action in Burma, who before the war had helped the Jews devise active methods of self-defence.[2] Asked to send a message for the twenty-fifth anniversary of the opening of the university, Churchill wrote, on 3 June 1950: 'The thought, the inspiration and the culture of the Jews has been one of the vital dominants in the world history.

1 Quoted in Kay Halle, *Irrepressible Churchill*, page 90.
2 Letter from Churchill to Mrs Orde Wingate (Laura Wingate), 14 March 1945: Churchill papers, 20/193.

There are none of the arts or sciences which have not been enriched by Jewish achievements.'[3]

Within Israel and among Jews generally the extent to which Churchill was a friend was much debated. There were those who felt, as did several of the Zionist leaders in 1945, that he could not be trusted. But in Jerusalem, a South-African born member of the Israeli Foreign Office, Michael Comay, wrote in September 1950 to the Israel ambassador in London, that Churchill 'is still a powerful friend to have, both in his official and personal capacities.'[4]

In April 1951 Churchill was invited by Weizmann to attend the opening of the Weizmann Forest in the Jerusalem hills. In sending his apologies, Churchill wrote to Israel's Minister Plenipotentiary in London: 'As a Zionist since the days of the Balfour Declaration I am much complimented to receive this invitation from so great a world statesman as Doctor Weizmann, whose son fell in the cause of freedom, which we now all labour to defend. It is with much regret therefore that I do not find it possible to come to the ceremony which signifies another stage in reclaiming the desert of so many centuries into a fertile home for the Jewish people. Please convey my warm thanks to the President and express my great regrets.'[5]

As Leader of the Opposition, Churchill watched Israel's progress with a supportive eye. He also kept an eye on Israel's adversaries. The three-year-old State was viewed with hatred by its Arab neighbours, of whom Egypt was the most powerful and the most determined to take action that would harm Israel's young and fragile economy. On 30 July 1951 Churchill spoke in the House of Commons about the Labour Government's 'weakness' in allowing Israel to suffer through Egypt's closing of the Suez Canal to Israeli ships.[6] He continued to castigate the Labour Government's Middle East policy, telling the electors of Huddersfield during the General Election campaign in 1951, 'It was a wonderful thing, which really ought to be preserved

---

3 Hebrew University Archive.
4 Letter of 24 September 1950: Israel State Archives.
5 Weizmann Archive.
6 Parliamentary Debates, *Hansard*, 30 July 1951.

as a model of what not to do, how they managed to excite equally the animosity of the Israelites and the Arabs.'[7]

On 26 October 1951 Churchill became Prime Minister for the second time. He was a month short of his 77th birthday. One of the first letters he wrote was to Weizmann, who had congratulated him on his return to power. 'Thank you so much for your letter and good wishes,' Churchill wrote. 'The wonderful exertions which Israel is making in these times of difficulty are cheering to an old Zionist like me. I trust you may work in with Jordan and the rest of the Moslem world. With true comradeship there will be enough for all. Every good wish my old friend.'[8]

On 17 January 1952, while on an official visit to Washington, Churchill addressed a joint session of Congress. 'From the days of the Balfour Declaration,' he said, 'I have desired that the Jews should have a National Home, and I have worked for that end. I rejoice to pay my tribute here to the achievements of those who have founded the Israelite State, who have defended themselves with tenacity, and who offer asylum to great numbers of Jewish refugees. I hope that with their aid they may convert deserts into gardens; but if they are to enjoy peace and prosperity they must strive to renew and preserve their friendly relations with the Arab world, without which widespread misery might follow for all.'[9]

At Carnegie Hall in New York on 29 April 1952, Churchill's daughter Sarah read out a message from her father on the fourth anniversary of the independence of Israel. The gathering was the first meeting of the American Zionist Council, an amalgamation of eight leading Zionist organisations in the United States. 'As a Zionist from the days of the Balfour Declaration,' Churchill's message read, 'I have watched with admiration the courageous effort of Israel to

---

7 Speech of 15 October 1951: Randolph S. Churchill (editor), *Stemming the Tide, Speeches 1951 and 1952 by Winston S. Churchill*, pages 146–51.

8 Weizmann Archive.

9 Speech of 17 January 1952: Randolph S. Churchill (editor), *Stemming the Tide, Speeches 1951 and 1952 by Winston S. Churchill*, pages 220–7.

establish her independence and prosperity. May this and future anniversaries be celebrated with growing confidence and good will by Israel's friends throughout the world.'[10]

Chaim Weizmann, who was just three days older than Churchill, died on 9 November 1952. On the following day, during a parliamentary debate on Egypt, Churchill declared: 'There is another country I must mention at this moment. Those of us who have been Zionists since the days of the Balfour Declaration know what a heavy loss Israel has sustained in the death of its President, Dr Chaim Weizmann. Here was a man whose fame and fidelity were respected throughout the free world, whose son was killed fighting for us in the late war, and who, it may be rightly claimed, led his people back into their promised land, where we have seen them invincibly established as a free and sovereign State.'[11]

Churchill also made a television tribute to Weizmann, one of his few television appearances. Among those watching was James de Rothschild, who wrote from his home in London: 'My dear Winston, Or perhaps on this occasion I should prefer to say my dear Prime Minister, I have just listened to you and watched you on our TV set and I feel that I really must write and tell you how enchanted I was with your appearance and with what you said.'

James de Rothschild added: 'I have not seen you in action now for nearly seven years (save perhaps at the Jockey Club meeting) and seven years is a cycle in man's life. But my dear Winston, you have not changed, the same voice, the same appearance, the same fire and the same cool logic. I was particularly touched and want to thank you personally for what you said about Weizmann; it will mean a lot to the many thousands & tens of thousands of Jews, it will mean a lot to those who are their friends, also perhaps to those who like them less. Yours affectionately, Jimmy.'[12]

---

10 *New York Herald Tribune*, 30 April 1952.
11 Parliamentary Debates, *Hansard*, 10 November 1952.
12 Letter of 10 November 1952: Churchill papers, 2/197.

Within a few days of Churchill's warm remarks about Weizmann, he learned that the Iraqi government was suggesting that Egypt extend its border with Israel from the Sinai desert into the Negev – also known as the Negeb – an area that had been part of Israel since the 1948 War of Independence. Churchill, who was shown the telegram reporting this, and who knew that more than half a million Jews forced to flee Arab lands had found refuge in Israel since independence, wrote to the Foreign Office: 'Surely there can be no question of Israel being asked to give up the Negeb, as its development might afford the only means of sustaining their great population of refugee immigrants?'[13]

The Permanent Under-Secretary of State at the Foreign Office, Sir William Strang, hastened to assure Churchill that the Foreign Office 'consider the Arab claim to be unrealistic and we recognise Israel's need of an area in which the population can expand and which, once developed, may be a source of wealth to the country.'[14] Churchill replied, 'I am very glad we are in full agreement.'[15] The largely barren Negev remained a part of Israel.

In the autumn of 1952, more than sixty years after he had first met the first Lord Rothschild at his father's house, Churchill made the acquaintance of another member of the Rothschild family – Major Edmund de Rothschild. Churchill did so after Joseph Smallwood, the Premier of Newfoundland, approached him with an ambitious plan to harness the power of the 245-foot high Grand Falls, on the Hamilton River in Labrador, to create a major source of electricity to serve not only eastern Canada but also the East Coast of the United States. Churchill, who thirty years earlier had put his political authority behind the Zionist electrical project in Palestine, turned to the Rothschild bank in the City of London, N. M. Rothschild & Sons, a bank he had first visited more than half a century earlier. There, one

13 Minute of 17 November 1952: Premier papers, 11/207.
14 Minute of 19 November 1952: Premier papers, 11/207.
15 Note of 20 November 1952: Premier papers, 11/207.

of the partners, Edmund de Rothschild, who had served in France, North Africa and Italy during the war, undertook to organise the financing of the scheme, establishing Brinco as the holding company.[16]

After retiring as Prime Minister three years later, Churchill purchased shares in Brinco. It was Edmund de Rothschild – Mr Eddie as he was known at the bank – who kept him informed of progress. After Churchill's death, Smallwood and Mr Eddie, having gone together to pay their respects at the Lying-in-State in Westminster Hall, decided to rename the Grand Falls the Churchill Falls – 'they bear the name today,' Mr Eddie later wrote, 'all 5,255 million kilowatts!'[17]

At the beginning of 1953, Churchill was in Washington for talks with President Truman, who had just given his final State of the Union address and was about to hand over the presidency to General Dwight D. Eisenhower. On 8 January, Truman and Churchill dined together at the British Embassy. During dinner Churchill impressed on Truman his strong support for Israel, and his equally strong criticism of Egypt for closing the Suez Canal to ships bound for Israeli ports. The guests then adjourned to the drawing room, where Truman began to play the piano. But, as Churchill's Principal Private Secretary, Jock Colville, wrote in his diary: 'Nobody would listen because they were all busy with post-mortems on a diatribe in favour of Zionism and against Egypt' that Churchill 'had delivered at dinner (to the disagreement of practically all the Americans present, though they admitted that the large Jewish vote would prevent them from disagreeing publicly).'[18]

Churchill had no qualms in urging support for Zionism, or in stating his support for it. Returning from the United States on the *Queen Mary*, he saw from the passenger list that Barnett Janner, with

16 Edmund de Rothschild, 'Brinco: The Early Days', in *The Atlantic Advocate*, July 1967.

whom he had worked on the pro-Zionist Committee in the House of Commons twenty years earlier, was on board. Inviting Janner to join him for coffee in his room, his first words when Janner entered were: 'I am a Zionist' – as if to say, Janner noted, 'Now that's that, let's get on with something else.'

Churchill was never an uncritical supporter of Israeli actions. On 14 October 1953, after an Israeli mother and her two children – the youngest only eighteen months old – had been killed by Palestinian Arab infiltrators from Jordan, an Israeli military force, Unit 101, commanded by Ariel Sharon, supported by a paratroop company, carried out a reprisal raid on the Jordanian Arab village of Kibya. Sixty-nine Arabs, mostly women and children, were killed. The British Embassy in Tel Aviv was instructed by the British Government to convey 'an expression of the horror' at the attack.[19]

Churchill was shown this telegram, but he made no comment. Nor, as some have believed, did he send a personal message to Ben-Gurion deploring the Kibya attack. Indeed, at a meeting of the Defence Committee on 14 October, during the discussion about stationing a British armoured brigade in Jordan, Churchill urged that it should be 'made clear' to Israel 'that the presence of our armoured force in Jordan would not represent any threat to their interests but would, in fact, provide a stabilising influence in that area.'[20]

At a Cabinet meeting on 17 November 1953, during the discussion on the recent tension between Jordan and Israel, caused by the infiltration of Palestinian Arab terrorists from across the Jordanian border and Israeli cross-border retaliation, Churchill distanced himself from calls, particularly from his fellow Conservative parliamentarians, for Britain to support a Jordanian request for British troops. He was 'inclined to think,' he told his Cabinet colleagues, 'that this particular source of trouble concerned the United Nations more than it concerned the United Kingdom.' To send a

17 Major Edmund de Rothschild, letter to the author, 9 July 1986.
18 Colville diary, 8 January 1953: Sir John Colville, *The Fringes of Power*, pages 663–4.
19 Telegram of 16 October 1953: Premier papers, 11/941.

small British force to Jordan, as Jordan wished, 'might merely provoke Israel.' If Britain 'had to intervene at all,' he said, 'it would be better to use overwhelming force which could provide an effective deterrent.'[21]

'Now the Foreign Office wants a war with Israel,' Churchill told his doctor the following morning, and added 'Ernie Bevin apparently made a treaty with Jordan. I don't want war.'[22] 'We should be careful,' Churchill reiterated in Cabinet on 19 November, 'to avoid a situation in which British troops became engaged in hostilities between Israel and Jordan.'[23]

Not Jordan, but Egypt, proved to be Israel's main adversary in 1954. When, in the third week of January, the Egyptian Government announced that it would intensify its blockade of Israel, and would continue to prevent Israeli ships, or even ships of other countries bound for Israel, from using the Suez Canal. On 21 January, Churchill told his Cabinet that such a blockade would lead to increased 'interference' with the passage of ships through the Suez Canal and the blacklisting by Egypt of many ships of all flags trading with the Levant. The Israeli Government was proposing to raise the matter in the United Nations Security Council 'and had asked whether they could count on our support and that of the United States Government.' He hoped 'we should give prompt and effective support to the Israel Government in this matter.' In Parliament, members of all political parties would welcome 'an initiative designed to assert the rights of free transit through the Canal; and it would be convenient if we could transfer the emphasis, in our current differences with Egypt, from the Base to the Canal.'

Commenting on this, the Foreign Secretary, Anthony Eden, told the Cabinet that it should realise 'that the Egyptian Government had legal grounds for their action, in that their war with Israel had not legally been terminated. It was therefore desirable that we should

20 Defence Committee meeting, 14 October 1953: Cabinet papers, 131/13
21 Cabinet Minutes, 17 November 1953: Cabinet papers, 128/26
22 Diary entry, 18 November 1953: Lord Moran, *Winston Churchill, The Struggle for Survival*, page 498.

not take any public position in this matter until we had assured ourselves that we should have the support of some of the other maritime Powers.' The Cabinet then 'invited' Eden to try to enlist the support of those maritime Powers for the protest that Israel proposed to make in the Security Council.[24]

When nothing had been achieved in this regard after five days, Churchill raised the matter again, stressing at the Cabinet of 26 January 'the importance of upholding the right of international passage through the Suez Canal and the Parliamentary advantages of putting this issue in the forefront of our differences with Egypt.' He hoped, therefore, 'that no effort would be spared in enlisting the support of leading maritime Powers for the protest which Israel wished to make in the Security Council against the Egyptian decision to intensify the blockade.'[25]

Britain was firmly behind Israel in its dispute with Egypt, which mirrored a wider effort by President Nasser to take control of the Suez Canal. But when Israeli-Jordanian relations worsened, with cross-border Palestinian terrorist attacks from Jordan and Israeli counter-attacks, the British Cabinet was far closer to Jordan, with whom it was allied, and whose army had been trained by British officers.

At the end of March 1954 the Jordanian-Israeli border again became the focus of Churchill's attention. On 17 March an Israeli bus, travelling up the precipitous hairpin bends of the Scorpion Ascent in the Negev, was attacked by a group of Palestinian Arabs who had infiltrated into Israel from Jordan. The driver and ten passengers were killed. The Israeli Government announced that they considered this a warlike act, responsibility for which 'falls squarely upon the government from whose territory this unit of murderers was sent forth across the border into Israeli territory to carry out this dastardly deed.'[26] There was a state of high tension between Israel and Jordan.

23 Cabinet Minutes, 19 November 1953: Cabinet papers, 131/13.
24 Cabinet meeting of 21 January 1954: Cabinet papers, 128/27.
25 Cabinet meeting of 26 January 1954: Cabinet papers, 128/27.
26 *The Times*, 18 March 1954.

On 31 March the British Cabinet discussed a plan, drawn up by the Chiefs of Staff, for military assistance to Jordan in the event of Jordanian hostilities with Israel. This plan was explained by the Minister of Defence, Field Marshal Viscount Alexander of Tunis, the former Commander-in-Chief of Britain's wartime forces in the Mediterranean and Italy. It involved, he explained, 'the invasion of Israel' by British forces from the south. Should the plan be communicated to the Jordanians, Alexander asked, to which the Chief of the Imperial General Staff, Field Marshal Sir John Harding, commented that the Chiefs of Staff did not wish to do so. He was 'much relieved' to hear this, Churchill remarked, adding that 'leakage of such a plan would have very grave consequences.'

Later in the discussion, Eden proposed that Churchill should send a message to David Ben-Gurion the Prime Minister of Israel, 'reminding him of our obligations under our Treaty with Jordan and urging him to avoid any provocative action.'[27] Eden prepared a draft of what he thought Churchill should send to the Israeli Foreign Minister, Moshe Sharett. Churchill accepted the draft and it was sent on 2 April, noting that 'We shall do what we can to influence the Arab States, but we look to you to make counsels of statesmanship and patience prevail on the Israel side.'[28]

In his reply, Sharett asked Britain to use its influence in Amman to bring about a cessation of terrorist raids across the Jordanian border. 'Through the clouds of the present local storms,' Sharett added, 'we see far-reaching vistas of beneficent co-operation between Britain and Israel in culture and trade, in the advancement and defence of democracy, and in all creative achievement.'[29]

Amid his work as Prime Minister, and despite the burden of a severe stroke in 1953, Churchill was always ready to respond to a Jewish request. In March 1954 the Manchester Zionist Council organised

27 Cabinet meeting of 31 March 1954: Cabinet papers, 128/27.
28 Draft letter initialled by Churchill, 2 April 1954: Premier papers, 11/941.
29 Letter of 13 April 1954: Premier papers, 11/941.

an exhibition, 'Manchester and Israel – a city's contribution to the birth of a State', to coincide with the fiftieth anniversary of Weizmann's arrival in Manchester fifty years earlier. 'The City of Manchester may be proud,' Churchill wrote, 'of its connection with Dr Weizmann, a man of vision and genius, whose lasting memorial will be the vigour and the prosperity of the State of Israel, which he did more than any other single man to inspire and create. I am indeed glad that Manchester should commemorate the fiftieth anniversary of this great man's arrival in our country, and I send my best wishes for the success of the exhibition which is being held.'[30]

During his second premiership, Churchill befriended a Yugoslav-born Jewish sculptor, Oscar Nemon, who had been commissioned by Queen Elizabeth II to make a bust of Churchill for Windsor Castle. As a guest at Chequers, Nemon recalled Churchill's words to Field Marshal Sir William Slim, the Chief of the Imperial General Staff: 'Field Marshal, I'm sending you to Egypt and I want to make one point clear. I am a Zionist and I want you to act accordingly.' Churchill then spoke of how the world owed 'an incalculable amount to the Jews,' telling his guests that the great inventions of the twentieth century had been made by Christians and Jews, 'as though God had revealed His secrets to them.' Churchill also spoke of the Jewish contribution in two world wars, mentioning Weizmann's work on explosives in the First World War, and Einstein's work on the development of atomic science with which 'we were able to put the seal' on the Second World War.

During this discussion at Chequers, Churchill spoke of the Jewish Nobel Prizewinners, whose contribution to humanity in many fields had been 'unique and absolute'. There were nations consisting of hundreds of millions of people who had been unable to produce a single Nobel Prizewinner, 'and are the beneficiaries every day from the genius and discoveries of the Jews.'

Speaking of the situation in Israel, Churchill expressed concern

30 *Jewish Chronicle*, 19 March 1954.

at the country's vulnerability, at a time of repeated terrorist infiltration from across the Jordanian border.'[31]

On 30 November 1954 Churchill celebrated his eightieth birthday. Among the hundreds of messages he received from overseas was a telegram from the Foreign Minister of Israel, Moshe Sharett (formerly Shertok) – whose request ten years earlier, to bomb the railway lines to Auschwitz, Churchill had endorsed. 'In one of the bleakest crises in the history of civilisation,' Sharett wrote, 'it was given to you, by supreme feat of personal determination and inspired national leadership, to save the cause of freedom, to give sublime expression to the faith and fervour of man in his resistance to tyranny, and to lead your own brave people and its allies from defeat to victory.'

Turning to an Israeli perspective, Sharett continued: 'Your staunch advocacy of the Zionist idea, your belief in its justice and ultimate triumph, and your joy in its consummation with the rise of an independent Israel, have earned for you the everlasting gratitude of the Jewish people. They will never forget your steadfast support of the policy of the Balfour Declaration, your forceful interventions on its behalf, your long and unbroken friendship with Chaim Weizmann, and your resolute step in giving their sons the long yearned-for chance of fighting the mortal enemy as a national unit under their own flag. Your continuing personal interest in the efforts and aspirations of Israel reverberates deeply in our people's hearts. May you long be spared to persevere in your noble endeavours.'[32]

In the first and second weeks of February 1955, Churchill was host to the Commonwealth Prime Ministers at their conference in London. In answer to a suggestion in a letter from James de Rothschild that Israel, which was then approaching its seventh year of independence, should be admitted to the Commonwealth,

---

31 Notes of a visit to Chequers: Oscar Nemon papers.
32 Government of Israel State Archives.

Churchill wrote supportively to Eden: 'This is a big question. Israel is a force in the world and a link with the USA.'[33]

In his letter, James de Rothschild recalled 'our stay in Jerusalem in 1921,' during which, he reminded Churchill, 'You then laid the foundations of the Jewish State by separating Abdullah's Kingdom from the rest of Palestine. Without this much-opposed prophetic foresight, there would not have been an Israel today.'[34]

On 18 February Churchill was at Buckingham Palace for a lunch to welcome the Shah of Iran to London. Sir John Shuckburgh, who in 1921 had been in charge of the Arab Department of the Colonial Office under Churchill, was among the guests. He recorded in his diary: 'I was drawn into some talk with him, and he said the Foreign Office was "riddled with Bevinism" on Middle East questions, i.e. anti-Jewish. He had heard (from James de Rothschild) that the Israelis would like to join the British Commonwealth. "Do not put that out of your mind. It would be a wonderful thing. So many people want to leave us; it might be the turning of the tide," Churchill said.'

Shuckburgh noted that Churchill also said to him: 'You ought to let the Jews have Jerusalem; it is they who made it famous.' He also said that large numbers of the refugees ought to be settled in the Negev. I'm not sure whether he was aware that this is something the Israelis are resisting.'[35]

The exhortation 'You ought to let the Jews have Jerusalem; it is they who made it famous' was one of Churchill's last pronouncements before he retired as Prime Minister. He had been a supporter of Jewish national aspirations for more than fifty years.

---

33 Note initialled 'WSC', 9 February 1955: Churchill papers, 2/197.

34 Letter of 1 February 1955: Churchill papers, 2/197.

35 Shuckburgh diary, 18 February 1955: John Shuckburgh, *Descent to Suez, Diaries 1951–56*, page 251.

CHAPTER TWENTY-SEVEN

'A GREAT NATION'

In retirement, Churchill kept a watchful eye on Israel's wellbeing. On 24 February 1956 he received the Israeli Ambassador, Eliahu Elath, who presented him with a portfolio of woodcuts of ancient Jerusalem as an eightieth birthday gift from the Prime Minister and Government of Israel. Returning to his Embassy, Elath telegraphed to his Foreign Minister, Moshe Sharett: 'It was obvious that the words of the dedication moved him more than the pictures themselves.' The dedication had spoken of Israel's 'admiration and gratitude for the man who saved the world from Nazi domination, this securing for all its peoples – Israel among them – the renewed hope of peace, freedom and progress.'

While Churchill was looking at the pictures, Elath reported, 'I told him about the fate of the Jewish Quarter in the Old City. He asked what had happened to the Western Wall. In the course of the conversation he inquired about painting in Israel.' Churchill also told the ambassador 'that he has been and remains our friend. He took joy in the establishment of our State and expressed his confidence in its splendid future. He went on to say: you are a nation of ideals and that is the greatest thing in the life of both the community and the individual. He added that he admires the fact that we have absorbed so many refugees and that we have succeeded in developing the land and conquering the wilderness.'

After assuring the ambassador that he would 'continue to see to it that no evil befalls Israel,' Churchill told him that the Israeli gift would take its place among all the others he received for his birthday, and that 'he was happy that future generations would thereby know that the sons of the prophets dwelling in Zion were among his many well-wishers from all over the world.'[1]

Churchill continued to champion Israeli enterprise. When James and Dorothy de Rothschild asked him to support a project to erect, on behalf of British Jewry, a large ornamental candelabra in front of the new parliament building in Jerusalem – of which they were major sponsors – he was keen to participate. His Private Secretary, Anthony Montague Browne, having consulted the Foreign Office, reported to Churchill: 'There would be no political objection to your subscribing to this fund if you wished. We are not very happy that the Israeli parliament should have set itself up in Jerusalem, which is supposed to be an international city, but this is rather a fine point.'[2]

Montague Browne, who had been seconded to Churchill from the Foreign Office, knew that the British Government still adhered, in theory at least, to the United Nations Partition Plan of 1947, whereby Jerusalem was intended to become an international enclave, separate from both Jewish and Arab Palestine. Undeterred by this, Churchill became a subscriber.

On 13 April 1956, during a speech at the Albert Hall in London, Churchill spoke of the mounting crisis in the Middle East, and of how Israel and Egypt were 'face to face'. It was 'perfectly sure' he said, that the United States, as well as Britain, would intervene to prevent aggression by one side or the other. The moment for this would probably never come, and yet, Churchill warned, 'it may come, and come at any moment.' If Israel was to be 'dissuaded from using' the life of their race to ward off the Egyptians until the Egyptians have learnt to use the Russian weapons with which they have been supplied,' he argued, 'and the Egyptians then attack, it will become not

1 Telegram of 24 February 1956: Government of Israel State Archives.
2 Note of 4 March 1956: Churchill papers, 2/341.

only a matter of prudence but a measure of honour to make sure that they are not the losers by waiting.'[3]

'I should like you to know,' wrote Eliahu Elath, the Israeli Ambassador to Britain, later that day, 'with what deep gratification my Government and the people of Israel will receive your friendly references to our country in your speech.' Elath added: 'We shall all hope and pray that these words, coming from you, will have their effect on those, in London and in Washington, in whose hands now lie the crucial decisions on the matters to which you referred, including that of the supply to Israel of adequate arms for her self-defence.'[4]

Turning to the current confrontation between Egypt and Israel, Churchill wrote to Eisenhower on 16 April, 'I am sure that if we act together, we shall stave off an actual war between Israel and Egypt,' and he went on to tell the President: 'I am, of course, a Zionist, and have been ever since the Balfour Declaration. I think it is a wonderful thing that this tiny colony of Jews should have become a refuge to their compatriots in all the lands where they were persecuted so cruelly, and at the same time established themselves as the most effective fighting force in the area. I am sure America would not stand by and see them overwhelmed by Russian weapons, especially if we had persuaded them to hold their hand while their chance remained.'[5]

On 26 July 1956 President Nasser of Egypt nationalised the Suez Canal. The catalyst for his action was the withdrawal of funds by both Britain and the United States for his Aswan Dam project. Both Britain and France, under whom the Canal had been operating for more than a century, were indignant, especially the British Prime Minister, Anthony Eden. 'I think that Britain and France ought to act together with vigour,' Churchill wrote to his wife four days later.[6]

On 5 August the Chancellor of the Exchequer, Harold

---

3 Speech of 13 April 1956: Randolph S. Churchill (editor), *The Unwritten Alliance, 1953–1959 by Winston S. Churchill*, pages 257–8.
4 Letter of 13 April 1956: Government of Israel State Archives.
5 Letter of 16 April 1956: Eisenhower papers.
6 Letter of 1 August 1956: Spencer-Churchill papers.

Macmillan, dined with Churchill at Chartwell, noting in his diary: 'I said that unless we brought in Israel it couldn't be done. Surely if we landed, we must seek out the Egyptian forces, destroy them and bring down Nasser's government. Churchill got out some maps and got quite excited.'[7]

The following day, Monday, 6 August, was a Bank Holiday. That day Churchill set off by car from Chartwell to Chequers. During the two and a half hour, seventy-five-mile journey, travelling with a secretary, he dictated a note on the Suez Crisis, which he handed to Eden on his arrival. As far as Israel was concerned, Churchill wrote: 'We should want them to menace and hold the Egyptians and not be drawn off against Jordan.'[8]

A conference of Suez Canal users was called, to decide upon a firm stance against Egypt. Israel, whose ships were still forbidden passage of the Canal by Egypt, was not invited. In a letter to her husband, Clementine Churchill wondered why not. 'I suppose why they did not bring Israel in,' Churchill replied, 'was that they were afraid that she would become uncontrollable. But she is there in the background, and I have no doubt that if it comes to war she will join in.' Churchill added: 'The unity of Islam is remarkable. There is no doubt that Libya, to whom we paid £5,000,000 a year, like Jordania, to whom we paid £10,000,000 or more, are whole-heartedly manifesting hostility.'[9]

As Churchill explained to Clementine in this same letter, he was at that very moment reading books about Benjamin Disraeli, for his own book *A History of the English-Speaking Peoples*. Ironically, the book had a Suez aspect, for it was Disraeli who in 1875 purchased a controlling share in the Suez Canal Company on behalf of the British Government. Because the Egyptian ruler, the Khedive Ismail, was bankrupt, Disraeli was able to purchase almost half the shares in the Suez Canal Company – although not a majority interest, this was effectively a controlling interest. Parliament was not in session at the

7 Harold Macmillan, diary entry for 5 August 1956: *Sunday Times*, 5 January 1987
8 'Note by Sir Winston', 6 August 1956: Churchill papers, 2/130.
9 Letter of 11 August 1956: Spencer-Churchill papers. Ten million pounds is the equivalent of £200 million today.

time; to secure the purchase, Disraeli, on his own initiative, borrowed four million pounds from the Rothschilds. It was a government expenditure that was to be of value both as a financial investment and to secure British control of the sea route to India.

In *A History of the English-Speaking Peoples* Churchill praised the 'courage and quickness of wit' with which Disraeli 'had been so generously endowed', and described him – not mentioning that his father had had him baptised – as 'a young Jewish Member of Parliament.'[10] Churchill commented that Disraeli 'never became wholly assimilated to English ways of life, and preserved to his death the detachment which had led him as a young man to make his own analysis of English society. It was this which probably enabled him to diagnose and assess the deeper political currents of his age.'[11] It was Disraeli – the Conservative – who introduced the Reform Bill of 1867, extending the vote to the working class, favouring the large industrial towns, and doubling the electorate to two million.

One November evening at Chartwell in 1947, Churchill had fallen asleep while painting and dreamed that he was talking with his father. During their conversation, which Churchill set down after he woke up, Lord Randolph said of Disraeli: 'I always believed in Dizzy, that old Jew. He saw into the future. We had to bring the English working man into the centre of the picture.'[12]

To help him with his Disraeli and Gladstone chapter of *A History of the English-Speaking Peoples*, which he worked on for several months at Emery Reves' villa, La Pausa, in the South of France, Churchill enlisted the aid of Maurice Shock, a young Jewish don who was teaching at University College, Oxford, and who was put up at a hotel in nearby Roquebrune. 'He is a very nice young man,' Churchill wrote to Clementine at the beginning of October from La Pausa, 'and I am glad to have had him at the hotel for the weekend.'

---

10 Winston S. Churchill, *A History of the English-Speaking Peoples*, Volume Four, page 224.
11 Winston S. Churchill, *A History of the English-Speaking Peoples*, Volume Four, page 44.
12 Winston S. Churchill, 'The Dream', first published by Randolph Churchill in the *Sunday Telegraph*, 30 January 1966, and then as chapter twenty in Martin Gilbert, *Winston S. Churchill*, Volume Eight, pages 364–72.

Among the other guests at La Pausa that weekend was Baroness Jean de Rothschild, with whom Churchill played his favourite card game, bezique. As he wrote to Clementine, 'Her husband – a Vienna Rothschild – is 72 and she about thirty years younger.'[13]

Clementine Churchill was staying at St Moritz, where she renewed her acquaintance with a New York Jew, Lewis Einstein, a widower, with whom she had lively discussions about Britain's rule in Cyprus, then in the throes of a national uprising. Einstein, who had entered the United States diplomatic service in 1903, had served in London, Paris, Peking, Constantinople and Prague, and was a writer and raconteur on topics as diverse as Renaissance art, Tudor manners and the diplomacy of the American Civil War. Churchill was pleased that his wife had found so congenial a friend, writing to her: 'I am very glad that he has turned up to give you company.'[14]

Following President Nasser's nationalisation of the Suez Canal, a British military response was regarded as inevitable, although when or how it would come was unclear. 'I expect we must look to Israel for the next move,' Churchill wrote to Clementine in mid-August.[15] In fact, a month later, it was the Prime Minister, Anthony Eden, who, in secret cooperation with France, persuaded Israel to join in Anglo-French military action against Egypt, and to do so in such a way as to give Britain and France an excuse to intervene militarily. The plan was for Britain and France, having encouraged Israel to attack Egypt, to occupy the Canal under the guise of preventing it from coming under Israeli control. This was the 'collusion' agreed upon at a meeting near Paris on 22 October between Israel, Britain and France, which only became known after the event.

Eight days later, on 30 October 1956, Israeli forces attacked Egypt in the Sinai desert, destroying the Egyptian forces there, and reaching to within a few miles of the Suez Canal. With Israel in the

13 Letter of 11 August 1956: Spencer-Churchill papers.
14 Letter of 3 August 1956: Spencer-Churchill papers.
15 Letter of 15 August 1956: Spencer-Churchill papers.

toils of war, Churchill confided to Emery Reves during a weekend at Chartwell in mid-November: 'I wish them well, and how I wish I were young again, to go to help them.'[16] But Israel's advance came to a halt, as previously arranged with Britain and France, when, following a twelve-hour Anglo-French ultimatum to Egypt, insisting that an Anglo-French force 'move temporarily' to the Suez Canal, British bombers struck at Egyptian airfields, while British troops set sail on the long journey from Malta towards Port Said, at the Canal's northern end.

On 3 November, as British forces were still on their way to Egypt, Churchill issued a public statement giving 'the reasons that lead me to support the Government on the Egyptian issue.' In spite of all the efforts of Britain, France and the United States, he wrote, 'the frontiers of Israel have flickered with murder and armed raids.' Egypt, 'the principal instigator of these incidents,' had 'rejected restraint.' Israel, 'under the gravest provocation' had 'erupted against Egypt.' Britain intended 'to restore peace and order' to the Middle East, 'and I am convinced that we shall achieve our aim.' Churchill was also 'confident' he added, 'that our American friends will come to realise that, not for the first time, we have acted independently for the common good.'[17]

Churchill's message was published in the British newspapers on the morning of 5 November at the very moment when British and French paratroops, in advance of the Anglo-French forces still on their way by sea, landed at the northern end of the Suez Canal, capturing Port Said. 'My dear Winston,' Eden wrote to Churchill, 'I cannot thank you enough for your wonderful message. It has had an enormous effect, and I am sure that in the US it will have maybe an even greater influence.' Eden added: 'These are tough days – but the alternative was a slow bleeding to death.'

'Thank you for your kind words,' Churchill replied. 'I am so glad it was a help.'[18]

---

16 Recollection of Emery Reves: in conversation with the author, 1980.
17 *The Times*, 5 November 1956.
18 Letters exchanged on 5 November 1956: Churchill papers, 2/216

On the morning of 6 November, the seaborne forces of Britain and France finally reached Port Said, landed, and advanced southward along both banks of the Canal. Later that same day, however, as the culmination of a week of intense American pressure, augmented by the refusal of many of Eden's own colleagues to support him, Eden agreed to a ceasefire. Pressure from Washington had been decisive.

Having completed the six volumes of his war memoirs, in 1956 Churchill prepared a single-volume abridgement. In it he decided to refer in the preface to acts by Jewish terrorists that had so scarred the last three years of the Palestine Mandate. 'I wrote a phrase,' recalled Anthony Montague Browne, 'to the effect that these were acts of black ingratitude to their saviours which would always be a blot on the creation of Israel. Emery Reves took exception to this,' but Churchill 'insisted that it should go in,' telling Montague Browne, 'The Jewish people know well enough that I am their friend.'[19]

The sentences as published, read: 'Few of us could blame the Jewish people for their violent views on the subject. A race that has suffered the virtual extermination of its national existence cannot be expected to be entirely reasonable. But the activities of terrorists, who tried to gain their ends by the assassination of British officials and soldiers, were an odious act of ingratitude that left a profound impression.'[20]

Following the Israeli occupation of the Sinai Peninsula with the collusion of Britain and France, President Eisenhower, and his Secretary of State, John Foster Dulles, denounced the Suez war as aggression, demanded the immediate and unconditional withdrawal of Israeli troops, and threatened sanctions. Emery Reves, with whom Churchill was staying at La Pausa, at the beginning of 1957, wrote to him in protest at the American position: 'If there has been since 1949 a state of belligerence, as Egypt asserts, then how

19 Anthony Montague Browne, recollections: notes for the author, 24 March 1987.
20 Winston S. Churchill, *The Second World War and an Epilogue on the Years 1945 to 1957*, pages 953–73.

can the occupation of the Sinai Peninsula in November be called "aggression"? Under the circumstances of belligerency the move of Israeli troops was an offensive, and certainly nations at war have the right to take the offensive and to attack. Under the theory of Israel and Egypt having been belligerents since 1949 the occupation of the Sinai Peninsula is legally the same operation as was the Anglo-American landing in Normandy.' It was clearly a military offensive, Reves wrote, 'but not "aggression" in the sense of the UN Charter.'[21]

From La Pausa, Churchill sent Reves's note to Harold Macmillan, with a covering letter: 'This seems to me to contain a point of real substance. It has been written by Reves, who you know is an Israelite. I do not see myself the answer to it on principle, and I hope it will influence your mind. I am astonished at Eisenhower and America's State Department.'[22]

Eisenhower's last message, Macmillan replied, seemed to show that the United States administration had abandoned the idea of voting for sanctions against Israel, and was thinking in terms of a solution that would give Israel 'reasonable guarantees.'[23] The United States was taking up the torch that Britain had set aside; but Eden, recovering in hospital in Boston from a major operation, wrote to Churchill about the support of Democrats and Republicans for this course: 'I don't feel that this will for a moment influence Dulles in his pursuit of Arab favours and at the cost of the French, British or Israeli interests.'[24]

On 30 November 1957 Churchill was eighty-three years old. Among his Christmas gifts that year were a case of Israeli oranges from Weizmann's widow Vera, and a Virginia ham from Bernard Baruch. In May 1958 the Technion at Haifa, to which four years earlier Churchill had sent a thirtieth anniversary message, opened a new

21 Note by Emery Reves, undated: Squerryes Lodge Archive.
22 Letter of 24 February 1957: Squerryes Lodge Archive.
23 Letter of 27 February 1957: Squerryes Lodge Archive.
24 Letter of 15 July 1957: Squerryes Lodge Archive.

auditorium. Churchill had agreed that it could be called the Churchill Auditorium. Representing him at the opening ceremony on 29 May was his daughter Sarah. 'They love you very much', she wrote, 'and the auditorium was designed to honour your achievements and exist as a constant reminder of your courage and inspiration.'[25]

Sarah reported to her father how much the Israeli Prime Minister, David Ben-Gurion, wanted to see him. A few months later, when Churchill was again at La Pausa, he saw in the local newspaper that Ben-Gurion was also in the South of France. Churchill invited him to lunch at La Pausa. 'I deeply appreciate your kind invitation,' Ben-Gurion replied, 'which to my regret arrived too late, when I was already on the high seas on my way back to Israel.' Ben-Gurion added: 'Like many others in all parts of the globe, I regard you as the greatest Englishman in your country's history and the greatest statesman of our time, as the man whose courage, wisdom and foresight saved his country and the free world from Nazi servitude.'[26]

Churchill wrote in reply: 'I often think of your Country, and I view with admiration the way in which you are undertaking your great tasks. I trust that we shall have another opportunity of meeting before long.'[27]

At the end of May 1961, while Churchill was in London, he received a request from Ben-Gurion, asking if the two men could meet. He readily agreed, and on 2 June 1961, at his home in London, received the man whom he had just missed in the South of France, and whom Sarah had so enjoyed meeting in Israel. At the meeting, Ben-Gurion was accompanied by his Private Secretary Yitzhak Navon (later President of Israel), and by the Israeli Ambassador to London, Arthur Lourie.

The conversation between Churchill and Ben-Gurion lasted about twenty minutes, Anthony Montague Browne reported to the

---

25 Letter of 30 May 1958: Churchill papers, 2/369.
26 Letter of 3 September 1959: Churchill papers, 2/128.
27 Letter of 11 September 1959: Churchill papers, 2/128.

Foreign Office later that day. Ben-Gurion told Churchill that in his view Iraq would 'survive' the overthrow of the monarchy 'and be strong enough to contain her own Communists.' He was 'more doubtful about the survival of Jordan which hung on the life of one brave man, to wit, the King.' Ben-Gurion also told Churchill 'that Egypt was slowly preparing for war, that they had twenty and possibly more MIG 19 fighters which were better than anything the Israelis had, and about 200 Russian Army and Air Force instructors.' He added that he had asked the Prime Minister, Harold Macmillan, 'to make available suitable weapons to deal with the air side.'[28]

Yitzhak Navon later recalled the subsequent conversation: 'Churchill said that he was always a friend of the Jewish people and Zionism, and Ben-Gurion responded with expressions of admiration for his friendship and his stand during the Second World War as a leader of the free world which was saved, thanks to him. He told of his stay in London during the Blitz and the impressions he gained of the courageous stand of the British people.' During their talk, Churchill mentioned that he had written an essay on Moses. Ben-Gurion expressed great interest and requested to receive a copy. Churchill gave Ben-Gurion a copy of his book *Thoughts and Adventures*, in which his essay on Moses had been reprinted in 1932. At the end of their meeting Churchill turned to Ben-Gurion and said: 'You are a brave leader of a great nation.'[29]

In September 1961, two months before Churchill's eighty-seventh birthday, Anthony Montague Browne asked him if he wanted to send a message to David Ben-Gurion on his seventy-fifth birthday. 'You have not done so in previous years,' Montague Browne pointed out.[30] The two men had, however, finally met, and Churchill wanted

28 Letter from Anthony Montague Browne to the Foreign Office, 2 June 1961: Churchill papers, 2/506.
29 Yitzhak Navon, letter to the author, 6 July 1987.
30 Note of 23 September 1961: Churchill papers, 2/519.

to send a message, which he did: 'On your 75th birthday I send you my congratulations and good wishes.'[31] Ben-Gurion replied to Churchill's telegram: 'My dear Sir Winston, I was deeply moved to receive your greeting on the occasion of my birthday, and rejoiced to see that you still remember such trifles. It recalled to my mind the few unforgettable moments I spent with you at the beginning of June, and I cherish as a precious possession your book of essays, which includes that on Moses. I hold you in esteem and affection, not only – not even mainly – because of your unfailing friendship to our people and your profound sympathy with its resurgence in our ancient homeland. Your greatness transcends all national boundaries.'

As to Churchill's realisation that the march of Soviet Communism would be the great danger in the post-war world, Ben-Gurion recalled Churchill's desire for the Western Allies to reach Berlin before the Soviet forces, telling Churchill: 'If your advice had been taken in the last year of the war, the grave crisis over the question of Berlin, which has aroused the apprehensions of the civilised world, would never have arisen, and some of the East European countries would have remained within the bounds of Western Europe.'

Ben-Gurion ended his letter: 'Your words and your deeds are indelibly engraved in the annals of humanity. Happy the people that has produced such a son.'[32]

'I have not failed to give Mr Ben-Gurion's letter to Sir Winston, to whom it afforded much pleasure,' Montague Browne informed the Israeli Ambassador, Arthur Lourie.[33] Two days later Churchill wrote direct to Ben-Gurion, at his desert home in the Negev: 'My dear Prime Minister, I am indeed obliged to you for your graceful and charming letter. It gave me great pleasure to read what you said, and I would like to assure you again of my

---

31 Telegram sent 27 September 1961: Churchill papers, 2/519.
32 Letter of 2 October 1961: Churchill papers, 2/506.
33 Letter of 12 October 1961: Churchill papers, 2/506.

very warm good wishes both for the State of Israel and for you personally.'[34]

In April 1962 Churchill made plans to take a cruise with Aristotle Onassis on board his yacht *Christina.* The cruise was to start from Monte Carlo on 5 April, and visit Libya, Lebanon and Greece. 'I fear much, however,' Montague Browne wrote to one of Macmillan's Private Secretaries, Philip de Zulueta, 'that Sir Winston will insist on visiting Israel. I had thought that our host, Mr Onassis, would have been debarred from going there because of his oil interests and his relations with the Arab countries, but I find that this is not so. I will do what I can to persuade Sir Winston not to go to Israel, but I cannot guarantee it in view of his long association with Israel and his outspoken feelings as a Zionist.'

Montague Browne added: 'I will let you know how things develop, and possibly as a last resort the Prime Minister might consider writing to Sir Winston if it is thought that it would be really harmful for Sir Winston to stop in Israel.'[35] In the event, the fears of the Foreign Office that Britain's Arab friends might be offended if Churchill were to visit Israel were not put to the test, as *Christina* sailed along the coast of Israel during the night. It was almost thirty years since Churchill had last been in Palestine. Aged eighty-seven, he was never to set foot on Israeli soil.

Churchill died at his London home on 24 January 1965. He was ninety years old. At a special meeting of the Knesset on the following day, he was eulogised by David Ben-Gurion. 'In his undaunted resistance and struggle against the Nazi kingdom of hell,' Ben-Gurion told the Israeli parliamentarians, 'Churchill was the perfect combination of a great man at a great hour. He joined battle and he prevailed. The longed-for decision was not the result of one man's war or the victory of a single nation. It was not through him alone that the sons of light

34 Letter of 14 October 1961: Churchill papers, 2/506.
35 Letter of 23 February 1962: Churchill papers, 1/155.

prevailed against the sons of darkness. Nevertheless, this one man was a symbol and a catalyst, a focal point of hope and a kingpin of forces in the struggle of giants. As far back as the beginning of the century, Sir Winston Churchill supported the cause of Zionism. Thirteen years later he spoke on Mount Scopus of a free and sovereign state, one that would be unconquerable. Churchill belonged to the entire world. His memory will light the way for generations to come in every corner of the globe.'[36]

Knesset members rose in tribute to the departed leader. A week later, having flown to London, President Zalman Shazar and David Ben-Gurion represented Israel at Churchill's funeral service in St Paul's Cathedral. So that they would not have to drive on the Sabbath they were found a hotel near the cathedral, and walked through the sombre, muted streets of London to the service.

In a tribute in the *Jewish Chronicle*, Harry Sacher, one of the British Zionist drafters of the Balfour Declaration, who had been present in Jerusalem when Churchill planted a tree at the site of the Hebrew University in 1921, wrote: 'We Jews are under a special obligation to Churchill, the faithful friend of Zionism.' Sacher went on to explain: 'For the MacDonalds, Zionism was a fantasy to be indulged when undemanding and to be betrayed when expedient. For Chamberlain it was an exotic irrelevance to be cast away in a diplomatic deal. For Bevin it was an unofficial strike to be crushed by a trade union boss. For Churchill it was the magical revival of a nation which had seen so many empires crumple to dust, which had persisted through so many trials and humiliations, which had renewed its ancient creative vitality and from which mankind might hope no little. It was characteristic that he called upon his countrymen to conceive the establishment of the State of Israel in the perspective of thousands of years. No petty calculation of ephemeral diplomatic loss or gain drew him to Zionism; for him it belonged to the great tide of history.'[37]

---

36 Knesset debates, 26 January 1965.
37 Harry Sacher, 'The Faithful Friend of Zionism,' *Jewish Chronicle*, 29 January 1965.

EPILOGUE

Throughout his life Churchill's pronouncements about Jews were thoughtful and supportive. Reflecting on Jewish ethics when he was in Jerusalem in 1921, he declared: 'We owe to the Jews in the Christian revelation a system of ethics which, even if it were entirely separated from the supernatural, would be incomparably the most precious possession of mankind, worth in fact the fruits of all other wisdom and learning put together. On that system and by that faith there has been built out of the wreck of the Roman Empire the whole of our existing civilisation.'

Churchill never deviated from this view. In a newspaper article about Moses, published in 1931, he wrote of the Israelites in the desert: 'This wandering tribe, in many respects indistinguishable from numberless nomadic communities, grasped and proclaimed an idea of which all the genius of Greece and all the power of Rome were incapable.' At the height of the Second World War persecutions, Churchill announced to the warring nations: 'Assuredly in the day of victory the Jew's sufferings and his part in the struggle will not be forgotten. Once again, at the appointed time, he will see vindicated those principles of righteousness which it was the glory of his fathers to proclaim to the world.'

Having got to know the Jews of Manchester before the First World War, Churchill was impressed by the nature of Jewish communal life, energy, self-help and determination. 'The Jews were a lucky community,' he wrote, 'because they had the corporate spirit of their race and faith. That personal and special driving power which they possessed would enable them to bring vitality into their institutions, which nothing else would ever give.' In his article in the *Illustrated Sunday Herald* in 1920 describing the 'struggle for the soul of the Jewish people between Bolshevism and Zionism,' he wrote: 'Some people like Jews and some do not, but no thoughtful man can doubt the fact that they are beyond all question the most formidable and the most remarkable race which has ever appeared in the world.'

A supporter of what he called 'the harmonious disposition of the world among its peoples,' Churchill was attracted by Jewish national aspirations. 'The Zionist ideal,' he declared in 1921, 'is a very great ideal, and I confess, for myself, it is one that claims my keen personal sympathy.' His responsibility for the Jewish community in Palestine was a direct one. As Colonial Secretary, his 1922 White Paper led to the immigration in fourteen years of 300,000 Jews. He knew first hand the implacable Arab opposition to Jewish immigration. At the same time he was an outspoken supporter of the right of the Jews to avail themselves of the Jewish National Home provisions of the Mandate: that they were in Palestine, in the words of his own White Paper, 'of right and not on sufferance, and that, with due weight given to the economic absorptive capacity of Palestine, they could build up their self-governing institutions there until they were a majority, at which point they would achieve statehood.'

Churchill's support for Jewish enterprise in Palestine was not to the liking of some of his opponents in Britain, or even to some of his friends. Churchill was a persistent opponent of anti-Semitism, whether during public calls for restrictions on Jewish immigration, and the anti-Jewish riots in South Wales – both before the First World War – or during Parliamentary debates, or in his family and social circle. In 1946, at a time when Jewish terrorism in Palestine stimulated strong anti-Jewish feeling in the British Parliament, he told the House of Commons: 'I am against preventing Jews from doing anything which other people are allowed to do. I am against that, and I have the strongest abhorrence of the idea of anti-Semitic lines of prejudice.'

From his early days as a parliamentarian he found himself working with many Jewish politicians, civil servants and businessmen: he respected them, and was at ease with them. A Jewish banker was his patron after the early death of his father. A Jewish refugee from Hitler was his European literary agent. A leading Jewish historian gave him advice on his biography of his ancestor John Churchill, Duke of Marlborough. A young Jewish philosopher was among those to whom he submitted his war memoirs for criticism before publication. A young Jewish historian was among his small team of researchers on his four-volume *A History of the English-Speaking Peoples.* One of his favourite sculptors was a Jew. He had been much impressed by Jewish enterprise in Palestine. He warned both his mother, and two of his closest friends, as well as the House of Commons, against anti-Semitic utterances.

Churchill was proud to have been an early supporter of the Zionist enterprise. He held in high regard both the Jewish religious ethic and the Zionist ideal. The Biblical story of the Israelites had always moved and inspired him. The struggle of the Jews through the centuries had much impressed him. During the war he had been deeply affected by the fate of the Jews and had sought the means to combat it, over and above the overriding imperative of the defeat of Germany on the battlefield. He had Jewish colleagues, Jewish helpers, and Jews whom he admired. As he himself had said, during a discussion of Jewish terrorism in Palestine: 'The Jewish people know well enough that I am their friend.'

Churchill saw the Jews as one of the historic peoples. He felt an affinity with the Jewish struggle: both the struggle to survive and the struggle for statehood. His own career seemed to flow in the eddies of Jewish history: the search for a safe haven from persecution before the First World War; the aspirations for a National Home during and after that war; the struggle to establish a homeland in Palestine between the wars; the curse of Nazism; the rebuilding of Jewish life and Jewish statehood after the Second World War; the survival of the State of Israel in its first decade; and, throughout, the place of the Jews in the world: these were the dominant aspects of Jewish history with which Churchill's career was inextricably bound.

MAPS

1. Great Britain

2. Cities in Europe in which Emery Reves placed Churchill's Articles, 1937–9

3. Western Europe

4. Central and Eastern Europe

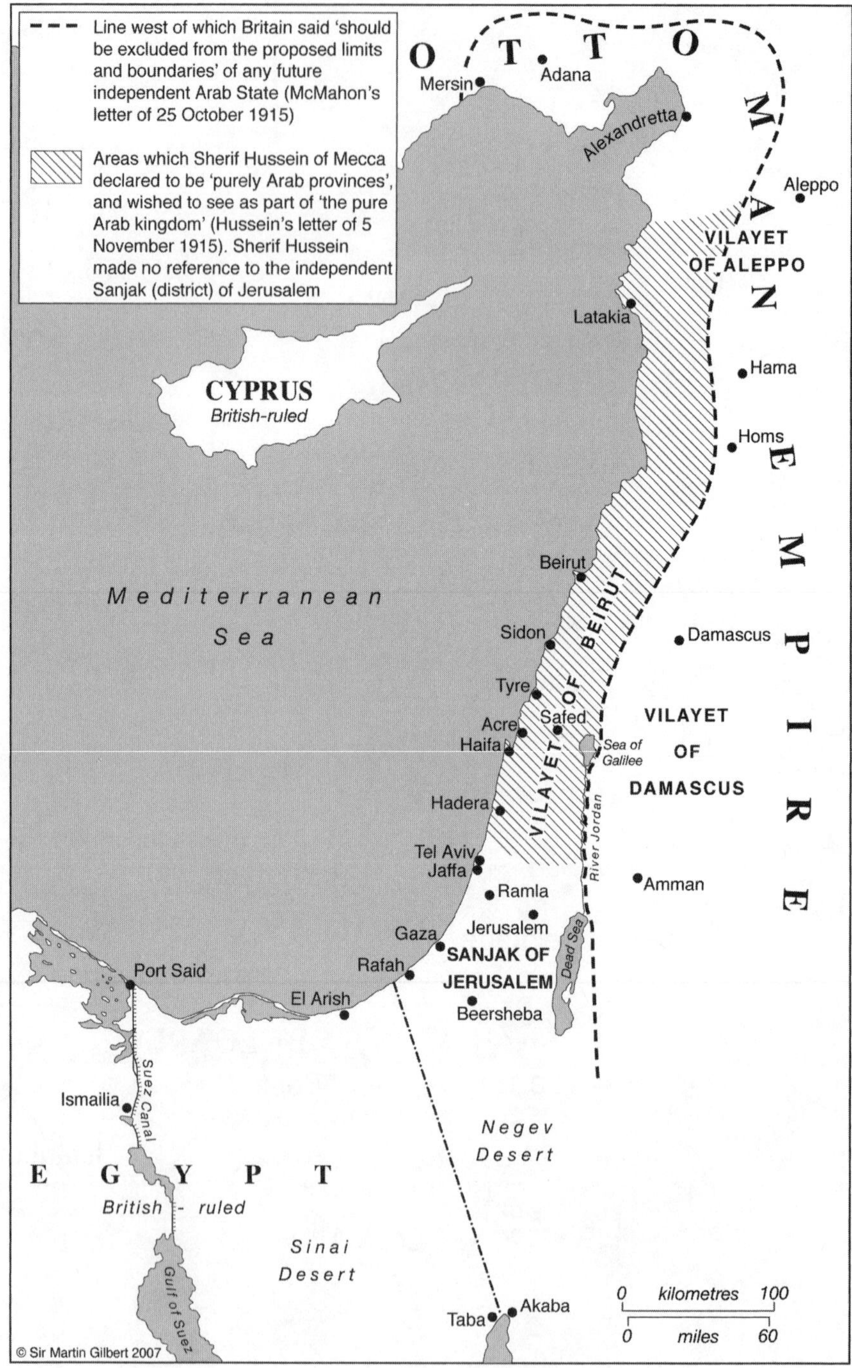

5. Britain's Promise to the Arabs, 1915

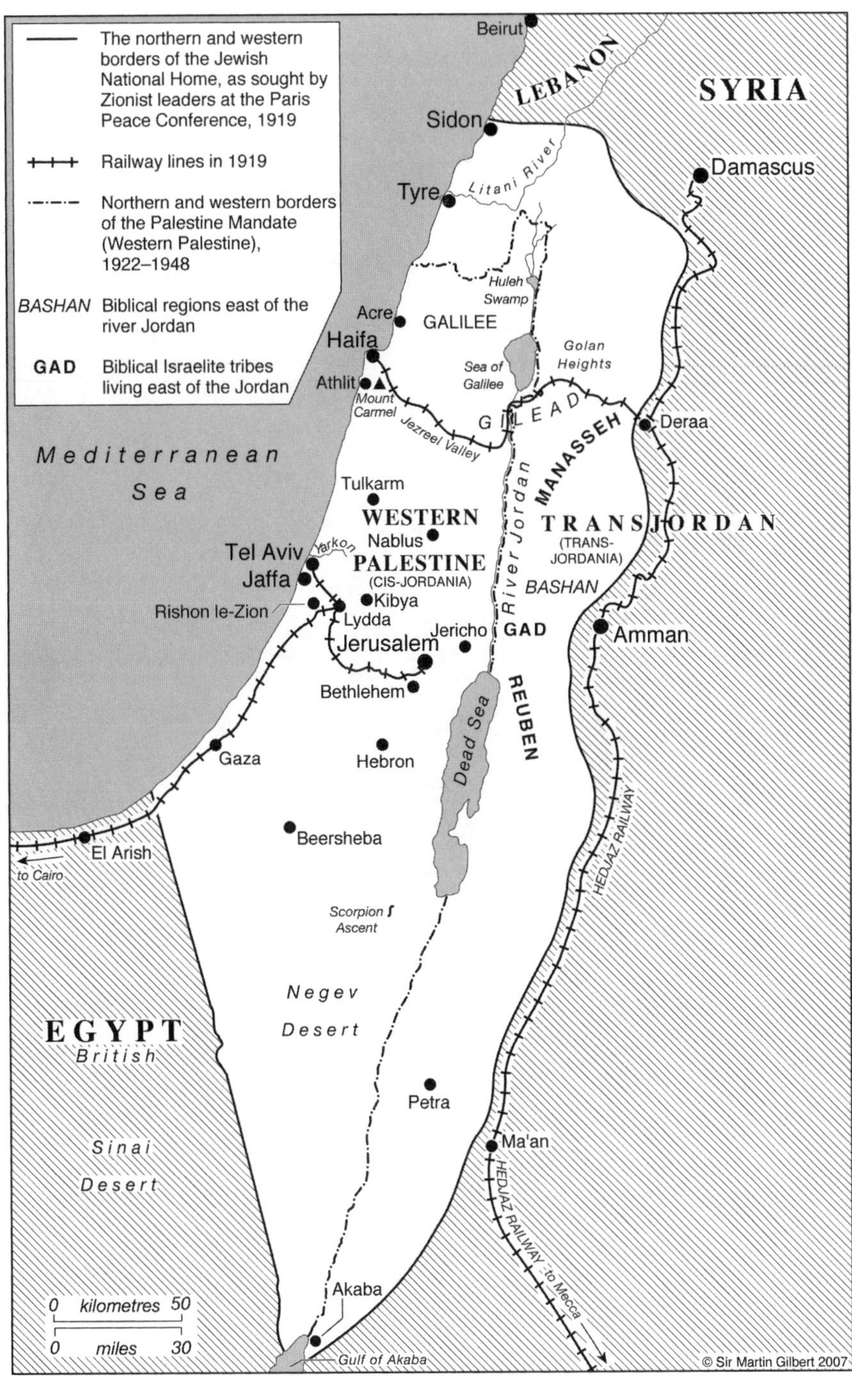

6. Zionist Desiderata for Palestine, 1919

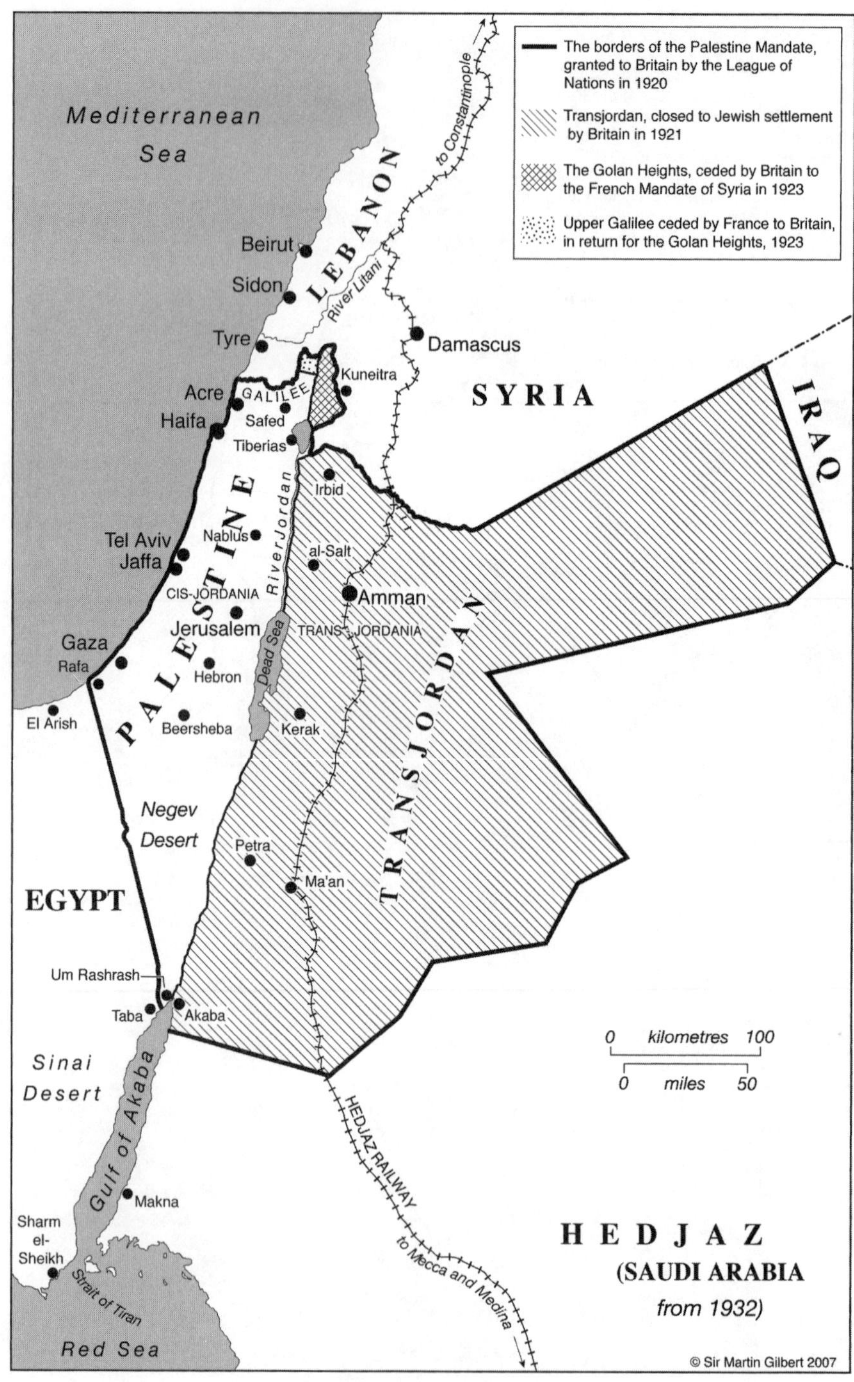

7. The British Mandate for Palestine, 1920–1948

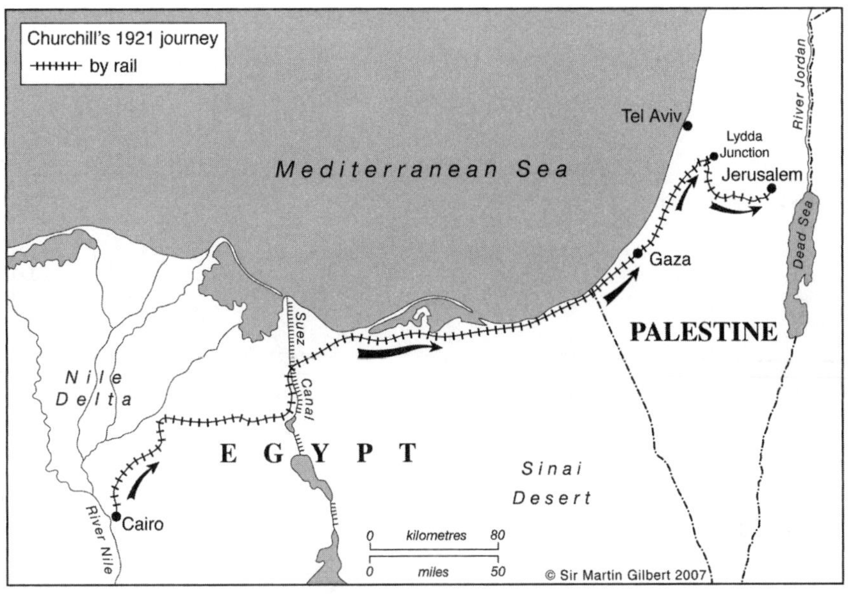

8. Churchill's Journey to Jerusalem, 1921

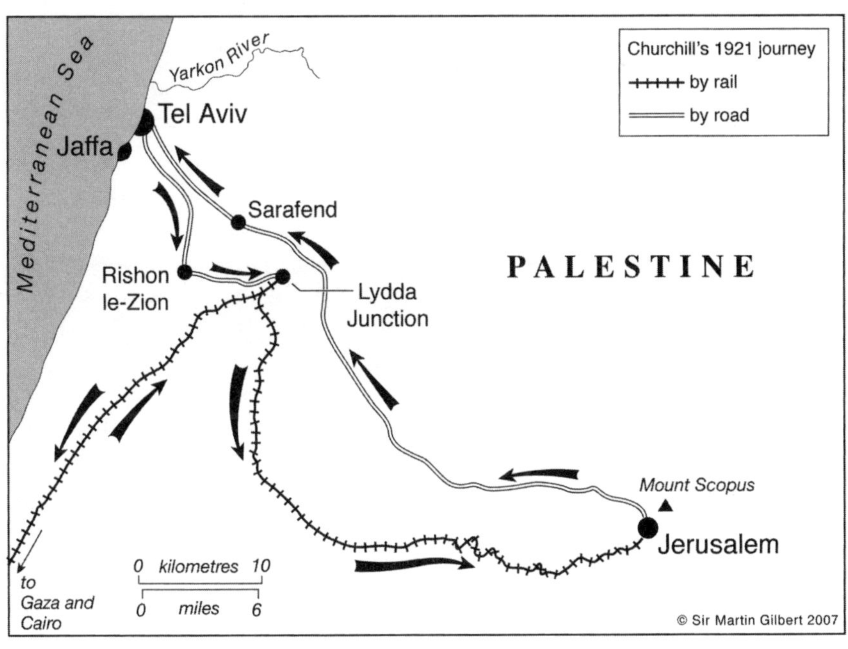

9. Churchill in Palestine, 1921

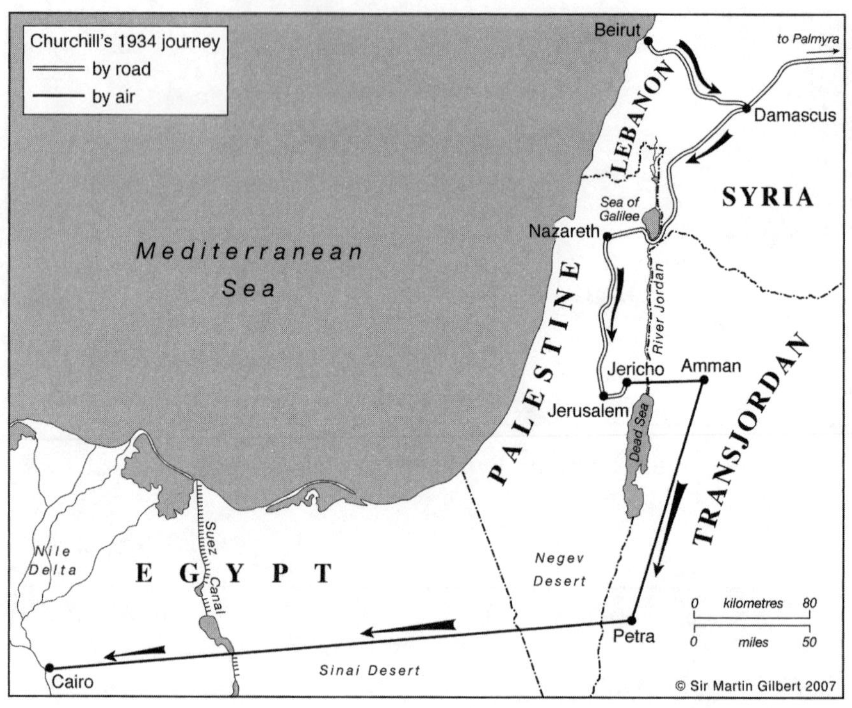

10. Churchill's Middle East Journey, 1934

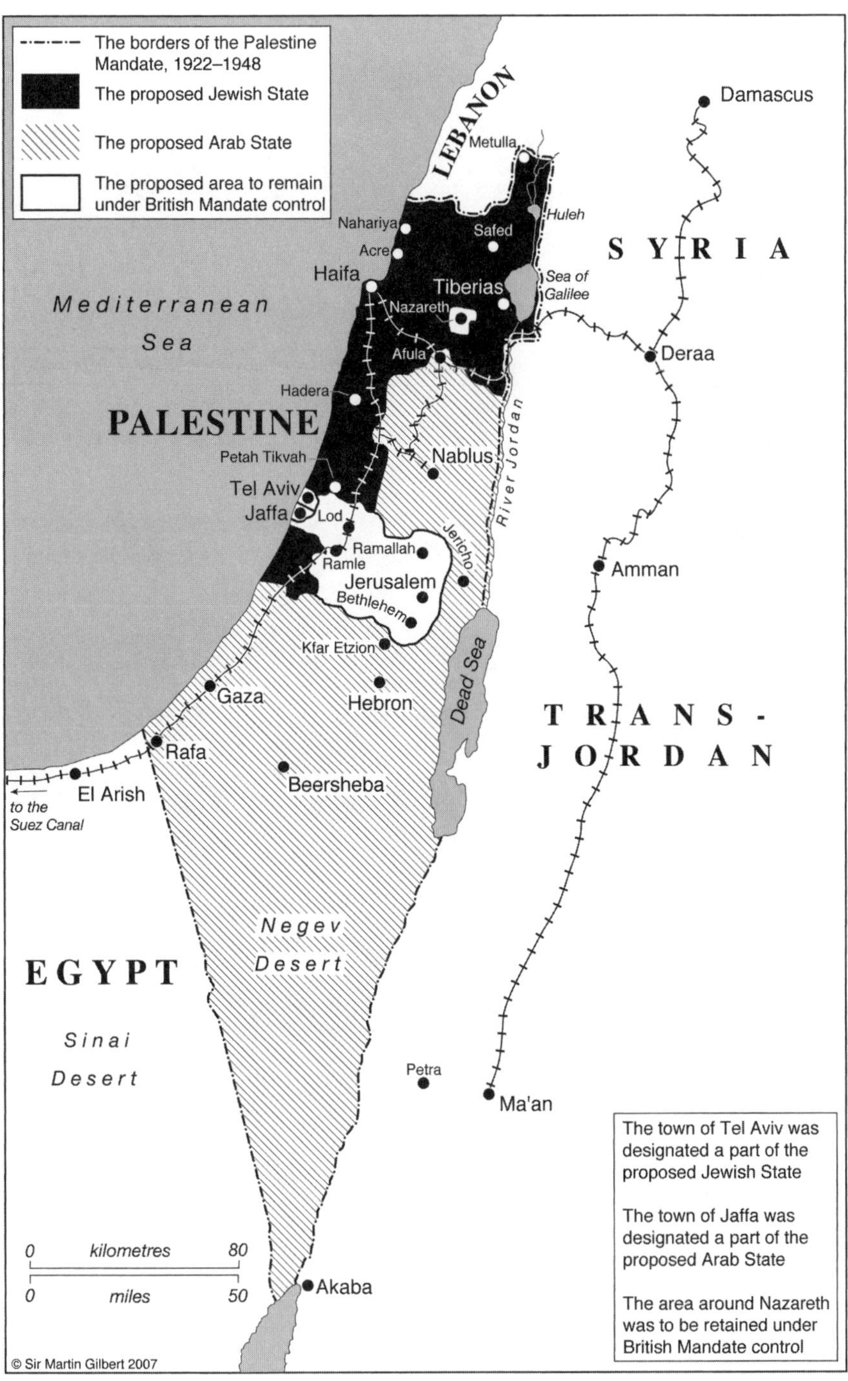

11. The Peel Commission Proposals for Palestine, 1937

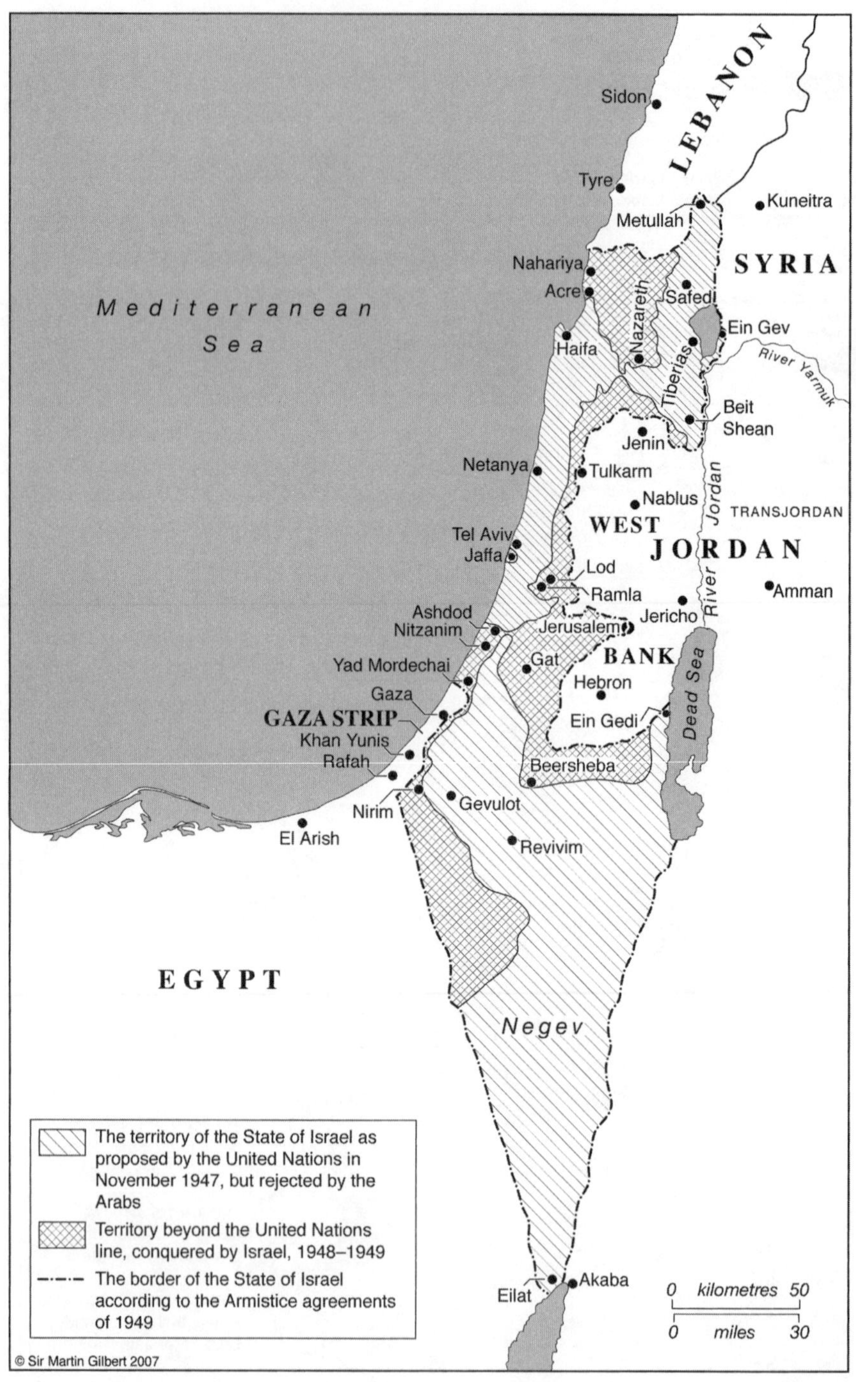

12. The United Nations Partition Plan, and the State of Israel, 1948–1967

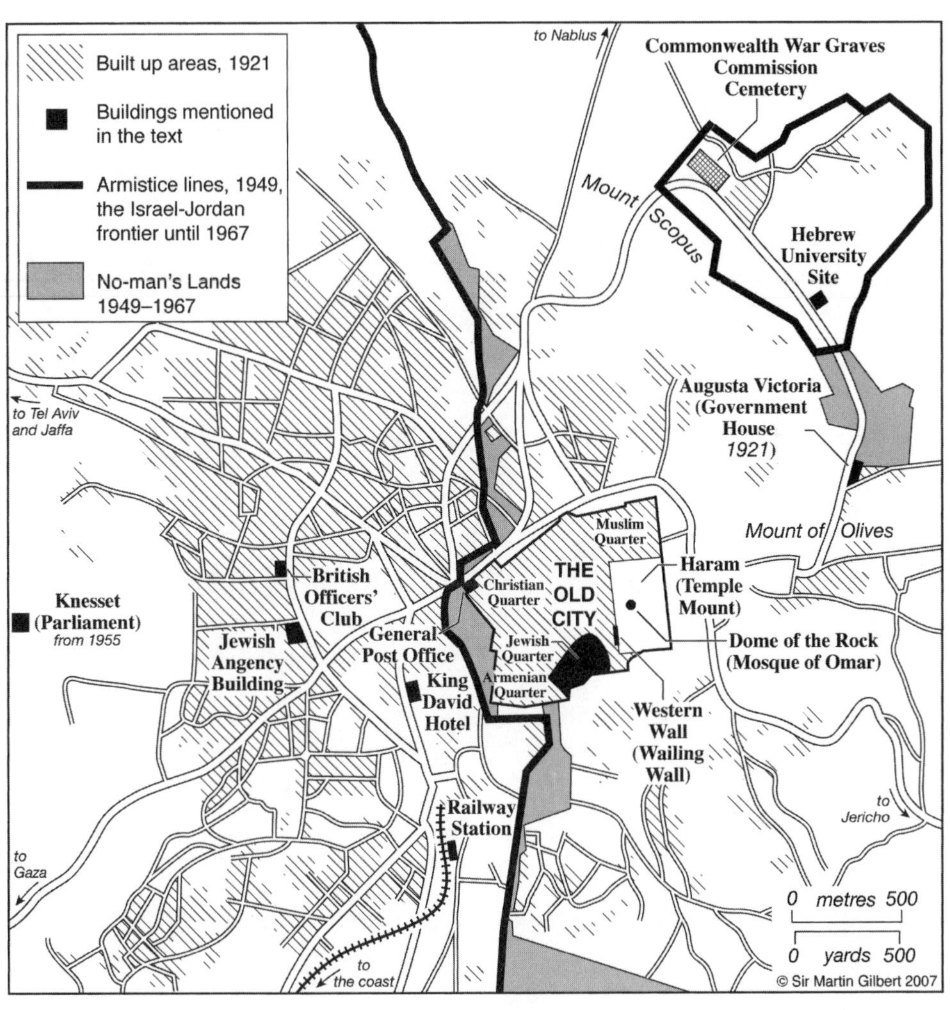

13. Jerusalem

BIBLIOGRAPHY

ARCHIVES CITED

Ben-Gurion Archives, Ben-Gurion University of the Negev
Board of Deputies of British Jews
Central Zionist Archives
Churchill College Archive, Churchill College, Cambridge (Sir Winston Churchill, Sir John Colville, Oscar Nemon, and Baroness Spencer-Churchill papers)
Government of Israel State Archives (Ginzach ha'Medina), Jerusalem
Israel Defence Force Archive (and Haganah Archive)
National Archives, London (Admiralty, Air Ministry, Cabinet, Colonial Office, Home Office, Foreign Office, Ministry of Munitions, Premier and War Office papers)
Reform Club, London
Squerryes Lodge Archive
State Department Archives, Washington (Office of Strategic Services papers)
Yad Chaim Weizmann (Weizmann Archive)

PRIVATE PAPERS OF

Neville Chamberlain
Winston Churchill (Churchill's grandson)
Albert Einstein
President Dwight D. Eisenhower
H.A.L. Fisher
Moses Gaster
Herbert Gladstone (Viscount Gladstone)
Sir Edward Grey (Viscount Grey of Falloden)
T.E. Lawrence ('Lawrence of Arabia')
David Lloyd George (Earl Lloyd George of Dwyfor)
Earl Mountbatten of Burma
Sir Samuel Hoare (Viscount Templewood)
Sir Herbert Samuel (Viscount Samuel)

Robert Shillingford
President Harry S. Truman
Chaim Weizmann

WORKS CITED

ARTICLES BY CHURCHILL

'Zionism versus Bolshevism: The Struggle for the Soul of the Jewish People, *Illustrated Sunday Herald*, 8 February 1920.

'The Palestine Crisis,' *Sunday Times*, 22 September 1929

'Fair Play to the Jews', *Sunday Chronicle*, 2 November 1930.

'Moses', *Sunday Chronicle*, 8 November 1931.

'The Truth About Hitler', *Strand Magazine*, November 1935.

'War Is Not Imminent', *Evening Standard*, 15 October 1936.

'The Communist Schism', *Evening Standard*, 16 October 1936.

'Europe's Peace', *Evening Standard*, 5 February 1937.

'Partition Perils in Palestine', *Evening Standard*, 23 July 1937.

'Why I Am Against Partition', *Jewish Chronicle*, 3 September 1937.

'Friendship with Germany', *Evening Standard*, 17 September 1937.

'Germany's Discipline for the Old Austria', *Daily Telegraph*, 6 July 1938.

'Palestine at the Crossroads', *Daily Telegraph*, 20 October 1938.

REFERENCE WORKS

Randolph S. Churchill (editor), *Europe Unite: Speeches 1947 and 1948 by Winston S. Churchill.* London: Cassell, 1950.

Randolph S. Churchill (editor), *Stemming the Tide, Speeches 1951 and 1952 by Winston S. Churchill*. London: Cassell, 1953.

Randolph S. Churchill (editor), *The Unwritten Alliance, 1953–1959 by Winston S. Churchill.* London: Cassell, 1961.

Randolph Churchill, *Winston S. Churchill*, Volumes One and Two, and their companion volumes of documents. London: William Heinemann, 1967, 1969.

Ronald I. Cohen, *Bibliography of the Writings of Sir Winston Churchill*, 3 volumes. London: Thoemmes Continuum, 2006.

Martin Gilbert, *Winston S. Churchill*, Volumes Three to Eight, and their companion volumes of documents. London: William Heinemann, 1971–88.

Martin Gilbert, *The Churchill War Papers*, volumes one, two and three. London: William Heinemann, 1993, 1995, 2000.

Statement of British Policy in Palestine (the Churchill White Paper), Command Paper 1700 of 1922.

Palestine Royal Commission Report (Peel Commission), Command Paper 5479 of 1937.

Palestine Partition Commission Report, Command Paper 5854 of 1938 (Woodhead Commission). London: His Majesty's Stationery Office, 1938.

OTHER WORKS

Michael Adler (editor), *British Jewry Book of Honour.* London: Caxton, 1922.

Michael Bar-Zohar, *Ben-Gurion, A Biography.* London: Weidenfeld and Nicolson, 1978.

Alex Bein (editor), *Arthur Ruppin: Memoirs, Diaries, Letters.* London: Weidenfeld and Nicolson, 1971.

David Ben-Gurion, *Rebirth and Destiny of Israel.* New York: Philosophical Library, 1954.

Charles E. Bohlen, *Witness of History.* New York: W.W. Norton, 1973.

Lord Boothby, *My Yesterday, Your Tomorrow.* London: Hutchinson, 1962

Professor Selig Brodetsky, *Memoirs: from Ghetto to Israel.* London: Weidenfeld and Nicolson, 1960.

Randolph S. Churchill, *Winston S. Churchill,* Volume Two. London: William Heinemann, 1967.

Winston S. Churchill, *The River War.* London: Longmans, Green, 2 volumes, 1899.

Winston S. Churchill, *Marlborough: His Life and Times,* Volume Four: London, George G. Harrap, 1938.

Winston S. Churchill, *The Second World War and an Epilogue on the Years 1945 to 1957.* London: Cassell, 1959.

Michael J. Cohen, *Churchill and the Jews.* London: Frank Cass, 1985.

John Colville, *The Fringes of Power, Downing Street Diaries, 1939–1955.* London: Hodder and Stoughton, 1985.

David Coombs with Minnie Churchill, *Sir Winston Churchill's Life Through His Paintings.* London: Chaucer Press, 2003.

William A. Eddy, *FDR Meets Ibn Saud.* Washington DC: America-Mideast Educational and Training Services, 1954 (reprinted 2005).

Ivan Fallon, *Billionaire: The Life and Times of Sir James Goldsmith.* New York, Little, Brown, 1992.

Martin Gilbert (editor), *Winston Churchill and Emery Reves, Correspondence, 1937–1964.* Austin, Texas: University of Texas Press, 1997.

Kay Halle, *Irrepressible Churchill, A Treasury of Winston Churchill's Wit.* Cleveland, Ohio: The World Publishing Company, 1966.

Ernst Hanfstaengel, *Hitler – The Missing Years.* London, Eyre & Spottiswoode, 1957.

John Harvey (editor), *The War Diaries of Oliver Harvey.* London: Collins, 1978.

Elsie Janner, *Barnett Janner: A Personal Portrait.* London: Robson Books, 1984.

Warren Kimball (editor), *Churchill and Roosevelt, the Complete Correspondence,* Three Volumes: Princeton, New Jersey, Princeton University Press, 1984.

A. W. Lawrence (editor), *T. E. Lawrence by His Friends.* London: Jonathan Cape, 1937.

Peter de Mendelssohn, *The Age of Churchill: Heritage and Adventure, 1874–1911.* London: Thames and Hudson, 1961.

Harford Montgomery Hyde, *Lord Alfred Douglas: A Biography.* London, Methuen, 1984.

Lord Moran, *Winston Churchill, The Struggle for Survival.* London: Constable, 1966.

Julia Namier, *Lewis Namier: A Biography.* London: Oxford University Press, 1971.

Vic Oliver, *Mr Showbusiness: An Autobiography of Vic Oliver.* London: George H. Harrap, 1954.

Oskar K. Rabinowicz, *Winston Churchill on Jewish Problems.* London, World Jewish Congress, British Section, Lincolns-Prager Publishers Ltd, 1956.

Robert Rhodes James (editor), *Chips, The Diaries of Sir Henry Channon.* London: Weidenfeld and Nicolson, 1967.

Kenneth Rose, *Elusive Rothschild.* London: Weidenfeld and Nicolson, 2003.

Y. Ya'ari-Poleskin, *Pinhas Rutenberg.* Tel Aviv: 1939. (Hebrew)

Joseph B. Schechtman, *The Jabotinsky Story: Fighter and Prophet, The Last Years, 1923–1940.* New York: Thomas Yoseloff, 1961.

Henry C. Semon and Thomas A. McIntyre (editors), *The Autobiography of Sir Felix Semon* London: Jarrolds, 1926.

Evelyn Shuckburgh, *Descent to Suez, Diaries 1951–56.* London: Weidenfeld and Nicolson, 1986.

Eugen Spier, *Focus: A Footnote to the History of the Thirties.* London: Oswald Wolff, 1963.

Chaim Weizmann, *Trial and Error: The Autobiography of Chaim Weizmann.* New York: Harper and Brothers, 1949.

The Yellow Spot: The Extermination of the Jews in Germany. London: Victor Gollancz, 1936.

ARTICLES

M. Donald Coleman, 'Churchill and the Jews', *Midstream*, May–June 1999.

Michel T. McMenamin, 'Winston Churchill and the Litigious Lord (Lord Alfred Douglas), *Litigation*, Winter 1995.

Harry Sacher, 'The Faithful Friend of Zionism', *Jewish Chronicle*, 29 January 1965.

Thomas W. Lippman, 'The Day FDR Met Saudi Arabia's Ibn Saud,' *The Link*, Volume 38, Issue 2, April–May 2005.

NEWSPAPERS AND MAGAZINES

Atlantic Monthly
Birmingham Post
Daily Telegraph
Egyptian Gazette
Friends News Sheet (Hebrew University of Jerusalem)
Illustrated Technion News
Jewish Chronicle
Jewish Guardian
Liberal Magazine
Manchester Guardian
New York Times
Palcor Bulletin
Palestine
Palestine Post
Picture Post
San Francisco Chronicle
The Times (London)
Zionist Review

Hansard (Parliamentary debates)

INDEX

compiled by the author

Acre: no Jewish land purchase allowed north of, 165

Abdullah, Emir: installed in Transjordan, 47, 109, 255, 292; and the Jews in Palestine, 52, 237; Churchill's discussions with, 55–6, 57; photograph 9

Aden: and 'the Victorious Vizier', 180

Akaba: 51

Akaba, Gulf of: 50

Albania: 154–5

Albanians: and Italy, 162

Albert Hall (London): 192, 294

Alexander, Field Marshal Sir Harold (later Viscount): and the Jewish Brigade Group, 218, 239; and the possible British 'invasion of Israel' (1954), 289

Algiers: 197

Aleppo: 47, 48, 127

Alexander, David: 21

Algeria: Churchill insists on repeal of anti-Jewish laws in (1943), 197

Aliens Bill: Churchill opposes, 7–10, 15–17, 19

Aliens Commission: 8

Allenby, General Sir Edmund (later Viscount): 33–4

Allied Declaration (17 December 1942): denounces German mass murder of Jews, 195–6

American Civil War: a Jewish authority on, 298

American Jews: and the Balfour Declaration: 28; recruited, 28; and the need to conciliate (1939), 165, 166–7; and the arming of Jews in Palestine, 173

American Zionist Council: 282

Amery, L.S. ('Leo'): 121; and the post-war future of Palestine, 203; photograph 10

Amman: 46, 102, 289

Anglo-American Commission (on Palestine): 250

Anglo-Jordanian Treaty of Alliance (March 1948): 268–9, 287, 289

Anglo-Persian Oil Company: 88–9, 144

Angriff (German newspaper): attacks Churchill, 147

Ankara: a telegram to, intercepted, 212

Anti-Nazi League: xvii, 136, 156

anti-Semitism: Churchill rejects, xvi, 6, 8, 308; and the anti-Bolshevik Russian armies, 30–3, 41; and the Arab delegation in London (1921), 75; and a proposed Zionist loan, 91; and a possible Churchill-Hitler meeting (1932), 98–9; the 'only argument against' (Palestine), 126; 'exploitation of', in Germany, 129; a query concerning, 137–8; and the 1939 Palestine White Paper, 159; and 'officers and others in high places', 190; Churchill's 'strongest abhorrence' of, 257; Churchill rebukes a friend for, 265

Antonescu, Ion: and the killing of Jews in Romania, 181

Arab Caliphate: and a Jewish State in, 183

Arab Federation: in prospect, 127; in conjunction with a Jewish State, 190, 202, 238

Arab League: Bevin's confidence in, 275
Arab Legion: in action against Israel (1948), 268; withdrawn, 269
Arab Revolt (of 1917–18): 46, 47, 51, 77
Arab States: and a partitioned Palestine, 125, 127; Britain's search for the friendship of (1939), 154, 157–8; their fears, 237; Britain to seek to influence, 289
Arab world: and Israel, 282
Arabs: Churchill's reflections on, 113, 115–6, 119, 120, 224; 'a lower manifestation', 116; 'children of the desert', 132; not to be alienated, 143–4, 154, 194; and the Second World War, 169, 181, 222, 224; one of their 'best friends', 180; Eden 'loves', 190; and the Jews of Europe, 232; British policy towards, 255; and John Foster Dulles, 301
Arabs (in Iraq): 'pro-German elements' among, 254
Arabs (in Palestine): 35, 67–8, 79; 'a handful of philosophic people', 81; attack Jews (1929), 91, 229; beneficiaries of Zionist enterprise, 92; and Britain's 'assurances' to, 94; incited, 102; incited by German and Italian propaganda, 109–110; attack Jews, and riot and go on strike against British policy (1936), 110, 115, 142, 157; and Arab immigration to Palestine, 111, 254; 'the dog in the manger', 120; continued revolt of, 130; 'always armed', 132; renewed violence of (1938), 140, 141, 149, 157; and the Jewish immigration 'Black Paper', 158, 161, 166, 179; and the arming of the Jews, 164, 172–3; and the Atlantic Charter, 184; Roosevelt suggests arming, 203; 'have done nothing for us in this war', 205; and a 'low grade gasp of a defeatist hour', 206; and post-war plans for Palestine, 231, 232; Britain to be 'at war' with, 259; and the coming into being of the State of Israel, 273; post-1922 growth in population of, recalled, 254, 277
Arabs (in Syria): 35; not to be 'upset', 222; in revolt, 228
Argentina: 12
'Arms and the Covenant': Churchill's call, 107
Ashley, Edwina (later lady Mountbatten); 5
Asquith, H.H.: 5–6, 124
Assyrians (in Iraq): 128
Aswan Dam: and the 'Suez Crisis' (1956), 295
Atchison, Topeka and Santa Fe Railway: shares in, 5
Athens: 139, 266
Atlantic Charter (1941): 184
Atlantic Ocean: 192
atomic science: 290
Attlee, Clement (later Earl): 121, 203, 204; Prime Minister (1945–51), 238, 249; Churchill's advice and suggestions to, 250–1, 251, 261; and the post-1945 possibility of Partition, 276; and Israel, 272; 'maladresse' of, 277
Auschwitz: the unknown destination (1942), 191; the appeal to bomb (1944), 211–13, 290; and an appeal for an Allied protest, 220
Australia: 69; soldiers from, 55, 174, 177; aborigines in, 120
Austria: 136, 137; annexed by Germany (1938), 145; Jewish emigration from (1939–40), 154, 178
Austria-Hungary: defeat of (1918), 58

BBC: broadcasts an account of Nazi brutality (1942), 194; broadcasts the Allied Declaration of 17 December 1942, 196; and 'that one, strong, unseen voice', 197–8; and 'the biggest outcry possible', 213; Churchill's draft statement for (1948), 268–9

Babi Yar (Kiev): mass murder of Jews at, 187
Baghdad: 46, 49; and a possible Arab Federation, 128; pressure from, 144; an Arab revolt in (1941), 205
Bailleul (France): 26
Bakstansky, Lionel: protests, 143
Baldwin, Stanley (later Earl): and an oil commission, 89; Churchill enters government of, 90; and Palestine, 108; and appeasement, 123
Balfour, A.J. (later Earl): 4, 11, 12, 25, 27, 42, 59–60, 71; and an anti-Semitic accusation, 86–7; and a Zionist loan, 90–1; compares size of Palestine to Wales, 124n.8; and the motives behind his Declaration, 165; Churchill's 'inheritance' from, 204; and 'the wrong type of Jews', 223; photograph 8
Balfour Day (1930): 93
Balfour Declaration (2 November 1917): 27–8, 35, 36; terms of, to be carried out, 45; first anniversary of, 51; demonstration against, 56; a 'gross injustice', 58; 'that most uncommon promise', 59; defended, 59–60, 69; an 'obligation', 69; 'negation' of, 71; challenged, 74; abused, 78; Churchill defends, 78–9, 84; and the protection of Jewish communities in Palestine, 92; modified (1929), 93–4; continued protests against, 110; 'spirit' of, 112; the 'prime and dominating pledge', 114, 117–8; and Partition, 127; the result of 'the dire need of war', 128; 'taking a great stand' on, 132; Churchill denounces 'betrayal' of, 158–62; Churchill a 'sincere advocate' of, 159; Churchill 'strongly wedded' to, 184; and Churchill's anniversary message (1942), 192–3; a supporter of, in Churchill's wartime administration, 203; thirty-third anniversary of, 273; and 'a Zionist since the days of', 281, 282, 283; and the Jewish National Home, 282; Churchill's 'steadfast support' for, 291; Churchill a Zionist 'ever since', 295; a drafter of, writes an obituary tribute to Churchill, 306
Baltic Sea: 188
Baltic States: 199
Baptists: 266
Baruch, Bernard M. ('Bernie'): 28–9, 103, 204, 222, 223, 250; a gift from, 301; photograph 26
Bashan, Land of: 56
Basra: 127
Basra-Baghdad-Haifa oil pipeline: 181
'Battle of Cable Street' (London, 1936): 137
Bavaria: 40, 83
Bay of Biscay: 188
'Be Good Jews': 15
Bedouin: 183
Beersheba: 50, 165
Begin, Menachem: 221, 253
Beirut: 102
Belgium: attacked (1914), 23; and the future of Palestine, 25–6; attacked again (1940), 171, 175; Government-in-Exile of, 195
Belgrade: Churchill's articles published in (1937–8), 139
Belzec: mass murder of Jews at (1942), 192
Ben-Gurion, David: xvii, 96, 119, 122; denounces Jewish acts of terror, 149; denounces restrictions on Jewish land purchase, 170–1; influenced by Churchill's wartime oratory, 174–6; rejects Jewish acts of terror, 221; Churchill's letter (of 1945) 'the greatest blow', 244; Prime Minister of Israel, 268, 272, 289; wants to see Churchill, 302; meets Churchill (1961), 302–3; 'a brave leader of a great nation', 303; Churchill's birthday telegram to, 303; Churchill's letter to, 304; at Churchill's funeral, 306; photographs 29, 30

Bengal: 134
Berlin: 83, 100, 138; an Anglo-American warning denounced from, 220; the Soviet conquest of (1945), recalled, 304
Berlin, (Sir) Isaiah: 272, 309
Bessarabia: Jewish refugees from, 206
Bet-Zouri, Eliahu: a Jewish assassin, 225
Betar (youth wing of the Revisionists): 124
Bethlehem: 81, 123
Bevin, Ernest: and Jewish immigration to Palestine, 184–5, 249–50; and the deportation of Jewish 'illegals' from Palestine, 265; and Israel, 272; releases final Cyprus detainees, 274; 'bias and prejudice' of, 275; 'maladresse' of, 277; and Jordan, 287; and Zionism, 306
'Bevinism': and the British Foreign Office, 292
Big Three (Churchill, Truman, Stalin): at Potsdam, 245, 246, 248–9
Birmingham Post: and criticism of Churchill in Berlin, 100
'Black Paper' (The 1939 Palestine White Paper): 158
Black Sea: 178, 188, 206
Blenheim, Battle of (1704): 97
Bletchley Park: 186, 187
Blum, Leon: 136, 174; photograph 16
Board of Deputies of British Jews: 21
Bohlen, Charles E.: 232–3
Bolsheviks: seize power, 28; Churchill's antagonism to, 37
Bolshevism: 'a Jewish movement', 37; and a 'sinister confederacy', 40; 'repudiated vehemently by the great mass of the Jewish race', 43; and Jewish immigration to Palestine, 62, 63, 64, 75, 76–7; and the Jaffa riots (1921), 73; and an anti-Bolshevik Zionist, 82–3; need to purge (in Palestine), 92; see also index entry for Communism
Bonham Carter, Lady Violet (later Baroness): 124, 125
Boothby, Robert: 270
Boston: 301
Bracken, Brendan (later Lord): 163, 270
Bratislava: war criminals executed in, 201
Brazil: soldiers of, in action in Italy, 239
Brinco: shares in, 285
Bristol University: 101
Britain: and the Bolshevik revolution, 28; 'National Jews' in, 39; Zionism 'a blessing to', 567; and 'good faith' of, to the Jews, 112; and the Munich Agreement, 141; and worsening violence in Palestine (1938–9), 141; troops of, in action in Normandy, 214; in Italy, 239; to 'be at war' with Jews and Arabs in Palestine (1946), 259; and the Arab Legion (1948), 268–9; its Treaty of Alliance with Transjordan (later Jordan),268–9; and the recognition of Israel, 272, 272–3, 274, 274, 278–9; and an air clash with Israel (1949), 274, 277; and an Israeli reprisal raid (1953), 286–7; and 'the invasion of Israel', (1954), 289; and the 'Suez Crisis' (1956), 294–6; and the Sinai Peninsula (1956–7), 300–1
British Army: Jewish volunteers in, 28
British East Africa Protectorate: 12, 17
British Empire: and a future Jewish State, 42
British Expeditionary Force: evacuates from Dunkirk, 174
British Jews: and Zionism, 42
British Mandate authorities (Palestine): 54
British Military Administration (Palestine): 34
British Military Cemetery (Jerusalem): 54
British West Indies: soldiers from, 55
Brodetsky, Selig: 23, 108

Brooke, General Sir Alan (later Viscount Alanbrooke): 208–9
Brussels: Churchill's articles published in, 139
Bucharest: Churchill's articles published in, 139
Buchenwald concentration camp: discovered, 240–1
Buckingham Palace (London): 292
Budapest: Churchill's articles published in, 139; a request to bomb deportation railway lines from, 212; bombing raid on, 212–3; Jews of, in danger, 220
Bulgaria: British pressure on (1939), 154; attempt to rescue Jewish children from, 193–4
Burma: 264, 280
Butcher, Sir John: opposes Zionism (1922), 78; an earlier supporter of Zionism (1917), 79

Cadogan, Sir Alexander: 203
Cairo: 50, 102, 144, 209, 224; Lord Moyne assassinated in, 225
Cairo Conference (1921): 50–1; (1944), 222
Canada: 12, 69, 91, 199; and the 'Churchill Falls', 284–5
Canadian troops: in action, 214
Campbell-Bannerman, Sir Henry: 16
Canaanites: 237
Carnegie Hall (New York): 282
Cassel, Sir Ernest: 2, 4, 5, 13, 308–9; and an anti-Semitic accusation, 86–7; photograph 5
Catholics: in Germany, 139
Cazalet, Captain Victor: 121, 122
Central British Fund (to help German Jews): 106
Central Europe: 'unhappy lands' of, 43
Central Powers (1914–1918): 58–9
Chamberlain, Sir Austen: 94
Chamberlain, Neville: 140, 143, 160; 'let us offend the Jews . . .', 157; 'this mortal blow', 161; 'Jews aren't a lovable people', 162; brings Churchill into government, 163; replaced by Churchill, 171, 176; his Cabinet's policy on 'illegal' Jewish refugees, 178; and Zionism, 306
Channon, Henry: 269
Chartwell, Westerham, Kent: 88–9, 101, 136, 146, 155, 271, 295, 296; a dream at, 297
Chequers: 199, 203, 207, 222, 225, 290, 296
Cheetham (Manchester): 14, 18
Chelmno: mass murder of Jews at (1942), 192
Cheka (Soviet secret police): and the Jews, 40
Christianity: 'sheltered', 54
Christians: and Jews, 290, 307
Christina (yacht): and Israel, 304–5
Churchill, Clementine (Churchill's wife): 5, 13–14, 26, 88, 89, 105, 297, 298; accompanies her husband to Jerusalem (1921), 50; (1934), 102; and Hitler's 'satanic design' (1942), 196; and 'the most horrible revelations' (1945), 241; and the 'Suez Crisis' (1956), 295, 296, 298; photographs 6, 9
Churchill, Jack (Churchill's brother): 2–3, 5, 203
Churchill, Lady Randolph (Churchill's mother): 3, 4, 6
Churchill, Lord Randolph (Churchill's father): 1–2, 13, 297; photograph 1
Churchill, Randolph (Churchill's son): 1 n.2, 4, 97, 98, 130; meets Weizmann, 95, 203; represents his father, 136; alerts his father, 188, 219; opposes Partition, 204–5; acts as a conduit for Jewish parachutists, 209; facilitates rescue of Jews from Yugoslavia, 210; defends his father, 244; advises his father, 247; photograph 21
Churchill, Sarah (Churchill's daughter): 97, 136–7; represents her father, 282, 302; photograph 25

Churchill, Winston S.:
challenges anti-Semitism, xvi, 6, 8, 30–3, 190, 257; opposes the Aliens Bill, 7–10. 15–17, 19; takes action against a pogrom in South Wales, 20–22; and the Balfour Declaration, 28; and Jewish Cabinet members, 29; and Jewish soldiers in the First World War, 30; his 'low opinion of the Arab', 48; and the future of the Negev Desert, 50, 102, 126, 183, 205, 223, 284; at the Cairo Conference, 50–1; in Gaza, 52–3; his reflections on Islam, 53–4; in Jerusalem, 54–64; hears and rebuts Arab objections to Zionism, 58–61, 72; hears and encourages the Zionists in Palestine, 61–3; meetings with Chaim Weizmann, (1921), 70–1; (1939–45), 163–4, 164, 166, 182, 203–5, 206, 222; his continued support for Zionist enterprise in Palestine (from 1921), 72; and an anti-Semitic accusation, 86–7; and a Zionist loan, 90–1; warnings about Germany under Hitler, 99–100; his 'impudence' criticised in Berlin, 100–1; and a 'singularly cruel offence', 102; and the Partition debate, 121–134; his 1934 visit to Palestine recalled (1937), 129; warns about the fate of the Jews in Vienna, 145; meets Gauleiter Foerster, 146; Hitler attacks, 146–7; Goebbels attacks, 147; seeks alternate places of refuge for Jews (1939), 154; and British rearmament, 155; opposes the 1939 Palestine White Paper, 158–62, 165, 183, 189, 206, 209, 242; First Lord of the Admiralty (September 1939-May 1940), 163–171; supports the arming of Jews in Palestine, 169–70, 172–4, 181–2, 183; the impact of his oratory (1940), 174–6; his condolence telegram to the Mayor of Tel Aviv (1940), 177; and an 'act of inhumanity', 179–80; not informed of suspension of Jewish immigration to Palestine, 180; sceptical of warnings concerning 'the whole Arab world', 181–2; plans for a post-war Jewish State in Palestine, 183, 184, 202–3, 204, 231, 234–6; and 'a crime without a name', 186; denounces the deportation of Jews from France (1942), 191–2; denounces 'these vile crimes', 192; supports reprisal bombing on behalf of captive Poles and Jews, 196–7; intervenes on behalf of Jewish refugees, 198, 206–7, 209–10, 214–5, 218–9; shows a film of 'atrocities inflicted on' Jews, 199; insists on a strong war crimes declaration, 200–1; opposes arming the Arabs of Palestine, 203; calls Jewish settlement in Transjordan 'a good idea', 204; suggests Transjordan might be part of a future Jewish State, 205; suggests Jews 'would be able to judge' war criminals, 204; and a renewed suggestion of Partition, 204, 205, 223; warns Weizmann about a Jewish 'campaign of abuse', 209; and Jewish terrorism, 209, 222, 223, 225–8, 256, 258–9, 262–3; supports bombing of railway lines to Auschwitz, 212; supports 'the biggest outcry possible', 213; helps a group of Hungarian Jewish escapees, 214–5; 'the most horrible crime ever committed', 215; persists in supporting war crimes trails, 215, 220; urges establishment of a Jewish Brigade Group in the British Army, 216–8, 239; wants to help save 'the multitudes', 220; accepts Weizmann's assurances about opposing Jewish terror, 222, 223; briefs Lord Gort, 223; and post-war Jewish immigration, 224; and the assassination of Lord Moyne, 225–8,

228–9; advises Weizmann to go to the United States, 230; discusses Palestine with Ibn Saud, 234–6; and the discovery of two concentration camps (1945), 239–41, 257; what he meant to 'the hunted, the persecuted', 242; correspondence with Weizmann (1945), 242–247; and American responsibility for Palestine, 246, 248, 258; and the possible abandonment of the Mandate, 251, 258, 263–4; Leader of the Opposition (1945–51), 238, 262; supports the Anglo-American Commission's Partition suggestion, 250–1, 251; and the King David Hotel bomb debate (July 1946), 253–60; and 'large causes which we have carried far', 259; and British military expenditure in Palestine, 263, 264–5; compares Jews and Greeks, 266–7; and Israel's War of Independence (1948–9): 268–9, 270, 275; his war memoirs, 271–2; criticises the Labour Government's Israel policies, 274–8; recalls the positive potential of Partition, 276–7; recalls the post-1922 immigration debate, 277–8; and Britain's recognition of Israel, 274, 279; and modern Israel, 280; and Jewish 'inspiration and culture', 280–1; and Egypt's closure of the Suez Canal to Israel-bound ships, 281, 285, 287–8; 'an old Zionist', 282, 283; and the 'Churchill Falls', 284–5; 'I am a Zionist', 286, 290, 295; and an Israeli reprisal raid (1953), 286–7; and a possible British 'invasion of Israel' (1954), 289; looks to Israel for 'statesmanship and patience', 289; and the world's 'incalculable' debt to the Jews, 290; two Jewish perspectives on, 291, 306; and the 'Suez Crisis' (1956), 294–6, 298–300; and 'murder and armed raids' against Israel, 299; and 'odious acts of ingratitude' by Jewish terrorists, 300; and the Sinai Peninsula (1956–7), 300–1; meets Ben-Gurion (1960), 302–3; Ben-Gurion's letter to (1961), 303–4; a possible visit to Israel (1962), 305; Ben-Gurion's obituary tribute to (1965), 305–6

Churchill, Winston (Churchill's grandson): told of 'that one, strong, unseen voice', 197–8

Churchill White Paper (1922): 84–5, 111, 113, 120, 122, 209, 253, 277–8, 308

Cis-Jordania (Western Palestine): 49

Cologne: 2

Colville, (Sir) John ('Jock'): 285

Colvin, Ian: 148

Comay: Michael, 281

Commonwealth (formerly British Commonwealth): and Israel, 291–2

Communism (and Bolshevism): and anti-Semitism, 30–3; and the Jews, 37–44; in Palestine, 64–5; and the Jews of Britain, 137–8; in Iraq, 303; 'march of' after 1945, 275, 304

concentration camps: 'pock-mark the German soil', 104

Conservative Party: 9, 44, 155; Churchill warns (1939), 160; and the arming of Jews in Palestine (1940), 174; shows 'little support' for a Jewish State, 222, 243, 246; hardens Churchill's heart, 223; and Churchill's advice to Weizmann, 230; defeated (1945), 238, 249; resents his 'alleged pro-Zionist leanings', 269; and the prospect of a Jewish State, 275; and Disraeli, 297

Constantinople: 25

Constituent Assembly (Russia): 28

Coote, Captain Maxwell: 52–3

Copenhagen: Churchill's articles published in, 139

Cordova: 116

Council of Aliens: Churchill's instruction to (1940), 177

Coupland, Professor Reginald: questions Churchill (1937), 112, 115, 118, 119
Cracow: war criminals executed in, 201
Cranborne, Viscount: 183, 190
Crimea: 229
Cripps, Sir Stafford: 257
Croft, Brigadier-General Lord: rebuked, 265
Cromie, Captain Francis: 37
Crusaders: 'dust of', 55
Curzon, Marquess: 46
Cyprus: Jewish detainees in, 250; last detainees released from, 274; continuing British rule in, 298
Cyrenaica: Jews 'not very smitten with', 249
Czechoslovakia: 126, 140, 141, 146, 159; Jewish emigrants from, 178; Government-in-Exile of, 195
Czechs: among the 'tortured peoples', 188

Dachau concentration camp: 155
Daily Telegraph: 13, 141, 145
Dalmatia: 210
Damascus: 46, 47, 48, 49, 102
Danes: and Germany, 162
Danube River: 271
Danzig, Free City of: 146
Dardanelles, the: naval attack on (1915), 25, 26
Darien (steamship): its passengers interned, 188
Davidson, Randall (Archbishop of Canterbury); his criticism of Zionism, 69–70
Dead Sea: and the waters of the Jordan, 81
Deakin, (Sir) William: 271, 272
Deedes, General (Sir) Wyndham: 33–4
Delhi: pressure from, 144
demobilisation (1919): 29–30
Denikin, General: warned against anti-Semitic violence, 31, 32, 41
Derby, 17th Earl of: 44
Displaced Persons camps (DP camps): 242, 265–6; and Palestine, 249–50; Jews from, to be deported from Palestine back to Europe, 265
Disraeli, Benjamin (Earl of Beaconsfield): Churchill writes about, 296–7
Dizengoff, Meir (Mayor of Tel Aviv): 64; photograph 11
Dorset: 144
Douglas, Lord Alfred: his anti-Semitic accusations, 86–88
Douglas, Lewis W. ('Lew'): 269
'Down with the Jews': a cry in Gaza, 53
Dreyfus, Captain Alfred: 3
Dreyfus, Dr Charles: 19
Dulberg, Dr Joseph: 12, 18; photographs 3, 4
Dulles, John Foster: and the Suez War (1956), 300; and 'Arab favours', 301
Dundee: 18, 86; and an anti-Semitic accusation, 88
Dunkirk evacuation (1940): 174–5
Dutch: and Germany, 162
Dzerzhinsky, Feliks: 40

East Africa: 17
Eastern Palestine: 49
Ebbw Vale: attacks on Jews at, 20
Eddy, Colonel William A.: and Ibn Saud's plan for the survivors of the Holocaust, 232
Eden, Anthony: and a protest to Romania, 181; 'loves Arabs and hates Jews', 189–90; supports declaration about Nazi crimes against Jews, 195, 196; hesitant about too explicit a war crimes declaration, 200; opposes Churchill's post-war plan for Palestine, 202, 203; and the Jewish request to bomb the railway lines to Auschwitz, 211–12, 216; and the fate of a group of Hungarian-Jewish escapees, 215; Churchill writes to, of 'the most horrible crime ever committed', 215; Churchill advocates a public protest, 220; and

Lord Moyne's murderers, 229; and Churchill's meeting with Ibn Saud, 235; and the discovery of Buchenwald, 240; and the 'Peace table', 248; and the Suez Canal, 287–8; and the 'Suez Crisis' (1956), 295–6, 298–300
Edward VII, King: as Prince of Wales, 2; as King, 5
Egypt: 50, 52, 59, 102, 116, 118, 144; to be appeased, 157; during the Second World War 174, 176, 182, 191, 208; the trial of Lord Moyne's assassins in, 228–9; and Palestine, 231; Britain to 'scuttle' from, 259, 264; invades Israel (1948), 268, 275, 276; negotiates an armistice with Israel (1949), 274, 280; closes Suez Canal to ships bound for Israel, 281, 285, 287–8; and the Negev, 284; an emissary to, 290; receives arms from the Soviet Union, 294, 295, 303; and the 'Suez Crisis' (1956), 294–6; and the Sinai Peninsula (1956–7), 300–1; preparing for war, 303
Eichmann, Adolf: and Jewish emigration, 178; forestalled, in Budapest, 213
Eichstatt Castle (Moravia): Churchill's Jewish host at, 13
Einstein, Albert: visits Churchill, 101; his visit recalled, 176; and atomic science, 290; photograph 15
Einstein, Lewis: congenial company, 298
Eisenhower, General Dwight D.: and the discovery of a concentration camp (1945), 239–41; as President, 285; and the 'Suez Crisis' (1956), 295; and the Sinai Peninsula (1956–7), 300–1
Elath, Eliahu: Churchill's talk with, 293–4; and the 'Suez Crisis' (1956), 295; photograph 28
electrification (of Palestine): 47, 64; Churchill supports, 75–83; and the Arabs, 81, 92; Churchill praises, 160, 254, 277–8; recalled, 285
Elizabeth II, Queen: 290
Empire Rival: Jews deported back to Europe on (1947), 265
English Zionist Federation: 17
Epping (constituency): 90
Eritrea: a suggested future Jewish colony, 189; Jewish terrorists deported to, 222
Estonians: 265–6
Evans-Gordon, Major William: 10
Evening Standard: Churchill criticises Partition in, 128–9; advice to British Jewry in, 137; and Churchill warning about the Nazi regime, 138; Churchill's appeal to Hitler in, 139

Farouk, King of Egypt: 208, 236
Fayyum (Egypt): 234, 238
Feisal, Emir (Feisal ibn-Hussein): 46, 52, 255
Feldblum, Igo: 'We Will Win', 218
Finns: 265–6
First World War: 25–9; Jewish soldiers in, 25, 30, 39, 124–5, 148; recalled, 58, 60; pledges made during, 78–9, 115
Fisher, H. A. L.: 84
Foerster, Gauleiter: 146
Foggia (southern Italy): 210
Fontainebleau Forest (near Paris): a memorial service in, 136
Forest, Baron de ('Tootie'): 3, 13, 23
France: and Syria, 35, 44, 222, 228; and the Jews of Russia, 39; and Palestine population density, 126, 128; and the Munich Agreement, 141; invaded (1940), 171, 175; round up of Jews in (1942), 191; and the 'Suez Crisis' (1956), 295, 298–300; and the Sinai Peninsula (1956–7), 300–1
Free Trade: 90
French Algerian troops: 35
French National Committee (De Gaulle): endorses the Allied Declaration of 17 December 1942, 195

Friedman, Elisha: 250
Friedman-Yellin, Nathan: agrees that Churchill will not be an assassin's target, 227–8

Gad, tribe of: 49
Gale, Ben: 171
Galilee: 50, 151 n.1, 164
Galilee, Sea of: 102
Gallipoli Peninsula, Battle for (1915): Jews fight on, 25, 125
Gapon, Father Georgi Apollonovich: 83
Gaster, Rabbi Dr Moses: 17–18
Gaza: 52–3
General Post Office (Jerusalem): demonstration at, 56
Geneva: 11, 85, 168
George Cross (medal): 2
German soldiers: graves of, 55
Germany: occupies southern Russia (1918), 28; Bolshevism in (1919–20), 40–1; a possible Muslim ally, 58; defeat of (in 1918), 58, 58–9; a warning against placing orders in, 76; Hitler's rise to power in, 97; Churchill visits (1929), 97–9; anti-Jewish legislation in, 99; Churchill's warnings about, 99–100, 103; and the Nuremberg Laws (1935), 106; continued persecution of Jews in (1936–9), 107, 129, 135; Jewish immigration to Palestine from, 108, 109, 131; foments Arab agitation, 109–10, 140–1, 161, 182; and Palestine population density, 126, 128; Churchill's continued warnings concerning, 138; onward march of, 141; false claims of, 144–5; expels Polish-born Jews, 147; Kristallnacht in, and its aftermath, 147–8, 149; Jewish emigration from (1939), 154; and 'the hush of fear', 162; invades Poland, 162, 163; at war with Britain, 176; Jewish emigration from (1940), 178; and Turkey, 182–3; and the revolt in Iraq (1941), 205; invades the Soviet Union (1941), 186; and the mass murder of Jews, 186–7; Allied bombing of (1942), 192; possible reprisal bombing of (1943), 196–7; Jews 'reluctant to go back' to, 232; Displaced Persons camps in (1945), 249–50
Gibson, Guy and Eve: 199
Gilead, Land of: 56
Gladstone, Herbert (later Viscount): 16
Goebbels, Josef: and 'you and me', 136; his newspaper attacks Churchill, 147
Golan Heights: Churchill drives across, 102
Goldschmidt-Rothschild, Baroness von: 105–6, 135
Goldsmith, Major Frank: 23–4
Gollancz, Victor: 107
Golomb, Eliahu: Churchill not to be an assassin's target, 227–8
Gort, Field Marshal Lord: 223
Goschen, Lord: 6
Government House (Jerusalem): 54, 55, 58
Grafftey Smith, (Sir) Laurence: 234–5
Graham Greene, Sir William: and an anti-Semitic accusation, 88
Grand Falls (Newfoundland): 284–5
Great Synagogue (Cheetham Hill, Manchester): 14
Greater Syria: and Palestine, 236–7
Greece: British pressure on (1939), 154; British support for (1941), 182; Government-in Exile of, 195; Hungarian Jewish refugees in, 218–9; Communist insurgency in, 228; Churchill's visit to (1944), 229; 30; a cruise to (1962), 305
Greeks: among the 'tortured peoples', 188; mass murder of, 241; and the Jews (Truman), 265–6, and the Jews (Churchill), 266–7
Gregorieff, General: and 'fearful massacres', 33

Grey, Sir Edward (later Viscount): 25
Grigg, Sir James: 216, 217
Gruner, Dov: his 'fortitude', 263
Grynszpan, Herschel: 147
Gunnersbury: 2, 3

Haganah (Jewish Agency defence force): sets an explosive charge, 179; and the Palestinian parachutists, 209 n.13; cooperates with British against Jewish terrorists, 221–2; ensures that Churchill will not be an assassin's target, 227–8
Haifa: a protest in, 54; within Arab artillery range, 127; and Partition, 151 n.1; and Jewish land purchase, 165; the fate of a a ship seized in, 178–9; Jews kill British police officers in, 221; a further act of Jewish terror in, 261–2
Haifa Congress of Palestinian Arabs: Churchill receives delegation from, 58–61
Hakim, Eliahu: a Jewish assassin, 225
Haking, General: a warning sent through, 32
Halifax, Third Viscount (later Earl): 140, 146, 154
Hall, Gilbert: 29, n.13
Hama (Syria): 47, 48
Hamilton River (Labrador): 284
Hammond, Sir Laurie: questions Churchill (1937), 119
Hanfstaengel, Ernst (Putzi): 98–9
Harding, Field Marshal Sir John: 289
Harrow School: 1, 2, 14
Harvey, Oliver (later Lord): 189–90
Hass, The Reverend Simon: 'We have no bread, but we have Churchill', 241
Hastings, (Sir) Patrick: and an anti-Semitic accusation, 86–7
Hebrew: 'a dead language', 58
Hebrew University of Jerusalem: 56, 280–1
Hedjaz: Muslims of, 58
Hedjaz Railway: 48, 49
Helsinki: Churchill's articles published in, 139
Herzl, Hans: Churchill helps, 23
Herzl, Theodor: 23
Hirsch, Baron Maurice de: 3, 4, 12
History of the English-Speaking Peoples, A (Winston S. Churchill): and Disraeli, 296–7
Hitler, Adolf: his road to power, 97; nearly meets Churchill, 98–9; appointed Chancellor, 99; and 'currents of hatred', 103; Churchill's critique of (1935), 103–5; and appeasement, 123; Churchill appeals to, 139; and Palestine, 141; and the position of Jews in Germany (in 1933), 145; enters Vienna (1938), 145; attacks Churchill by name (1938), 146–7; a secret speech by (1938), 148; enters Prague (1939), 159; and the 'hush of fear' (1939), 162; and the Second World War, 174, 187; 'unspeakable evils' of, 187; his 'vile regime', 193; his 'satanic design', 196; 'wrongs inflicted by', 199; and the Jews (in Truman's perspective), 266; and Churchill's war memoirs, 272
Hoare, Sir Samuel (later Viscount Templewood): and 'Winston's mistakes', 171
Hohenstaufen Castle (Rhineland): 54
Holland (The Netherlands): 171, 275; Government-in-Exile of, 195
Holman, General Sir H. C.: a warning sent through, 31, 33
Holocaust: 'probably the greatest and most horrible crime ever committed', 271; 'virtual extermination' during, 300
Holy Land: 'a natural home in' (for the Jews), 255
Holy Places (Jerusalem): 72, 123
Homs (Syria): 47, 48
horse chestnuts: 27
Horthy, Admiral Miklos: 155, 212
Hotel du Lac (Fayyum, Egypt); 234

House of Commons: Churchill opposes Aliens Bill in, 9–10; anti-Semitism and the 'Russian National Cause', 32; Churchill descants in, on his visit to a Jewish village, 65–6; Palestine debate in (1922), 78–84; Churchill temporarily out of, 86–90; a debate in, regretted, 140; a delegation from, to go to Buchenwald, 240–1; and the King David Hotel bomb debate, 253–60
House of Lords: 2; Zionism under attack in, 76–7, 84; a delegation from, to go to Buchenwald, 240–1
Huddersfield: 281
Huguenots: 129
humanity: "considerations of", 180
Hungary: 40, 83; Jews from, to be rescued, 209–10; Jews of, deported to Auschwitz, 211; BBC broadcasts warnings to, 213; renewed danger in, 220; wartime fate of Jews in, recalled, 271
Hussein, Sherif of Mecca: 46; one of his sons ruler of Iraq, 255
Husseini, Haj Amin al-: incites Arabs against Jews, 102; and British policy, 112; Churchill advises 'violent methods' against, 130; prevents emigration of Bulgarian Jewish children, 194
Husseini, Musa Kazem Pasha al-: 70
Hyde Park Hotel (London): 74

'I owe you the gift of life itself': 219
I Was Hitler's Prisoner (Stefan Lorant): 155–6
Ibn Saud, King: 67; and a future Jewish State in Palestine, 182, 183, 202, 231–6, 237; photographs 23, 24
Illustrated Sunday Herald: Churchill's article in, 38–44, 307–8
India (British India): 3, 4, 35, 46, 143–4; Muslims of, 58, 144; soldiers from, in Italy, 239; Britain to leave, 259, 264; and the Suez Canal, 297
Indian Ocean: 178
Indonesia: 274, 275
inhumanity: an act of, 179
'International Jews': 40
Iran: 144; Shah of, 292
Iraq: an Arab throne in, 47, 180, 236, 255; Muslims of, 58; Palestinian Arab help from, 122; to be appeased, 157; the anti-British revolt in (1941), 205, 222, 254; and Palestine, 231; troops from, invade Israel (1948), 268; suggests an Egyptian expansion into the Negev, 284; monarchy overthrown in, 303
Irgun: acts of terror by, 221, 253; arrests of, 222; 'the vilest gangsters', 270
Irish Treaty (1922): 82
Iron Guard (Romania): 181
Islam: Churchill's perspective on, 53–4, 67, 115–6; not to be alienated, 143–4, 157, 194; and Roosevelt's meeting with Ibn Saud (1945), 233, 234; the 'remarkable' unity of, 296
Islington, Lord: anti-Zionist, 76
Ismay, General Sir Hastings (later Lord): 228
Israel: laying the 'foundation' of, 57; comes into being (1948), 268; its War of Independence (1948–9), 176, 280; Britain's refusal to recognise, 272, 274; and a military clash with Britain (1949), 274; 'tough fibre of the Zionist community' in, 275; and Churchill as a 'powerful friend', 281; 'wonderful exertions' of, 282; a 'tribute' to the founders of, 282; 'courageous efforts' of, 282–3; 'free and sovereign', 283; and Egypt's closure of the Suez Canal to ship bound for, 281, 285, 287–8; and a British 'invasion' of, in prospect (1954), 289; 'counsels of statesmanship' required of, 289; its 'vigour and prosperity', 290; 'vulnerability' of, 290–1; Churchill's 'personal interest' in, 291; 'a force in the world', 292;

and Churchill's 'prophetic insight' (in 1921), 292; Churchill 'has been and is' a friend of, 293; 'a nation of ideals', 293; 'no evil to befall', 293; and the 'Suez Crisis' with Egypt (1956), 294–6, 298–9; 'a refuge', 295; 'how I wish I were young again', 299; and the Sinai Peninsula (1956–7), 300–1; oranges from, 301; Churchill's 'very warm good wishes' for, 304; Churchill's possible visit to (1962), 305
Israelis: 275–6
Israelites: 307
Istanbul: Jewish refugees reach, 206–7, 226
Italy: 13, 55; foments Arab agitation, 109–10, 140–1, 161, 182; its armies, 162; at war, 176, 177; Jewish refugees flown to safety in, 210; Jewish Brigade Group fights in, 218, 239; soldiers of, fight alongside the Allies, 239

Jabotinsky, Vladimir: opposes Partition (1937), 124–7, 130; biographical sketch of, 124–5; photograph 14
Jaffa: 64; violence in an around, 73; Britain to retain, 123; a Jewish terrorist act in, 261
Janner, Barnett (later Lord): 94, 285–6
Japan: and the Second World War, 187, 246–7, 271
Japanese Government Loan: 4–5
Jericho: Churchill visits, 102; Churchill receives a report from, 110
Jerusalem: 17; Churchill in, 24 n.4, 109, 255; not mentioned in promise to Arabs, 47, 48; Arabs attack Jews in (1920), 125; (1929), 91; Mufti of, incites Arabs against Jews, 102; Britain to retain, 123, 151 n.1; not a 'significant' geographic area, 126; Jewish land purchase near, curtailed, 165; acts of Jewish terror in, 221, 261, 264; and Athens, 266; Jewish Quarter in, attacked (1948), 268, 269; Arab shelling of, 270; Egyptian forces reach southern suburbs of (1948), 276; Churchill's 1921 visit, recalled, 292; and the State of Israel, 292; woodcuts of, 293; and the United Nations Partition Plan (1947), 294
Jewish Agency for Palestine: 119, 122, 163, 164, 171, 174, 177, 179, 193, 206–7, 209, 213, 215; its appeals for action, 220; rejects Jewish terror, 221, 227, 228; and the assassination of Lord Moyne, 225, 227; and failed promises, 247; after the King David Hotel bomb, 258–9
Jewish agricultural villages (in Palestine): 60, 64, 65–6; to be defended, 66, 79; 'thriving', 72; and Communist elements', 73; 'desert . . . converted into gardens', 80
Jewish Brigade Group: to be established (1944), 216–8; in action (1945), 239; recalled, 271
Jewish Chronicle: 9, 20, 28 n.11; and Churchill's 'flashy generalisations', 43–4; and Churchill's discussion of Partition, 132–4; Churchill's messages to (1941 and 1942), 187, 193; Churchill's obituary tribute in, 306
Jewish Colonisation Association: and land purchase in Palestine, 77
Jewish commonwealth (in Palestine): a post-war prospect, 206
Jewish communal clubs (Manchester): 14
Jewish ethics: 38, 95–6; 'principles of righteousness' of, 187
Jewish Hospital Fund (Manchester): 14
Jewish immigration (to Palestine): opposed, 58–9, 67–8, 110; to be safeguarded, 68; limits on, 68–9, 69, 71–2, 75, 79, 253; Churchill questioned about, 111–5, 116–7; continued discussion of, 121, 122, 129; Churchill urges need to 'go slowly', 131, 142–3, 151;

Jewish immigration (to Palestine): – *continued*
Churchill seeks ten-year quota for, 152–3, 154; and the 1939 Palestine White Paper (the 'Black Paper'), 158–63, 166, 167; and the interception of 'illegal' immigrants (1939–40), 168, 177–80; Arab opposition to, 184, 189, 232, 233; and the *Patria*, 178–9, 181; and the *Darien*, 188–9; Churchill's refusal to allow 'absolute cessation' of, 189; a scheme to facilitate (1944), 206–7; a fifteen-year plan for (1944), 224; and the assassination of Lord Moyne, 225–6; restrictions on (1945–48), 242, 247, 250; harsh measures against, 265; 'we should never have stopped', 270; Churchill reflects on, 277–8; Churchill's support for, 308
Jewish Legion (First World War): 125
Jewish National Home (in Palestine): 25, 35, 36; to be facilitated, 45; to be in Western Palestine, 47; and Transjordan, 49, 55–6; 'will be a blessing', 56–7; to be 'abolished', 59; 'manifestly right', 60; meaning of, 69; and land purchase, 69–70, 130; 'of right and not on sufferance', 74, 85; and '25,000 promiscuous people', 76–7; accepted by the League of Nations (9122), 84–5; and a British Government loan (1928), 90; to be protected, 92; and Britain's 'obligation', 94; Churchill questioned about, 111–123; the 'Jewish Commonwealth', 125; 'moral grounds' of, 130; its achievements praised (1939), 160; two suggested 'colonies' for, 189, 249; not to be abandoned, 262; has come into existence, 275; 'I have worked to that end', 282
'Jewish, Negro, Management, Labor': '. . . goes haywire' (Truman), 266
Jewish people: 'struggle for the soul' of, 42; 'everlasting gratitude' of, 291; 'I am their friend', 300
Jewish Quarter (of Jerusalem): attacked (1948), 268, 269; Churchill asks about, 293
Jewish refugees: a plan to help (1933), 101; British policy towards (1939), 154; enhance British science, 176; interned, 176–7; Churchill seeks to help, 197, 198, 214–5, 218–9; Ibn Saud's view of, 231–2; Palestine effectively barred to (1945–47), 245, 247; in Tel Aviv, 254; their suggested return to their pre-war homes, 257; final release of, from detention in Cyprus (1949), 272; 'asylum' for, in Israel, 282, 293; and the Negev, 292
Jewish soldiers: in the First World War, 25, 30, 39, 124–5; in the Second World War, recruitment and arming of, requested, 163–4, 172–3, 181–2, 182–3, 190, 216–8; and parachutists behind German lines, 209; and the proposed Jewish Brigade Group (1944), 216–8; in action in Italy, 239
Jewish State (in Palestine): envisaged (before 1948), 42, 71, 112–3, 114–5, 164, 305; at risk, 121–2, 130; and Partition, 123–4; and Jabotinsky, 125–6; endangered by Partition, 126–7, 128; eventually 'over the whole of Palestine', 131; the attraction of, even in a partitioned Palestine, 132; dangers to, under Partition, 132–3; wartime discussion and prospects of (1940–45), 182, 184–5, 190, 224–5, 234; and the post-war 'permanent settlement', 199; Transjordan and the Negev possible parts of, 205; and the Conservative Party, 222; Ibn Saud opposes, 231–6, 237; a 'deadly blow', 237; 'a form of Nazi-Fascism', 237; and Churchill's immediate post-war discussions, 242–9; and the

British Labour Party, 265; 'an event in world history', 274–5; 'hour of glory' of, 280
Jewish Territorial Organisation: and Uganda, 12
Jewish terrorist acts (in Palestine): 221–2, 223, 250, 251, 253, 256, 258–9, 261–2; and the policies of the British Labour Government, 256, 261; and a 'small . . . fanatical minority', 262–3; after Britain announces transfer of Mandate to the United Nations, 264; and Churchill's war memoirs, 300
Jews: Churchill 'too fond of', xv; 'racial prejudice' against, 8; 'corporate spirit' of, 15; 'corporate responsibility' of, 18; 'you must not have too many of them', 29; and Bolshevism, 31, 31–2, 37; 'whom we are pledged to introduce into Palestine', 35; 'the most remarkable race', 38; 'a people of peculiar genius', 39; 'evil prominence' of, 40; 'importers of western leaven', 51; 'Cut their throats', 53; an Arab perspective on, 58–9; have 'a far more difficult task', 72; the 'necessity of killing', 75; 'extraneous and alien' to Palestine, 76; worldwide 'hereditary antipathy' to, 78; to be protected (in Palestine), 79; not 'a cause of reproach', 82; persecuted (in Germany), 97; 'how can any man help how he is born', 99; 'pitiless ill-treatment' of, 100; 'declared a foul and odious race', 104; and the Nuremberg Laws (1935), 196; immigration to Palestine of, 109; 'abominable persecution' of, 136: and the 'battle of Cable Street' (1936), 137; Churchill's advice to, 137, 138; and Hitler's desire for conquest, 139; to be 'blotted out', 140; Nazi propaganda concerning, 144–5; persecution of, in Vienna, 145; in Danzig, 146; Hitler's desire concerning (1938), 148; and the 'hush of fear' (1939), 162; and the Palestine Land Transfer Regulations (1939), 164; the proposed arming of, in Palestine (1940), 169–70, 176; interned, in Britain (1939–40), 176–7; to be deported from Palestine (1940), 177–80; their fate, in Poland, 181, 199; their fate, in Romania, 181; in the German-occupied Soviet Union, 186–7, 199; in France, 191; 'principles of righteousness' of, 187, 193; Eden 'hates', 190; Churchill denounces 'these vile crimes' against, 192; 'none has suffered more cruelly', 193; and possible British reprisal raids on Germany (1943), 196–7; 'terrible sufferings inflicted on', 199; a film of 'atrocities inflicted on', 199; to be able to judge war criminals, 204, to get post-war compensation, 204; have 'a wonderful case' with regard to a post-war Jewish State, 205; hostility of British officers towards, 205; volunteer to parachute behind German lines, 209; Churchill urges 'sympathetic consideration' of projects for, 216; deserve the 'satisfaction' of their own military force, 217; and 'a new set of gangsters worthy of Nazi Germany', 226; 'must have a place to live in – that is to say, in Palestine', 236; 'merely aliens' in Palestine, 237; and the discovery of the concentration camps, 239; and 'the surviving remnant of European Jewry', 245, 249–50; a 'senseless, squalid war with', 264; 'have no sense of proportion' (Truman), 265–6; and Greeks, 266–7; the 'case for', 270, 'inspiration and culture' of, 280–1; the world's 'incalculable' debt to, 290; and Jerusalem, 292; and 'a special obligation' to Churchill, 306

Jezreel Valley: 165
Jockey Club (London): 283
John the Baptist: 1
Jordan, Kingdom of (see earlier index entries for Transjordan): negotiates an armistice with Israel (1949), 274; 'I trust you may work in with', 282; in conflict with Israel (1953–4), 286–7, 288–9; Palestinian Arab acts of terror launched from, 286–7, 288, 290; and the 'Suez Crisis' (1956), 296; the survival of, 303
Jordan River: 12, 42, 47, 48, 50, 52, 56; water power of, 76, 80, 81, 160; and Partition, 124; and the First World War, 125; and the Revisionists' territorial agenda, 125. 126–7
Joshua (Israelite leader): 237
Joynson-Hicks, Sir William (later Viscount Brentford): opposes Zionists, 74, 78
Jutland, Battle of (1916): and an anti-Semitic accusation, 86–7

Kamenets-Podolsk: Jews murdered in, 186
Kaplan, Fanya: 40
Karachi: pressure from, 144
Karski, Jan: his report and its impact, 194–5
Kaunas (Kovno): Churchill's articles published in, 139
Kedourie Agricultural School (Palestine): a strike at, 110
Kenya: a possible Jewish homeland in, 12
Keppel, Alice: photograph 5
Kerensky, Alexander: 83
Khalifs: 'dust of', 55
Kibya (Jordan): an Israeli reprisal raid on (1953), 286–7
Kielce (Poland): Jewish survivors of the Holocaust killed in (1946): 251–2
Kiev: 187
King David Hotel (Jerusalem): Churchill stays at (1934), 24 n.4, 102; Jewish act of terror at (1946), 253
Kishinev: pogroms in, 10
Kleist, Major Ewald von: 146
Knesset, the (Israel's parliament): Churchill contributes to a gift for (1956), 294; Ben Gurion's obituary tribute in (1965), 305–6
Koran, the: Ibn Saud quotes, 235
Kristallnacht pogrom (1938): 147–8, 149
Kun, Bela (Commissar for Foreign Affairs, Hungary): 40
Kuwatli, Shukri al- (President of Syria): 236

Labour Government (1945–51): comes to power, 249, abandons the Mandate, 264; refuses to recognise Israel, 272; has 'largely destroyed' bridges of goodwill, 278; recognises Israel, 279; and Egypt's closure of the Suez Canal to ships bound for Israel, 281
Labour Party (Britain): 107, 128, 166; 'committed', 204; 'friends' of the Zionists, 224; leaves Churchill's wartime coalition, 243; 'have lost all zeal', 246; abandons its earlier pro-Zionist stance, 255–6, 270
Labour Zionism (Palestine): 64–5
Labrador: 284
Land Ordinance for Palestine: see index entry for Palestine Land Transfer Regulations (1939–40)
La Pausa (South of France); Churchill at, 297–8, 302; Ben-Gurion invited to, 302
Laski, Harold: and a 'terrible book', 107; Churchill's assurance to (1943), 199; tells Churchill 'I owe you the gift of life itself', 219; the butt of anti-Semitism, 265
Laski, Nathan: 7, 9, 199, and 'the blessings of millions of Jews', 161
Last Post: sounded, 55

Latvia: 126
Latvians: 265–6
Lawrence, Colonel T.E. ('Lawrence of Arabia'): advises Churchill, 46, 47, 50, 51, 52, 53
Lawrence-Feisal Agreement (1921): 46–7
League of Nations: and the Palestine Mandate: 58, 77, 84–5; and collective security, 107; and a Jewish 'independent autonomous State', 132; and the possible return of the Palestine Mandate to, 142; Palestine population figures submitted to, 152; opposes the 1939 Palestine White Paper, 166, 167, 168
League of Nations Union: 136
Lebanon: 102, 183, 190, 236, 255; invades Israel, 268; negotiates an armistice with Israel (1949), 274, 280; a cruise to, 305
Legislative Council (Palestine): proposed, 108
Leicester West (constituency): 86; and an anti-Semitic accusation, 88
Lenin, V.I.: 28, 37, 40, 83
Levy, Louis: Churchill seeks help from, 136–7
Levy-Lawson, Harry (later Viscount Burnham): 13
Liberal Party (Britain): 16, 17, 29, 128, 152, 166
liberation (1945): 198
Libya: possible Jewish settlement in, 233, 234; and the 'Suez Crisis' (1956), 296; a cruise to, 305
Lindemann, Professor Frederick: and a plan to help German Jews, 101; meets Gauleiter Foerster, 146
Lindsay, Sir Ronald: 'the chickens will come home to roost', 93
Lisbon: Jewish escapees in, 214
Litani River: 50
Lithuania: 126
Lloyd, Lord: opposes arming of Jews, 172–3, 174; and Jewish deportees, 178; and Arab 'virtue', 180
Lloyd George, David (later Earl Lloyd-George): 26, 29, 32, 33, 35, 36, 45, 46, 54, 71; his government defeated (1922), 86; and the Palestine White Paper (1939), 166
London: 62, 69; an anti-Semitic accusation circulated in, 87; 'Battle of Cable Street' in (1936), 137; and the impact of Churchill's oratory, 174, 176; the Allied Declaration of 17 December 1942 broadcast from, 195; a warning broadcast from (10 October 1944); the Blitz in, recalled, 303; Churchill's funeral in, 306
London University: 197–8
Lorant, Stefan: supports Churchill, 155–6; photograph 20
Lothian, Lord: 165, 166, 167, 173
Lourie, Arthur: 302, 304
Loveday, Dr Thomas: and a German-Jewish applicant, 101
Luxembourg: Churchill's articles published in, 139; invaded, 171; Government-in-Exile of, 195
Lydda: 64
Lyons: Jews deported from (1942), 191
Lytton, Earl of: 177

Ma'an: 49
Maccabees: 'dust of', 55
MacDonald, Malcolm: 151, 152; and the 'Black Paper', 158, 160; and the Palestine Land Ordinance, 164, 169; and 'illegal' immigration, 168; 'cruel penalties' imposed by, 173–4; and Zionism (with his father Ramsay), 306
MacDonald, Ramsay: 93, 100
McMahon, Sir Henry: his pledge, 48
MacMichael, Sir Harold: 207; an assassination attempt on, 221
Macmillan, Harold (later Earl of Stockton): and the 'Suez Crisis' (1956), 295–6; and the Sinai Peninsula (1956–7), 301; an Israeli request to, 303

Madrid: 197
Makhno, Nestor: and 'fearful massacres', 33
Malaya: 275
'Malay run amok, a': 155
Manasseh, tribe of: 49
Manchester North-West: Churchill's parliamentary constituency, 7, 11, 13, 14, 17, 18–19; Jews of, recalled, 56; and Chaim Weizmann, 290; and Jewish communal life, 307
Manchester Liberal Party: 7
Manchester Zionist Committee: 19
Manchester Zionist Council: 289–90
Manchester Guardian: and the Nuremberg Laws, 106; and Nazi propaganda concerning the Jews in Germany, 144–5
Mandates Commission (of the League of Nations): opposes the 1939 Palestine White Paper, 166, 167, 168
Mandel, Georges: 136
Maritza (steamship); its refugee passengers travel on to Palestine, 207
Marks, Sir Simon (later Lord): 278
Marks and Spencer: 272
Marlborough, First Duke of: 97–8, 171
Marlborough, Ninth Duke of: 13
Marseille: 50
Marsh, (Sir) Edward: 17
Marshall Diston, Adam: Churchill's instructions to, 138
Martin, (Sir) John: 180, 220, 244, 246
Marx, Ernst von: 24
Masterton-Smith, Sir James: and an anti-Semitic accusation, 88; and an oil consultancy, 88
Mauritius: Jews deported from Palestine to, 178, 179; Jews not to be deported to, 188–9
Maurois, Andrè (Emile Herzog): 26
Mayfair: 5
Maxwell, Sir Alexander: 137
May, Doris; 149
Mecca: 67
'Mechanised Attila' the (Hitler): 174
Medina: 97
Medina, Sir Solomon de: 97–8
Mediterranean Sea: 12, 48, 50, 52, 56, 124; a suggested future Jewish colony on, 189; the United States to be 'drawn into', 248
Meighen, Arthur: questions Churchill, 69
Mein Kampf (Hitler): Churchill refers to, 103
Melchett, Second Baron: Churchill's advice to, on Zionist policy, 130–2; a possible High Commissioner for Palestine, 207, 208; and the fate of Hungarian Jews, 216; Churchill confides in, 269–70
Mesopotamia (Iraq): British Mandate for, 35, 45; for further index entries, see: Iraq
Middle East Department (Colonial Office): 45–6, 74
Millerand, Alexandre: fears 'high-handed' Jews, 46
Mond, Sir Alfred: his warning, 75
Monte Carlo: 305
Montefiore, Leonard: 106
Moran, Lord: 287
Montague Browne, (Sir) Anthony: 294, 300, 302–5
Moravia (Austria-Hungary): 13
Morgenthau, Henry, Jr: 265
Mormons: 266
Morning Post: and an anti-Semitic accusation, 86–7
Morton, (Sir) Desmond: 137–8
Moscow: 30, 37; the Allied Declaration of 17 December 1942 broadcast from, 195; Churchill in, 220
Moscow Declaration (on war crimes, 1 November 1943): 201
Moses: Churchill's article on, 95–6, 303, 304
Mosque of Omar (Jerusalem): 56
Mosley, Sir Oswald: 137
Mount Carmel (Haifa): 183
Mount of Olives (Jerusalem): 54

Mount Scopus (Jerusalem): 54, 56; Churchill's speech on, recalled, 305
Mount Sinai: 95
Moyne, Lord: with Churchill in Jerusalem (1934), 102; and the 'Arab world', 181; critical of Zionist aspirations, 184; Churchill's instruction to, to allow Jewish 'illegals' to remain in Palestine, 188–9; Churchill advises Weizmann to meet, 224–5; assassinated, 225; aftermath of assassination of, 225–8, 228–9
Munich: Churchill in (1932): 98–9
Munich Agreement (October 1938): 141, 159; Churchill's criticisms of, resented, 269
Muslims: in British India, 35; and 'the Moslem world', 282
Mussolini, Benito: 118, 123, 141, 155

Nablus: 102
Namier, Professor (Sir) Lewis: 97, 171, 309
Nasser, President (of Egypt): 288, and the 'Suez Crisis' (1956), 294–6
Nathan, Sir Frederic: 24, 26, 27
'National Jews': in Britain, 39, 43; in Russia, 39
'National Government' (in Palestine): called for, 59
'National Home of Israel': 61
Navon, Yitzhak: 302, 303
Nazareth: 102
Nazi Party: its road to power in Germany, 97
'Nazi kingdom of hell': Churchill's 'undaunted resistance and struggle against' (Ben Gurion), 305
Nazism: 'utter degradation' of, 191–2
Nazi-Soviet Pact (1939): 162
Nazism: Churchill's sustained critique of (1935), 103–5
Negev desert: 50, 102; and Partition, 123, 124; 'no room' for substantial Jewish immigration in, 126; to be part of a future Jewish State, 183, 205, 223; an integral part of Israel, 284; a Palestinian Arab act of terror in, 288; a place for Jewish refugees, 292
'Negro, Management, Labor': 'goes haywire' (Truman), 266
Nemon, Oscar: his recollections, 290–1; photograph 27
Neuman, Halina: 'his speeches kept us alive', 241–2
New Commonwealth Society: 136
Newfoundland: 69, 284, 285
New York: 250; Jewish refugees reach (1945), 265; population of, as an example, 278; Churchill speaks to American Zionists in (1949), 280; (1952), 282–3
New York American: Churchill praises Zionists in, 92
New York Stock Exchange: and an anti-Semitic accusation, 86–7
New York Times: 'his speeches kept us alive', 241–2
New Zealand: 69; soldiers from, 55, 239
Newmarket: 3
'No Israelite need apply': 82
Nobel Prizewinners: Einstein, 101; other Jews, 290
Normandy Landings (D-Day, 6 June 1944): preparations for, 200, 206; aftermath of, 214; and the Sinai Peninsula (1956–7), 300–1
North Africa: fighting in (1942), 190; under Allied control (1943), 198; Muslims of, a British plan 'unfair' to, 233
North Wales: 272
Norton (Sir) Clifford, 194
Norway: deportation of Jews from (1942), 195; Government-in-Exile of, 195
Novi Sad: killings at (1941), 271–2
Nuremberg Laws (1935); 106

Odessa: 33, 83
Office of Strategic Services (OSS): reports on Churchill and Weizmann, 230; reports on Churchill and Ibn Saud, 236–7, 238

Ohrdruf (concentration camp): discovered, 239–41
Old Testament: 1
Oldham: 7
Oliver, Vic (Victor Oliver von Samek): 136–7
Onassis, Aristotle: 304–5
oranges: a gift from Israel, 301
Ormsby-Gore, William (later Second Baron Harlech): and Partition, 123. 124
Oslo: Churchill's articles published in, 139
Ottoman Empire (Turkey): 11, 12, 2; dismembered, 35

Palace Theatre (Manchester): 14
Palestine: at the time of John the Baptist: 1; Jewish aspirations for, 18, 25; expellees from, recruited, 25; and the Balfour Declaration, 27–8, 36; and Churchill's War Office responsibilities for (1919–1921), 33–6; not mentioned in promise to Arabs, 47, 48; Muslims of, 58; Arab fears concerning, 58–9; 'a great event is taking place here', 63; Churchill's visits to (1921), 52–66; (1934), 102–3; Jews on way to, killed in Poland (1946), 251–2; see also index entry for Palestine Mandate
Palestine Certificates: 180, 188, 199, 207
Palestine Government: and the profits of electrification, 81
Palestine Land Transfer Regulations (1939–40): 164–5, 168–9,170–1, 171
Palestine Mandate (British Mandate for Palestine): 35, 36, 42; to be 'a symbol of Jewish unity', 43; 'dangerous in the extreme', 44; Churchill's Ministerial responsibilities for (1921–1922), 45–85; Arab claims to, abandoned, 46; electrification scheme for, 47; discussions on the Zionist future in, 55–6; to 'turn into a paradise', 57; Arab desiderata for, 58–9; and Jewish immigration, 67–8, 142; and representative institutions, 68; Jewish land purchase in, 77, 114, 118–9, 164–5, 168–9; defended, 78–84; a 'bright future' for, 80; 'new sources of wealth' in, 84; Arabs attack Jews in (1929), 91; Jews and Arabs beneficiaries in, 91–2, 254; and the British 'obligation', 94; Arabs incited against Jews in (1929–39), 102; Jewish immigration to (from 1933), 108; Churchill speaks in controversial debate on (1936), 108–10; Churchill questioned in secret on the meaning of (1937), 110–120; possible abandonment of, 116, 118, 119, 142, 246, 259–60; possible partition of, 121–34; 'great developments' in, 129; renewed Arab violence in (1938), 140–1; Jewish acts of terror in, 140, 141, 149, 208–9, 253, 258–9, 261–2; population estimates for (1938 and 1939), 149, 152, 152 n.2; Churchill attacks British Government policy in (1938–9), 149–53, 157; and British Government immigration restrictions (1939), 157–8; and the arming of Palestinian Jews for war service, 163–4, 169–70, 172–3, 176, 182–3, 190, 191, 218, 254–5, 271; Jewish 'illegals' to be deported from, 177–80; 'illegals' to remain in, 188–9; and the Palestine Regiment (of Jews and Arabs), 191; and renewed Jewish immigration (1944), 206–7; acts of Jewish terror in, 221–2, 223, 250, 251, 253, 256, 258–9; Jews in, no 'irritating' of, 230; post-war plans for, discussed, 231–8; Jews in, 'a great danger to the Arabs', 235; Jews preparing to establish 'a form of Nazi-Fascism' in, 237; beckons, for the survivors of

the concentration camps, 242; continued restrictions on Jewish immigration to, 250; Britain to be 'relieved' of, 251, 258, 263–4; 'thankless, painful, costly . . .', 258; Britain to be 'at war' with Jews and Arabs of, 259: Jews in, to be protected, 261; British military expenditure in, 263; comes to an end (1948), 268; the issue of immigration to, recalled, 277–8; Jewish terrorism in, recalled, 300
Palestine Police Force: and Jewish acts of terror, 262
Palestine Post: 161
Palestine Royal Commission (Peel Commission): Churchill gives secret evidence to, 110–20; publishes its report, 123; and the Negev, 124; and Arab emigration, 126; debated in the House of Commons, 128; recalled, 142, 150, 249–50
Palestine White Paper: (1922), 84–5, 111, 113, 120, 122, 209, 253, 277–8, 308
Palestine White Paper: (1929), 93–41
Palestine White Paper: (1939), 158–62, 163, 164, 165, 166–7; and Arab sensitivities, 179; to be forestalled, 183, 189, 206, 209, 242; and the post-war future of Palestine, 202, 205; continued 'injustice of' (1945), 242–3, 245; 'a negation of Zionist policy,' 254
Palestinian Arab Delegation (to London, 1921): 70, 72–3, 74, 77; re-iteration of an assurance to, 84–5
Palestinian Arabs: terrorist acts by, after 1948, 286, 288
Palestine Regiment (of Jews and Arabs): established (1943), 191, 218
Palmyra: 102
Papen, Franz von: 97
Paris: 3, 34, 46; and Churchill's plea for fair play and equal rights, 135–6, 137; Churchill's literary agent in, 138–9; Churchill's articles published in, 139; and the 'Suez Crisis' (1956), 298
Paris Peace Conference (1919): 34
Partition (of Palestine): the debate for and against, 121–34, 151 n.1; 'a fraud', 122–3; proposed, 123; 'a counsel of despair', 129; Churchill's continued opposition to, 130–1, 132–3, 150; Churchill to support Jewish view of, 205; Weizmann reports rumours of its future limitations, 223; and Greater Syria, 236; plans for, renewed (1945–7), 250, 251
Passfield, Lord (formerly Sidney Webb): modifies the Balfour Declaration, 93–4
Passfield White Paper (1929): 93–4
Patria (steamship): fate of passengers on (1940), 146, 178–9, 181
Peel, Lord: 110; questions Churchill in secret, 111–2, 112–3, 117, 120
Peel Commission: see index entry for: Palestine Royal Commission
Perth (Scotland): 269
Petlura, Simon: and 'fearful massacres', 33
Petra: Churchill visits, 102
Petrograd (formerly St Petersburg, later Leningrad): 28, 30, 40, 83
Pharisees: 1
Phipps, Sir Eric: 103, 104
Picture Post: Churchill supported by, 155–6
Pim, Captain (Sir) Richard: 249
pogroms: in Russia, 10–11, 31–3; in Britain, 19–22; in Ukraine, 33; in Germany, 109, 147–8, 162; in Poland, 251–2
Poland: 'another persecution' in, forecast, 100; economic pressure on Jews in, 113; 'a reservoir of distress', 126; British guarantee to (1939), 160; German invasion of, 162, 163; fate of Jews in, 181; the destination of Jewish deportees, 191, 195; at Potsdam, 248; post-war killing of Jews in, 251–2; post-war frontiers of, 274

Poles: among the 'tortured peoples', 188; mass murder of, 241; and the Jews, 265–6
Polish Government in London (1940–45): 195, 196
Polish troops: in action, 214, 239
Port Lympne (Kent): 5
Port Said (Egypt): 299
Portal, Air Chief Marshal Sir Charles: 197
Potsdam Conference (1945): 246, 247–9
Press Association: Churchill's draft statement for (1948), 268–9
Prague: Churchill's articles published in (1937–8), 139; Hitler occupies (1929), 159; war criminals executed in (post-1945), 201
Protestants: in Germany, 139
Protocols of the Learned Elders of Zion: 44
Pyrenees: Churchill insists on opening for Jewish refugees, 197

Queen Mary (passenger liner); a 'Zionist' on, 285–6
Quincy, USS (heavy cruiser): Ibn Saud and Churchill visit Roosevelt on, 231–4, 238

Rabin, Yitzhak: 28 n.12
Ramleh: 123
Rashid Ali: his revolt in Iraq (1941), 205
Red Army: 42
Red Sea: 189
representative government (for Palestine): to be withheld, 74
Reform Bill (1867): 297
Reform Club (London): Churchill resigns from, 23
Reid, Thomas: interrupts, 276–7
Reik, Havivah: a parachutist, 209
Reuben, Tribe of: 49
Reves, Emery (Imre Revesz): helps Churchill, 138–9, 309; sends Churchill information, 148; and Churchill's war memoirs, 271, 300; tells Churchill of the fate of his family, 271–2; Churchill at the villa of, 297–8; and the 'Suez Crisis' (1956), 298–9; and the Sinai Peninsula (1956–7), 300–1; photographs 17, 25
Revisionists (headed by Jabotinsky): 124, 125; want both sides of the River Jordan, 126–7
Riga: Churchill's articles published in, 139
Rishon le-Zion: Churchill visits, 64, 65–6; Churchill recalls, 92
River War, The: 53–4
Riyadh: 235; pressure from, 144
Roberts, (Sir) Frank: 220
Roquebrune (South of France): 297
Roman Empire: 38, 54, 115, 307
Romania: 126; British pressure on (1939), 154; British guarantee to (1939), 160; and Jewish refugees (1940), 178; fate of Jews in, 181; Jewish refugees from (1944), 206, 226
Rommel, General Erwin: 191
Roosevelt, President Franklin D.: and Palestine, 183–4; and Jewish refugees, 198; and future war crimes trials, 200; suggests arming the Arabs of Palestine, 203; and the post-war future of Palestine, 206, 223, 230, 231–4, 244; his assurance to Ibn Saud, 233–4; and 'something to keep the wolf from the door', 244; has 'let them down', 247; photograph 23
Rothschild, a: persecuted in Vienna (1938), 145
Rothschild, First Baron ('Natty'): 2, 4, 9, 10, 12, 284; photograph 1
Rothschild, Second Baron (Lionel Walter): 27
Rothschild, Dorothy de ('Dollie'): 124, 144, 272, 294
Rothschild, Edmund de ('Eddie'): 284–5; photograph 30
Rothschild, James de ('Jimmy'): 57, 94, 106, 121, 122, 124, 144; and 'the dignity of man', 196; and Churchill's

tribute to Weizmann, 283; suggests Israel join the Commonwealth, 291–2; obtains Churchill's charitable support, 294; photographs 9, 19
Rothschild, Baroness Jean de: 298
Rothschild, Leopold: 2
Rothschild, Lionel: 2–3, 13
Rothschild, Nathaniel, 2
Rothschild, Third Baron (Victor): 2; photograph 22
Rothschild, N.M. (bankers): and the 'Churchill Falls', 284
Rothschilds, the: and the Suez Canal Company (1875), 296–7
Rowan, (Sir) Leslie: 261
Royal Air Force: and appeasement, 155; and a clash over Sinai, 274, 277
Royal Navy: and oil, 88; and 'illegal' immigrants to Palestine, 168, 178, 265
Royal Naval Volunteer Reserve: 23
Rubitzov, Nehemia: enlists, 28 n.12
Rumbold, Sir Horace: 110; questions Churchill, 113–5, 115–6, 118
Runneymede Memorial: 188 n.5
Ruppin, Dr Arthur: 63–4
Russia: the Jews of, and the Balfour Declaration, 28, 79; and the Bolshevik revolution, 28, 37; and anti-Semitism, 30–3; a possible Muslim ally, 58
Russian Co-operative Societies: 39
Russian Empire: 7, 10, 11, 16; Jews from, in Palestine, 12; revolution in, 28; 'National Jews' in, 39
Russians: mass murder of, 241
Rutenberg, Pinhas: his hydro-electric scheme, 47; accompanies Churchill, 64–5; Churchill supports, 75–83; an anti-Bolshevik, 82–3; and the geographic needs of Palestine, 122; the parliamentary debate about, recalled, 259; photograph 13

SS: and Jewish emigration (1940), 178; and the mass murder of Jews (1941), 186; brutality of, reported to London (1942), 194–5; and the Jews of Hungary, 211, 214; negotiations with, rejected, 215
Sacher, Harry: his tribute to Churchill (1965), 306
St James's Palace Conference (1939): 154
St Moritz: 298
St Paul's Cathedral: 306
Sanaa (Yemen): 127
Samuel, Sir Herbert (later Viscount): 25, 26; High Commissioner for Palestine, 45, 46, 50, 52, 53, 68, 70, 208; 'face the facts', 71–2; and the Jaffa riots (1921), 73; warned, 75; rebukes, and rebuked, 155; photographs 9, 10
San Francisco: Churchill's declaration in, 91–2
San Remo Conference (1920): 45
Sarachi, Chatin: 154
Sarafend: Churchill sees Jewish labourers at, 64
Sassoon, (Sir) Philip: 5
Sassoon, Reuben: 5
Sassoon, Siegfried: 29
Sassoon, Sybil (later Lady Cholmondeley): 5
Saudi Arabia: Churchill critical of Wahabism in, 67; to be appeased, 157; and Palestine, 231–6; and oil, 273
Savoy Hotel (London): 269
Scholem, Siegfried: 84 n.25
Scorpion Ascent (Negev): 288
'Season, the': Jewish Agency and British cooperate against Jewish acts of terror, 221–2
Seal (Sir) Eric: 172
Second World War: begins (1 September 1939), 162; the 'seal' put on (1945), 290
Second World War, The (Winston S. Churchill): Churchill at work on, 271–2, 300
Selborne, Earl of: 229
Semon, Sir Felix: 3

Senesh, Hanna: a parachutist, 209
Serbs: among the 'tortured peoples', 188; mass murder of, 241
Sharon, Ariel: carries out a reprisal raid, 286
Shazar, President Zalman: at Churchill's funeral, 306
Shertok, Moshe (later Moshe Sharett): 206–7, 211, 289, 291, 293
Shibly al-Jamal: and 'the necessity of killing Jews', 74–5
Shock, (Sir) Maurice: 297, 309
Shuckburgh, (Sir) John: 46, 47, 48, 71, 74, 77, 180, 292
Sieff, Marcus: his memorandum, 272–3; 'you have given a lead', 278
Silverman, Sidney: his question, 257
Sinai Desert: 102, 274, 300–1
Sinclair, Sir Archibald: 76, 121, 122, 152, 224
Sirhowy Valley (South Wales): 21
Slim, Field Marshal Sir William (later Viscount): 290
Slovakia: 211
Smallwood, Joseph: 284, 285
Smith, General Bedell: tells Churchill about Buchenwald, 239–40
Smuts, General Jan Christiaan: 247, 280
Soames, Christopher: 270
Sobibor: mass murder of Jews at (1942), 192
South Africa: 4, 5; soldiers from, 55, 239
South of France: 270, 271, 297–8, 302
South Wales Pogrom in, 19
Soviet Union (also known as Soviet Russia): 160; Jews train in, to be farmers in Palestine, 64; and the Nazi-Soviet Pact, 162; invaded by Germany, 186; and a group of Hungarian Jewish escapees, 214–5; unwilling to join Churchill in a warning, 220; Churchill's wife in, 241; recognises Israel, 268, 274; supports Israel, 273, 275–6; arms Egypt, 294, 295, 303
Spain: Churchill's comment on Arab 'civilisation' in, 116; Churchill's protest to, on behalf of Jews seeking refuge in, 197; the future of Jewish refugees in, 198
Spears, General Sir Edward Louis: xv; Churchill warns, 190
Spier, Eugen: xvii; and Churchill's 'Focus', 135; interned, 177; photograph 18
Stalin, Joseph: and future war crimes trails, 200; at Potsdam, 246, 248–9; and the Jews (in Truman's perspective), 266
Stanley, Oliver: 169, 193–4; helps Jewish refugees, 206–7; sceptical of Weizmann as High Commissioner for Palestine, 208; and the assassination of Lord Moyne, 225, 226; sees Weizmann, 247–8; and the 'Peace table', 248
Stanley, Venetia (later Mrs Edwin Montagu): 6
Star of David: Churchill supports as a Jewish regimental flag, 217; in action, 239
State Department (Washington): Churchill challenges fears of, 214–5; and the Sinai Peninsula (1956–7), 300–1
Steed, Henry Wickham: 156
Stern, Sir Albert: 26
Stern Gang: acts of terror by, 221; arrests of, 222; and the murder of Lord Moyne, 225, 227–8
Stockholm: Churchill's articles published in, 139
Stowmarket: 2
Straits of Gibraltar: an avenue of rescue, 198
Strand (magazine): Churchill's article on Germany in, 103–5
Strang, Sir William; 284
Sudan: Jewish terrorists deported to, 222
Sudetenland (Czechoslovakia): 140, 141
Suez Canal: 102, 144; and the Second World War, 182, 191; closed to ships

bound for Israel, 281, 285, 287–8; nationalised, 295; and the 'Suez Crisis' (1956), 295–6, 298–300
Suez Canal Company: 296–7
Suez Canal Zone: 259
Sun (newspaper): an accusation in, 9, 10
Sunday Chronicle: Churchill writes about Moses in, 95–6
Sunderland: 37
Swiss: and Germany, 162
Swiss Alps: 13
Switzerland: 211
Sydenham, Lord: attacks Zionists, 76–7
Syria: 35, 44, 48, 59, 102, 118; post-war independence for, 183, 255; and Greater Syria, 237; invades Israel, 268, 275

Tallin: Churchill's articles published in, 139
Talmud Torah School (Manchester): Churchill visits, 14
Technion (Haifa): 'they love you very much', 301–2
Tel Aviv: Churchill visits, 64; within Arab artillery range, 127; 'a great city', 160; bombed, by Italy (1940), 177; Jews kill British policemen in, 221; and rumours about Partition, 223; kidnappings in, 251; Churchill praises, 254; a Jewish act of terror near, 261; Churchill's war memoirs published in, 271; government in, 273, 274
television: Churchill's tribute to Weizmann on (1952), 283
Temple, William, Archbishop of Canterbury: 192, 216
'Temple of Zion': 1
Territorialists: 11, 17
'Terrorist Jews': 40
Thoughts and Adventures (Winston S. Churchill): a gift to Ben-Gurion, 304
Tiberias: 151 n.1
Times, The (London): 156; and the Nuremberg Laws, 106; and the deportations from France (1942), 191; a protest to (1948), 270
Tito, Marshal (Josip Broz): 209–10
Topusko (Yugoslavia): 210
Toulon: 135
Transjordan: Churchill's settlement for, 47, 109, 180, 236, 255; Weizmann's hopes for, 49; Churchill's pledge concerning, 55–6; Churchill visits, 102; self-governing, 118; Attlee suggests (1943) that Jews settle in, after the war, 204; Churchill calls Jewish settlement in 'a good idea', 204; Churchill suggests might be part of a future Jewish State, 205; invades Israel, 268, 275; Britain's Treaty of Alliance with (March 1948), 268–9, 287, 289; population of, and that of Palestine, 277; for subsequent index entries, see Jordan, Kingdom of
Treaty of Versailles (1919): 146
Tredegar: Jews attacked in, 19–20
Teblinka: mass murder of Jews at (1942), 192
Tring Park: Churchill visits, 2
Tripolitania: a suggested future Jewish colony, 189; Jews 'not very smitten with', 249
Trotsky, Leon Davidovich: 42, 43, 83; and 'you and me', 136
Truman, President Harry S.: 245, 246; cannot be fought, 247; 'very sympathetic', 247; at Potsdam, 249; fulminates in his diary against the Jews, 265–6; his piano playing interrupted, 285
Tulcia (Romania): Jewish refugees leave (1940), 178
Tulkarm: a strike at, 110
Tulloch, Major: his report from Jericho, 110
Turkey: 11, 25; soldiers from, 55; British pressure on (1939), 154; British guarantee to (1939), 160; and the Second World War, 182–3;

Turkey: – *continued*
and the proposed rescue of Jews from Bulgaria, 193–4; facilitates Jewish immigration to Palestine, 207

Uganda: an alternative Jewish homeland in, 12
Ukraine: pogroms in, 31, 33, 41
Ukrainian People's Republic: 33
Unit 101 (in Israel): carries out a reprisal raid, 286
United Nations (United Nations Organisation): during the Second World War, 196, 213; and a possible attack on the Jews in Palestine by Arab States, 255; the Palestine Mandate to be returned to, 259–60, 263–4; Palestine Mandate returned to (1947), 264; Partition Resolution in (November 1947), 276–7, 294
United Nations Assembly: Britain's policy towards Israel in, 273, 286
United Nations Charter: 301
United Nations Security Council: Churchill wishes to support Israel in, 287, 288
United States: and Jewish recruiting (1917–18), 28, 79; Churchill visits (1929), 91; Jews in, 93; 'public opinion' in, 112; 'Red Indians' in, 120; a German liner on way to, 137; and the Palestine White Paper (1939), 159; Churchill's broadcast to (1939), 162; 'powerful factor' of Jews in, 165; Jewish concerns in, 173, 198; a goodwill mission to, 199; and the post-war future of Palestine, 202, 206, 223, 246; and anti-Zionist Jews, 204, 222; and Churchill's proposal of Weizmann as High Commissioner for Palestine, 208; a Jewish 'campaign of abuse' in American newspapers, 209; and a bombing raid on Budapest, 212–3; troops of, in action in Normandy, 214; and the Jewish Brigade Group, 217; and Hungarian Jewish refugees in Greece, 218–9; joins Churchill in a warning, 220; government of, 'more or less academic' in attitude to Zionism, 224; Jews of, and Lord Moyne's assassination, 229; Ibn Saud's hopes in, 233; and Saudi oil, 235; soldiers from, in action in Italy, 239; 'should have their turn' in Palestine, 248, 250–1; Churchill in (1946), 250; to 'share' the burden of Palestine, 258, 259, 263–4, 264; and the British Labour Party's policies in Palestine, 256; recognises Israel, 268, 274; and Churchill's war memoirs, 271; and Israel, 273, 275–6, 280, 285, 287; 'large Jewish vote' in, 285; Israel a 'link with', 292; and the 'Suez Crisis' (1956), 294–6; and the Sinai Peninsula (1956–7), 300–1
United States Congress: Churchill speaks about Israel in (1952), 282
University College, Oxford: 297

Vermont: and the size of Palestine, 124 n.8
Vichy France: 136, 191, 197, 255
Victoria, Queen-Empress: 5
Victoria Cross: won by Jews, 30, 39
Victoria Island (British Columbia, Canada): and the size of Palestine, 124 n.8
Victoria Memorial Jewish Hospital (Manchester): 14, 18–19
victory: the ultimate hope for the surviving Jews of Europe, 213–4
Vienna: Churchill's articles published in (1937), 139; Hitler enters (March 1938), 145
Veesenmayer, SS General Edmund: 212
Villa Cassel (Swiss Alps): 13
Vilnius (Vilna): Churchill's articles published in, 139
Virginia: a gift from, 301
Volkischer Beobachter (German newspaper): attacks Churchill, 103

Waddesdon Manor: 124
Wahabism: Churchill critical of, 67
Wales: and Palestine, 124 n.8
Waley Cohen, Sir Robert: Churchill represents, 88–90
war crimes trials: in prospect (1942), 195; Churchill supports an Allied declaration about, 200; Churchill suggests Jews 'would be able to judge' war criminals, 204; and the deportation of Jews from Hungary, 213; Churchill insistent on, 215, 220
War Industries Board (Washington): 29
War Refugee Board (Washington): 219
War of the Spanish Succession (1701–14): 97
Warsaw: Churchill's articles published in (1937–8), 139; war criminals executed in (after 1945), 201
Warsaw Ghetto: Jews in, revolt (1943), 197–8; 'his speeches kept us alive', 241–2
Washington D.C.: Churchill's visits to, 187, 206; the Allied Declaration of 17 December 1942 broadcast from, 195; and the post-war future of Palestine, 202; a warning broadcast from (10 October 1944); Churchill defends Israel in (1952), 282; (1953), 285
Wauchope, Sir Arthur: 102
Wavell, General Sir Archibald: rebuked, 179; opposes a Jewish force in the British Army, 181–2
Wedgwood, Josiah: 94, 121, 122
Weimar: a concentration camp near, 240
Weizmann, Dr Chaim: in Manchester, 11; during the First World War, 24–5, 26–7, 290; while Churchill at the War Office (1919–21), 33–4, 41, 183; 'fiery energies' of, 42; and Churchill's tenure of the Colonial Office, 48–50; territorial desires of, 49–50; his desires frustrated, 56; and Churchill's visit to Palestine (1921), 64; in dispute with Churchill, 70–1; seeks assurances, 71; congratulates Churchill (1922), 85; seeks a British Government loan, 90–1; and Churchill's son, 95; favours Partition, 121–2, 123–4, 132; seeks the Negev, 123, 124; denounces Jewish acts of terror, 140; and the Palestine White Paper (1939), 158, 161; wartime meetings with Churchill, 163–4, 164, 166, 182, 203–5, 206, 222–5; and the Palestine Land Transfer Regulations, 164, 170; and the arming of Jews in Palestine, 173; and Jewish deportees to Mauritius, 178; and the creation of a Jewish force in the British Army, 181–2; and Jewish immigration to Palestine, 184; and the fate of his son Michael, 188; and 'your suffering people', 193; and the post-war future of Palestine, 202, 203–5; and a possible High Commissioner for Palestine, 207–8; Churchill warns, about a Jewish 'campaign of abuse' in British and American newspapers, and Jewish terrorism, 209; obtains Churchill's help to rescue Jews, 209–10; seeks bombing of railway lines to Auschwitz, 211–12; his letter to Churchill's Private Office, 220; rejects Jewish acts of terror, 221; gives Churchill assurances about opposing Jewish terror, 222; Churchill advises to see Lord Moyne, 225; and the assassination of Lord Moyne, 225–6, 227; Churchill advises him to go the United States, 230; his correspondence with Churchill (1945), 242–3, 243–4, 244–5, 246–7; 'very bitter', 245; feels let down, 247; 'the ablest and wisest', 259; Churchill's 'Conscience', 270; 'an old friend of mine', 276;

Weizmann, Dr Chaim: – *continued*
and Churchill's praise for Israel, 278; and Britain's recognition of Israel, 279; as President of Israel, 281, 282; dies, 283; 'a man of vision and genius', 290; photograph 12
Weizmann, Flight-Lieutenant Michael: his fate, 188, 259, 276, 281, 283
Weizmann, Vera: a gift from, 301
Weizmann Forest (Israel): 281
'Weizmann organism': 27
Welldon, Bishop: 14
West Bank: 164
West Ham (London): 23
Westminster, Abbey (constituency): 90
Westminster Hall (London): 285
Western Desert (1942): 192
Western Front (1914–18): 25, 26, 28
Western Palestine: and the Jewish National Home, 52, 55–6, 57, 121; to be partitioned, 123, 151 n.1; plans for a future Jewish State in, 183; Jews confined to a 'territorial ghetto' in, 245
Western Wall (Wailing Wall, Jerusalem): Churchill asks about, 293
Wigmore Hall (London): 196
Wilson, President Woodrow: 29
'Win We Will': 218
Windham, Judge Ralph: kidnapped, 262, 263
Windsor Castle: 290
Wingate, Orde: a memorial to, 280
Winnipeg: 5
'Winning Winnie': 218
Winter Palace (Petrograd): 47
Winterton, Lord: not to be appointed, 229
Wise, Dr Stephen: and Roosevelt's possible 'moonshine', 244
Wiskemann, Elizabeth: her ingenuity, 212–3
Wolfson, Sir Isaac (later Lord): photograph 18
Women's International Zionist Organization (WIZO): 196
Wood, Sir Kingsley: 154
Woodhead, Sir John: his Palestine Commission (1937–8), 134, 142, 151, 152
Woodhead Commission: a member of, and the Partition debate, 277
World Union of Revisionists: 125
World Zionist Organisation: 227, 247

Yarkon River: 47, 76
Yellow Spot, The: a 'terrible book', 107
Yiddish newspapers; Churchill's articles published in, 139
Young, Major Hubert: 47, 71, 77
Yugoslavia: British pressure on (1939), 154; Government-in-Exile of, 195; Jews rescued from (1944), 209–10; and the fate of Emery Reves' family in, 271–2
Yugoslavs: 265–6

Zangwill, Israel: 11
Zaslani, Reuven (later Reuven Shiloah): 209 n.13
Zion: 'sons of the prophets dwelling in', 293–4
Zion Mule Corps: 25, 125
Zionism: 11–12, 38, 41–3; 'deep significance' of, 41–2; Churchill's strong endorsement of, 43; and the 'Arab world', 46; and an electrification scheme for Palestine, 47, 75–82; territorial desires of, 49–50; Arab opposition to, 51, 53, 54, 56, 58–61, 71–2; Churchill's 'heart full of sympathy for', 56–7; to be given 'a fair chance', 60–1; seeks 'sincere friendship' with the Arabs, 62; 'a very great ideal', 69; under attack in the House of Lords, 76–7; defended, 78–84; a 'good gift' of, 80; and the 'British obligation' (after 1917), 94; and a 'mistake' in Palestine, 119; the 'great cause' of, 130–1, 193; Neville Chamberlain's 'mortal blow' against, 161; Britain's 'promises' to, 180; Churchill

'strongly wedded' to, 184; the 'bitter pill', for the Arabs of Syria, 222; and American Jews, 222–3; and 'the smoke of assassins' pistols', 226, 229; Roosevelt and Churchill at variance on, 234; future of, and the United States (1945–7), 246, 250–1; a possible convert to (Bernard Baruch), 250; a 'cherished hope', 254; and the British Labour Party, 255–6; 'not abandoned', 256–7; 'large causes which we have carried far', 259; supporters of (1948), 275–6, 282, 283; Churchill's 'diatribe in favour' of, 285; Churchill 'always a friend of', 303; Churchill's 'outspoken' support of, 305; and 'the perspective of a thousand years', 306
Zionist Association: 75
Zionist Executive: 33, 34
Zionist Federation of Great Britain: 143
Zionist Organisation: 34, 48, 184
Zionist Political Committee (London): 243–4, 245
'Zionist State': opposed, 44
Zola, Emile: Churchill applauds, 3
Zulueta, (Sir) Philip de: and a possible Churchill visit to Israel (1962), 305

ABOUT THE AUTHOR

Sir Martin Gilbert was knighted in 1995 "for services to British history and international relations." The author of an eight-volume biography of Winston Churchill, among his other books are *Churchill: A Life, The First World War, The Second World War*, and *The Somme.* He lives in London, England.